Haskell High Performance Programming

Boost the performance of your Haskell applications using optimization, concurrency, and parallel programming

Samuli Thomasson

[PACKT] open source *
PUBLISHING   community experience distilled

BIRMINGHAM - MUMBAI

Haskell High Performance Programming

First published: September 2016

Production reference: 1190916

Published by Packt Publishing Ltd.
Livery Place
35 Livery Street
Birmingham B3 2PB, UK.

ISBN 978-1-78646-421-7

www.packtpub.com

Credits

Author
Samuli Thomasson

Reviewer
Aaron Stevens

Commissioning Editor
Kunal Parikh

Acquisition Editor
Sonali Vernekar

Content Development Editor
Priyanka Mehta

Technical Editor
Ravikiran Pise

Copy Editor
Safis Editing

Project Coordinator
Izzat Contractor

Proofreader
Safis Editing

Indexer
Tejal Daruwale Soni

Graphics
Abhinash Sahu

Production Coordinator
Melwyn Dsa

Cover Work
Melwyn Dsa

About the Author

Samuli Thomasson is a long-time functional programming enthusiast from Finland who has used Haskell extensively, both as a pastime and commercially, for over four years. He enjoys working with great tools that help in getting things done nice and fast.

His current job at RELEX Solutions consists of providing technical solutions to a variety of practical problems. Besides functional programming, Samuli is interested in distributed systems, which he also studies at the University of Helsinki.

I am grateful to my awesome friends, who have stuck around and provided their support during the writing process, and my family for always being there and their understanding.

About the Reviewer

Aaron Stevens is a scientific software engineer with Molex LLC in Little Rock, Arkansas, where he combines his passion for programming with his education in electrical systems engineering to develop innovative techniques to characterize high-speed electronics in the lab and in production. He specializes in signal processing, statistical process-control methods, and application construction in Python and C#, and he enjoys discovering new methods to explore complex data sets through rich visualizations.

Away from the office, Aaron enjoys practicing with a variety of programming languages, studying linguistics, cooking, and spending time with his family. He received his BS in mathematics and BS in electrical systems engineering from the University of Arkansas in Little Rock.

www.PacktPub.com

eBooks, discount offers, and more

Did you know that Packt offers eBook versions of every book published, with PDF and ePub files available? You can upgrade to the eBook version at www.PacktPub.com and as a print book customer, you are entitled to a discount on the eBook copy. Get in touch with us at customercare@packtpub.com for more details.

At www.PacktPub.com, you can also read a collection of free technical articles, sign up for a range of free newsletters and receive exclusive discounts and offers on Packt books and eBooks.

https://www2.packtpub.com/books/subscription/packtlib

Do you need instant solutions to your IT questions? PacktLib is Packt's online digital book library. Here, you can search, access, and read Packt's entire library of books.

Why subscribe?

- Fully searchable across every book published by Packt
- Copy and paste, print, and bookmark content
- On demand and accessible via a web browser

Table of Contents

Preface
xi

Chapter 1: Identifying Bottlenecks
1

Meeting lazy evaluation
1

Writing sum correctly
3

Weak head normal form
5

Folding correctly
6

Memoization and CAFs
7

Constant applicative form
8

Recursion and accumulators
9

The worker/wrapper idiom
9

Guarded recursion
10

Accumulator parameters
12

Inspecting time and space usage
12

Increasing sharing and minimizing allocation
15

Compiler code optimizations
17

Inlining and stream fusion
17

Polymorphism performance
18

Partial functions
19

Summary
20

Chapter 2: Choosing the Correct Data Structures
21

Annotating strictness and unpacking datatype fields
22

Unbox with UNPACK
23

Using anonymous tuples
25

Performance of GADTs and branching
26

Handling numerical data
28

Handling binary and textual data
29

Representing bit arrays   29
Handling bytes and blobs of bytes   31
Working with characters and strings   33
   Using the text library   33
Builders for iterative construction   34
   Builders for strings   35

Handling sequential data   **36**
   Using difference lists   37
      Difference list performance   38
      Difference list with the Writer monad   38
   Using zippers   39
      Accessing both ends fast with Seq   40

Handling tabular data   **42**
   Using the vector package   43

Handling sparse data   **47**
   Using the containers package   47
   Using the unordered-containers package   48

Ephemeral data structures   **49**
   Mutable references are slow   49
   Using mutable arrays   50
   Using mutable vectors   51
      Bubble sort with vectors   53

Working with monads and monad stacks   **55**
   The list monad and its transformer   55
   Free monads   57
   Working with monad transformers   59
   Speedup via continuation-passing style   59

Summary   **61**

Chapter 3: Profile and Benchmark to Your Heart's Content   **63**
Profiling time and allocations   **63**
   Setting cost centres manually   64
   Setting cost centres automatically   68
   Installing libraries with profiling   70
   Debugging unexpected crashes with profiler   70

Heap profiling   **71**
   Cost centre-based heap profiling   73
   Objects outside the heap   76
   Retainer profiling   80
   Biographical profiling   83

Benchmarking using the criterion library   **84**
Profile and monitor in real time   **88**
  Monitoring over HTTP with ekg   89
Summary   **92**

Chapter 4: The Devil's in the Detail   93

The anatomy of a Haskell project   **94**
  Useful fields and flags in cabal files   96
  Test suites and benchmarks   98
  Using the stack tool   99
  Multi-package projects   101
Erroring and handling exceptions   **101**
  Handling synchronous errors   102
  The exception hierarchy   104
  Handling asynchronous errors   105
  Throw and catch in other monads besides IO   106
Writing tests for Haskell   **107**
  Property checks   107
  Unit testing with HUnit   108
  Test frameworks   109
Trivia at term-level   **110**
  Coding in GHC PrimOps   112
  Control inlining   114
    Using rewrite rules   115
    Specializing definitions   116
    Phase control   117
Trivia at type-level   **117**
  Phantom types   118
  Functional dependencies   118
  Type families and associated types   120
Useful GHC extensions   **121**
  Monomorphism Restriction   122
  Extensions for patterns and guards   123
  Strict-by-default Haskell   124
Summary   **125**

Chapter 5: Parallelize for Performance   127

Primitive parallelism and the Runtime System   **128**
  Spark away   130
  Subtle evaluation – pseq   131
  When in doubt, use the force   131

The Eval monad and strategies   **132**
Composing strategies   134
Fine-tune granularity with chunking and buffering   136
The Par monad and schedules   **136**
spawn for futures and promises   138
Non-deterministic parallelism with ParIO   139
Diagnosing parallelism – ThreadScope   **140**
Data parallel programming – Repa   **141**
Playing with Repa in GHCi   142
Mapping and delayed arrays   143
Reduction via folding   144
Manifest representations   145
Delayed representation and fusion   146
Indices, slicing, and extending arrays   146
Convolution with stencils   149
Cursored and partitioned arrays   151
Writing fast Repa code   153
Additional libraries   154
Example from image processing   154
Loading the image from file   155
Identifying letters with convolution   155
Extracting strings from an image   157
Testing and evaluating performance   159
Summary   **161**
Chapter 6: I/O and Streaming   **163**
Reading, writing, and handling resources   **164**
Traps of lazy I/O   164
File handles, buffering, and encoding   165
Binary I/O   166
Textual I/O   168
I/O performance with filesystem objects   168
Sockets and networking   169
Acting as a TCP/IP client   169
Acting as a TCP server (Unix domain sockets)   170
Raw UDP traffic   172
Networking above the transport layer   173
Managing resources with ResourceT   173
Streaming with side-effects   **175**
Choosing a streaming library   175

Simple streaming using io-streams 176
Creating input streams 177
Using combinators and output streams 179
Handling exceptions and resources in streams 179
An example of parsing using io-streams and attoparsec 181
Streaming using pipes 184
Composing and executing pipes 185
For loops and category theory in pipes 186
Handling exceptions in pipes 187
Strengths and weaknesses of pipes 187
Streaming using conduits 188
Handling resources and exceptions in conduits 189
Resuming conduits 190
Logging in Haskell **191**
Logging with FastLogger 191
More abstract loggers 192
Timed log messages 193
Monadic logging 195
Customizing monadic loggers 196
Summary **197**
Chapter 7: Concurrency and Performance **199**
Threads and concurrency primitives **200**
Threads and mutable references 200
Avoid accumulating thunks 202
Atomic operations with IORefs 202
MVar 203
MVars are fair 204
MVar as a building block 205
Broadcasting with Chan 206
Software Transactional Memory **208**
STM example – Bank accounts 208
Alternative transactions 210
Exceptions in STM 210
Runtime System and threads **211**
Masking asynchronous exceptions 212
Asynchronous processing **213**
Using the Async API 215
Async example – Timeouts 215
Composing with Concurrently 217

Lifting up from I/O   **218**
  Top-level mutable references   218
  Lifting from a base monad   219
  Lifting base with exception handling   220
Summary   **222**
Chapter 8: Tweaking the Compiler and Runtime System (GHC)   **223**
  Using GHC like a pro   **224**
    Operating GHC   224
      Circular dependencies   226
    Adjusting optimizations and transformations   227
      The state hack   227
      Floating lets in and out   228
      Eliminating common subexpressions   229
      Liberate-case duplicates code   230
    Compiling via the LLVM route   230
    Linking and building shared libraries   231
    Preprocessing Haskell source code   232
    Enforcing type-safety using Safe Haskell   233
  Tuning GHC's Runtime System   **234**
    Scheduler and green threads   235
      Sparks and spark pool   235
      Bounded threads and affinity   236
      Indefinite blocking and weak references   236
    Heap, stack, and memory management   237
      Evaluation stack in Haskell   238
    Tuning the garbage collector   238
      Parallel GC   239
    Profiling and tracing options   240
      Tracing using eventlog   241
      Options for profiling and debugging   241
  Summary of useful GHC options   **241**
    Basic usage   242
    The LLVM backend   242
    Turn optimizations on and off   242
    Configuring the Runtime System (compile-time)   242
    Safe Haskell   243
  Summary of useful RTS options   **243**
    Scheduler flags   243
    Memory management   243
    Garbage collection   244

Runtime System statistics   244
Profiling and debugging   244
Summary   **244**
Chapter 9: GHC Internals and Code Generation   **247**
Interpreting GHC's internal representations   **248**
Reading GHC Core   248
Spineless tagless G-machine   251
Primitive GHC-specific features   **253**
Kinds encode type representation   254
Datatype generic programming   **255**
Working example – A generic sum   256
Generating Haskell with Haskell   **259**
Splicing with $(...)   260
Names in templates   261
Smart template constructors   262
The constN function   263
Lifting Haskell code to Q with quotation brackets   264
Launching missiles during compilation   264
Reifying Haskell data into template objects   264
Deriving setters with Template Haskell   265
Quasi-quoting for DSLs   267
Summary   **269**
Chapter 10: Foreign Function Interface   **271**
From Haskell to C and C to Haskell   **271**
Common types in Haskell and C   272
Importing static functions and addresses   273
Exporting Haskell functions   275
Compiling a shared library   276
Function pointers and wrappers   278
Haskell callbacks from C   279
Data marshal and stable pointers   **280**
Allocating memory outside the heap   281
Pointing to objects in the heap   281
Marshalling abstract datatypes   282
Marshalling in standard libraries   283
Summary   **284**

Chapter 11: Programming for the GPU with Accelerate   285

Writing Accelerate programs   286
Kernels – The motivation behind explicit use and run   287
Working with elements and scalars   288
Rudimentary array computations   290
Example – Matrix multiplication   291
Flow control and conditional execution   293
Inspecting generated code   293

Running with the CUDA backend   294
Debugging CUDA programs   295

More Accelerate concepts   296
Working with tuples   297
Folding, reducing, and segmenting   297
Accelerated stencils   298
Permutations in Accelerate   299
Using the backend foreign function interface   300

Summary   300

Chapter 12: Scaling to the Cloud with Cloud Haskell   301

Processes and message-passing   302
Creating a message type   302
Creating a Process   303
Spawning and closures   304
Running with the SimpleLocalNet backend   305
Using channels   306
Establishing bidirectional channels   308
Calling a remote process   309

Handling failure   310
Firing up monitors   311
Matching on the message queue   311
Linking processes together   312
Message-passing performance   312

Nodes and networking   313

Summary   315

Chapter 13: Functional Reactive Programming   317

The tiny discrete-time Elerea   318
Mutually recursive signals   320
Signalling side-effects   321

Dynamically changing signal networks 322
Performance and limitations in Elerea 324
Events and signal functions with Yampa **324**
Adding state to signal functions 325
Working with time 326
Switching and discrete-time events 327
Integrating to the real world 330
Reactive-banana – Safe and simple semantics **331**
Example – First GUI application 332
Graphical display with wxWidgets 332
Combining events and behaviors **335**
Switching events and behaviors 336
Observing moments on demand 336
Recursion and semantics 337
Adding input and output 338
Input via polling or handlers 338
Reactimate output 339
Input and output dynamically 340
Summary **340**
Chapter 14: Library Recommendations **343**
Representing data **343**
Functional graphs **344**
Numeric data for special use **345**
Encoding and serialization **346**
Binary serialization of Haskell values 347
Encoding to and from other formats 348
CSV input and output 349
Persistent storage, SQL, and NoSQL **350**
acid-state and safecopy 350
persistent and esqueleto 351
HDBC and add-ons 352
Networking and HTTP **353**
HTTP clients and servers 353
Supplementary HTTP libraries 354
JSON remote procedure calls 355
Using WebSockets 355
Programming a REST API 355
Cryptography **356**

Web technologies   **356**
Parsing and pretty-printing   **357**
    Regular expressions in Haskell   358
    Parsing XML   359
Pretty-printing and text formatting   **359**
Control and utility libraries   **361**
    Using lenses   361
    Easily converting between types (convertible)   363
    Using a custom Prelude   363
Working with monads and transformers   **365**
    Monad morphisms – monad-unlift   366
Handling exceptions   **366**
Random number generators   **367**
Parallel and concurrent programming   **368**
Functional Reactive Programming   **368**
Mathematics, statistics, and science   **369**
Tools for research and sketching   **369**
The HaskellR project   **370**
Creating charts and diagrams   **370**
Scripting and CLI applications   **371**
Testing and benchmarking   **372**
Summary   **372**
Index   **375**

Preface

Haskell is an elegant language. It allows us to express in code exactly what we mean, in a clean and compact style. The nice features, including referential transparency and call-by-need evaluation, not only help the programmer be more efficient, but also help Haskell compilers to optimize programs in ways that are otherwise plain impossible. For example, the garbage collector of GHC is notoriously fast, not least thanks to its ability to exploit the immutability of Haskell values.

Unfortunately, high expressivity is a double-edged sword. Reasoning the exact order of evaluation in Haskell programs is, in general, not an easy task. A lack of understanding of the lazy call-by-need evaluation in Haskell will for sure lead the programmer to introduce space leaks sooner or later. A productive Haskell programmer not only has to know how to read and write the language, which is a hard enough skill to achieve in itself, they also need to understand a new evaluation schema and some related details. Of course, in order to not make things too easy, just knowing the language well will not get you very far. In addition, one has to be familiar with at least a few common libraries and, of course, the application domain itself.

This book will give you working knowledge of high-performance Haskell programming, including parallelism and concurrency. In this book, we will cover the language, GHC, and the common libraries of Haskell.

What this book covers

Chapter 1, *Identifying Bottlenecks*, introduces you to basic techniques for optimal evaluation and avoiding space leaks.

Chapter 2, *Choose the Correct Data Structures*, works with and optimizes both immutable and mutable data structures.

Chapter 3, Profile and Benchmark to Your Heart's Content, profiles Haskell programs using GHC and benchmarking using Criterion.

Chapter 4, The Devil's in the Detail, explains the small details that affect performance in Haskell programs, including code sharing, specializing, and simplifier rules.

Chapter 5, Parallelize for Performance, exploits parallelism in Haskell programs using the RePa library for data parallelism.

Chapter 6, I/O and Streaming, talks about the pros and cons of lazy and strict I/O in Haskell and explores the concept of streaming.

Chapter 7, Concurrency Performance, explores the different aspects of concurrent programming, such as shared variables, exception handling, and software-transactional memory.

Chapter 8, Tweaking the Compiler and Runtime System, chooses the optimal compiler and runtime parameters for Haskell programs compiled with GHC.

Chapter 9, GHC Internals and Code Optimizations, delves deeper into the compilation pipeline, and understands the intermediate representations of GHC.

Chapter 10, Foreign Function Interface, calls safely to and from C in Haskell using GHC and its FFI support.

Chapter 11, Programming for the GPU with Accelerate, uses the Accelerate library to program backend-agnostic GPU programs and executes on CUDA-enabled systems.

Chapter 12, Scaling to the Cloud with Cloud Haskell, uses the Cloud Haskell ecosystem to build distributed systems with Haskell.

Chapter 13, Functional Reactive Programming, introduces three Haskell FRP libraries, including Elerea, Yampa, and Reactive-banana.

Chapter 14, Library Recommendations, talks about a catalogue of robust Haskell libraries, accompanied with overviews and examples.

What you need for this book

To run most examples in this book, all you need is a working, relatively recent, installation of GHC and some Haskell libraries. Examples are built for nix-like systems, although they are easily adapted for a Windows machine.

The recommended minimum version for GHC is 7.6. The Haskell libraries needed are introduced in the chapters in which they are used. In *Chapter 4*, *The Devil's in the Detail*, we use the Haskell Stack tool to perform some tasks, but it isn't strictly required, although it is recommended to install Stack.

In *Chapter 11*, *Programming for the GPU Using Accelerate*, executing the CUDA versions of examples requires a CUDA-enabled system and the installation of the CUDA platform.

Who this book is for

To get the most out of this book, you need to have a working knowledge of reading and writing basic Haskell. No knowledge of performance, optimization, or concurrency is required.

Conventions

In this book, you will find a number of text styles that distinguish between different kinds of information. Here are some examples of these styles and an explanation of their meaning.

Code words in text, database table names, folder names, filenames, file extensions, pathnames, dummy URLs, user input, and Twitter handles are shown as follows: "We can include other contexts through the use of the `include` directive."

A block of code is set as follows:

```
mySum [1..100]
    = 1 + mySum [2..100]
    = 1 + (2 + mySum [2..100])
    = 1 + (2 + (3 + mySum [2..100]))
    = ...
    = 1 + (2 + (... + mySum [100]))
  = 1 + (2 + (... + (100 + 0)))
```

When we wish to draw your attention to a particular part of a code block, the relevant lines or items are set in bold:

```
mySum [1..100]
    = 1 + mySum [2..100]
    = 1 + (2 + mySum [2..100])
    = 1 + (2 + (3 + mySum [2..100]))
    = ...
    = 1 + (2 + (... + mySum [100]))
  = 1 + (2 + (... + (100 + 0)))
```

Any command-line input or output is written as follows:

```
> let xs = enumFromTo 1 5 :: [Int]
> :sprint xs
```

New terms and **important words** are shown in bold. Words that you see on the screen, for example, in menus or dialog boxes, appear in the text like this: "Clicking the **Next** button moves you to the next screen."

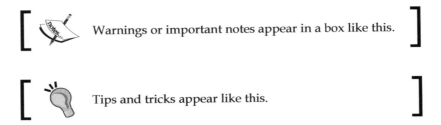

Warnings or important notes appear in a box like this.

Tips and tricks appear like this.

Reader feedback

Feedback from our readers is always welcome. Let us know what you think about this book—what you liked or disliked. Reader feedback is important for us as it helps us develop titles that you will really get the most out of.

To send us general feedback, simply e-mail feedback@packtpub.com, and mention the book's title in the subject of your message.

If there is a topic that you have expertise in and you are interested in either writing or contributing to a book, see our author guide at www.packtpub.com/authors.

Customer support

Now that you are the proud owner of a Packt book, we have a number of things to help you to get the most from your purchase.

Downloading the example code

You can download the example code files for this book from your account at http://www.packtpub.com. If you purchased this book elsewhere, you can visit http://www.packtpub.com/support and register to have the files e-mailed directly to you.

You can download the code files by following these steps:

1. Log in or register to our website using your e-mail address and password.
2. Hover the mouse pointer on the **SUPPORT** tab at the top.
3. Click on **Code Downloads & Errata**.
4. Enter the name of the book in the **Search** box.
5. Select the book for which you're looking to download the code files.
6. Choose from the drop-down menu where you purchased this book from.
7. Click on **Code Download**.

You can also download the code files by clicking on the **Code Files** button on the book's webpage at the Packt Publishing website. This page can be accessed by entering the book's name in the **Search** box. Please note that you need to be logged in to your Packt account.

Once the file is downloaded, please make sure that you unzip or extract the folder using the latest version of:

- WinRAR / 7-Zip for Windows
- Zipeg / iZip / UnRarX for Mac
- 7-Zip / PeaZip for Linux

The code bundle for the book is also hosted on GitHub at `https://github.com/PacktPublishing/Haskell-High-Performance-Programming`. We also have other code bundles from our rich catalog of books and videos available at `https://github.com/PacktPublishing/`. Check them out!

Downloading the color images of this book

We also provide you with a PDF file that has color images of the screenshots/diagrams used in this book. The color images will help you better understand the changes in the output. You can download this file from `http://www.packtpub.com/sites/default/files/downloads/HaskellHighPerformanceProgramming_ColorImages.pdf`.

Errata

Although we have taken every care to ensure the accuracy of our content, mistakes do happen. If you find a mistake in one of our books—maybe a mistake in the text or the code—we would be grateful if you could report this to us. By doing so, you can save other readers from frustration and help us improve subsequent versions of this book. If you find any errata, please report them by visiting http://www.packtpub.com/submit-errata, selecting your book, clicking on the **Errata Submission Form** link, and entering the details of your errata. Once your errata are verified, your submission will be accepted and the errata will be uploaded to our website or added to any list of existing errata under the Errata section of that title.

To view the previously submitted errata, go to https://www.packtpub.com/books/content/support and enter the name of the book in the search field. The required information will appear under the **Errata** section.

Piracy

Piracy of copyrighted material on the Internet is an ongoing problem across all media. At Packt, we take the protection of our copyright and licenses very seriously. If you come across any illegal copies of our works in any form on the Internet, please provide us with the location address or website name immediately so that we can pursue a remedy.

Please contact us at copyright@packtpub.com with a link to the suspected pirated material.

We appreciate your help in protecting our authors and our ability to bring you valuable content.

Questions

If you have a problem with any aspect of this book, you can contact us at questions@packtpub.com, and we will do our best to address the problem.

1
Identifying Bottlenecks

You have probably at least once written some very neat Haskell you were very proud of, until you test the code and it took ages to give an answer or even ran out of memory. This is very normal, especially if you are used to performance semantics in which performance can be analyzed on a step-by-step basis. Analyzing Haskell code requires a different mental model that is more akin to graph traversal.

Luckily, there is no reason to think that writing efficient Haskell is sorcery known only by math wizards or academics. Most bottlenecks are straightforward to identify with some understanding of Haskell's evaluation schema. This chapter will help you to reason about the performance of Haskell programs and to avoid some easily recognizable patterns of bad performance:

- Understanding lazy evaluation schemas and their implications
- Handling intended and unintended value memoization (CAFs)
- Utilizing (guarded) recursion and the worker/wrapper pattern efficiently
- Using accumulators correctly to avoid space leaks
- Analyzing strictness and space usage of Haskell programs
- Important compiler code optimizations, inlining and fusion

Meeting lazy evaluation

The default evaluation strategy in Haskell is lazy, which intuitively means that evaluation of values is deferred until the value is needed. To see lazy evaluation in action, we can fire up GHCi and use the `:sprint` command to inspect only the evaluated parts of a value. Consider the following GHCi session:

```
> let xs = enumFromTo 1 5 :: [Int]
> :sprint xs
xs = _
```

```
> xs !! 2
3
> :sprint xs
xs = 1 : 2 : 3 : _
```

 The code bundle for the book is also hosted on GitHub at `https://github.com/PacktPublishing/Haskell-High-Performance-Programming`. We also have other code bundles from our rich catalog of books and videos available at `https://github.com/PacktPublishing/`. Check them out!

Underscores in the output of `:sprint` stand for unevaluated values. The `enumFromTo` function builds a linked list lazily. At first, `xs` is only an unevaluated thunk. Thunks are in a way pointers to some calculation that is performed when the value is needed. The preceding example illustrates this: after we have asked for the third element of the list, the list has been evaluated up to the third element. Note also how pure values are implicitly shared; by evaluating the third element after binding the list to a variable, the original list was evaluated up to the third element. It will remain evaluated as such in memory until we destroy the last reference to the list head.

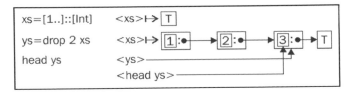

The preceding figure is a graphical representation of how a list is stored in memory. A **T** stands for a thunk; simple arrows represent pointers.

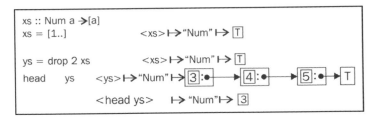

The preceding scenario is otherwise identical to the previous one, but now the list is **polymorphic**. Polymorphic values are simply functions with implicit parameters that provide the required operations when the type is specialized.

Be careful with :sprint and **ad hoc** polymorphic values! For example, xs' = enumFromTo 1 5 is by default given the type Num a => [a]. To evaluate such an expression, the type for a must be filled in, meaning that in :sprint xs', the value xs' is different from its first definition. Fully polymorphic values such as xs'' = [undefined, undefined] are okay.

A shared value can be either a performance essential or an ugly space leak. Consider the following seemingly similar scenarios (run with **ghci +RTS -M20m** to not throttle your computer):

```
> Data.List.foldl' (+) 0 [1..10^6]
500000500000

> let xs = [1..10^6] :: [Int]
> Data.List.foldl' (+) 0 xs
<interactive>: Heap exhausted;
```

So what happened? By just assigning the list to a variable, we exhausted the heap of a calculation that worked just fine previously. In the first calculation, the list could be garbage-collected as we folded over it. But in the second scenario, we kept a reference to the head of the linked list. Then the calculation blows up, because the elements cannot be garbage-collected due to the reference to xs.

Writing sum correctly

Notice that in the previous example we used a strict variant of left-fold called foldl' from Data.List and not the foldl exported from Prelude. Why couldn't we have just as well used the latter? After all, we are only asking for a single numerical value and, given lazy evaluation, we shouldn't be doing anything unnecessary. But we can see that this is not the case (again with ghci +RTS -M20m):

```
> Prelude.foldl (+) 0 [1..10^6]
<interactive>: Heap exhausted;
```

To understand the underlying issue here, let's step away from the fold abstraction for a moment and instead write our own sum function:

```
mySum :: [Int] -> Int
mySum      [] = 0
mySum (x:xs) = x + mySum xs
```

By testing it, we can confirm that mySum too exhausts the heap:

```
> :load sums.hs
> mySum [1..10^6]
<interactive>: Heap exhausted;
```

Because mySum is a pure function, we can expand its evaluation by hand as follows:

```
mySum [1..100]
    = 1 + mySum [2..100]
    = 1 + (2 + mySum [2..100])
    = 1 + (2 + (3 + mySum [2..100]))
    = ...
    = 1 + (2 + (... + mySum [100]))
  = 1 + (2 + (... + (100 + 0)))
```

From the expanded form we can see that we build up a huge sum chain and then start reducing it, starting from the very last element on the list. This means that we have all the elements of the list simultaneously in memory. From this observation, the obvious thing we could try is to evaluate the intermediate sum at each step. We could define a mySum2 which does just this:

```
mySum2 :: Int -> [Int] -> Int
mySum2 s []     = s
mySum2 s (x:xs) = let s' = s + x in mySum2 s' xs
```

But to our disappointment mySum2 blows up too! Let's see how it expands:

```
mySum2 0 [1..100]
    = let s1 = 0 + 1 in mySum2 s1 [2..100]
    = let s1 = 0 + 1
          s2 = s1 + 2
          in mySum2 s2 [2..100]
    ...
    = let s1 = 0 + 1
          ...
          s100 = s99 + 100
          in mySum2 s100 []
    = s100
    = s99 + 100
    = (s89 + 99) + 100
    ...
    = ((1 + 2) + ... ) + 100
```

Oops! We still build up a huge sum chain. It may not be immediately clear that this is happening. One could perhaps expect that *1 + 2* would be evaluated immediately as *3* as it is in strict languages. But in Haskell, this evaluation does not take place, as we can confirm with `:sprint`:

```
> let x = 1 + 2 :: Int
> :sprint x
x = _
```

Note that our `mySum` is a special case of `foldr` and `mySum2` corresponds to `foldl`.

Weak head normal form

The problem in our `mySum2` function was too much laziness. We built up a huge chain of numbers in memory only to immediately consume them in their original order. The straightforward solution then is to decrease laziness: if we could force the evaluation of the intermediate sums before moving on to the next element, our function would consume the list immediately. We can do this with a system function, `seq`:

```
mySum2' :: [Int] -> Int -> Int
mySum2' []     s = s
mySum2' (x:xs) s = let s' = s + x
                   in seq s' (mySum2' xs s')
```

This version won't blow up no matter how big a list you give it. Speaking very roughly, the `seq` function returns its second argument and ties the evaluation of its first argument to the evaluation of the second. In `seq a b`, the value of a is always evaluated before b. However, the notion of evaluation here is a bit ambiguous, as we will see soon.

When we evaluate a Haskell value, we mean one of two things:

- **Normal Form (NF)**: A fully evaluated value; for example when we `show` a value it will eventually be fully evaluated

- **Weak Head Normal Form (WHNF)**: Evaluated up to the first data constructor. `seq` evaluates its argument to WHNF only

Consider the following GHCi session:

```
> let t = const (Just "a") () :: Maybe String
> :sprint t
t = _
> t `seq` ()
> :sprint t
t = Just _
```

Even though we seq the value of t, it was only evaluated up to the Just constructor. The list of characters inside was not touched at all. When deciding whether or not a seq is necessary, it is crucial to understand WHNF and your data constructors. You should take special care of accumulators, like those in the intermediate sums in the mySum* functions. Because the actual value of the accumulator is often used only after the iterator has finished, it is very easy to accidentally build long chains of unevaluated thunks.

We could have annotated strictness more cleanly with the strict cousin of ($), the ($!) operator: mySum2' s (x:xs) = mySum2' xs $! s + x.

($!) is defined as f $! x = x `seq` f x.

Folding correctly

Now going back to folds, we recall that both foldl and foldr failed miserably, while (+) . foldl' instead did the right thing. In fact, if you just turn on optimizations in GHC then foldl (+) 0 will be optimized into a tight constant-space loop. This is the mechanism behind why we can get away with Prelude.sum, which is defined as foldl (+) 0.

What do we then have the foldr for? Let's look at the evaluation of foldr f a xs:

```
foldr f a [x1,x2,x3,x4,...]
    = f x1 (foldr f a [x2,x3,x4,...])
    = f x1 (f x2 (foldr f a [x3,x4,...]))
    = f x1 (f x2 (f x3 (foldr f a [x4,...])))
    ...
```

Note that, if the operator f isn't strict in its second argument, then foldr does not build up chains of unevaluated thunks. For example, let's consider foldr (:) [] [1..5]. Because (:) is just a data constructor, it is for sure lazy in its second (and first) argument. That fold then simply expands to 1 : (2 : (3 : ...)), so it is the identity function for lists.

Monadic bind (>>) for the IO monad is another example of a function that is lazy in its second argument:

```
foldr (>>) (return ()) [putStrLn "Hello", putStrLn "World!"]
```

For those monads whose actions do not depend on later actions, (that is, printing "Hello" is independent from printing "World!" in the IO monad), bind is non-strict in its second argument. On the other hand, the list monad is an example where bind is generally non-strict in its second argument. (Bind for lists is strict unless the first argument is the empty list.)

To sum up, use a left-fold when you need an accumulator function that is strict in both its operands. Most of the time, though, a right-fold is the best option. And with infinite lists, right-fold is the only option.

Memoization and CAFs

Memoization is a dynamic programming technique where intermediate results are saved and later reused. Many string and graph algorithms make use of memoization. Calculating the Fibonacci sequence, instances of the knapsack problem, and many bioinformatics algorithms are almost inherently solvable only with dynamic programming. A classic example in Haskell is the algorithm for the nth Fibonacci number, of which one variant is the following:

```
-- file: fib.hs

fib_mem :: Int -> Integer
fib_mem = (map fib [0..] !!)
  where fib 0 = 1
        fib 1 = 1
        fib n = fib_mem (n-2) + fib_mem (n-1)
```

Try it with a reasonable input size (10000) to confirm it does memoize the intermediate numbers. The time for lookups grows in size with larger numbers though, so a linked list is not a very appropriate data structure here. But let's ignore that for the time being and focus on what actually enables the values of this function to be memoized.

Looking at the top level, fib_mem looks like a normal function that takes input, does a computation, returns a result, and forgets everything it did with regard to its internal state. But in reality, fib_mem will memoize the results of all inputs it will ever be called with during its lifetime. So if fib_mem is defined at the top level, the results will persist in memory over the lifetime of the program itself!

The short story of why memoization is taking place in fib_mem stems from the fact that in Haskell functions exist at the same level with normal values such as integers and characters; that is, they are all values. Because the parameter of fib_mem does not occur in the function body, the body can be reduced irrespective of the parameter value. Compare fib_mem to this fib_mem_arg:

```
fib_mem_arg :: Int -> Integer
fib_mem_arg x = map fib [0..] !! x
  where fib 0 = 1
        fib 1 = 1
        fib n = fib_mem_arg (n-2) + fib_mem_arg (n-1)
```

Running fib_mem_arg with anything but very small arguments, one can confirm it does no memoization. Even though we can see that map fib [0..] does not depend on the argument number and could be memorized, it will not be, because applying an argument to a function will create a new expression that cannot implicitly have pointers to expressions from previous function applications. This is equally true with lambda abstractions as well, so this fib_mem_lambda is similarly stateless:

```
fib_mem_lambda :: Int -> Integer
fib_mem_lambda = \x -> map fib [0..] !! x
  where fib 0 = 1
        fib 1 = 1
        fib n = fib_mem_lambda (n-2) + fib_mem_lambda (n-1)
```

With optimizations, both fib_mem_arg and fib_mem_lambda will get rewritten into a form similar to fib_mem. So in simple cases, the compiler will conveniently fix our mistakes, but sometimes it is necessary to reorder complex computations so that different parts are memoized correctly.

 Be wary of memoization and compiler optimizations. GHC performs aggressive inlining (Explained in the section, *Inlining* and *stream fusion*) as a routine optimization, so it's very likely that values (and functions) get recalculated more often than was intended.

Constant applicative form

The formal difference between fib_mem and the others is that the fib_mem is something called a **constant applicative form**, or **CAF** for short. The compact definition of a CAF is as follows: *a supercombinator that is not a lambda abstraction.* We already covered the not-a-lambda abstraction, but what is a supercombinator?

A supercombinator is either a constant, say `1.5` or `['a'..'z']`, or a combinator whose subexpressions are supercombinators. These are all supercombinators:

```
\n -> 1 + n
\f n -> f 1 n
\f -> f 1 . (\g n -> g 2 n)
```

But this one is not a supercombinator:

```
\f g -> f 1 . (\n -> g 2 n)
```

This is because `g` is not a free variable of the inner lambda abstraction.

CAFs are constant in the sense that they contain no free variables, which guarantees that all thunks a CAF references directly are also constants. Actually, the constant subvalues are a part of the value. Subvalues are automatically memoized within the value itself.

A top-level `[Int]`, say, is just as valid a value as the `fib_mem` function for holding references to other values. You should pay attention to CAFs in your code because memoized values are space leaks when the memoization was unintended. All code that allocates lots of memory should be wrapped in functions that take one or more parameters.

Recursion and accumulators

Recursion is perhaps the most important pattern in functional programming. Recursive functions are more practical in Haskell than in imperative languages, due to referential transparency and laziness. Referential transparency allows the compiler to optimize the recursion away into a tight inner loop, and laziness means that we don't have to evaluate the whole recursive expression at once.

Next we will look at a few useful idioms related to recursive definitions: the worker/wrapper transformation, guarded recursion, and keeping accumulator parameters strict.

The worker/wrapper idiom

Worker/wrapper transformation is an optimization that GHC sometimes does, but worker/wrapper is also a useful coding idiom. The idiom consists of a (locally defined, tail-recursive) worker function and a (top-level) function that calls the worker. As an example, consider the following naive primality test implementation:

```
-- file: worker_wrapper.hs

isPrime :: Int -> Bool
```

```
isPrime n
    | n <= 1     = False
    | n <= 3     = True
    | otherwise = worker 2
       where
          worker i | i >= n       = True
                   | mod n i == 0 = False
                   | otherwise    = worker (i+1)
```

Here, `isPrime` is the wrapper and `worker` is the worker function. This style has two benefits. First, you can rest assured it will compile into optimal code. Second, the worker/wrapper style is both concise and flexible; notice how we did preliminary checks in the wrapper code before invoking the worker, and how the argument n is also (conveniently) in the worker's scope too.

Guarded recursion

In strict languages, tail-call optimization is often a concern with recursive functions. A function f is tail-recursive if the result of a recursive call to f is the result. In a lazy language such as Haskell, tail-call "optimization" is guaranteed by the evaluation schema. Actually, because in Haskell evaluation is normally done only up to WHNF (outmost data constructor), we have something more general than just tail-calls, called guarded recursion. Consider this simple moving average implementation:

```
-- file: sma.hs
sma :: [Double] -> [Double]
sma (x0:x1:xs) = (x0 + x1) / 2 : sma (x1:xs)
sma          xs = xs
```

The `sma` function is not tail-recursive, but nonetheless it won't build up a huge stack like an equivalent in some other language might do. In `sma`, the recursive call is guarded by the (:) data constructor. Evaluating the first element of a call to sma does not yet make a single recursive call to sma. Asking for the second element initiates the first recursive call, the third the second, and so on.

As a more involved example, let's build a **reverse polish notation (RPN)** calculator. RPN is a notation where operands precede their operator, so that *(3 1 2 + *)* in RPN corresponds to *((3 + 1) * 2)*, for example. To make our program easier to understand, we wish to separate parsing the input from performing the calculation:

```
-- file: rpn.hs
data Lex = Number Double Lex
         | Plus Lex
         | Times Lex
         | End
lexRPN :: String -> Lex
```

```
lexRPN = go . words
  where go ("*":rest) = Times (go rest)
        go ("+":rest) = Plus (go rest)
        go (num:rest) = Number (read num) (go rest)
        go         [] = End
```

The `Lex` datatype represents a formula in RPN and is similar to the standard list type. The `lexRPN` function reads a formula from string format into our own datatype. Let's add an `evalRPN` function, which evaluates a parsed RPN formula:

```
evalRPN :: Lex -> Double
evalRPN = go []
  where
    go stack (Number num rest)
      = go (num : stack) rest
    go (o1:o2:stack) (Plus rest)
      = let r = o1 + o2 in r `seq` go (r : stack) rest
    go (o1:o2:stack) (Times rest)
      = let r = o1 * o2 in r `seq` go (r : stack) rest
    go [res] End
      = res
```

We can test this implementation to confirm that it works:

```
> :load rpn.hs
> evalRPN $ lexRPN "5 1 2 + 4 * *"
60.0
```

The RPN expression (5 1 2 + 4 * *) is *(5 * ((1 + 2) * 4))* in infix, which is indeed equal to 60.

Note how the `lexRPN` function makes use of guarded recursion when producing the intermediate structure. It reads the input string incrementally and yields the structure an element at a time. The evaluation function `evalRPN` consumes the intermediate structure from left to right and is tail-recursive, so we keep the minimum amount of things in memory at all times.

[Linked lists equipped with guarded recursion (and lazy I/O) actually provide a lightweight streaming facility – for more on streaming see *Chapter 6, I/O and Streaming*.]

Accumulator parameters

In our examples so far, we have encountered a few functions that used some kind of accumulator. mySum2 had an Int that increased on every step. The go worker function in evalRPN passed on a stack (a linked list). The former had a space leak, because we didn't require the accumulator's value until at the end, at which point it had grown into a huge chain of pointers. The latter case was okay because the stack didn't grow in size indefinitely and the parameter was sufficiently strict in the sense that we didn't unnecessarily defer its evaluation. The fix we applied in mySum2' was to force the accumulator to WHNF at every iteration, even though the result was not strictly speaking required in that iteration.

The final lesson is that you should apply special care to your accumulator's strictness properties. If the accumulator must always be fully evaluated in order to continue to the next step, then you're automatically safe. But if there is a danger of an unnecessary chain of thunks being constructed due to a lazy accumulator, then adding a seq (or a bang pattern, see *Chapter 2, Choose the Correct Data Structures*) is more than just a good idea.

Inspecting time and space usage

It is often necessary to have numbers about the time and space usage of Haskell programs, either to have an indicator of how well the program performs or to identify unnecessary allocations. The GHC Runtime System flag -s enables printing allocation and garbage-collection statistics when the program finishes.

Let's try this with an example program, which naively calculates the covariance of two lists:

```
-- file: time_and_space.hs
import Data.List (foldl')

sum' = foldl' (+) 0

mean :: [Double] -> Double
mean v = sum' v / fromIntegral (length v)

covariance :: [Double] -> [Double] -> Double
covariance xs ys =
    sum' (zipWith (\x y -> (x - mean xs) * (y - mean ys)) xs ys)
    / fromIntegral (length xs)

main = do
    let xs = [1, 1.1 .. 500]
        ys = [2, 2.1 .. 501]
    print $ covariance xs ys
```

To enable passing options for the Runtime System, we must compile with -rtsopts:

```
$ ghc -rtsopts time_and_space.hs
```

For the time being, we ignore optimizations GHC could do for us and compile the program without any:

```
$ ./time_and_space +RTS -s
20758.399999992813
    802,142,688 bytes allocated in the heap
      1,215,656 bytes copied during GC
        339,056 bytes maximum residency (2 sample(s))
         88,104 bytes maximum slop
              2 MB total memory in use (0 MB lost due to
  fragmentation)
```

			Tot time	(elapsed)	Avg pause	Max pause
Gen 0	1529 colls,	0 par	0.008s	0.007s	0.0000s	0.0004s
Gen 1	2 colls,	0 par	0.001s	0.001s	0.0003s	0.0006s

```
  INIT    time    0.000s  (  0.000s elapsed)
  MUT     time    1.072s  (  1.073s elapsed)
  GC      time    0.008s  (  0.008s elapsed)
  EXIT    time    0.000s  (  0.000s elapsed)
  Total   time    1.083s  (  1.082s elapsed)

  %GC     time      0.8%  (0.7% elapsed)

  Alloc rate    747,988,284 bytes per MUT second

  Productivity  99.2% of total user, 99.3% of total elapsed
```

On the first line of output from the Runtime System, we see that we allocated over 800 megabytes of memory. This is quite a lot for a program that only handles two lists of 5,000 double-precision values. There is definitely something in our code that could be made a lot more efficient. The output also contains other useful information, such as the total memory in use and, more importantly, some statistics on garbage collection. Our program spent only 0.8% of time in GC, meaning the program was doing productive things 99.2% of the time. So our performance problem lies in the calculations our program performs themselves.

If we look at the definition of covariance, we can spot the many invocations to mean in the argument lambda to `zipWith`: we actually calculate the means of both lists thousands of times over. So let's optimize that away:

```
covariance' :: [Double] -> [Double] -> Double
covariance' xs ys =
    let mean_xs = mean xs
        mean_ys = mean ys
        in
    sum' (zipWith (\x y -> (x - mean_xs) * (y - mean_ys)) xs ys)
    / fromIntegral (length xs)
```

With `covariance'` we get down to three megabytes of allocation:

```
3,263,680 bytes allocated in the heap
  915,024 bytes copied during GC
  339,032 bytes maximum residency (2 sample(s))
  112,936 bytes maximum slop
        2 MB total memory in use (0 MB lost due to fragmentation)
```

	Tot time (elapsed)	Avg pause	Max pause		
Gen 0	5 colls,	0 par	0.002s	0.002s	0.0003s
0.0005s					
Gen 1	2 colls,	0 par	0.001s	0.001s	0.0005s
0.0010s					

```
INIT    time    0.000s  ( 0.000s elapsed)
MUT     time    0.003s  ( 0.003s elapsed)
GC      time    0.003s  ( 0.003s elapsed)
EXIT    time    0.000s  ( 0.000s elapsed)
Total   time    0.008s  ( 0.006s elapsed)
```

```
%GC      time       35.3%  (44.6% elapsed)


Alloc rate   1,029,648,194 bytes per MUT second


Productivity  63.1% of total user, 79.6% of total elapsed
```

That's over a 250-fold decrease in heap allocation! With the new version, we now have a considerable amount of time going to GC, about a third. This is about as good as we can get without enabling compiler optimizations; if we compile with -O, we would get to under two megabytes of heap allocation. And if you tried the original covariance performance with optimizations on, you should get exactly the same performance as with the newer hand-optimized variant. In fact, both versions compile to the same assembly code. This is a demonstration of the sophistication of GHC's optimizer, which we will take a deeper look at in a later chapter.

GHCi tip:

By setting +s in the interpreter, you can get time and space statistics of every evaluation, which can be handy for quick testing. Keep in mind though that no optimizations can be enabled for interpreted code, so compiled code can have very different performance characteristics. To test with optimizations, you should compile the module with optimizations and then import it into GHCi.

Increasing sharing and minimizing allocation

In the covariance example, we observed that we could improve code performance by explicitly sharing the result of an expensive calculation. Alternatively, enabling compiler optimizations would have had that same effect (with some extras). Most of the time, the optimizer does the right thing, but that is not always the case. Consider the following versions of rather a silly function:

```
-- file: time_and_space_2.hs


goGen        u = sum [1..u] + product [1..u]
goGenShared  u = let xs = [1..u] in sum xs + product xs
```

Try reasoning which of these functions executes faster. The first one builds two possibly very large lists and then immediately consumes them, independent of each other. The second one shares the list between sum and product.

The list-sharing function is about 25% slower than the list-rebuilding function. When we share the list, we need to keep the whole list in memory, whereas by just enumerating the elements we can discard the elements as we go. The following table confirms our reasoning. The list-sharing function has a larger maximum residency in system memory and does more GC:

U = 10000	Time	Allocated heap	Copied during GC	Maximum residency	Total memory	Time in GC
goGen	0.050ms	87 MB	10 MB	0.7 MB	6 MB	60%
goGenShared	0.070ms	88 MB	29 MB	0.9 MB	7 MB	70%

Recall that, in the covariance example, the compiler automatically shared the values of *sin x* and *cos x* for us when we enabled optimizations. But in the previous example, we didn't get implicit sharing of the lists, even though they are thunks just like the results of *sin x* and *cos x*. So what magic enabled the GHC optimizer to choose the best sharing schema in both cases? The optimizer is non-trivial, and unfortunately, in practice it's not feasible to blindly rely on the optimizer always doing "the right thing." If you need to be sure that some sharing will take place, you should test it yourself.

Let's go back to our previous example of sum and product. Surely we could do better than spending 60% of the time in GC. The obvious improvement would be to make only one pass through one list and calculate both the sum and product of the elements simultaneously. The code is then a bit more involved:

```
goGenOnePass u = su + pu
   where
     (su, pu) = foldl f (0,1) [1..u]
     f (s, p) i = let s' = s+i
                      p' = p*i
                  in s' `seq` p' `seq` (s', p')
```

Note the sequential use of seq in the definition of goGenOnePass. This version has a much better performance: only 10% in GC and about 50% faster than our first version:

U = 10000	Time	Allocated heap	Copied during GC	Maximum residency	Total memory	Time in GC
GoGenOnePass	0.025ms	86 MB	0.9 MB	0.05 MB	2 MB	10%

The takeaway message is that once again algorithmic complexity matters more than technical optimizations. The one-pass version executed in half the time of the original two-pass version, as would be expected.

With the Bang Patterns (`BangPatterns`) language extension (available since GHC 6.6) the `f` binding could have been written more cleanly as `f (!s, !p) i = (s + i, p * I)` with very slightly degraded performance (0.7%). Annotating a binding with a bang means that evaluation of that binding will be bound to the evaluation of its surrounding tuple.

Compiler code optimizations

Haskell compilers perform aggressive optimization transformations on code. GHC optimization passes are highly sophisticated, so much that one rarely needs to worry about performance. We have seen some of the effects of `ghc -O1` in our examples so far; in all cases,`-O1`increased performance relative to no optimizations, or `-Onot`, and in some optimizations passes were the difference between constant and exponential complexity.

Inlining and stream fusion

GHC performs aggressive **inlining**, which simply means rewriting a function call with the function's definition. Because all values in Haskell are referentially transparent, any function can be inlined within the scope of its definition. Especially in loops, inlining improves performance drastically. The GHC inliner does inlining within a module, but also to some extent cross-module and cross-package.

Some rules of thumb regarding inlining:

- If a definition is only used once, and isn't exported, it will always be inlined.
- When a function body is small, it will almost certainly be inlined no matter where or how often it is used.
- Bigger functions may be inlined cross-module. To ensure that foo is always inlined, add a `{-# INLINE foo #-}` pragma near the definition of `foo`.

With these easy rules, you rarely need to worry about problems from bad inlining. For completeness's sake, there is also a `NOINLINE` pragma which ensures a definition is never inlined. `NOINLINE` is mostly used for hacks that would break referential transparency; see *Chapter 4, The Devil's in the Detail*.

Another powerful technique is **stream fusion**. Behind that fancy name is just a bunch of equations that are used to perform code rewriting (see *Chapter 4, The Devil's in the Detail* for the technicalities).

When working with lists, you may be tempted to rewrite code like this:

```
map f . map g . map h
```

Rather than to use intermediate lists:

```
map (f . g . h)
```

But there is no other reason than cosmetics to do this, because with optimizations GHC performs stream fusion, after which both expressions are time- and space-equivalent. Stream fusion is also performed for other structures than [], which we will take a look at in the next chapter.

Polymorphism performance

In principle, (ad hoc) polymorphic programs should carry a performance cost. To evaluate a polymorphic function, a dictionary must be passed in, which contains the specializations for the type specified on the caller side. However, almost always GHC can fill in the dictionary already at compile time, reducing the cost of polymorphism to zero. The big and obvious exception is code that uses reflection (**Typeable**). Also, some sufficiently complex polymorphic code might defer the dictionary passing to runtime, although, most of the time you can expect a zero cost.

Either way, it might ease your mind to have some notion of the cost of dictionary passing in runtime. Let's write a program with both general and specialized versions of the same function, compile it without optimizations, and compare the performance. Our program will just iterate a simple calculation with double-precision values:

```
-- file: class_performance.hs

class Some a where
    next :: a -> a -> a

instance Some Double where
    next a b = (a + b) / 2

goGeneral :: Some a => Int -> a -> a
goGeneral 0 x = x
goGeneral n x = goGeneral (n-1) (next x x)

goSpecialized :: Int -> Double -> Double
goSpecialized 0 x = x
goSpecialized n x = goSpecialized (n-1) (next' x x)

next' :: Double -> Double -> Double
next' a b = (a + b) / 2
```

I compiled and ran both versions separately with their own `main` entry points using the following command lines:

```
ghc class_performance.hs
time ./class_performance +RTS -s
```

On my machine, with 5,000,000 iterations, the general version does 1.09 GB of allocation and takes 3.4s. The specialized version does 1.01 GB of allocation and runs in about 3.2s. So the extra memory cost was about 8%, which is considerable. But by enabling optimizations, both versions will have exactly the same performance.

Partial functions

Here's a puzzle: given the following definition, which is faster, `partial` or `total`?

```
partialHead :: [a] -> a
partialHead (x:_) = x

totalHead :: [a] -> Maybe a
totalHead []     = Nothing
totalHead (x:_) = Just x

partial = print $ partialHead [1..]

total = print $ case totalHead [1..] of
                  Nothing -> 1
                  Just n  -> n
```

The `total` variant uses a head that wraps its result inside a new data constructor, whereas the `partial` one results in a crash when a case is not matched, but in exchange doesn't perform any extra wrapping. Surely the partial variant must be faster, right? Well, almost always it is not. Both functions have exactly the same time and space requirements.

Partial functions are justified in some situations, but performance is rarely if ever one of them. In the example, the `Maybe`-wrapper of total will have a zero performance cost. The performance cost of the case analysis will be left, however, but a similar analysis is done in the partial variant too; the error case must be handled anyway, so that the program can exit gracefully. Of course, even GHC is not a silver bullet and you should always keep in mind that it might miss some optimizations. If you absolutely need to rely on certain optimizations to take place, you should test your program to confirm the correct results.

Summary

In this chapter, we learned how lazy evaluation works, what weak head normal form is, and how to control it by increasing strictness with different methods. We considered the peculiarities of right-fold, left-fold, and strict left-fold, and in which situations one fold strategy works better than another. We introduced the concept of CAF along with memoization techniques, utilized the worker/wrapper pattern, and used guarded recursion to write clean and efficient recursive programs.

We used the `:sprint` command in GHCi to inspect unevaluated thunks and the Runtime System option `-s` to inspect the heap usage and GC activity of compiled programs. We took a look at inlining, stream fusion, and the performance costs of partial functions and polymorphism.

In the next chapter, we will take a look at other basic data and control structures, such as different array structures and some monads. But first, we will learn about the performance semantics of Haskell data types and related common optimization techniques.

2
Choosing the Correct Data Structures

Perhaps the next most important topic in Haskell performance after lazy evaluation is data structures. I say the next most important because although data structures form a wider area than lazy evaluation, the unique performance aspects of lazy evaluation should deserve more attention. Still, structuring data efficiently is a must for performance, and in Haskell this often requires taking laziness into account, too.

Haskell gives the programmer lots of variety and clutches to structuring data, ranging from low-level primitives to ingenious, purely functional data structures. The traditional (re-)implementation costs associated with quick'n'dirty versus highly optimized solutions are really low in Haskell, and therefore there are even fewer reasons for complex premature optimizations in Haskell than in many other languages.

This chapter will help you to understand the performance semantics of Haskell values in general and to write efficient programs for processing numbers, text, and arbitrary data in different classic container data types. By the end of this chapter, you will know how to choose and design optimal data structures in applications. You will be able to drop the level of abstraction in slow parts of code, all the way to mutable data structures if necessary.

This chapter will cover the following points:

- Datatype design: boxed and unboxed, strict fields and unpacking fields
- Efficiently processing numeric, binary, and textual data
- Using common sequential, tabular, and mapping container data types
- Employing mutable state in Haskell: IO and ST monads
- Monad and monad transformer performance

Annotating strictness and unpacking datatype fields

Recall that in the previous chapter, we used `seq` to force strict evaluation. With the `BangPatterns` extension, we can force functions arguments. Strict arguments are evaluated WHNF just before entering the function body:

```
{-# LANGUAGE BangPatterns #-}

f !s (x:xs) = f (s + 1) xs
f !s     _  = s
```

Using bangs for annotating strictness in fact predates the `BangPatterns` extension (and the older compiler flag `-fbang-patterns` in GHC 6.x). With just plain Haskell98, we are allowed to use bangs to make datatype fields strict:

```
> data T = T !Int
```

A bang in front of a field ensures that whenever the outer constructor (`T` above) is in WHNF, the inner field is as well in WHNF. We can check this:

```
> T undefined `seq` ()
*** Exception: Prelude.undefined
```

There are no restrictions to which fields can be strict, be it recursive or polymorphic fields, although it rarely makes sense to make recursive fields strict. Consider the fully strict linked list:

```
data List a = List !a !(List a)
            | ListEnd
```

With this much strictness, you cannot represent parts of infinite lists without always requiring infinite space. Moreover, before accessing the head of a finite strict list you must evaluate the list all the way to the last element. Strict lists don't have the streaming property of lazy lists.

By default, all data constructor fields are pointers to other data constructors or primitives, regardless of their strictness. This applies to basic data types `Int`, `Double`, `Char`, and so on, which are not primitive in Haskell. They are data constructors over their primitive counterparts `Int#`, `Double#`, and `Char#`:

```
> :info Int
data Int = GHC.Types.I# GHC.Prim.Int#
```

There is a performance overhead, the size of pointer dereference between types, say, Int and Int#, but an Int can represent lazy values (called thunks), whereas primitives cannot. Without thunks, we couldn't have lazy evaluation. Luckily, GHC is intelligent enough to unroll wrapper types as primitives in many situations, completely eliminating indirect references.

The hash suffix is specific to GHC and always denotes a primitive type. The GHC modules do expose the primitive interface. Programming with primitives, you can further micro-optimize code and get C-like performance. However, several limitations and drawbacks apply, which we shall consider in *Chapter 4, The Devil's in the Detail*.

Unbox with UNPACK

The most powerful trick available to make efficient datatypes in Haskell is to unpack their fields, also known as unboxing. Those terms are almost synonymous; unboxing means very generally peeling off layers of indirection, while unpacking refers to methods of unboxing in GHC. An unpacked field is no longer a pointer to a data constructor. Instead, the value is stored in memory next to the constructor, where the pointer to a value (or a thunk) is normally stored.

Use the {-# UNPACK #-} pragma before a field to unpack it. An unpacked field must also be strict, that is, prefixed with a bang, otherwise it could be a pointer to a thunk, and there would be no way to know whether the value is evaluated or not.

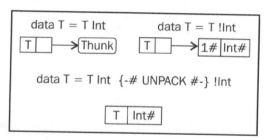

The preceding diagram illustrates how a value such as T (1 + 2) would be represented in memory given different definitions for T. Without strictness annotation, the field points to a thunk. When the field is strictly defined, the contents will be calculated, but the `field` is still a pointer to the value.

In the unpacked version, the contents of field are stored in place of the pointer.

Note that, if compiled with -O and above optimization level, there is an error in the image, as an optimization passed in GHC automatically unpacks strict fields when possible. The strict field version then produces exactly the code of the version with explicit unpacking. However, in performance-critical datatypes, and especially in library code, it is good practice to use explicit unpacking, because automatic unboxing isn't always a good idea.

There are some restrictions to which kinds of values can be declared unpacked. Most importantly, sum types, parametrically polymorphic values, and functions are ruled out. So these are all invalid data declarations:

```haskell
data S = S {-# UNPACK #-} !(Maybe Int)   -- invalid!

data F = F {-# UNPACK #-} !(Int -> Int) -- invalid!

data P a = P {-# UNPACK #-} !a           -- invalid!
```

On the other hand, these are valid:

```haskell
data T = T {-# UNPACK #-} !(Int, Int)

data R a = R { field_a :: a
             , field_t :: {-# UNPACK #-} !T
             }
data GADT a where
  Empty :: GADT ()
  Some  :: a - > {-# UNPACK #-} !Int - > Some Int
```

That last type requires enabling the GADTs extension, for **general algebraic datatypes**.

Then how about this one?

```haskell
data W = W {-# UNPACK #-} !Int {-# UNPACK #-} !W
```

It compiles just fine. W is not a sum type nor polymorphic, so it will be unpacked. But you cannot actually do anything with W – it's impossible to construct values of type W: W 1 undefined as they will produce an error, while let w = W 1 w produces a loop! So as a corollary of other requirements of unboxing, we have that inductive fields cannot be unpacked.

Now let's find out the effect of unpacking on performance in a tight loop with the following little program:

```haskell
-- file: strict_and_unpacked.hs

{-# LANGUAGE BangPatterns #-}
```

```
data PairP = PairP Int Int deriving (Show)

data PairS = PairS !Int !Int deriving (Show)

data PairU = PairU {-# UNPACK #-} !Int {-# UNPACK #-} !Int deriving
  (Show)

iter :: Int -> (a -> a) -> a -> a
iter end f x = go 0 x
    where go !n x | n < end    = go (n + 1) $! f x
                  | otherwise = x
```

With 1000 iterations of a function that does simple arithmetic on the fields, we obtain the following heap usage for the different data types:

PairP	370 KB
PairS	50 KB
PairU	50 KB

The difference is very big indeed! But do note that unboxing doesn't always increase performance. For example, consider a record with a lot of fields. If those fields contain large chunks of unboxed data, then to make a copy of the record would mean duplicating all of that unboxed data too. Comparing to if those fields were lazy, that is, represented by pointers, we would only need to make copies of those pointers.

Using anonymous tuples

Tuples may seem harmless at first; they just lump a bunch of values together. But note that the fields in a tuple aren't strict, so a two-tuple corresponds to the slowest PairP data type from our previous benchmark.

If you need a strict Tuple type, you need to define one yourself. This is also one more reason to prefer custom types over nameless tuples in many situations. These two structurally similar tuple types have widely different performance semantics:

```
data Tuple = Tuple {-# UNPACK #-} !Int {-# UNPACK #-} !Int
data Tuple2 = Tuple2 {-# UNPACK #-} !(Int, Int)
```

If you really want unboxed anonymous tuples, you can enable the UnboxedTuples extension and write things with types, like (# Int#, Char# #). But note that a number of restrictions apply to unboxed tuples, as to all primitives. The most important restriction is that unboxed types may not occur where polymorphic types or values are expected, because polymorphic values are always considered as pointers.

Performance of GADTs and branching

Generalized algebraic datatypes are great. Existential quantification, which is more or less, comes with GADTs, but it's relatively easy to destroy performance with existential quantification.

Consider the following slightly contrived GADT, capable of representing all integral types and Chars:

```
-- file: gadts.hs

{-# LANGUAGE GADTs #-}

data Object a where
    Number :: Integral a => a -> Object a
    Character :: Char -> Object Char
```

Turns out, this datatype is quite benign. The following two folds, when compiled with at least-o, have exactly the same performance:

```
foldl (+) 0 [1..1000000 :: Int]

foldl (\a (Number b) -> a + b) 0
        [ Number x  | x <- [1..1000000 :: Int] ]
```

But this is an extremely simplified example, where GHC in fact discards our intermediate Number constructors altogether and just produces a tight loop over integers. And due to the extra type information present in the GADT, we can switch the function we fold into:

```
f :: a -> Object a -> a
f a x = case x of
            Character _ -> a
            Number n -> a + n
```

GHC would inline f and specialize it with type Int → Object Int → Int, learn that branch Character is never reached in the specialized version, discard it, and we'd end up with the same tight loop. Which is pretty nice!

But if we add an extra constructor to Object:

```
Number' :: Integral a => a -> Object a
```

And add an extra branch to f:

```
case x of
    ...
    Number' n -> a - n
```

Then GHC will be forced to consider two branches, right? Well in general, the answer would be yes. But in our simple example, GHC will still happily produce the same tight loop. What is happening is that GHC fuses the list of `Object` values from the list comprehension, learning that no values are constructed with the `Number'` constructor, inferring that the new branch is still redundant.

But if we forced either the folding function or the object list and its elements to not inline (with `NOINLINE` or producing the objects elsewhere), or indeed constructed values with multiple constructors, then GHC would be forced to consider all type-correct branches.

So, in general, GADTs are optimized pretty well. But what about existentials? Consider using this `ObjectE` instead of `Object`:

```
data ObjectE where
    NumberE :: Integral a => a -> ObjectE
```

Here we're just saying that we don't care which number type a given object is, only that it has an `Integral` instance. But if we compare the performance of this fold over `[ObjectE]`:

```
foldl (\a (NumberE b) -> a + fromIntegral b) 0
    [ NumberE x | x <- [1..1000000 :: Int] ]
```

To the performance of a similar fold over `[Object Int]`, the numbers are as follows:

- `[Object Int]`: 51 KB allocated and execution time about 5ms
- `[ObjectE]`: 32,000 KB allocated and execution time about 30ms

That is, because of an existential, our program got six times slower, and additionally started allocating space linear to input size. What exactly is going on here?

The problem is that by wrapping our numbers inside an existential, we are deliberately forgetting the type. The `type` class constraint lets us retain some information, but with an extra cost of a layer of indirection. Existentials force this indirection to persist through all GHC optimizations, and that's why our code was so slow. Furthermore, with that added indirection, GHC can no longer unbox our numbers as efficiently, which explains the extra allocations we observed.

The lessons here are that existentials have an overhead, and that extra type information available in GADTs helps not only the programmer, but also the compiler, by opening up extra possibilities for optimizations. GADT's are useful and fast, while existentials are just useful.

Handling numerical data

Like all general-purpose programming languages, Haskell too has a few different number types. Unlike other languages, the number types in Haskell are organized into a hierarchy via type classes. This gives us two things:

- Check sat compiletime we aren't doing anything insane with numbers
- The ability to write polymorphic functions in the number type with enhanced type safety

An example of an insane thing would be dividing an integer by another integer, expecting an integer as a result. And because every integral type is an instance of the `Integral` class, we can easily write a `factorial` function that doesn't care what the underlying type is (as long as it represents an integer):

```
factorial :: Integral a => a -> a
factorial n = product [1..n]
```

The following table lists basic numeric types in Haskell:

Type	Size
`Int`	Signed integers, machine-dependent
`Word`	Unsigned integers, machine-dependent
`Double`	Double-precision floating point, machine-dependent
`Float`	Single-precision floating point, machine-dependent
`Integer`	Arbitrary precision integers
`Integral a => Ratio a`	Rational numbers (Rational = Ratio Integer)
`Int/Word{8,16,32,64}`	Signed (Int) or unsigned (Word) integers with fixed size(from 8 to 64 bits)
`RealFloat a => Complex a`	Complex numbers
`HasResolution a => Fixed a`	Arbitrary size, fixed-precision numbers (a represents precision, like E0, E1, and so on)

Apart from Integer and its derivatives, the performance of basic operations is very much the same. Integer is special because of its ability to represent arbitrary-sized numbers via **GNU Multiple Precision Arithmetic Library (GMP)**. For its purpose, Integer isn't slow, but the overhead relative to low-level types is big.

Because of the strict number hierarchy, some things are a bit inconvenient. However, there are idiomatic conventions in many situations. For example:

- Instead of `fromIntegral . length`, use `Data.List.genericLength`
- Instead of `1 / fromIntegral (length xs)`, write `1 % length xs`

- Use `float2Double` and `double2Float` from `GHC.Float` to convert between Floats and Doubles

Loops that use intermediate numbers usually benefit from strictness annotations. GHC often unboxes strict number arguments, which leads to efficient code. Strict arguments in non-recursive functions, however, are usually not a good idea, resulting in longer execution times due to suboptimal sharing.

GHC flags that often give better performance for number-heavy code include `-O2`, `-fexcess-precision`, and `-fllvm`. The last flag compiles via LLVM, which requires the LLVM libraries installed (and currently (GHC 7 series) only version 3.5 is supported).

Handling binary and textual data

The smallest piece of data is a bit (0 or 1), which is isomorphic to `Bool` (`True` or `False`). When you need just one bit, a Bool should be your choice. If you need a few bits, then a tuple of Bools will fit the purpose when performance is not critical. A `[Bool]` is sometimes convenient, but should only be chosen for convenience in some situations.

For high-performance binary data, you could define your own data type with strict Bool fields. But this has an important caveat, namely that Bool is not a primitive but an algebraic data type:

```
data Bool = False | True
```

The consequence is that you cannot unpack a Bool similar to how you could an Int or Double. In Haskell, Bool values will always be represented by pointers. Fortunately for many bit-fiddling applications, you can define a data type like this:

```
data BitStruct = BitStore !Bool !Bool !Bool
```

This will get respectable performance. However, if you need a whole array of bits it quickly becomes inconvenient to define a field per bit.

Representing bit arrays

One way to define a bit array in Haskell that still retains the convenience of Bool is:

```
import Data.Array.Unboxed
type BitArray = UArray Int Bool
```

This representation packs 8 bits per byte, so it's space efficient. See the following section on arrays in general to learn about time efficiency – for now we only note that `BitArray` is an immutable data structure, like `BitStruct`, and that copying small BitStructs is cheaper than copying BitArrays due to overheads in `UArray`.

Consider a program that processes a list of integers and tells whether they are even or odd counts of numbers divisible by 2, 3, and 5. We can implement this with simple recursion and a three-bit accumulator. Here are three alternative representations for the accumulator:

```
-- file: bitstore.hs

{-# LANGUAGE BangPatterns #-}

import Data.Array.Unboxed
import Data.Bits (xor)
type BitTuple = (Bool, Bool, Bool)
data BitStruct = BitStruct !Bool !Bool !Bool deriving Show
type BitArray = UArray Int Bool
```

And the program itself is defined along these lines:

```
go :: acc -> [Int] -> acc
go acc              []      = acc
go (two three five) (x:xs) = go ((test 2 x `xor` two)
(test 3 x `xor` three)
(test 5 x `xor` five)) xs

test n x = x `mod` n == 0
```

I've omitted the details here. They can be found in the `bitstore.hs` file.

The fastest variant is BitStruct, then comes BitTuple (30% slower), and BitArray is the slowest (130% slower than BitStruct). Although BitArray is the slowest (due to making a copy of the array on every iteration), it would be easy to scale the array in size or make it dynamic. Note also that this benchmark is really on the extreme side; normally programs do a bunch of other stuff besides updating an array in a tight loop.

If you need fast array updates, you can resort to mutable arrays discussed later on. It might also be tempting to use `Data.Vector.Unboxed.Vector Bool` from the `vector` package, due to its nice interface. But beware that that representation uses one byte for every bit, wasting 7 bits for every bit.

Handling bytes and blobs of bytes

The next simplest piece of information after bits is a byte, which is eight bits. In Haskell, the Word8 type represents a byte. Often though, whole words are more useful. The Word type has the same size as Int, defined by the underlying architecture. Types Word16, Word32, and Word64 consist of respective numbers of bits.

Like a bit array, a byte array could be represented as a UArray. But a more standard solution is to use ByteString from the bytestring package. The bytestring package uses a blazingly fast pointer representation internally, while the API looks just like the API for standard lists.

Let's test how fast it really is:

```
-- file: bytestring-perf.hs

import qualified Data.ByteString as B
import System.IO (stdin)

go :: Int -> Int -> IO Int
go 0 s = return $! s
go n s = do bs <- B.hGet stdin (1024 * 1024)
            go (n-1) $! B.length bs + s

main = go 2048 0 >>= print
```

This program reads two gigabytes of binary data from its standard input in one megabyte chunks and prints the total of bytes read. Test it with this:

```
$ ghc -rtsopts -O bytestring-perf.hs
$ time ./bytestring-perf +RTS -s < /dev/zero
```

On my machine, the program takes 0.25 seconds and allocates about 2.1 gigabytes in heap – meaning there was hardly any space overhead from our use of ByteString and speed was respectable as well.

The Data.ByteString.ByteString datatype is strict, meaning that all bytes of a ByteString will be in memory. The Data.ByteString.Lazy module defines its own ByteString, which is lazy:

```
data ByteString = Empty
                | Chunk {-# UNPACK #-} !S.ByteString ByteString
```

Note that you can unbox strict ByteStrings in your own data types as well.

Using lazy ByteStrings, we could rewrite our program as follows:

```
-- file: bytestring-lazy-perf.hs

import qualified Data.ByteString.Lazy as B
import qualified Data.ByteString as S
import System.IO (stdin)

size = 2048 * 1024 * 1024

go :: Int -> [S.ByteString] -> Int
go s (c:cs) | s >= size = s
            | otherwise = go (s + S.length c) cs

main = do
    bs <- B.hGetContents stdin
    print $ go 0 (B.toChunks bs)
```

This program has very similar memory footprint to the strict ByteString version, but is about 20% slower. That slowdown comes from different chunk sizes. hGetContents uses a hard-coded chunk size of 32 KB (described in the documentation of ByteString). In our previous example, we used a chunk size of 1024 KB, which is a better fit when a lot of bytes are read in. If you changed the chunk size of the strict program variant to 32 KB, the difference between the strict and lazy variants would be negligible, though lazy ByteStrings produce more GC traffic.

Thanks to lazy ByteStrings, we could use hGetContents to get an infinite ByteString and turn our loop into a pure function. Pure code is in general more valuable than just raw performance.

Starting with bytestring 0.10.0.0, the Data.ByteString.Short module provides byte arrays with zero memory overhead. A normal ByteString has a memory overhead of a few Word, and a ByteString, once allocated, cannot be moved by GC. This means that multiple small ByteString could contribute to heap fragmentation, or wasted space. ShortByteString, on the other hand, can be moved by GC, but their API is not nearly as complete as the ByteString API, and should only be used for internal optimization.

Working with characters and strings

The standard Char data type is defined to hold any character of the ISO 10646 character set. Char represents every character with 31 bits.

The text representation chosen in `Prelude` and base libraries is `String = [Char]`. This representation has the convenient property that an understanding of, and operations on, lists carries over to Strings. Furthermore, it's trivial to write programs that process infinite data sequentially without any extra libraries.

Other than being convenient for the programmer, linked lists have a huge overhead, making them ill-suited for high performance string processing. Furthermore, String isn't totally **Unicode-correct** because some strings' lengths depend on their case.

We could fix performance with a `UArray ix Char`. However, this still wouldn't get us Unicode-correctness.

The `bytestring` package provides a simple 8-bit character interface for ByteStrings in separate `Char8` modules (one for strict and lazy ByteStrings), which may sometimes be all you need if you are sure you're working with 8-bit (ISO 8859) encoded strings.

Using the text library

The library of choice for general text processing nowadays is `text`. Its API is designed to resemble String functions, but is faster and Unicode-correct. The Text datatype stores values UTF-16 encoded. That's 16 bits for most characters and 32 bits for obscure characters. Compare this to 31 bits in a Char.

 Note that due to the different representations, there is an overhead when converting Strings and Texts. It doesn't always make sense to convert from String to Text or vice versa.

Similar to the `bytestring` library, the `text` library provides strict and lazy variants under different modules. I/O operations with strict and lazy Text are provided under corresponding modules.

Unlike the `bytestring` library, the `text` library uses internally an array representation and employs a technique called **stream fusion** to eliminate the need for intermediate values. Basically this means that pipelines such as `T.length . T.toUpper . T.init` will be optimized into a single loop over the input value when optimizations are enabled. Functions that are fused away are indicated in the documentation of text with the phrase Subject to fusion.

The `text-icu` package provides bindings for the mature **International Components for Unicode (ICU)** library on top of text.

Builders for iterative construction

Builder abstractions can be used to efficiently compose multiple small chunks into one big ByteString, Text, or even String. The `text` and `bytestring` packages provide modules, `Data.ByteString.Builder` and `Data.Text.Lazy.Builder`, which define Builder types that compose as monoids.

Say we have a data type, `Tree`, defined by:

```
data Tree = Tree !(Int, Tree) !(Int, Tree)
          | Leaf !ByteString
```

We want a ByteString serialization of `Tree` values, so that for an example value (this requires enabling the OverloadedStrings extension):

```
Tree (1,Leaf "one") (2, Tree (3,Leaf "three") (4,Leaf "four"))
```

This encodes as `[1:"one",2:[3:"three",4:"four"]]`.

We can accomplish this with the following function:

```
-- file: builder-encoding.hs

import Data.ByteString (ByteString)
import qualified Data.ByteString.Builder as B
import Data.Monoid ((<>))
import System.IO (stdout)

encodeTree :: Tree -> B.Builder
encodeTree (Tree (l1, t1) (l2, t2)) = B.charUtf8 '['
    <> B.intDec l1 <> B.charUtf8 ':'<> encodeTree t1
    <> B.charUtf8 ','
    <> B.intDec l2 <> B.charUtf8 ':'<> encodeTree t2
    <> B.charUtf8 ']'
encodeTree (Leaf bs) = B.charUtf8 '"'
    <> B.byteString bs <> B.charUtf8 '"'
```

I also added a `main` to test the encoder:

```
main = B.hPutBuilder stdout $ encodeTree $
    Tree (1,Leaf "one") (2, Tree (3,Leaf "three") (4,Leaf "four"))
```

The **ByteString Builder** skips all unnecessary intermediate data structures. A ready Builder value can be rendered as a lazy ByteString, meaning it can be consumed lazily. So it's completely possible to create even infinite ByteStrings with Builder. As a final bonus, if you are writing the resulting ByteString into a `Handle`, you can use `hPutBuilder`, which puts the result straight in the handle's buffer, skipping all intermediate allocations.

The `Data.Text.Lazy.Builder` API is similar to the ByteString Builder API. The biggest difference is that text Builders can be constructed only from Chars, and lazy and strict Texts, so they're clearly fit for textual data only.

Builders for strings

Strings are only lists of characters, and lists admit a rather elegant `Builder` type:

```
type Builder = [Char] -> [Char]
```

Turning a `String` into a `Builder` is accomplished by applying concatenation partially, and to execute the `Builder` we just apply it to the empty list, `[]`:

```
string :: String -> Builder
string str = (str ++)
toString :: Builder -> String
toString b = b []
```

With this representation, builders are concatenated with normal function composition (`.`). Now we can write the previous tree-encoding example using our string builder:

```
-- file: string-builder.hs

data Tree = Tree !(Int, Tree) !(Int, Tree)
          | Leaf !String

encodeTree :: Tree -> Builder
encodeTree (Tree (l1, t1) (l2, t2)) =
    string "[" . string (show l1) . string ":" . encodeTree t1 .
    string "," . string (show l2) . string ":" . encodeTree t2 .
string "]"
    encodeTree (Leaf str) = string "\"" . string str . string "\""

main = putStrLn $ toString $ encodeTree $
Tree (1,Leaf "one") (2, Tree (3,Leaf "three") (4,Leaf "four"))
```

It's not hard to see that this builder also creates its result lazily. Coincidentally, the standard Show type class defines its serializations via:

```
type ShowS = String -> String
```

This is exactly the same as our Builder.

Handling sequential data

The standard list, [], is the most used data structure for sequential data. It has reasonable performance, but when processing multiple small values, say Chars, the overhead of a linked list might be too much. Often, the convenient nature of [] is convincing enough.

The wide range of list functions in Data.List are hand-optimized and many are subject to fusion. List fusion, as it is currently implemented using the foldr/build fusion transformation, is subtly different from stream fusion employed in ByteString and Text (concatMap is a bit problematic with traditional stream fusion). Still, the end result is pretty much the same; in a long pipeline of list functions, intermediate lists will usually not be constructed.

Say we want a pipeline that first increases every element by one, calculates intermediate sums of all elements up to current element, and finally sums all elements. From the previous chapter, we have learned to write optimally strict recursive functions, so we end up with the following implementation:

```
-- file: list-fusion.hs

inc :: [Int] -> [Int]
inc (x:xs) = x + 1 : inc xs
inc     [] = []

summer :: Int -> [Int] -> [Int]
summer a (x:xs) = let r = a + x in r `seq` r : summer r xs
summer _     [] = []

main = print $ sum $ summer 0 $ inc [1..100000]
```

If you run this program, you will find out that it allocates a whopping 24 megabytes of heap space and does quite a lot of GC, being productive only about 80% of the time. The problem here is that our pipeline is constructing a 100,000-element list three times over, which is quite expensive.

Sure, we could write our pipeline as a single fold, but that would be harder to extend or maintain. A much better option is to use the `map` and `scanl` functions, which are subject to fusion:

```
print $ sum $ scanl (+) 0 $ map (+1) [1..100000]
```

This version is not only much shorter than the original, but faster and allocates heap for only 6.5 megabytes, which is very close to just allocating 100,000 64-bit integers (6.1 megabytes).

The lesson here is that for fusion to kick in, library functions and higher-order functions should be preferred over custom recursive functions. This holds for every library that provides fusion: `lists`, `text`, `bytestring`, and others.

Using difference lists

We already met a difference list in the String builder section, which was a function from String to String, or from list of characters to list of characters. String builder is an example of a difference list. Generalizing over the element type (Char), we obtain the general definition of difference lists.

Here is a definition of difference lists wrapped in a new type and conversion function from and to a list:

```
-- file: dlist.hs

newtype DList a = DList ([a] -> [a])

fromList :: [a] -> DList a
fromList xs = DList (xs ++)

toList :: DList a -> [a]
toList (DList list) = list []
```

We can't use function composition to compose `DList` directly, so we give `DList` a monoid instance:

```
instance Monoid (DList a) where
    mempty = DList id
    mappend (DList x) (DList y) = DList (x . y)
```

 You might also want to consider using the `DList` package from the Hackage archive in your own code, instead of rolling your own difference list.

Difference list performance

Composing difference lists with (.) instead of lists directly with (++) can be magnitudes faster when there is lots of appending. (++) associates to right, so the following:

```
a ++ b ++ c ++ d
```

Will parse as:

```
a ++ (b ++ (c ++ d))
```

And by the definition of (++), each of a, b, c, and d are traversed only once. But if instead we first appended b to a, then c, and then d, the result would associate to left:

```
((a ++ b) ++ c) ++ d
```

This will unnecessarily build lots of intermediate thunks. If instead we used difference lists and appended them with (.), the result would look like this:

```
(a ++) . ((b ++) . ((c ++) . (d ++))) $ []
```

This would reduce to:

```
a ++ ((b ++) . ((c ++) . (d ++)) $ [])
```

And so on, turning (++) right-associative again.

Difference list with the Writer monad

A difference list is often a much better choice as the logging type in a Writer monad. Here is a simple benchmark of using lists versus difference lists:

```
-- file: dlist.hs

import Control.Monad.Writer

type DListWriter = Writer (DList Int)
type ListWriter  = Writer [Int]

action :: Int -> ListWriter ()
action 15000 = return ()
action n     = action (n + 1) >> tell [n]

action' :: Int -> DListWriter ()
action' 15000 = return ()
action' n     = action' (n + 1) >> tell (fromList [n])
main = do
    forM (snd $ runWriter (action 1)) print -- []
    forM (toList $ snd $ runWriter (action' 1)) print -- DList
```

The list-based version starts printing the numbers at an almost readable speed and gradually gains speed, while the difference list-based version spits out numbers immediately.

Using zippers

Another neat pattern that uses lists is the zipper. The core idea is that of focusing on some element, that is, viewing the structure from different angles. For simplicity, we'll consider only the list zipper here, though zippers can be defined for trees or actually any data structure. For lists, we can define a zipper as:

```
-- file: zipper.hs

type Zipper a = ([a], [a])
```

The idea here is that we have split the actual list in two right before the element we are focusing on. Elements that precede the focused element are kept in the first list, while the focused element and the elements that follow it are kept in the second list. Furthermore, the first list is in reverse order relative to the order of the actual list. The following diagram illustrates this:

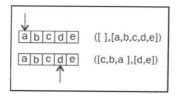

It's easy to define operations for moving the focus forwards or backwards:

```
forward, backward :: Zipper a -> Zipper a
forward  (xs, y:ys) = (y:xs, ys)
backward (x:xs, ys) = (xs, x:ys)
```

The get function yields the element under focus, and set replaces the focused element:

```
get :: Zipper a -> a
get (_, y:_) = y

set :: a -> Zipper a -> Zipper a
set x (xs, _:ys) = (xs, x:ys)
```

Accessing both ends fast with Seq

The `Data.Sequence` module (from the `containers` package) provides a general-purpose sequential data structure **Seq**, characterized by its O(1) inserts and deletes at both ends of the sequence. General indexing is of the same complexity as indexing in a **Map**.

Seq is a purely functional data structure (based on non-trivial structures called **finger trees**) and also quite fast. If you need fast indexing and inserting in both ends of a sequence, then Seq is one of the easiest and fastest options you have.

Say we are observing sensor events, and would like to keep a buffer of the latest *n* events only. Using Seq, we can easily create such a circular buffer, which supports O(1) inserts, as follows:

```
-- file: circular.hs

import Data.Sequence as Seq
import Data.Foldable (toList)

data Circular a = Circular !Int (Seq.Seq a)
```

We will use the Integer in `Circular` to store the maximum size. Then we'll need a way to create an empty buffer and a way to extract the current contents from the buffer:

```
create :: Int -> Circular a
create n = Circular n Seq.empty

values :: Circular a -> [a]
values (Circular _ s) = toList s
```

That was pretty simple. Appending a new observation is almost as easy too, except that we must handle possible buffer overflow:

```
observe :: Circular a -> a -> Circular a
observe (Circular n s) x
    | Seq.length s < n   = Circular n $ s  |> x
    | _ :< s'<- viewl s = Circular n $ s' |> x
```

The `viewl` and `viewr` functions are used to inspect the first and last, or left-most and right-most, elements of a Seq:

```
data ViewR a = EmptyR | Seq a :> a
data ViewL a = EmptyL | a :< Seq a
```

We can confirm that our buffer works as expected:

```
> :load circular.hs
> values $ foldl' observe (create 7) [1..10000000 :: Int]
[9999994,9999995,9999996,9999997,9999998,9999999,10000000]
```

If you compile that fold with optimizations and inspect the heap profile with +RTS -s, you would find out that processing 10 million observations with buffer size of 7 spends about 3.5% time in GC, clocks in with 2.3 GB of heap allocation, and on my machine completes in under 350ms.

So at least we have acceptable speed. However, for a buffer size of 7 elements we could have probably done better with an unboxed array or vector and a simple linear-time (in buffer size) observe function. But with bigger buffer sizes, linearity will be costly and Seq will clearly dominate.

In the following graph, I have plotted heap allocation when folding 10 million integers with different buffer sizes:

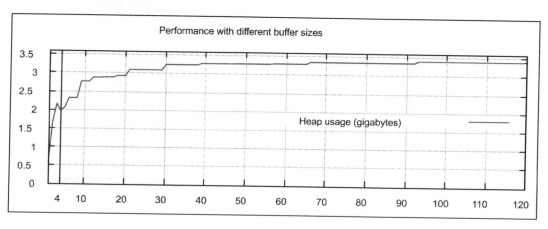

We see that after the buffer size is larger than about 10 elements, the amortized constant time operations of Seq start to pay off. Note that there are size ranges where heap usage doesn't really change at all – and such ranges become even longer when buffer size gets larger! With small buffer sizes, overhead from modifying the internal finger-trees is far greater than added value. There is even a peak at buffer size 3, implying that it would be more efficient to represent size 3 as 4. This is also a consequence of the underlying finger-trees, which behave sub optimally in such small sizes.

Note that if we make the `sequence` field in the `Circular` datatype strict (or almost equally, replace (`$`) with (`$!`) in `observe`), then performance would actually decrease by about 10%. This is very much counterintuitive, because we will anyways always need to evaluate the sequence to WHNF. Let me paraphrase this in a way that's easier to explain: why does deferring the evaluation of a Seq from the constructing site onto the consuming site have such a big impact?

Once again, the answer boils down to a combination of usual optimizations in GHC, namely inlining and rewriting. Seq is based on finger-trees and has an interesting structure and many operations that are often inlined all the way to our own functions that use Seq operations. Now if we enforce strictness in something that the GHC inliner rewrites to something completely different, we are limiting code transformations that GHC could otherwise perform with full laziness.

Handling tabular data

If you need O(1) general indexing, a table-like data structure is virtually your only option. The Haskell report specifies the `array` package, which provides tables indexed by anything with an instance for a `Ix` typeclass.

Immutable arrays come in two flavors (we'll discuss mutable arrays later):

- `Data.Array.Array`: Immutable arrays of boxed values
- `Data.Array.Unboxed.UArray`: Immutable arrays of unboxed values

A common use case for Immutable arrays is memoization. For example, a table of Fibonacci numbers could be constructed as follows:

```
-- file: fib-array-mem.hs
import Data.Array

fib :: Int -> Array Int Integer
fib n = arr where
  arr = listArray (1,n) $ 1 : 1 : [ arr!(i-2) + arr!(i-1)
                                  | i <- [3..n] ]
```

We can also index by a tuple, which gives the array extra dimensions. The symmetric Pascal matrix will serve as an example:

```
pascal :: Int -> Array (Int, Int) Integer
pascal n = arr where
  arr = array ((1,1),(n,n)) $
    [ ((i,1),1) | i <- [1..n] ] ++
    [ ((1,j),1) | j <- [1..n] ] ++
    [ ((i,j),arr!(i-1,j) + arr!(i,j-1)) | i <- [2..n], j <- [2..n] ]
```

These self-referential definitions look very nice, and with arbitrary-sized integers the performance is pretty much as good as it could be.

But what if we only needed a table of the first 90 Fibonacci numbers? The 90th Fibonacci number fits into an Int64, so we could switch to that and use UArray instead of Array. But then we could not have had the nice self-referential definition, because array construction would block trying to index its unfinished self. In this case, you should build the list so that it doesn't reference the array, or convert the boxed array into an unboxed array via an intermediate list:

```
toUArray :: (Ix i, IArray UArray e) => Array i e -> UArray i e
toUArray a = listArray (bounds a) (elems a)
```

This conversion comes at the cost of an intermediate list, though.

The array package is quite low-level, but the speed will be there at the cost of doing a lot of index fiddling yourself. For multi-dimensional arrays, much of that index-fiddling is unfortunately unavoidable. But for single-dimensional arrays, there is a better choice.

Using the vector package

The Data.Vector modules in the vector package provide sweet and speedy high-level Int-indexed arrays, implemented on top of Data.Array. They too come in boxed and unboxed flavors.

The sweetness of vector is in the API, which is loaded with higher-order functions, convenient helpers, monad-lifted operations, and of course all the common operations for list-like structures.

The speed comes once again from fusion; in terms of raw speed, operations on vector have an upper bound set by arrays that vectors use internally. However, a sufficiently large composition of vector operations will almost always outperform a similar naive array-based program.

Say we have a sensor from which we have stored numeric observations at different times, and now we want to analyze that data. For performance, we choose to use unboxed vector for storing the data in memory. Also, we import randomIO for testing purposes:

```
-- file: vector-testing.hs

import qualified Data.Vector.Unboxed as U
import System.Random (randomIO)
```

A neat thing about unboxed Vectors is that unboxed vectors support tuple-valued elements. Internally, they are represented with two vectors. This defines some types:

```
type Obs = U.Vector (TimeStamp, Double)

type TimeStamp = Int
```

We can extract the value Vector of our observation vector using U.unzip in constant time and no copying:

```
-- | O(1)
values :: Obs -> U.Vector Double
values obs = snd (U.unzip obs)
```

Note that U.map snd would be bad, because mapping constructs a new vector, in general.

Now let's try something more interesting: a **windowing** function, which gives us the slice between two timestamps. The following implementation of a window function is linear in time and constant in space:

```
-- | O(n+m), no copying.
window :: TimeStamp -> TimeStamp -> Obs -> Obs
window from until v =
    let (_, start)   = U.span ((< from) . fst) v
        (between, _) = U.span ((<= until) . fst) start
        in between
```

We could improve this by a more involved binary search, for example. But for demonstration, I used just U.span, which also does no copying by reusing the original vector. Because the time step between two observations (TimeStamps) can be arbitrary, logarithmic time complexity is the best we could get.

Implementing value average is straightforward:

```
-- | O(n)
average :: Obs -> Double
average obs = U.sum (values obs) / fromIntegral (U.length (values obs))
```

Let's test out the performance by generating a data set of a million random observations and then calculating averages at different windows:

```
main = do
    obs <- U.generateM (1024 ^ 2) $ \i -> randomIO >>= \v -> return (i, v)
    print $ average $ window 1 (1024 ^ 2) obs
```

```
print $ average $ window 2 (1023 ^ 2) obs
print $ average $ window 3 (1022 ^ 2) obs
print $ average $ window 4 (1021 ^ 2) obs
```

Compile and run with Runtime System statistics:

```
$ ghc -rtsopts -O vector-testing.hs && time ./vector-testing +RTS -s

[...]


2,090,993,872 bytes allocated in the heap
341,188,752 bytes copied during GC
59,032,744 bytes maximum residency (7 sample(s))
2,863,512 bytes maximum slop
138 MB total memory in use (0 MB lost due to fragmentation)


Tot time (elapsed)  Avg pause  Max pause
Gen  0      4003 colls,     0 par    0.372s   0.372s    0.0001s
0.0013s

Gen  1         7 colls,     0 par    0.177s   0.177s    0.0253s
0.0447s


INIT    time    0.000s  (  0.000s elapsed)
MUT     time    1.426s  (  1.428s elapsed)
GC      time    0.548s  (  0.548s elapsed)
EXIT    time    0.006s  (  0.006s elapsed)
Total   time    1.983s  (  1.983s elapsed)


%GC     time    27.7%  (27.7% elapsed)


Alloc rate   1,465,833,131 bytes per MUT second


Productivity  72.3% of total user, 72.3% of total elapsed
```

Wow, this looks pretty bad: lots of GC, only 70% productivity, and a 60-megabyte memory footprint! The data itself is only 16 megabytes on a 64-bit machine, which implies that a lot of unnecessary things are going on.

Turns out, optimization level -O is insufficient for lots of important optimizations to kick in. Switching to -O2 gives significant improvements:

```
$ ghc -rtsopts -O2 vector-testing.hs && ./vector-testing +RTS -s
```

[..]

```
1,862,402,704 bytes allocated in the heap
818,920 bytes copied during GC
16,779,344 bytes maximum residency (2 sample(s))
2,070,704 bytes maximum slop
19 MB total memory in use (0 MB lost due to fragmentation)
```

```
         Tot time (elapsed)  Avg pause  Max pause
Gen  0    3576 colls,    0 par   0.014s   0.014s    0.0000s
0.0000s
Gen  1       2 colls,    0 par   0.001s   0.001s    0.0006s
0.0010s
```

```
INIT    time    0.000s  (  0.000s elapsed)
MUT     time    1.227s  (  1.229s elapsed)
GC      time    0.016s  (  0.015s elapsed)
EXIT    time    0.001s  (  0.001s elapsed)
Total   time    1.247s  (  1.245s elapsed)

%GC     time      1.3%  (1.2% elapsed)

Alloc rate    1,517,508,130 bytes per MUT second

Productivity  98.7% of total user, 98.9% of total elapsed
```

With -O2, we got down to 1.3% GC and 19 megabytes of memory footprint. For even better results, we could combine with optimizations for numerical code.

It's certainly a good idea to always use -O2 for production and performance testing, especially for vector code. Compile times will be significantly longer, however, so in development -O or even no optimization passes at all is advisable.

Handling sparse data

Vectors and arrays are excellent for dense data, that is, when you're not doing inserts in between elements, and the range of indices is reasonable. But if you need, for example, inserts and indexing in arbitrary indices, a tabular structure won't perform well. In such cases, you need some sort of a map or similar structure.

Haskell doesn't have any sparse structures built-in, nor does the Haskell report define any. This has some nice consequences:

- Keeps the core language small
- Gives Haskellers complete freedom over the implementation
- Allows writing code that doesn't care much about the specific underlying data structure

There are many excellent libraries, implementing a wide range of sparse data structures, in Hackage, not to mention type classes capturing general properties of those structures. Unfortunately, the ecosystem is a bit too scattered, so it is sometimes hard to determine which library would give the best performance, cleanest code, and most flexibility, or whether the package is maintained.

Using the containers package

The go-to package for immutable sparse data structures is `containers`. It provides reasonably efficient implementations for maps and sets, very basic tree and graph structures, and the sequence mentioned previously. The structures are purely functional, which is a nice property in itself, encouraging us to write code in a functional style:

```
Ord a => Data.Map.{Lazy,Strict}.Map k v
Ord a => Data.Set.Set a

Data.IntMap.{Lazy,Strict}.IntMap v
Data.IntSet.IntSet a

Data.Tree.Tree a
Data.Graph.Graph = Array Int [Int]
Data.Sequence.Seq a
```

However, you shouldn't expect these structures, say Map, to perform equally with traditional imperative-style structures (hashmaps), especially when used more or less imperatively. The Map from `containers` is based on binary trees. IntMap, which constrains its keys to Ints, uses Patricia trees and is considerably more efficient than Map Int.

The imperative map implementation is usually a hash table because of its O(1) lookups compared to the **O(log n)** of tree-based maps. However, hash tables rely on mutable state, and so are not so convenient in functional settings.

Functional structures have their unique advantages:

- Updates reuse parts of the previous structure, so keeping older versions lying around is cheap
- Automatic thread-safety

Furthermore, with lazy evaluation, a map lazy in its values allows for an intuitive memoization pattern:

```
-- file: map-fib.hs

import Data.IntMap as IM

fib :: Int -> IntMap Int
fib n = m where
    m = IM.fromList $ (1,1) : (2,1) :
        [ (i, IM.findWithDefault 0 (i-1) m + IM.findWithDefault 0 (i-
2) m)
        | i <- [3..n] ]
```

 Unless you need to have thunks as values, you should use the strict variants of Map and IntMap for efficiency.

Using the unordered-containers package

The `containers` package requires an `Ord` instance from the keys in a Map and from values in a Set. For string-valued data this is problematic, because a comparison might be too expensive. And for some data, an `Ord` instance is an impossibility:

```
Hashable k => Data.HashMap.Lazy.HashMap k v
Hashable k => Data.HashMap.Strict.HashMap k v
Hashable a => Data.HashSet.HashSet
```

The `unordered-containers` package provides pure functional hash maps and sets, requiring a `Hashable` instance. The same performance considerations apply to `HashMap` and `HashSet` as the data structures from `containers`: they are persistent in nature but won't beat mutable-state variants in terms of raw speed.

Ephemeral data structures

Lazy evaluation, functional code, and persistent data structures are nice and all, but they are not meant to wholly replace imperative strict evaluation, imperative code, and ephemeral structures. Nor vice versa. Instead, all complement each other. Although the default evaluation in Haskell is strict and a functional style is strongly encouraged, Haskell is more than capable of providing for programming in imperative style:

> *"In short, Haskell is the world's finest imperative programming language."*
>
> – *Simon Peyton Jones (in his paper Tackling the Awkward Squad)*

Imperative programming calls for sequential processing. In Haskell, we tackle sequential steps with monads. The monad of choice for ephemeral data structures is **IO** or **ST**. ST (for **state threads**) behaves a bit more nicely than IO in that you cannot launch missiles from ST. An ST action can be executed in pure code, or converted to an IO action:

```
import Control.Monad.ST

runST :: (forall s. ST s a) -> a
stToIO :: ST RealWorld a -> IO a
```

The s type variable in ST actions can be largely ignored. It is only used to separate the states of separate ST actions.

The ST monad comes in two flavors, strict (Control.Monad.ST) and lazy (Control.Monad.ST.Lazy). The lazy ST monad executes only actions whose values are required. The following code works with a lazy ST monad, but not with a strict one:

```
st :: Int
st = runST $ do
    mapM_ return [1..]
    return 9001
```

Unless you need lazy semantics, strict ST will be faster.

Mutable references are slow

Data.IORef and Data.STRef are the smallest bits of mutable state ; they are, references to mutable variables, one for IO and other for ST. There is also a Data.STRef.Lazy module, which provides a wrapper over strict STRef for lazy ST.

However, because IORef and STRef are references, they imply a level of indirection. GHC intentionally does not optimize them away, as that would cause problems in concurrent settings. For this reason, IORef or STRef shouldn't be used like variables in C, for example. Performance will for sure be very bad.

Let's verify the performance hit by considering the following ST-based sum-of-range implementation:

```
-- file: sum_mutable.hs

import Control.Monad.ST
import Data.STRef

count_st :: Int -> Int
count_st n = runST $ do
    ref <- newSTRef 0
    let go 0 = readSTRef ref
        go i = modifySTRef' ref (+ i) >> go (i - 1)
    go n
```

And compare it to this pure recursive implementation:

```
count_pure :: Int -> Int
count_pure n = go n 0 where
    go 0 s = s
    go i s = go (i - 1) $! (s + i)
```

The ST implementation is many times slower when at least -O is enabled. Without optimizations, the two functions are more or less equivalent in performance; there is similar amount of indirection from not unboxing arguments in the latter version. This is one example of the wonders that can be done to optimize referentially transparent code.

Using mutable arrays

To get rid of indirection when it isn't desired, mutable arrays from the array package can be used. Those too live either in IO or ST, but unlike references arrays can contain unboxed values. The main mutable array modules and types are:

- Data.Array.IO: Mutable boxed (IOArray) and unboxed arrays (IOUArray) in IO

- Data.Array.ST: Mutable boxed (STArray) and unboxed arrays (STUArray) in ST

- Data.Array.Storable: Mutable arrays in contiguous memory (StorableArray)

The purpose of StorableArray is to serve as a convenient medium for interfacing with C. In general, it is a bit slower than the others. We'll consider StorableArray in *Chapter 10, Foreign Function Interface.*

Using STUArray we can write sum-of-range, which is as efficient as the optimized pure function:

```
-- file: sum_array_mutable.hs

{-# LANGUAGE FlexibleContexts #-}

import Control.Monad.ST
import Data.Array.ST

count_stuarray :: Int -> Int
count_stuarray n = runST $ do
    ref <- newArray (0,0) 0 :: ST s (STUArray s Int Int)
    let go 0 = readArray ref 0
        go i = do s <- readArray ref 0
                  writeArray ref 0 $ s + i
                  go (i-1)
    go n
```

The obvious caveat here is that the code is more involved:

*   Had to use an array for a single variable
*   Needed an explicit type signature for the intermediate array (the array interface is highly overloaded, for better or worse)
*   Needed to enable FlexibleContexts so that go type-checks (due to the s type parameter in ST)

The advantage of mutable arrays is that they are pretty low-level. It's trivial to reason about the time and space usage of strict array code.

Using mutable vectors

Roman Leshchinskiy's wonderful vector package provides a mutable API. Similar to immutable, the mutable API is charged with stream fusion as well. Furthermore, mutable and immutable vectors are tightly entwined, so sometimes conversions from one to the other can be done in place.

When working with mutable vectors, the types can seem a bit baffling. The `Data.Vector.Mutable` and `Data.Vector.Unboxed.Mutable` modules each define two types, `IOVector` and `STVectors`, which are analogous to mutable array types. However, `IOVector` and `STVector` are just synonyms defined in terms of a more general type, `MVector s`:

```
type IOVector    = MVector RealWorld
type STVector s = MVector s
```

`MVector` is the sole mutable (boxed) vector type; the immediate benefit is that fewer API functions need to be overloaded via an adhoc type class, yielding very good type inference. All of the mutable vector API is written in terms of `MVector`, for example:

```
slice :: Int -> Int -> MVector s a -> MVector s a
```

Operations that must mutate the vector are wrapped in the underlying monad (IO or ST). Thus, type signatures of mutating operations are a bit more involved:

```
read :: PrimMonad m => MVector (PrimState m) a -> Int -> m a
write :: PrimMonad m => MVector (PrimState m) a -> Int -> a ->
m ()
```

These operations execute in a monad, `m`, capable of primitive state-transformer actions. So the monad must be IO, ST, or some monad transformer stack with IO or ST at the bottom. That's the `PrimMonad m =>...` part.

The `PrimState m` might be baffling if you're not very familiar with associated types. Associated types are like ordinary class functions, but lifted to type-level:

```
class Monad m => PrimMonad m where
    type PrimState m

instance PrimMonad IO where
    type PrimState IO = RealWorld

instance PrimMonad (ST s) where
    type PrimState (ST s) = s
```

So respectively for IO and ST, we have:

```
MVector (PrimState m) a === MVector RealWorld a = IOVector a
MVector (PrimState m) a === MVector s a          = STVector s a
```

Associated types are not rocket science. Unfortunately, function arrow syntax for type level functions does not exist in Haskell, so syntax is a little funny.

Unboxed mutable vectors work the same way as boxed mutable vectors. The only addition is an `Unbox a =>` constraint on the element (and the unboxed `MVector` is a type-family instead of a datatype). `Unbox` comes with instances for primitive types and tuples (and it is possible to add your own instances), and is also a requirement in the immutable unboxed API.

Bubble sort with vectors

Bubble sort is not an efficient sort algorithm, but because it's an in-place algorithm and simple, we will implement it as a demonstration of mutable vectors:

```
-- file: bubblesort.hs

import Control.Monad.ST
import Data.Vector as V
import Data.Vector.Mutable as MV
import System.Random (randomIO) -- for testing
```

The (naive) bubble sort compares values of all adjacent indices in order, and swaps the values if necessary. After reaching the last element, it starts from the beginning or, if no swaps were made, the list is sorted and the algorithm is done:

```
bubblesortM :: (Ord a, PrimMonad m)
            => MVector (PrimState m) a -> m ()
bubblesortM v = loop where

    indices = V.fromList [1 .. MV.length v - 1]

    loop = do swapped <- V.foldM' f False indices - (1)
              if swapped then loop else return () - (2)

    f swapped i = do                                 - (3)
       a <- MV.read v (i-1)
       b <- MV.read v i
       if a > b then MV.swap v (i-1) i >> return True
                else return swapped
```

At (1), we fold monadically over all but the last index, keeping state about whether or not we have performed a swap in this iteration. If we had, at (2) we rerun the fold ; if not, we can return. At (3) we compare an index and possibly swap values.

We can write a pure function that wraps the stateful algorithm:

```
bubblesort :: Ord a => Vector a -> Vector a
bubblesort v = runST $ do
    mv <- V.thaw v
    bubblesortM mv
    V.freeze mv
```

`V.thaw` and `V.freeze` (both `O(n)`) can be used to go back and forth with mutable and immutable vectors.

Now, there are multiple code optimization opportunities in our implementation of bubble sort. But before tackling those, let's see how well our straightforward implementation fares using the following `main`:

```
main = do
    v <- V.generateM 10000 $ \_ -> randomIO :: IO Double
    let v_sorted = bubblesort v
        median   = v_sorted ! 5000
    print median
```

We should remember to compile with `-O2`. On my machine, this program takes about 1.55s, and Runtime System reports 99.9% productivity, 18.7 megabytes allocated heap and 570 kilobytes copied during GC.

So now with a baseline, let's see if we can squeeze more performance from vectors. This is a non-exhaustive list:

- Use unboxed vectors instead. This restricts the types of elements we can store, but it saves us a level of indirection. Down to 960ms and approximately halved GC traffic.
- Large lists are inefficient, and they don't compose with vectors stream fusion. We should change indices so that it uses `V.enumFromTo` instead (alternatively turn on `OverloadedLists` extension and drop `V.fromList`). Down to 360ms and 94% less GC traffic.
- Conversion functions `V.thaw` and `V.freeze` are O(n), that is, they modify copies. Using in-place `V.unsafeThaw` and `V.unsafeFreeze` instead is sometimes useful. `V.unsafeFreeze` in the `bubblesort` wrapper is completely safe, but `V.unsafeThaw` is not. In our example, however, with `-O2`, the program is optimized into a single loop and all those conversions get eliminated.
- Vector operations (`V.read`, `V.swap`) in `bubblesortM` are guaranteed to never be out of bounds, so it's perfectly safe to replace these with unsafe variants (`V.unsafeRead`, `V.unsafeSwap`) that don't check bounds. Speed-up of about 25 milliseconds, or 5%.

To summarize, applying good practices and safe usage of unsafe functions, our Bubble sort just got 80% faster. These optimizations are applied in the `bubblesort-optimized.hs` file (omitted here).

We noticed that almost all GC traffic came from a linked list, which was constructed and immediately consumed. Lists are bad for performance in that they don't fuse like vectors. To ensure good vector performance, ensure that the fusion framework can work effectively. Anything that can be done with a vector should be done.

As a final note, when working with vectors (and other libraries) it's a good idea to keep the Haddock documentation handy. There are several big and small performance choices to be made. Often the difference is that of between O(n) and O(1).

Working with monads and monad stacks

Monads are very useful abstractions, and like any sufficiently complex abstraction, many monads too incur some overhead. Two notable exceptions are IO and ST, which are eliminated during compilation. A single simple monad such as **Reader** or **Writer** has very minimal overhead, but monad stacks can incur unfortunate slowdowns. In most cases, the convenient nature of programming in a monad stack far outweighs the small overhead, because cost centers are rarely located in monad operations (excluding IO and ST).

 If you have an expensive subroutine in a State monad, it might be possible to convert it to ST for a big speedup. However, `State` is more expressive than ST so conversion is not always feasible.

The list monad and its transformer

The monad instance of lists admits attractive backtracking. For example, consider special Pythagorean triplets from Project Euler problem 9: find three natural numbers $a < b < c$ such that $a^2 + b^2 = c^2$ and $a + b + c = n$, where $n = 1000$ (there exists exactly one such triplet). A naive implementation using the `list` monad can be given as follows:

```
-- file: backtracking-list.hs

import Control.Monad (guard)

special_pythagorean :: Int -> [(Int,Int,Int)]
special_pythagorean n = do
    a <- [1     .. n]
    b <- [a + 1 .. n]
    c <- [b + 1 .. n]
    guard (a + b + c == n)
```

```
    guard (a ^ 2 + b ^ 2 == c ^ 2)
    return (a, b, c)

main = print $ head $ special_pythagorean 1000
```

Algorithmically, this solution is pretty bad. But the implementation itself is fairly efficient. GHC is smart enough to optimize all intermediate lists away, producing a program with three nested loops. Most values get unboxed, too.

Previously we observed that lists don't perform well if used like lists and arrays are used in imperative languages, that is, treating them as just some list-like values. Instead, in a functional style, lists are more useful when used as a control structure. Indeed, the list monad goes by another name, the **stream** monad. If you ever take a look at how stream fusion in bytestring, vector, text, or built-in iterators in imperative languages such as Python and Java are implemented, what you'll find is just a linked list in disguise.

The list monad can be turned into a monad transformer, named ListT, albeit it is tricky to get right. A correct implementation can be found in the list-t package.

With ListT, we can add streaming to any monad. For example, we could implement a random noise generator with a repeating pattern and random delays with a ListT IO. First, some imports:

```
-- file: noise.hs

import ListT                        -- package list-t
import System.Random                -- package random
import Control.Monad.Trans (lift) -- package mtl
import Control.Concurrent (threadDelay)
```

We write the noise generator to take the pattern as an argument:

```
noise :: [Double] -> ListT IO Double
noise pat = do
    pat'<- ListT.repeat pat
    x      <- ListT.fromFoldable pat'
    lift $ do delay <- randomIO
              threadDelay (mod delay 300000)
              randomRIO (x - 0.5, x + 0.5)

main = let generator = noise [1,5,10,5]
           in ListT.traverse_ print generator
```

Monadic code in `ListT` looks just like monadic code in `[]`, with the addition of interleaved IO actions via `lift`. In `main`, we create a generator and consume it one element at a time. The next item is generated only when it is really required, hence we don't loop indefinitely but recurse productively.

In the `list-t` package, there is a `MonadPlus` instance for `Monad m => ListT m`. `MonadPlus` gives us the empty list (`mzero`) and list concatenation (`mplus`) lifted to `ListT m` for any monad `m`. Of course, we can also use other generic combinators, for example, to make derived generators:

```
Control.Monad.mfilter (> 5) (noise [1,5,10,5])

Control.Monad.liftM (+) (noise [1,2,3]) (noise [7,6,8])
```

However, that second example is a bit questionable, because it incurs random delays from both generators sequentially.

Free monads

Another general example of data as a control structure is the `Free` monad:

```
data Free f a = Pure a
              | Free (f (Free f a))
```

The key observation is that if `f` is a (law-abiding) functor, then `Free f` is automatically always a monad.

With `Free`, we can define embedded languages in Haskell quite conveniently. Let's take a silly example: a language capable of reading and writing strings, and launching missiles, that is, to perform arbitrary I/O actions. We could write an abstract datatype like so:

```
data Language = Write String Language
              | Read (String -> Language)
              | Missiles (IO ()) Language
              | End
```

Then, expressions could be written like so:

```
Write "Launch?"
   (Read (\s -> if s == "y" then Missiles launch End
                            else Write "No launch" End))
```

But this doesn't look very nice. Certainly not nearly as readable as direct Haskell. We could roll our own parser, but fortunately there is `Free`:

```
-- file: free.hs
{-# LANGUAGE DeriveFunctor #-}
import Prelude hiding (read)
import Control.Monad.Free -- package free
```

We begin our `Free` adventure with that preamble. `Free` will capture the recursive nature in our `Language` datatype for us when we write it as:

```
data Language next = Write String next
                   | Read (String -> next)
                   | Missiles (IO ()) next
                   deriving (Functor)
type Program = Free Language
```

We need `DeriveFunctor` to derive the `Functor` instance. Alternatively, we could have written it by hand. To lift statements in our language to the free monad `Program`, we write the following definitions:

```
read :: Program String
read = liftF (Read id)

write :: String -> Program ()
write string = liftF (Write string ())

missiles :: IO () -> Program ()
missiles io = liftF (Missiles io ())
```

With these statements, we can write programs in monadic style in our `Program` monad. The following example program repeatedly asks for a command until receiving a `"launch"` command, after which it launches some missiles and exits gracefully:

```
program :: Program Int
program = do
    write "Waiting for command (launch)"
    input <- read
    case input of
        "launch" -> do missiles $ putStrLn "Missiles launched!"
                       return 0
        _        -> do write $ "Unknown command: " ++ input
                       program
```

An interpreter for this `Free` language is implemented very similarly, as in the case of a direct ADT:

```
interpret :: Program a -> IO a
interpret (Pure res)     = return res
interpret (Free program) = case program of
    Write string next -> putStrLn string >> interpret next
    Read go           -> getLine >>= interpret . go
    Missiles m next   -> m >> interpret next
```

Note that nothing prevents us from writing a safe interpreter that doesn't launch missiles, or an interpreter that doesn't live in the IO monad. Using `Free`, we got monadic do-syntax for free, as well as all standard monad machinery in our little embedded language. Also, similarly to `ListT`, there is a `FreeT` monad transformer, with which side-effects in arbitrary inner monads can be allowed inside the embedded language.

Working with monad transformers

In general, monads from the `transformers` package behave very nicely. Overhead is pretty much predicted by the number of layers in the stack. Monadic functions inline well and GHC is able to do lots of optimizations. The **monad transformer library (mtl)** isn't much worse nowadays, but the extra flexibility in mtl doesn't always come for free.

If you need to speed up a monad stack, you might want to consider unrolling it. The **RWS** monad/transformer from `mtl` is an example of unrolling. **RWS** combines **Reader**, **Writer**, and **State** on a single level:

```
RWS r w s a                     ~  r -> s -> (a, s, w)
ReaderT r (StateT s (Writer w)) a  ~  r -> s -> ((a, s), w)
```

Composing monads and side-effects efficiently is ongoing research. Also, new approaches such as extensible effects have emerged, but speed remains an issue.

Speedup via continuation-passing style

Implementing monads in **continuation-passing style (CPS)** can have very good results. Unfortunately, no widely-used or supported library I'm aware of would provide drop-in replacements for ubiquitous **Maybe**, **List**, **Reader**, **Writer**, and **State** monads.

It's not that hard to implement the standard monads in CPS from scratch. For example, the `State` monad can be implemented using the `Cont` monad from `mtl` as follows:

```haskell
-- file: cont-state-writer.hs
{-# LANGUAGE GeneralizedNewtypeDeriving #-}
{-# LANGUAGE MultiParamTypeClasses #-}
{-# LANGUAGE FlexibleInstances #-}
{-# LANGUAGE FlexibleContexts #-}

import Control.Monad.State.Strict
import Control.Monad.Cont

newtype StateCPS s r a = StateCPS (Cont (s -> r) a)
deriving (Functor, Applicative, Monad, MonadCont)

instance MonadState s (StateCPS s r) where
    get   = StateCPS $ cont $
\next curState → next curState curState

    put newState = StateCPS $ cont $
\next curState → next () newState

runStateCPS :: StateCPS s s () -> s -> s
runStateCPS (StateCPS m) = runCont m (\_ -> id)
```

In case you're not familiar with the continuation-passing style and the `Cont` monad, the details might not make much sense: instead of just returning results from a function, a function in CPS applies its results to a continuation. So in short, to "get" the state in continuation-passing style, we pass the current state to the "next" continuation (first argument) and don't change the state (second argument). To "put," we call the continuation with the unit (no return value) and change the state to a new state (second argument to next).

`StateCPS` is used just like the `State` monad:

```haskell
action :: MonadState Int m => m ()
action = replicateM_ 1000000 $ do
    i <- get
    put $! i + 1

main = do
    print $ (runStateCPS action 0 :: Int)
    print $ (snd $ runState action 0 :: Int)
```

That `action` operation is, in the CPS version of the state monad, about 5% faster and performs 30% less heap allocation than the state monad from `mtl`. This program is limited pretty much only by the speed of monadic composition, so these numbers are at least very close to the maximum speedup we can have from CPSing the state monad. Speedups of the writer monad are probably near these results.

Other standard monads can be implemented similarly to StateCPS. The definitions can also be generalized to monad transformers over an arbitrary monad (a la `ContT`). For extra speed, you might wish to combine many monads in a single CPS monad, similarly to what RWST does.

Summary

We began this chapter with GHC primitives such as `Int#` and figured out the effects of strictness and unpacking annotations (`bangs` and `UNPACK`-pragmas) in data type definitions. We noted that tuples are lazy and that Bool is an algebraic data type, but we also noted that arrays and vectors represent Bool intelligently as single bits internally.

Then we considered working with numeric, binary, and textual data. We witnessed the performance of the `bytestring`, `text`, and `vector` libraries, all of which get their speed from fusion optimizations, in contrast to linked lists, which have a huge overhead despite also being subject to fusion to some degree. However, linked lists give rise to simple difference lists and zippers. The builder patterns for `lists`, `bytestring`, and `text` were introduced. We discovered that the `array` package is low-level and clumsy compared to the superior `vector` package, unless you must support Haskell 98. The Map type in `containers` was a binary tree, whereas some hashing-based (functional) implementations resided in unordered containers. We used the IO and ST monads to program with mutable state. Finally, we touched upon the subject of side-effect composition.

In the next chapter, we will profile and benchmark Haskell code using the GHC profiler and criterion. Our aim is to identify space leaks and cost centers. We will learn how to structure and annotate programs for easy profiling.

3
Profile and Benchmark to Your Heart's Content

So far we haven't used much else but heap usage statistics to gauge the performance of Haskell programs. For a quick overview of the overall performance of a program, a simple +RTS -s is often sufficient. However, often it is necessary to know which parts of the code specifically are taking up the most time and space.

In this chapter we extend our toolset with more sophisticated profiling and benchmarking facilities. We will learn to inspect and set cost centres, to benchmark robustly when semantics are mostly lazy. Finally we'll also look at monitoring performance while the program is still running.

- Profiling time, allocation and space usage
- Profiling the heap: break-downs and subset selection
- Benchmarking Haskell programs with the criterion library
- Monitoring still-executing programs in real-time with ekg

Profiling time and allocations

Profiling in the presence of lazy evaluation does not differ much from profiling always-strict programs. The profiler that comes with GHC assigns time and space usages to cost centres. Cost centres annotate expressions, and can be set either manually or automatically by GHC. Cost centres can occur enclosed in other cost centres recursively, forming cost centre stacks. All time and space costs accumulate in each enclosing cost centre.

Cost centres can be set manually via annotations, or automatically by GHC via compiler flags. Depending on how often the cost centre is entered, the choice of cost centre can have a big impact on overall execution time. Fortunately, allocation profiling is not affected by chosen cost centers.

Setting cost centres manually

Let's start our profiling journey with a basic example. The following program uses the simple moving average function we wrote in the first chapter:

```
-- file: prof-basics.hs

sma :: [Double] -> [Double]
sma (x0:x1:xs) = (x0 + x1) / 2 : sma (x1:xs)
sma         xs = xs

main =
    let a = [1..1000000]
        b = sma a
        c = sum b
        in print c
```

We compile and execute this program with Runtime System statistics but no profiling yet, to see what the performance is without any overhead from profiling:

```
ghc -O -rtsopts prof-basics.hs

./prof-basics +RTS -s
5.000009999995e11

264,106,248 bytes allocated in the heap
255,768 bytes copied during GC
44,312 bytes maximum residency (2 sample(s))

...

INIT    time    0.000s  (  0.000s elapsed)
MUT     time    0.105s  (  0.105s elapsed)
GC      time    0.002s  (  0.002s elapsed)
EXIT    time    0.000s  (  0.000s elapsed)
Total   time    0.111s  (  0.108s elapsed)
```

From the statistics output, we learn that our program executes in about 110ms and allocates 260 Megabytes of heap.

We would now like to know which of the parts a, b, or c is consuming the most resources. To do this, we can set cost centres with {-# SCC identifier #-} pragmas and so modify our main accordingly:

```
main =
    let a = {-# SCC "list-" #-} [1..1000000]
        b = {-# SCC "sma-"  #-} sma a
        c = {-# SCC "sum-"  #-} sum b
    in print c
```

SCC stands for **Set Cost Centre**. To enable profiling support, we must compile with the -prof flag and also enable the -p Runtime System option:

```
ghc -fforce-recomp -O -rtsopts -prof prof-basics.hs

./prof-basics +RTS -s -p
5.000009999995e11

440,172,808 bytes allocated in the heap
377,968 bytes copied during GC
46,040 bytes maximum residency (2 sample(s))
...


INIT    time    0.000s  (  0.000s elapsed)
MUT     time    0.169s  (  0.173s elapsed)
GC      time    0.003s  (  0.003s elapsed)
RP      time    0.000s  (  0.000s elapsed)
PROF    time    0.000s  (  0.000s elapsed)
EXIT    time    0.000s  (  0.000s elapsed)
Total   time    0.175s  (  0.177s elapsed)
```

Using ghc -fforce-recomp forces re-compilation. This is useful when changing compiler flags but not touching the source code itself. Normally GHC will look at the source code files, and if they haven't changed since the last compilation, GHC won't recompile.

Immediately we notice the overhead from profiling: the number of allocations nearly doubled and execution time also increased from 110ms to 180ms. Also, in the statistics there are two new lines: time spent in RP and time spent in PROF. However, those are both zero and the overhead is accumulated in MUT, where the meat of our program is.

We note that compiling with profiling adds overhead to all code. Also, it doesn't matter whether we used the -p Runtime System flag or not; the overhead is inherent in the program itself when we ask to compile with profiling support.

For this reason, one should compile with profiling only when actually profiling.

By default, -p writes the profiling report into a file named <program>.prof, in this case prof-basics.prof. The contents of that file are:

```
prof-basics +RTS -s -p -RTS


total time  =        0.17 secs    (170 ticks @ 1000 us, 1 processor)
total alloc = 264,104,200 bytes   (excludes profiling overheads)


COST CENTRE MODULE   %time %alloc


list-      Main      72.9   63.6
sma-       Main      22.9   36.3
sum-       Main       4.1    0.0
```

| | | | | individual | | inherited | |
COST CENTRE MODULE		no.	entries	%time	%alloc	%time	%alloc
MAINMAIN		47	0	0.0	0.0	100.0	100.0
CAF	Main	93	0	0.0	0.0	100.0	100.0
list-	Main	96	1	72.9	63.6	72.9	63.6
sma-	Main	95	1	22.9	36.3	22.9	36.3
sum-	Main	94	1	4.1	0.0	4.1	0.0
CAF	GHC.IO.Handle.FD	90	0	0.0	0.0	0.0	0.0
CAF	GHC.IO.Handle.Text	88	0	0.0	0.0	0.0	0.0
CAF	GHC.Conc.Signal	85	0	0.0	0.0	0.0	0.0
CAF	GHC.Float	84	0	0.0	0.0	0.0	0.0
CAF	GHC.IO.Encoding	2	0	0.0	0.0	0.0	0.0
CAF	GHC.IO.Encoding.Iconv 62		0	0.0	0.0	0.0	0.0

The report contains lots of useful information:

- First, the profiling report conveniently gives us the amount of allocations excluding profiling overheads, which unsurprisingly is exactly what we observed compiling without profiling support.

- Second, the cost centres that accrued individual costs are listed. In this case, this is all of our manually set cost centres.

- Lastly, the hierarchy of all cost centres are listed. GHC assigns by default one top-level cost centre stack, named **Constant Applicative Form (CAF)**, for every module. We see that in addition to Main.CAF, some GHC-internal module CAFs are also exposed.

- Both individual and accumulated (inherited) costs are shown.

There are also other Runtime System flags besides `-p` that control time and allocation profiling. To get a complete list, we can do executable `+RTS -?`. Sometimes more detailed information can be useful. The extra Runtime System options for time and allocation profiling are:

```
executable:  -p  Time/allocation profile (output file
   <program>.prof)
executable:  -P  More detailed Time/Allocation profile
executable:  -Pa Give information about *all* cost centres
```

We can reduce allocations in our sma function with seq:

```
sma :: [Double] -> [Double]
sma (x0:x1:xs) = let r = (x0 + x1) / 2 in r `seq` r : sma (x1:xs)
sma        xs = xs
```

Profiling this stricter version of the program, we now get slightly improved performance. The important bits of the report are:

```
total time  =        0.16 secs  (160 ticks @ 1000 us, 1
   processor)
total alloc = 232,104,232 bytes  (excludes profiling overheads)


COST CENTRE MODULE  %time %alloc


list-    Main   80.6   72.4
sma-     Main   16.9   27.6
sum-     Main    2.5    0.0
```

Including profiling overheads, we shaved off some 10% of the time, and allocations in sma dropped from 36.3% to 27.6%. (The real speed-up is probably somewhat more, because the number of entered cost centres didn't change, meaning the profiling overhead probably stayed the same. That constant factor eats into the percentage increase.)

Setting cost centres automatically

It's not necessary to add cost centres manually with SCC annotations. The GHC flag -fprof-auto adds an SCC annotation for us for every binding that is not marked INLINE. Be warned though that automatic cost centres might increase the profiling overhead a lot! Of course, the same applies to manual cost centres, but those are easier to control.

This is what our cost centres would have looked like (with the original lazy sma) if we had not specified any cost centres manually:

```
ghc -O prof-basics.hs -prof -fprof-auto


./prof-basics +RTS -p


total time  =       0.17 secs   (168 ticks @ 1000 us, 1 processor)
total alloc = 264,104,296 bytes  (excludes profiling overheads)


COST CENTRE MODULE   %time %alloc


main.a      Main     77.4   63.6
sma         Main     20.2   36.3
main.c      Main      2.4    0.0
```

				individual		inherited	
COST CENTRE	MODULE	no.	entries	%time	%alloc	%time	%alloc
MAIN	MAIN	47	0	0.0	0.0	100.0	100.0
main	Main	95	0	0.0	0.0	0.0	0.0
CAF	Main	93	0	0.0	0.0	100.0	100.0
main	Main	94	1	0.0	0.0	100.0	100.0
main.a	Main	99	1	77.4	63.6	77.4	63.6
main.b	Main	97	1	0.0	0.0	20.2	36.3
sma	Main	98	1000000	20.2	36.3	20.2	36.3
main.c	Main	96	1	2.4	0.0	2.4	0.0

Here we note a few differences from manual cost centres:

- -fprof-auto added cost centres for a, b, and c, but also the sma function binding. We see that we entered a total of 1,000,000 times into the sma function.

- The costs associated with sma are now included in the sma function, instead of the binding where we added the manual cost centre. But the accumulated costs in the binding haven't changed.

 Prior to GHC 7.4.1, -fprof-auto was known as -auto-all, which is apparently still recognized, at least in the GHC 7 series, but deprecated nonetheless.

Within the strict sma, the added r binding will get assigned a cost centre:

| | | | | | individual | | inherited | |
COST CENTRE	MODULE	no.	entries	%time	%alloc	%time	%alloc
CAF	Main	93	0	0.0	0.0	100.0	100.0
main	Main	94	1	0.0	0.0	100.0	100.0
main.a	Main	99	1	69.4	72.4	69.4	72.4
main.b	Main	97	1	0.0	0.0	27.1	27.6
sma	Main	98	1000000	26.5	27.6	27.1	27.6
sma.r	Main	100	999999	0.6	0.0	0.6	0.0
main.c	Main	96	1	3.5	0.0	3.5	0.0

That new cost centre adds so much overhead when invoked a million times that time-wise we don't see any improvement over the lazy version when compiled with profiling. However, allocations aren't affected.

What if we had both automatic and manual cost centres for the a, b, and c bindings? The profiling overhead would have increased even more. In fact, it would have increased so much that the strict version is 10% slower than the lazy one when profiling!

The takeaway here is that not much can be deduced from profiling just time. Allocation profiling is more valuable because profiling doesn't interfere with the amount of allocations done (apart from doing its own allocation and subsequently subtracting those in the report).

With -O and higher, GHC routinely lifts constant expressions to the toplevel, but this is not normally reflected in the cost centre stack. With the -fprof-cafs flag, we ask GHC to assign individual cost centres to CAFs lifted to the toplevel. The upside of -fprof-cafs is that the profiling report then more closely resembles the real structure of the program, the cost centre stacks don't get so deep, and profiling overheads reduce. The downside is that one might need to take a look at the Core (obtained via -ddump-simple) in order to figure out what the lifted CAFs correspond to.

Installing libraries with profiling

Profiling programs that depend on extra modules requires that those modules were built with profiling support. The libraries that come with Haskell Platform have been built with profiling. Some distributions have enabled profiling in their Haskell packages and some provide the profiling libraries in separate packages.

Haskell libraries that you have installed via cabal-install, or stack, do not in general have profiling enabled. To profile code that uses such libraries, it is necessary to re-install them with profiling. One can also create a cabal sandbox, which we will not cover here.

Enabling profiling for dependencies using stack is easy:

```
stack build --executable-profiling --library-profiling
```

Stack conveniently re-builds all necessary packages that didn't previously have profiling enabled.

Using cabal-install re-installs is more tedious. The fastest and most straightforward way is to enable library-profiling: True in your ~/.cabal/config, remove ~/.ghc, and then install packages you want to use.

Debugging unexpected crashes with profiler

The Runtime System features the -xc flag, which shows the current cost centre stack when an exception is raised. GHC 8 is the earliest release where actual callstack information is available. In earlier versions, we can simulate callstacks with cost centres to trace the sources of unexpected exceptions.

Consider the following silly program:

```
-- file: crash.hs

f = head
g = f . tail
```

```
h = g . tail

main = print $ h [1,2]
```

Obviously this program will raise a runtime exception. Let's look at the cost centre stack:

```
ghc -prof -fprof-auto crash.hs
[1 of 1] Compiling Main                ( crash.hs, crash.o )
Linking crash ...

./crash +RTS -p -xc
*** Exception (reporting due to +RTS -xc): (THUNK_1_0), stack
  trace:
GHC.List.CAF
--> evaluated by: Main.g,
called from Main.h,
called from Main.main,
called from Main.CAF
--> evaluated by: Main.main,
called from Main.CAF
crash: Prelude.head: empty list
```

The cost center stack prints with the most recent entry first. We can trace the error to definition g, but not further into f, where the erroneous call to head is. This is because, for GHC, f is the same as head, and therefore f doesn't get a cost centre of its own. In fact, it isn't possible to even have a cost centre for f with an explicit **Set Cost Centre (SCC)** annotation. If we had written f x = head x, then f would have been assigned a cost centre.

Heap profiling

From the profiling report (+RTS -p) we were able to infer how much different cost centres allocated space, along with a rough estimate of time spent in cost centres in total during the program's lifetime. What if we wanted to see how space usage varies across that lifetime? That would be useful to pinpoint space leaks that manifest themselves only at certain events.

GHC includes a heap profiler, which put simply snapshots heap usage at small fixed intervals and generates a time-dependent report in the form of a .hp file. To enable the heap profiler for an executable, the same -prof flag for GHC is enough. Some limited heap profiling is also supported when compiled without profiling. The same cost centres used for time and allocation profiling are also used for heap profiling, if the heap profile is generated or narrowed down based on cost centres.

To extract a heap report, we need to use some of the `-h` family of Runtime System options. Those options are as follows:

```
-h<break-down> Heap residency profile (hp2ps) (output file
   <program>.hp)
   break-down: c = cost centre stack (default)
               m = module
               d = closure description
               y = type description
               r = retainer
               b = biography (LAG,DRAG,VOID,USE)
```

A subset of closures may be selected thusly:

```
-hc<cc>,...   specific cost centre(s) (top of stack only)
-hC<cc>,...   specific cost centre(s) (anywhere in stack)
-hm<mod>...   all cost centres from the specified modules(s)
-hd<des>,...  closures with specified closure descriptions
-hy<typ>...   closures with specified type descriptions
-hr<cc>...    closures with specified retainers
-hb<bio>...   closures with specified biographies
   (lag,drag,void,use)
```

This help message is quite dense. Basically, there are two separate concepts: `break-down` and `closure` subset selection.

The `break-down` subset defines the kinds of thing we associate heap residencies with. That is, the space taken by heap objects is accumulated in one of the following:

- **cost centres (-hc)**: Pin-point heap residency to automatic or manual (SCC) cost centers.
- **per-module (-hm)**: Pin-point residency to Haskell modules.
- **closure descriptions (-hd)**: Constructors and GHC internals.
- **Type description (-hy)**: Types such as Double, String, Maybe, and so on. Unknown and polymorphic types are given some approximation.
- **Retainers (-hr)**: We'll discuss retainers shortly.
- **Biography (-hb)**: The state a heap object is in, also discussed later.

The usual strategy is to break the heap profile down by cost centres (`-hc`). The complementary concept to heap break-down is closure subsets. By restricting profiling to some subsets of closures, we can narrow down the parts of the program we are actually interested in. The same options apply for subset selection as for break-down.

There can be only one break-down option, but multiple closure subset selections. With break-down, we choose the level at which we wish to inspect the program; with closure subsets, we define the parts of the program we are interested in.

For example, this combination will generate a heap profile broken down by cost centres in the `Main` module of all values of type Double:

```
+RTS -hc -hmMain -hyDouble
```

You can also compile without profiling and still use the `-h` Runtime System option, at least with a recent GHC. This eliminates the profiling overhead, leaving only minimal overhead from taking residency samples from the heap, but then the profiler options are limited to a `-h` only. When profiling is disabled, a `-h` (long form `-hT`) is pretty much identical to `-hd` when profiling is enabled.

Cost centre-based heap profiling

Let's take a real example of heap profiling. The following program calculates the Taylor polynomial of degree 800 for the sin function. The approximation is given by this formula:

$$sinx \approx \sum_{n=0}^{800} \frac{(-1)^n}{(2n+1)!} x^{2n+1}$$

This is implemented by this program:

```
-- file: heap-profiling.hs

sin' :: Double -> Double
sin' x = go 0 x where
  go n x
    | n > precision = x
    | otherwise     = go (n + 1) $ x +
      (-1) ** n * x ** (2 * n + 1) / factorial (2 * n + 1)

  precision = 800

  factorial n = product [1..n]

main = print $ sum $ map sin' [0,0.1..1]
```

To extract a heap profile of this program, we compile it with:

```
ghc -rtsopts -prof -fprof-auto heap-profiling.hs

./heap-profiling +RTS -hc -i0.05
```

The `-i0.05` flag sets the interval we want to sample the heap. By default, this is 0.1 seconds. We halve it for our program to extract enough details.

By default, when just `-h` is given, the heap profile is generated based on cost centres (`-hc`). The report is written in this case to a file named `heap-profiling.hp`. It is hard to deduce anything meaningful from the `.hp` file directly. Instead, GHC comes with a binary called `hp2ps`, which produces nice graphs from heap profile reports. We can generate a PostScript file from a `.hp` file with `hp2ps`:

```
hp2ps -c -d -e8in heap-profiling.hp
```

I included some additional arguments there to make the output more readable:

- Colorized output with `-c`
- Sorting by standard deviation (`-d`) will push more static bars to the bottom of the graph
- The Encapsulated PostScript option (`-e`) will output in portrait mode (the default is landscape)

The graph is written in a file called `heap-profiling.ps`. It looks like this:

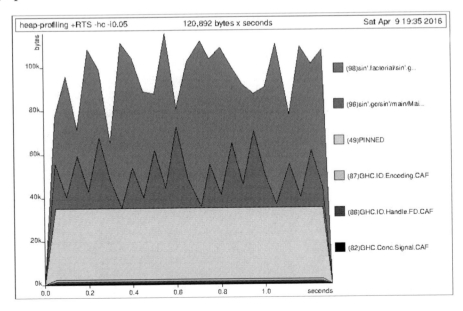

We see 11 spikes from 11 invocations of sin'. Due to the sampling interval, the spikes are not exactly even, and you might get fewer than 11 spikes on your machine. Crank up the sampling interval if there aren't enough details visible. If we decreased the interval a lot, we would see a lot more details. But this increases overhead, and finer details are not always better because they can obscure the bigger picture.

Looking at this graph, we can rest assured that our program isn't leaking memory over time. However, when we think about the space complexities of calculating a factorial or a series expansion (a sum, basically), those are constant-space. So our program is behaving suboptimally.

The problems in our program should be pretty easy to spot now. First, our factorial function is based on product, which, similar to sum, requires at least optimization-level -O to act in constant-space. The other thing is that, in go, the argument x is non-strict, which results in a chain of thunks being built.

With -O, strictness analyzer is smart enough to fix both of these problems. But if we don't want to rely on optimizer magic, we could fix our program with a bang and a strict fold:

```
-- file: heap-profiling-optimized.hs
{-# LANGUAGE BangPatterns #-}

import Data.List (foldl')

sin' :: Double -> Double
sin' x = go 0 x where
  go n !x
    | n > precision = x
    | otherwise     = go (n + 1) $ x +
        (-1) ** n * x ** (2 * n + 1) / factorial (2 * n + 1)

  precision = 800

  factorial n = foldl' (*) 1 [1..n]

main = print $ sum $ map sin' [0,0.1..1]
```

The optimized program produces a solid heap profile. The pinned data is data that the garbage collector cannot touch. Primitive data types are allocated pinned. From the new heap profile we can infer that we are not doing unnecessary allocations anymore:

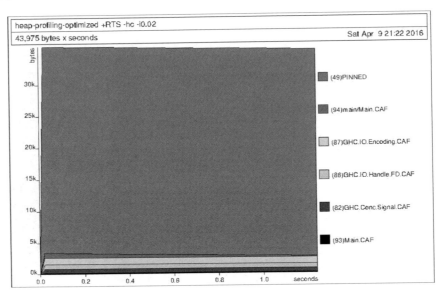

Objects outside the heap

The heap profiler cannot catch all data. Data allocated in the C land belongs to this category. The internal representation of a `ByteString` type is such that some allocations happen outside what is reachable for the heap profiler. This can be puzzling, as the following example illustrates.

A simple key-based encryption schema is obtained by taking a key k of length n and plain text of any length. Split the plain text into chunks, $p_0...p_m$, each with length n, truncating the last chunk. The first cipher text block is given by $b_0 = k$ `xor` p_0, and for the rest, $b_n = b_{\{n-1\}}$ `xor` p_n.

In Haskell, one way to implement this cipher is:

```
-- file: encryption.hs

import qualified Data.ByteString as B
import Data.Bits (xor)
import System.Environment (getArgs)
```

```
encrypt :: B.ByteString -> B.ByteString -> B.ByteString
encrypt key plain = go key plain
  where
    keyLength = B.length key

    go k0 b
       | B.null b  = B.empty
       | otherwise =
           let (b0, bn) = B.splitAt keyLength b
               r0       = B.pack $ B.zipWith xor k0 b0
               in r0 `B.append` go b0 bn
```

Here we just loop over the ByteString type, split it into two halves, the first of which is of the same size as our key (or less if we have reached the end of the ByteString type). We XOR the first half and the key (the first round) or previous chunk (subsequent rounds). This becomes a chunk of output. Splitting a ByteString type is O(1), and I intentionally included some naive O(n) appending and intermediate lists there.

Decryption is symmetric to encryption. Here is the implementation:

```
decrypt :: B.ByteString -> B.ByteString -> B.ByteString
decrypt key plain = go key plain
  where
    keyLength = B.length key

    go k0 b
       | B.null b  = B.empty
       | otherwise =
           let (b0, bn) = B.splitAt keyLength b
               r0       = B.pack $ B.zipWith xor k0 b0
               in r0 `B.append` go r0 bn
```

Now let's see how well our implementation performs. Here's a simple main program that reads the key and input data from files:

```
main = do
    [action, keyFile, inputFile] <- getArgs
    key <- B.readFile keyFile
    input <- B.readFile inputFile
    case action of
        "encrypt" -> B.writeFile (inputFile ++ ".out") $ encrypt
          key input
        "decrypt" -> B.writeFile (inputFile ++ ".out") $ decrypt
          key input
```

Let's compile with profiling and optimizations:

```
ghc -O -rtsopts -prof -fprof-auto encryption.hs
```

To test at a good enough scale, I used a key size of 1 MB and plain text size of 24 MB. Those can be generated as random samples:

```
dd if=/dev/urandom of=key.bin bs=1M count=1
dd if=/dev/urandom of=plain.bin bs=1M count=24
```

Then run the program and convert the heap report into a graph:

```
./encryption +RTS -h -RTS encrypt key.bin plain.bin
hp2ps -c -e8in encryption.hp
```

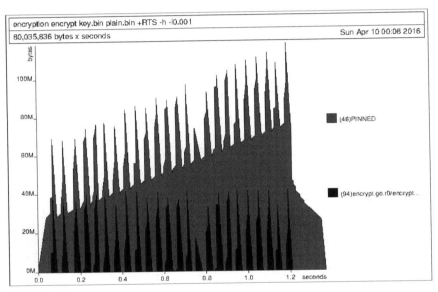

(Note that, when reproducing this graph yourself, you might need to play with the interval setting to get similar granularity. For instance, try a slightly bigger value, for example -i0.005.)

This profile is quite peculiar. Those spikes are attributed to what is happening with `B.pack $ B.zipWith ...` as that naively constructs from two ByteString a third ByteString via an intermediate list (which isn't optimized away in this case). But it doesn't make sense that there needs to be about 80 MB allocated simultaneously; there's a key of size 1 MB, one 24 MB plain text, and then the resulting ciphertext, also with size of 24 MB, so a total of about 30 MB is unknown. What is that extra?

Empty.

Empty.

Empty.

Empty.

Empty.

Empty.

Empty.

Empty.

Empty.

Empty.

Empty.

Empty.

Empty.

Empty.

Empty.

Empty.

Empty.

Empty.

Empty.

Empty.

Empty.

Doing the math from the graph, we see that, for every 1 MB of output ciphertext produced, an extra 1 MB is allocated. The culprit is `B.append` and non-tail non-productive recursion.

When we call `B.append`, it will evaluate its first argument to `whnf`, collapsing the list representation and allocating the first 1 MB. Evaluating its second argument will allocate the next 1 MB. But the catch is that `B.append` is a copying operation, so it also allocates the 1 MB for the output in addition. Both the output and the blocks will be allocated until the final output ciphertext can be constructed, resulting in twice as much space used as necessary.

A better option, as discussed in the previous chapter, is to use the `Data.ByteString.Builder` module to produce the output. The necessary changes are minimal. An implementation of the encryption step is given here:

```haskell
-- file: encryption-optimized.hs

import qualified Data.ByteString as B
import qualified Data.ByteString.Lazy as L
import qualified Data.ByteString.Builder as Builder
import Data.Bits (xor)
import System.Environment (getArgs)

encrypt :: B.ByteString -> B.ByteString -> B.ByteString
encrypt key plain = L.toStrict $ Builder.toLazyByteString $ go key plain
  where
    keyLength = B.length key

    go k0 b
        | B.null b  = mempty
        | otherwise =
            let (b0, bn) = B.splitAt keyLength b
                r0       = mconcat $ map Builder.word8 $ B.zipWith xor k0 b0
            in r0 `mappend` go b0 bn
```

The heap profile is now very concise, as shown in the following screenshot:

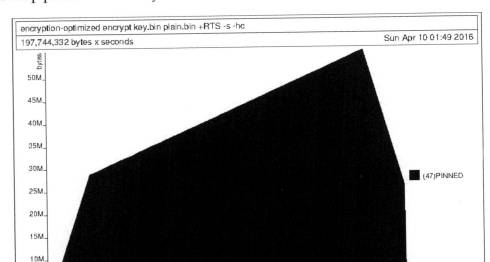

This is about as good as we can get with strict ByteStrings. Of course, the schema allows for streaming so using lazy ByteStrings would be more appropriate.

Retainer profiling

Retainer profiling (+RTS -hr) is designed to help track down space leaks. The retainer profiler breaks down the heap by retainer sets. The system stack, thunks, and explicitly mutable objects are retainers. All live objects are retained by one or more retainer objects.

Let's take an example:

```
let xs = [1..100000]
    a  = sum xs
```

Here a is a retainer for xs. xs is not yet nothing but an unevaluated, cheap thunk (as is a). If we asked for length xs, forcing the evaluation of xs, then xs becomes a large evaluated structure in the heap, which is retained by a. The retainer profiler spots such retaining and reports a as a retainer for a lot of data. Of course, if we evaluated a to WHNF, then it would stop being a retainer, because constructors are not retainers.

Let's take another illustratives example and actually do some retainer profiling. The following performs two calculations on two distinct lists:

```
-- file: mean.hs

mean  xs = sum xs / fromIntegral (length xs)

sumlg xs = sum (map log xs)

main = do
    print $ mean [1..1000000]
    print $ sumlg [1..1000001]
```

Asking for a retainer profiling, we need to compile with profiling, execute with the Runtime System flag -hr, and finally generate a graph from the heap profile:

```
ghc -rtsopts -prof -fprof-auto mean.hs
./mean +RTS -hr -i0.02
hp2ps -e8in -c mean.hp
```

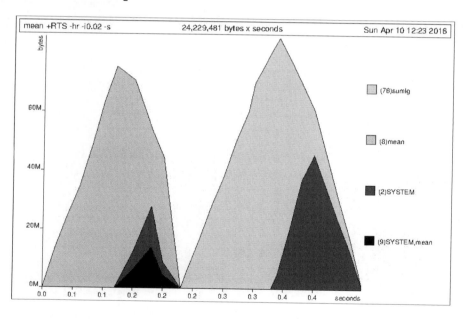

Looking at the program and the heap profile graph, the shape looks like what one would expect with no optimizations enabled: first, the first list is fully evaluated and retained as a whole, and then discarded as we have retrieved its mean. Then a similar process takes place for the second list. What is not quite clear though is what the (2)SYSTEM and (9)SYSTEM mean retainer sets are.

When we look at the graph more closely, we see that those system-things become retainers after the heap usage at our `mean` and `sumlg` functions have peaked, implying that our functions have pretty much done their work. After the peak, the list is consumed and it is up to the garbage collector to dispose of the list. There is a slight delay there, which is why the list shows up in a `SYSTEM` retainer before it is garbage-collected.

The retainer sets are numbered. A dump of all retainer sets is written to the file `<program>.prof`. The retainer sets in the graph correspond to these lines in that file:

```
SET 76 = {<Main.sumlg,Main.main,Main.CAF>}
SET 8 = {<Main.mean,Main.main,Main.CAF>}
SET 2 = {<SYSTEM.SYSTEM>}
SET 9 = {<SYSTEM.SYSTEM>, <Main.mean,Main.main,Main.CAF>}
```

We see that the retainers are given as cost centre stacks. This is crucial when pinpointing retainers to correct calle-sites.

Recall the ByteString encryption example from before. What would the retainer profile for that unoptimized program look like? Much to our surprise, it is in crucial ways different from the cost centre-based heap profile. Look at this:

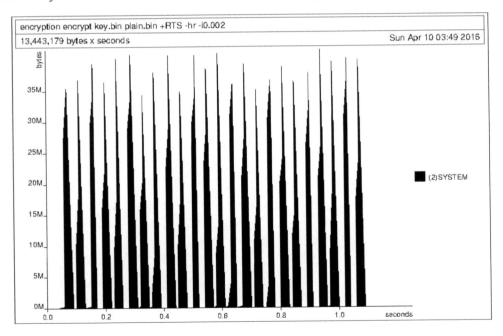

Only some spikes (from the intermediate list) – where are the large ByteStrings? There sure were some in the other heap profile!

This is a shortcoming of the heap profiler, or a consequence of the foreign pointer representation used in the `bytestring` library. The retainer profiler is unable to follow ByteStrings to their retainers, and in fact it isn't a given that the cost centre-based report is always totally correct either. This is something that needs to be kept in mind when using libraries, such as `bytestring`, that use foreign pointers in their data structures.

It is a good idea to always check the Runtime System memory statistics with `+RTS -s`, as that will always give exact memory usage.

Biographical profiling

The last kind of break-down we can ask from GHC is the biographical breakdown. Biographical profiling sorts heap objects into four categories:

- **State LAG**: From creation of the object to its first use
- **State USE**: From first use of the object until its last use
- **State DRAG**: From final use of the object until the last reference is dropped
- **State VOID**: Object is never used in its lifetime

Here's an example biographical profile of the ByteString encryption program from before. Like in the retainer profile, here too the big ByteStrings are not shown. The now familiar spikes are shown as lagging, as expected of a large list that is constructed and then consumed. Then some big data structures seem to show up at the end of the program execution. Something that is used and something that is lagging:

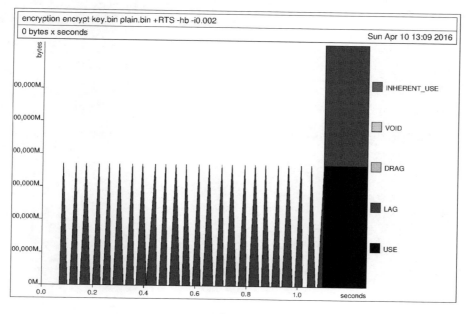

I used the following Runtime System options in generating this graph:

```
./encrypt key.bin plain.bin +RTS -hb -i0.002
```

Again, experiment with the interval setting to find the correct granularity on your machine.

Looking at this graph, it's hard to say much about anything. A more useful use case for biographical profiling is to use biographical data in the subset selection, and break-down using some other criteria, such as cost centres.

A usual example would be to find cost centres that produce heap objects in DRAG or VOID states. This is achieved with:

```
program +RTS -hc -hbdrag,void
```

Then we could find retainers for those cost centres with the +RTS -hr -hccc1,cc2, and so on program. Note that GHC cannot currently do both biographical and retainer profiling simultaneously, so +RTS -hr -hbdrag,void is unfortunately not allowed.

Benchmarking using the criterion library

Profiling aside, benchmarking the time a calculation takes to perform is a direct indicator of real-world performance. Benchmarking Haskell applications is pretty much dominated by the criterion library. There is a system called nofib, which is used to benchmark GHC itself, but for applications criterion is superior. Criterion even produces interactive web pages describing the results of benchmarks, which is a nice feature.

This text is written for criterion-1.1.1.0. Obviously, the criterion package needs to be installed:

```
cabal install criterion        # or: stack install criterion
```

A criterion benchmark suite is created as a normal Haskell program. An example is this:

```
-- file: benchmark.hs

import Criterion.Main
import Data.List (foldl')

main = defaultMain [
    bgroup "sum" [ bench "sum"    $ whnf sum             [1..1000000]
        , bench "foldr" $ whnf (foldr (+) 0)  [1..1000000]
```

```
  , bench "foldl"  $ whnf (foldl  (+) 0)  [1..1000000]
  , bench "foldl'" $ whnf (foldl' (+) 0)  [1..1000000]
  ]
]
```

What is going on here is that:

- We imported `Criterion.Main`, which imports the most used criterion functions.

- We used `Criterion.Main.defaultMain` as our program, giving it a list of type `[Benchmark]`.

- With `bgroup :: String → [Benchmark] → Benchmark` we defined a group of sum benchmarks.

- For `whnf :: (a → b) → a → Benchmarkable` we gave different implementations of `sum` to create something benchmarkable for us. Like the name suggests, the result `b` is evaluated to WHNF, which marks the end of the benchmark run.

- With `bench :: String → Benchmarkable → Benchmark` we defined benchmarks from something benchmarkable, giving them some descriptive names.

When we compile with optimizations and run this program, we get the following results:

```
benchmarking sum/sum
time                309.2 ms    (281.0 ms .. 344.2 ms)
0.996 R²    (0.983 R² .. 1.000 R²)
mean                310.4 ms    (300.6 ms .. 316.5 ms)
std dev             9.535 ms    (4.148 ms .. 12.65 ms)
variance introduced by outliers: 16% (moderately inflated)

benchmarking sum/foldr
time                66.14 ms    (62.61 ms .. 69.17 ms)
0.994 R²    (0.988 R² .. 0.998 R²)
mean                67.27 ms    (65.21 ms .. 71.28 ms)
std dev             4.686 ms    (2.113 ms .. 7.483 ms)
variance introduced by outliers: 17% (moderately inflated)

benchmarking sum/foldl
time                318.8 ms    (276.3 ms .. 365.7 ms)
0.988 R²    (0.939 R² .. 1.000 R²)
mean                315.6 ms    (294.8 ms .. 329.6 ms)
std dev             23.17 ms    (9.738 ms .. 32.22 ms)
```

```
variance introduced by outliers: 18% (moderately inflated)

benchmarking sum/foldl'
time                 20.16 ms   (20.10 ms .. 20.22 ms)
1.000 R²     (1.000 R² .. 1.000 R²)
mean                 20.17 ms   (20.14 ms .. 20.25 ms)
std dev              110.4 µs   (47.27 µs .. 202.3 µs)
```

No-one is surprised to see that `foldl'` is fast or that `foldr` is not too far behind. But recall how in the first chapter we noted that `sum [1..n]` and similarly `foldl (+) 0 [1..n]` were equivalent to `foldl' (+) 0 [1..n]`. So why are these now so much slower in our benchmark?

Simply because `whnf` by design doesn't inline `sum` or `foldl` cannot be optimized: they're forced to consider the list as a black box. This forces the benchmark situation to be such that the `benchmarkable` function cannot make assumptions about its argument at compiletime, often simulating the real use case.

But inlining is often crucial for performance, so you shouldn't blindly perform microbenchmarks on, for example, parts of vector code that as a whole would be largely fused away.

To confirm our suspicion, let's add a few more benchmarks where the list is now inside the `benchmarkable` function:

```
bgroup "foldl"
[ bench "_"  $ whnf (\_ -> foldl (+) 0 [1..1000000])
  undefined
, bench "()" $ whnf (\() -> foldl (+) 0 [1..1000000]) ()
, bench "num" $ whnf (\n -> foldl (+) 0 [1..n]) (1000000)
, bench "num (strict)" $ whnf (\n -> foldl' (+) 0 [1..n])
  (1000000)
]
```

Running the benchmarks now with HTML output (benchmark – output `results.html`) we get a webpage which, among benchmark-specific analysis, contains this graph:

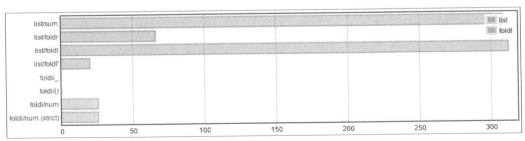

Now we see clearly that, when the list is generated within the `benchmarkable` function, `foldl` is equivalent to `foldl'`. And if we defined the list as a constant within the function, then GHC deduces that it is a constant and lifts it into a CAF which is memoized, resulting in a sum implementation that sums a million elements in a few petty nanoseconds.

Benchmark results should be taken with a grain of salt, especially ones that seem too fast. It is hardly ever trivial to guess which expressions are optimized into what. The rule of thumb is that, when the result of the `benchmarkable` function depends on the environment (the second argument to `whnf`), then the time taken to evaluate the result will resemble the real cost.

Apart from evaluation to WHNF, other benchmarkable things supported by `criterion` are:

```
nf   :: NFData b => (a → b) → a → Becnhmarkable
nfIO :: NFData a => IO a → Benchmarkable
whnfIO :: IO a → Benchmarkable
```

So there is another pure benchmark, something that requires the result to be some `NFData`, and `IO` action variants for both pure benchmarks.

NFData stands for **Normal Form Data**, which is a stronger notion than **Weak Head Normal Form**. In normal form, the structure is fully evaluated, meaning there are no unevaluated thunks, even deep down the structure. NFData is provided by the `deepseq` package. The only method in the `NFData` typeclass is `rnf :: a → ()`, implementations of which are just recursive calls to `rnf` and `seq`. Starting with GHC 7.2, instances can be derived for anything for which the Generic typeclass (from GHC.Generics) is derived. Refer to the documentation of the `deepseq` package for the details.

With normal form, we can benchmark the total evaluation of big algebraic data structures such as trees. However, it should be kept in mind that, in real scenarios, it is rarely the case that a big lazy structure needs to be evaluated fully. What this means is that such a benchmark doesn't accurately describe real amortized execution times.

Criterion works so that it executes a benchmark for a few different numbers of iterations. For a well-behaving, predictable benchmarkable function or action, execution times increase linearly when the number of iterations increases. Criterion uses linear regression to measure this, giving an ordinary least-squares regression estimate for a single execution, R^2 goodness-of-fit of the regression, along with mean execution time and standard deviation.

A general guideline for reading results from a criterion benchmark is to look at whether R^2 is close to 1. If it's much less than 1, it means that either there's something wrong with the benchmark itself or that indeterminism in the benchmarkable thing is producing a lot of deviation in single execution times. The ordinary least squares regression estimate is probably closer to the expected execution time than the mean execution time is, because outside disturbances in the benchmarking environment can result in outliers that affect the mean more than the regression estimate.

Although the default regression predicts execution time from iterations, other combinations are possible with the `--regress` criterion command line argument or the respective regressions `config` field, regressions. For example, `--regress allocated:iters` performs a regression of allocations given iterations. Extra regressions produce additional output, such as:

```
allocated:          1.000 R²   (1.000 R² .. 1.000 R²)
iters               23.999     (23.995 .. 24.004)
y                   275.081    (-20091.728 .. 19504.093)
```

Another R2 goodness-of-fit is given for the regression, along with the slope and y-intercept of the fitted line. Like many other regression metrics, measuring allocations from within the program requires enabling the Runtime System parameter `+RTS -T`. Refer to the criterion documentation to learn about other available regression metrics.

The criterion library is designed such that it should be relatively easy to adapt it to cover wildly different use cases. All necessary datatypes and utility functions are exported and all exported identifiers are extensively documented. JUnit-style reporting is also supported.

Profile and monitor in real time

The heap profile report file `<program>.hp` is generated as the program executes, so it's perfectly fine to take a snapshot of the file at any time and visualize it with hp2ps, even if the program is still busy executing. Because very basic heap profiling (`-hT`) is possible without having compiled with profiling support, it is possible to produce running heap profiles with a very small overhead.

Increasing the sample interval `-i` to something relatively big, such as a couple of seconds, it is very feasible to extract heap profiles from long-running programs even in production environments.

A quick-and-dirty trick that isn't for the light-hearted is the `-s` Runtime System option. This option prints garbage collector statistics every time a cleanup takes place, in realtime. This includes bytes allocated, bytes copied, bytes live, time elapsed, and how long the garbage collector took. To make some sense of the output, it might make sense to limit the number of generations in the garbage collector to 1 (the default is 2). So `+RTS -S -G1`.

Monitoring over HTTP with ekg

We are now familiar with profiling and benchmarking applications executing locally. We also know how to extract garbage collector information from programs running locally, but what if the program was running on a server? Things are no longer so convenient.

It would be nice to be able to monitor the performance of programs running on servers in realtime, and perhaps to store performance history in some timeseries database for later investigations.

A package called `ekg` provides a ready solution for the first wish, namely real-time monitoring, and also a quite mature set of features for collecting statistics from Haskell programs. It provides a REST API out-of-the-box, which can be used to fetch data into time-series databases.

The first step with a new library is again to install it. This also installs the `ekg-core` library, which contains metrics. The `ekg` library provides the monitoring application:

```
cabal install ekg
```

Now we get to an example. A silly example, but still an example: a program that repeatedly asks for a number and prints the factorial of that number. For some reason or other, we want to monitor the performance of our command-line application via HTTP. Implementing this program is very straightforward:

```
-- file: ekg-fact.hs

{-# LANGUAGE OverloadedStrings #-}

module Main where

import Control.Monad
import System.Remote.Monitoring

main = do
    forkServer "localhost" 8000
    forever $ do
```

```
input <- getLine
print $ product [1..read input :: Integer]
```

Adding real-time monitoring over HTTP to our command-line program was a matter of adding one `import` and one extra line in `main`. When compiling, we should enable the `-T` Runtime System option to enable `ekg` to collect GC statistics. It is also a good idea to enable at least `-O`. On multithreaded systems, we may likely also want a threaded runtime, so that the program doesn't need to share the same system core with the monitoring subsystem. All in all, we have:

```
ghc -O -threaded -rtsopts -with-rtsopts='-N-T' ekg-fact.hs
```

ekg-fact

Now we can open a browser at `http://localhost:8000` and get a real-time view of the performance of our program. A portion of the page is shown here:

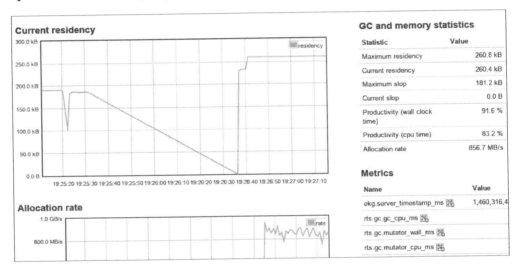

It's possible to add our own metrics for `ekg` to monitor. As an example, let's add to our program a metric that counts the number of factorials we have calculated:

```
{-# LANGUAGE OverloadedStrings #-}
module Main where

import Control.Monad
import System.Remote.Monitoring
import System.Metrics
import qualified System.Metrics.Counter as Counter
```

```
main = do
    server <- forkServer "localhost" 8000
    factorials <- createCounter "factorials.count"
                                (serverMetricStore server)
    forever $ do
        input <- getLine
        print $ product [1..read input :: Integer]
        Counter.inc factorials
```

First we needed to `import` metric modules from the `ekg-core` package. Then we created a new `Counter`type metric with `createMetric`. After calculating a factorial, we increase that counter by one.

The JSON API that comes with `ekg` is quite simple. We can retrieve all metrics by just requesting the root with content-type JSON:

```
curl -H "Accept: application/json" http://localhost:8000

{
  "ekg": {
  "server_timestamp_ms": { "type": "c", "val": 1460318128878 }
},
"rts": {
  "gc": {
    "gc_cpu_ms": { "type": "c", "val": 624 },
[...]
```

If we are only interested in one metric, say our new `factorials.count` metric, we can only request it specifically, like so:

```
curl -H "Accept: application/json"
http://localhost:8000/factorials/count
{"type":"c","val":12}
```

It's not hard to imagine integrating ekg-monitoring to time series databases. Using the REST API is straightforward, but the `ekg` library is so flexible that a push-model wouldn't be too hard either.

Summary

We started this chapter by profiling programs by cost centres, which can be set automatically (`-fprof-auto`) or manually (SCC-annotations). We learned that there is overhead in profiling, which is why execution times are an inaccurate metric when profiling. Allocations remained a good measure of performance in any case. We used the heap profiler to produce informative graphs about memory usage over time, and to spot unwanted allocations and retainers.

We explored different options in the GHC heap profiler: break-downs and subset selections, both of which draw more or less from the same pool of parameters. The default break-down was by cost not yet finished.

Finally, we looked at two additional libraries, `criterion` for benchmarking and `ekg` for monitoring. In discussing criterion, we stumbled upon the concept of normal form, which will also come up later on when we discuss parallelism. Adding real-time graphical garbage garbage collector monitoring via HTTP to a Haskell application was a real breeze with `ekg`, and the library fully supports custom metrics and extending the monitoring system.

In the next chapter, we will pull everything together from these first three chapters and discuss some of the fine details of developing Haskell at scale: structuring bigger projects using cabal and stack. We will look at some less common performance tricks such as lazy patterns and rewrite rules, revisit and introduce some concepts such as inlining and specializing, and briefly discuss practical type-level programming.

The Devil's in the Detail

In this chapter, we pull together knowledge and techniques from previous chapters and learn to apply those techniques in large and complex projects. In particular, we will use `cabal-install` and stack to help us cope with multi-file projects and even projects with multiple subprojects. We learn how, and especially how not, to throw and recover from exceptions in Haskell.

Having good test coverage is as important in a Haskell project as it is in projects written in any other language. But because Haskell's type-system is so expressive, the number of necessary test cases is greatly reduced. Also, new extensions for the type-system in GHC are constantly being experimented with. Consequently, there is a bunch of language extensions considered more or less experimental, and some extensions are just not enabled by default yet in the current standard (Haskell 2010).

This chapter concludes the first part of this book. Already from the three previous chapters, you are well equipped to create and optimize programs in vanilla Haskell and to use some high-quality libraries effectively. After this chapter, you will know how to structure Haskell projects of any size, handle exceptions correctly, and test code. In addition, we will look at the usual use cases for some new language extensions. The following topics will be covered in this chapter:

- Structuring larger projects using `cabal-install` and stack
- Writing tests for Haskell code
- Throwing errors and handling exceptions
- Best practices, tips, and tricks for writing robust, predictably fast Haskell
- Going beyond Haskell 2010 with modern language features

The anatomy of a Haskell project

A typical Haskell project consists of one or several of the following sections:

- Library (modules); A no-brainer for library authors. But most applications are also structured so that most code resides in distinct modules.
- One or more executables.
- Tests and benchmarks.
- Other source files and assets.

All of these are supported by Cabal. Starting with a new project from scratch, we can use `cabal init` to create a `.cabal` file with basic information such as the package name and maintainer details already filled in. Moreover, if you already have a bunch of Haskell source files in your working directory, then Cabal will add those to the `.cabal` file and even guess package dependencies for you.

The structure often found in projects that have both a library and an executable is to place library code and the executable's source files under different subdirectories. If we have a single library module, dubbed `Lib`, and a `main`, the structure would be:

```
some-package/
    src/Lib.hs
    app/main.hs
```

This is assuming the file contents are:

```
-- file: some-package/src/Lib.hs

{-# LANGUAGE OverloadedStrings #-}
module Lib where
import Data.ByteString as B
import qualified Data.ByteString.Char8 as C8
foo :: B.ByteString -> IO ()
foo = C8.putStrLn . B.append "foo"


-- file: some-package/app/main.hs

{-# LANGUAGE OverloadedStrings #-}
import Lib
main = foo "bar"
```

Invoking `cabal init -n -is` library under some-package, will create a `.cabal` file for us. The generated file looks like this (omitting some uninteresting lines):

```
-- Initial some-package.cabal generated by cabal init.  For further
-- documentation, see http://haskell.org/cabal/users-guide/

name:                some-package
version:             0.1.0.0
license:             BSD3
license-file:        LICENSE
build-type:          Simple
-- extra-source-files:
cabal-version:       >=1.10

library
  exposed-modules:     Lib
  -- other-modules:
  -- other-extensions:
  build-depends:       base >=4.8 && <4.9, bytestring >=0.10 &&
    <0.11
  hs-source-dirs:      src
  default-language:    Haskell2010
```

We notice a few things here. Firstly, the `build-type` is `Simple`. This holds for almost every package, so no need to worry about it. Then we have an `extra-source-files` field. In this field, we can list the non-Haskell, non-C source files required to build the package, and files that should be distributed with the package (such as a README).

Next, we have a section labeled as `library`. There can be only one `library` section per package. The `library` section is usually of most interest, because that's where all the interesting code is located. There are other parameters besides the ones listed here, but those most often used are:

- `default-language`: The language standard used in this package (currently either Haskell 98 or Haskell 2010).

- `build-depends`: Other packages this package depends on and their accepted version ranges.

- `exposed-modules`: Modules that are exposed for users of the library.

- `other-modules`: Modules that are hidden from users of the library. Unless it breaks internal consistency, it is advised to export internal modules too, because it is hard to predict all possible use cases of a library.

- `hs-source-dirs`: The directory under which module files are located.

Now that we can build the library, we need to tell Cabal how to build the executable as well. Unfortunately, current `cabal init` will not add both library and executable definitions for us, so we need to write one of them manually. Fortunately, a minimal `executable` section is only four lines appended to our `.cabal` file:

```
executable foo
    main-is:            app/main.hs
    build-depends:      base, some-package
    default-language:   Haskell2010
```

A single package can provide multiple executables, which is why we had to specify a name for it (`foo`). Then we need to specify which file contains `main` (`app/main.hs`) and the dependencies. Note that we had to explicitly depend on our package (some-package) to use our library modules. Last, the `default-language` needs also be specified for executables.

At this point, we can use `cabal build` to build both the library and executable, use `cabal install` to install the executable(s) under `~/.cabal/bin`, create a *Hackage-ready source distribution* with `cabal sdist`, and so on.

Useful fields and flags in cabal files

We can specify many other things in the cabal file as well. For example, in our example package, we had the `OverloadedStrings` extension enabled in all files. We could make this a default by adding the following line to the `library` and `executable` sections:

```
default-extensions: OverloadedStrings
```

It is also good practice to list conditionally used extensions (via LANGUAGE pragmas) in the `other-extensions` field.

Any cabal file section can be disabled by setting its `buildable` field to `false`, for example:

```
executable foo-win
    buildable: False
    [...]
```

Cabal supports conditionals and a few built-in functions such as `os(name)`, meaning we can, for example, conditionally enable some sections (or set any fields for that matter). The preceding code would be better written as:

```
executable foo-win
    if !os(windows)
        buildable: False
    [...]
```

But note that the following would not work. The executable wouldn't be built under any conditions:

```
executable foo-win
  buildable: False
  if os(windows)
    buildable: True
  [...]
```

The reason is that, in a technical sense, Cabal doesn't override a field when the same field has been declared multiple times. Instead, the occurrences are combined and, for one reason or an other, False takes precedence over `True` in cabal flags.

The combination of list-like fields such as `build-depends`, `default-extensions`, and so on is simply the union of all declarations. To build a `Lib.Windows` module only when building for a Windows machine, we could do this:

```
library
  exposed-modules: Lib
  build-depends: base <4.9, transformers >= 0.3 && < 0.6
  if os(windows)
    exposed-modules: Lib.Windows
    build-depends: transformers < 0.5
```

Note that we were able to tighten the version bounds within a conditional block. On the other hand, it is not possible to loosen bounds; bounds are simply concatenated, so the final bounds for transformers become `>=0.3 && <0.6 && <0.5`.

In addition to built-in functions, cabal supports defining flags within the cabal file itself. Package flags can be used in conditionals. To define a `development` flag, we add a new `flag` section into the cabal file:

```
flag development
  description: Enable development features
  default: False
```

The new flag can now be used, for example, in conjunction with the `ghc-options` field to enable profiling in development mode:

```
library
  [...]
  if flag(development)
    ghc-options: -prof -fprof-auto
```

A detail that's good to keep in mind if you're conditioning on `build-depends` or `*-extensions` with a flag is that by default Cabal will resolve on flags when looking for a plausible build plan. First Cabal tries the default flag value(s) and if that fails, it tries to negate flags until a build plan is found. If this behavior is not desired, a `manual: True` field can be added for the flag.

Flags are explicitly enabled via the `-f` argument for configure and its super commands:

```
cabal configure -fdevelopment
cabal install -f-development
```

The former enables the `development` flag, while the latter disables it.

Test suites and benchmarks

Cabal supports declaring test and `benchmark` suites within a cabal file. These are defined as sections, like `executables`. Examples of both are:

```
test-suite test-props
   type:           exitcode-stdio-1.0
   main-is:        properties.hs
   hs-source-dirs: tests
   build-depends:  base, some-package


benchmark bench-foo
   type:           exitcode-stdio-1.0
   main-is:        benchmarks.hs
   hs-source-dirs: tests
   build-depends:  base, some-package, criterion
```

Like executables, both test and `benchmark` suites require an identifier. It's possible to define multiple `test-suites` and `benchmarks` with different names. The usual usage of cabal `test-suites` and `benchmarks` consists of the `exitcode-stdio-1.0` type, which requires a `main-is` field, and basically just tells Cabal that, to run this test or benchmark, the accompanying program should be executed and the exit code inspected. If the program exits cleanly, the suite finished successfully.

And, just like the other sections, tests and benchmarks must have their `build-depends` explicitly listed. This is sometimes quite annoying, if the list of dependencies is the same for the library and its `test-suite`. Unfortunately, there is no simple solution to avoid this duplication.

If you only need to test the public API, then it makes sense for the `test-suite` to depend only on the `base` and the library. But often the internals need testing, in which case the only option is to list the often almost identical lists of dependencies. Many times, the version bounds are left out from the `test-suite`, because the library's dependencies already enforce those.

To run tests and benchmarks, we invoke `cabal` as:

```
cabal configure --enable-tests --enable-benchmarks
cabal build
cabal test
cabal bench
```

 If you want try these commands now, create dummy `tests/` `properties.hs` and `tests/benchmarks.hs` files with a `main` in them. We'll look at testing a bit later in this chapter.

Using the stack tool

Since its release in Spring 2015, the stack tool and `stackage.org` service by **FP Complete** have provided a lovely solution for the notorious "Cabal Hell" problems. In many ways, the stackage ecosystem is superior to cabal, or cabal with sandboxing. The core feature of stack is internally consistent releases of Haskell packages and reusable builds, along with many other cool features such as managing GHC versions and building Docker images.

As an aside, the notorious challenge with Haskell package management, relative to package management in many other languages, is mostly blamed on cross-module inlining – it's impossible for two different versions of the same package to coexist in the same dependency graph.

In normal Haskell development, transitioning from a cabal-based workflow to a stack-based one is for the most part as simple as changing all occurrences of cabal commands for stack commands. The subcommands and arguments don't need touching. For example, `cabal test` translates to `stack test`, `cabal install` to `stack install`, and so on.

Stack does not subsume cabal; in fact, the only feature of `cabal-install` that is wholly subsumed by stack is sandboxing. Otherwise, stack just calls out to cabal with some extra arguments. This also means that the cabal files are just as important with or without stack.

To use stack to build our toy project we cabalized previously, we need to create a stack.yaml file for it. This is accomplished with stack init:

```
stack init --prefer-lts
```

That --prefer-lts is optional, and just tells stack to choose a long-term support snapshot of Haskell packages from stackage as the basis of the project. Our stack.yaml file now looks something along these lines:

```
# For more information, see: http://docs.haskellstack.org/en/stable/
yaml_configuration.html

resolver: lts-5.11

packages:
- '.'

extra-deps: []

flags: {}
```

The syntax is just normal YAML syntax. On the first non-comment line, we specify the resolver (**lts-5.11**). This is a snapshot of popular and maintained packages guaranteed to work together. On the next line, we specify which cabal packages belong to this project. In this case, it's just the current directory ('.').

Often a project needs to use packages that are outside the stackage snapshot. Using the extra-deps array, we can augment the snapshot with arbitrary packages from Hackage. The catch here is that we need to specify explicit versioning, for example:

```
extra-deps:
- acme-missiles-0.3
```

With the flags section, we tell stack to build packages with specific values of cabal flags. For example, we can enable the development flag in our project by default:

```
flags:
  some-package:
    development: true
```

For more configurables and stack commands, refer to the stack manual at http://docs.haskellstack.org/en/stable/README.

Multi-package projects

When a project evolves into something bigger and complexity increases, it sometimes makes sense to split the project into multiple cabal packages. The Cabal infrastructure doesn't care how you organize your packages, as long as every cabal file is named by the project (the `name` field within the file) and resides in a directory with no other cabal files.

In general, two tactics are seen in the wild to organize multi-package projects (assuming a version control system):

- Separate repositories for every package, possibly with a super-repository that links to single repositories (for example with Git submodules)

- A catch-em-all mega-repository with subdirectories for every package

The choice is largely dependent on the nature of the project and people's preferences. In the end, the workflows in both organization schemas are very similar. The packages can be installed individually using `cabal-install` or declared in `stack.yaml` packages field. For example, the **Yesod** framework is structured as a mega-repository and the accompanying `stack.yaml` looks like this:

```
resolver: lts-5.6
packages:
  - ./yesod-core
  - ./yesod-static
  - ./yesod-persistent
  - ./yesod-form
  - ./yesod-auth
  - ./yesod-test
  - ./yesod-bin
  - ./yesod
[...]
```

More information on cabal and stack can be found in their manuals. Also, the `stackage.org` site has pointers to many useful pieces of information. In the next section, we will leave structuring concerns behind and get back to coding instead.

Erroring and handling exceptions

Haskell very intentionally does not have a `null`/`None`/`nil` value like many popular languages have, both strongly typed (Java) or not (Perl). Null values are exceptionally bad for program safety. Null values are not expressed in types, giving nulls no choice but to hide from the unsuspecting programmer and pop into sight in production.

Nulls are one of the main causes of bugs and security holes in today's software, which is why Haskell has opted for a *no-null policy*. This might sound restrictive at first, but actually the alternative representations for possibly failing computations in Haskell are various and rich.

First, there are infinite ways to embed the possibility of failing into the datatype: Maybe, Either, `YourAwesomeDataType`, and so on.

Second, with the wonderfully extensive abstraction machinery in Haskell we can compose and recover from failing situations on a very high level. Although these functors, monoids, monads, and whatnots have scarily abstract names "borrowed" from Category Theory, a branch of very abstract mathematics, their incarnations in Haskell are easy to grasp and their benefits are many.

The worst way to handle any error in Haskell is to use error or undefined. Undefined particularly should almost always be considered heresy – error is always better because at least an error message can be given. Both error and undefined indicate an anomalous program state, from which recovery should not be attempted. Moreover, they are pure and asynchronous; a nightmare for referential transparency.

Handling synchronous errors

The exceptions interface shipped with GHC is in the `Control.Exception` module. All exceptions (including error and undefined) are represented as a `SomeException`, which is a datatype defined as:

```
data SomeException = forall e. Exception e => SomeException e
```

Different exceptions are defined as their own datatypes, such as:

```
data IOException
data AssertionFailed = AssertionFailed String
data PatternMatchFail = PatternMatchFail String
data ErrorCall = ErrorCall String -- when called error
```

Unlike some other languages, Haskell does not have any built-in try...catch style constructs to handle exceptions. Instead, exceptions are thrown and handled with just normal functions.

Synchronous errors in the IO monad are thrown with `throwIO :: Exception e => e → IO a`. This is the best option to fail when working in IO, because the exception is guaranteed to be thrown at that point in the IO action.

Because there are no special try...catch style constructs in Haskell, for better or worse we can get creative with patterns for catching and recovering from errors. For example, using `catch` is rarely the best or even a good option.

Often we want to perform some action to acquire a resource, such as a file handle; do something with that resource; and release the resource when we are done or an exception was raised in the middle. We capture this pattern in a single function, `bracket`:

```
bracket :: IO a → (a → IO b) → (a → IO c) → IO c

bracket openFile closeFile (\fileHandle → doSomething)
```

In other situations, we want to only perform some cleanup action after a computation has finished, no matter what happened. For this we have:

```
finally :: IO a → IO b → IO a
```

Sometimes we would like to perform a computation but not really do anything with the exception yet – just return it for later inspection further down the program. For this we have `try`, which wraps the result in an `Either`:

```
try :: Exception e => IO a → IO (Either e a)
```

Despite it being convenient to catch virtually all exceptions, this sort of catching should be handled with great care. Especially if you are retrying a computation when it raises an exception, you shouldn't blindly discard all exceptions and try again; what if the user wants to abort and your program ignores the `UserInterrupt` exception? Or the operating system wants to kill your program gracefully, but your program ignores that wish too? Only catch exceptions you are prepared to handle!

Also, catching multiple exceptions does not require catching all exceptions. Using `catches` and multiple different `Handler` exceptions from one computation can be handled differently:

```
catches :: IO a → [Handler a] → IO a

data Handler a = forall e. Exception e => Handler (e → IO a)
```

An example of handling user interruption differently from an IO exception is:

```
catches someComputation
    [ Handler $ \UserInterrupt -> handleUserInterrupt
    , Handler $ \(e :: IOException) -> handleIOException ]
```

Note that, although exception handlers can be chained with multiple `catch` statements, the semantics are different from using a single `catch`, in that, in chained invocations of `catch`, previous handlers could throw exceptions that get caught in the next handlers.

The exception hierarchy

What is common for all exceptions is that they all must implement `Show` and `Exception`, the latter of which is given by:

```
class (Typeable e, Show e) => Exception e where
    toException :: e → SomeException
    fromException :: SomeException → Maybe e
```

It is possible (and you are encouraged) to define your own exception types. The simplest custom exception would be:

```
data MyException = MyException deriving (Show, Typeable)
instance Exception MyException
```

Looking at the `Exception` class, it would seem like the `toException` would be redundant – it has exactly the same signature as the `SomeException` constructor has.

The point in calling the `SomeException` constructor via `toException` is that, this way, arbitrary hierarchies of exceptions can be built. What is meant by exception hierarchy is that, when exceptions A and B are under C, we can create exception handlers for only A, only B, or both A and B as only C.

Say we are building an application that we would like to throw exceptions in some situations. Furthermore, we want to catch some of those exceptions within the application, while some application exceptions should be caught further up.

We start with an exception type that will represent all application exceptions. Our `SomeApplicationException` resembles the root `SomeException` type, in that both just wrap some other (ad hoc polymorphic) exception:

```
-- file: errors.hs
data SomeApplicationException =
    forall e. Exception e => SomeApplicationException e
    deriving Typeable

instance Show SomeApplicationException where
    show (SomeApplicationException e) =
        "application: " ++ show e

instance Exception SomeApplicationException
```

In all, three things are going on here:

- We derived a `Typeable` instance for our custom exception type. This is necessary for coercion to and from `SomeExceptions`.
- We wrote a `Show` instance for the type. Because our exception is now an existential, we cannot derive `Show`.

- We added an instance for `Exception`. The default implementations of the methods will suffice here.

Next, say our application includes some sub-procedures we call workers. These workers can fail and throw exceptions. We would like to separate these worker exceptions from other exceptions in our application, but still have it so that catching application exceptions catches `worker` exceptions as well.

To achieve that, we again create a new exception type and make it an instance of `Typeable`, `Show`, and `Exception`. But this time, the `Exception` instance is more involved:

```
data WorkerException = WorkerException String deriving (Show,
  Typeable)

instance Exception WorkerException where
    toException = toException . SomeApplicationException
    fromException x = do
        SomeApplicationException e <- fromException x
        cast e
```

What is going on in that instance is that `toException` first wraps the `worker` exception into an application exception, and dually in `fromException`, we coerce to an `application` exception and then inside of that into a `worker` exception.

Now we can throw a `WorkerException`, and it will get caught by a `worker` exception handler, an `application` exception handler, and a generic (`SomeException`) handler:

```
> let worker = throwIO $ WorkerException "flood"

> catch worker (\e@(WorkerException _) -> print e)
WorkerException "flood"

>     catch worker (\e@(SomeApplicationException _) -> print e)
application: WorkerException "flood"
```

Handling asynchronous errors

Exceptions thrown with `throwIO` are always synchronous – they are thrown at exactly that point in the computation. Exceptions thrown with `throw :: Exception e => e → a` are always asynchronous – they are thrown when and where an attempt to evaluate the result a is made. The error and undefined functions are specializations of `throw`.

Asynchronous exceptions are particularly vicious in a purely functional language, because the code or thread that raises the exception depends on where and when an expression is evaluated, and evaluation can be deferred indefinitely. Raising exceptions from pure code should be avoided in general; for instance, total functions should be preferred to partial functions in most cases.

It is impossible to catch any exceptions from pure code. All catching must happen in either IO or STM monads (or monad stacks with either IO or STM at the bottom). Catching asynchronous exceptions in IO is no different from catching synchronous exceptions. But care must be taken that the computation from which exceptions are caught really raises the exception and doesn't only defer it in a thunk.

For example, this does not make sense:

```
> catch (return $ head []) (\(SomeException _) -> return 0)
*** Exception: Prelude.head: empty list
```

The exception is not raised within the computation, but it's returned from it and raised outside the catch. On the other hand, if we force the evaluation within the computation, the exception is raised within the catch:

```
> catch (evaluate $ head []) (\(SomeException _) -> return 0)
0
```

Throw and catch in other monads besides IO

The Control.Exception family of throw and catch functions is limited to living in IO. This is not really a problem for throwing exceptions in monad stacks over IO (we can use lift) or in failure monads such as [], Maybe, or Either. However, because the exception handler callback in Control.Exception.catch and others is also limited to IO, it means we can't utilize other parts of the monad stack within the handler.

Instead of writing manual reconstructions for the monad stack from IO, a better option is to use the exceptions package. The exceptions package generalizes throw and catch for monad stacks via type-classes:

```
class Monad m => MonadThrow m where
  throwM :: Exception e => e -> m a

class MonadThrow m => MonadCatch m where
  catch :: Exception e => m a -> (e -> m a) -> m a
```

Instances are provided in particular for monad transformers from the mtl package. Many convenient utility functions are also provided; see the documentation of the Control.Monad.Catch module from the exceptions package.

Also, a special `CatchT` monad transformer and a `Catch` monad are provided by `exceptions`. `CatchT` and `Catch` can be used for mocking exception throwing and catching in pure code. Note that catching is limited to exceptions thrown via `throwM`, because "real" exceptions thrown with throw can only be caught in impure code.

Writing tests for Haskell

There are many libraries for testing Haskell code. Besides classic unit tests with **HUnit** and **spec** testing in Ruby-style with **Hspec**, we can verify properties using **SmallCheck** and **QuickCheck** with exhaustive and randomized test cases, respectively.

Property checks

With QuickCheck we can test properties in a randomized fashion. We don't need to generate the test cases ourselves, as QuickCheck takes care of that. Here's a quick example of testing a simple arithmetic property:

```
stack ghci --package QuickCheck
> import Test.QuickCheck as QC
> QC.quickCheck $ \x y -> x > 0 ==> x + y >= y
```

All testable properties in `QuickCheck` are given as instances of the `Testable` class. As a quick reference, the core interface looks like this:

```
quickCheck :: Testable prop => prop → IO ()

class Testable prop where [...]

instance Testable Property
instance Testable Bool
instance (Arbitrary a, Show a, Testable prop) => Testable (a →
    prop)
```

The last instance is perhaps most interesting. That's what allows us to test functions of variadic arguments directly with QuickCheck, like in our example.

QuickCheck generates test cases via the `Arbitrary` class. Instances for all the core types are given, provided they're sensible. Test case generators live in the `Gen` monad. Here is an example for clarification purposes:

```
class Arbitrary a where
    arbitrary :: Gen a
    shrink :: a → [a]
```

```
data D2 = D2 Double Double deriving (Eq, Show)

instance Arbitrary D2 where
  arbitrary = do
    x ← arbitrary
    y ← arbitrary
    return (x, y)
```

If you need more exhaustive checking than random test cases, then SmallCheck is a better choice. SmallCheck provides quantifiers, so we can express things such as *"forall x exists y"* and so forth. Here is an example GHCi session using SmallCheck:

```
stack ghci --package smallcheck
> import Test.SmallCheck as SC
> smallCheck 2 $ forAll $ \x -> exists $ \y -> x + y > (x :: Int)
Completed 22 tests without failure.
```

Like QuickCheck, SmallCheck supports testing properties as variadic functions. The smallCheck function requires an extra argument as its first argument, namely the depth of generated test cases. If the test case has a reasonably bounded search space, such as Booleans, then it's possible to set the max depth to maxBound. SmallCheck then does an exhaustive check for the property.

For the simple cases, SmallCheck works a lot like QuickCheck. The default quantification context is forAll, which resembles that of QuickCheck. However, the test cases of QuickCheck are much better optimized for inexhustive testing, covering most usual corner cases, and QuickCheck automatically attempts to shrink the size of counter-examples.

Unit testing with HUnit

Sometimes it is more interesting or just easier to write the test cases yourself. Although you can write some testing in IO using QuickCheck, the HUnit package is more suited for that too:

```
stack ghci --package HUnit

> import Test.HUnit as HU
> let mytests = test $ do { x <- getLine; assert (x == "success") }
> runTestTT mytests
success
Cases: 1  Tried: 1  Errors: 0  Failures: 0
```

The `Testable` class of testable properties in HUnit is slightly different from that of QuickCheck and SmallCheck. In particular, it's a lot simpler:

```
class Testable t where
    test :: t → Test

instance Testable Test
instance Testable t => Testable [t]
instance Assertable t => Testable (IO t)
```

One of the two main ways to build test cases in HUnit is to write them as `IO` actions that result in something `Assertable`. There is a Bool instance for `Assertable`, meaning that you can return a Boolean indicating the success or failure of the test case. However, it's more informative to perform asserts with explicit failure messages and just return unit, `()`, which is also an instance of `Assertable`.

The other way if there's no need to perform `IO` is to use one of the (seemingly) pure assertion functions:

```
[1,2,3] ~=? sort [2,1,3] :: Test
sort [2,1,3] ~?= [1,2,3] :: Test
```

Internally (~=?) and (~?=) live in IO, thus they're not really pure. They are counterparts for (@=?) and (@?=) that return Assertion, that is, `IO ()`.

Test frameworks

To use either property checking (QuickCheck/SmallCheck) or unit testing (HUnit) in the test suite of an application, the use of a test framework simplifies things. A good test framework should also support some sort of resource management. Currently there are two main choices for a test framework in Haskell: **Hspec** and **Tasty**.

Hspec is based on **RSpec** for Ruby, and Hspec tests look deceptively similar to RSpec. The `Hspec` library provides only the framework, leaving testing itself to any of the testing libraries discussed so far. The introduction and resource guide for Hspec at `http://hspec.github.io` is comprehensive and beginner-friendly. Integrations and extensions to Hspec are provided for many libraries.

The other of the two big test frameworks for Haskell, Tasty, is relatively new and is designed to be extremely extensible. Aside from having integrations for all the main testing libraries, Tasty supports integrating Hspec tests directly as Tasty tests. The excellent documentation for Tasty is maintained at `http://documentup.com/feuerbach/tasty`.

GHC also supports program coverage reporting. To extract a coverage report from running an arbitrary Haskell program (such as a test suite), the program must be compiled with `-fhpc`. Or, if using cabal, configure with `--enable-coverage`. If using stack, build with `--coverage`.

When you run a program with coverage reporting, a `<program>.tix` file is generated. GHC comes with the **hpc** command-line utility, which is used to inspect, combine, and do coverage reporting with `.tix` files. The hpc utility needs to know where source code files to the program are located. The easiest way to jump through the necessary hoops is to use `stack hpc` instead. To generate a report both in terminal and HTML outputs from a `foo.tix` file, we can just execute:

```
$ stack hpc report foo.tix

Generating combined report
100% expressions used (4/4)
100% boolean coverage (0/0)
     100% guards (0/0)
     100% 'if' conditions (0/0)
     100% qualifiers (0/0)
```

Trivia at term-level

In this section, we look at lazy patterns, using the magic hash, controlling inlining and using rewrite rules. These are small things used rarely in applications, but nevertheless are very convenient where applicable.

We'll start with lazy patterns. Where strict pattern annotations use bangs and mean "Evaluate this argument to WHNF immediately," lazy pattern annotations use tildes and imply "Don't even bother pattern-matching unless a binding is really requested." So this errors:

```
> let f (a,b) = 5
> f undefined
*** Exception: Prelude.undefined
```

But with a lazy pattern match, we are all okay:

```
> let f ~(a,b) = 5
> f undefined
5
```

A more realistic use case for lazy patterns is the classic server-client setting. The client makes requests sequentially and can change the request based on previous responses. We can express this in Haskell elegantly with just linked lists. The server is slightly simpler than the client: it just applies a computation on every request – it is a map or a fold. The following server expects a number as the request and responds with the square of that number:

```
-- file: lazypat.hs
server :: [Int] -> [Int]
server (y:ys) = process y : server ys
  where process n = n ^ 2
```

The client is slightly more involved, because of the initial request it has to make. This is also where a lazy pattern match will come in handy, as we will see soon. But first, let's try it without. This `client` function is otherwise similar to the server, but it also takes the next (`initial`) request as an argument:

```
client :: Int -> [Int] -> [Int]
client initial (x:xs) = initial : client (next x) xs
  where next n = n `mod` 65534
```

Now, we need just "tie the knot" between requests and responses, client and server. This happens like so:

```
requests :: [Int]
requests = client initial responses
    where initial = 2

responses :: [Int]
responses = server requests
```

But our program has a slight problem. Our client will never get to make even a single request!

To see why our program deadlocks, we should look at the `client`: it pattern-matches on the responses before producing the first request. The easiest fix in this case is to use a lazy pattern on the responses:

```
client :: Int -> [Int] -> [Int]
client initial ~(x:xs) = initial : client (next x) xs
  where next n = n `mod` 65534
```

With that fix, we can now observe requests and responses as expected:

```
> :load lazypat.hs
> take 10 responses
[4,16,256,65536,4,16,256,65536,4,16]
```

With `:sprint`, we can inspect requests made and responses:

```
> :sprint responses
responses = 4 : 16 : 256 : 65536 : 4 : 16 : 256 : 65536 : 4 : 16 :
          _

> :sprint requests
requests = 2 : 4 : 16 : 256 : 2 : 4 : 16 : 256 : 2 : 4 : _
```

Coding in GHC PrimOps

When the speed of some hopefully small piece of code is extremely critical and nothing else seems to help, one way to speed it up if using GHC is to code that code in raw primitives. **PrimOps** in GHC are built into the compiler and are always identified by a hash suffix on both type and term levels.

Primitives are defined in the `ghc-prim` package, but it is recommended to not use the `ghc-prim` package directly and instead import the `GHC.Exts` module from base. Also, to use any PrimOps, we need to enable the **MagicHash** language extension, and the **UnboxedTuples** extension is needed for primitive tuples.

Let's take a worked example upfront: an array that supports compare-and-swap (CAS) operations on its elements. As our first take, we'll deliberately use the `IO` constructor directly to show that `IO` in Haskell is really not that magical after all. Here we go:

```
-- file: primops.hs

{-# LANGUAGE MagicHash #-}
{-# LANGUAGE UnboxedTuples #-}

import GHC.Exts
import GHC.Types (IO(IO))

data CASArrayIO a = CASArrayIO (MutableArray# RealWorld a)
```

Here we enabled some extensions, imported the officially supported `primops` module `GHC.Exts`, and for demonstration the `IO` constructor from `ghc-prim:GHC.Types`. Then we defined a data type for CAS arrays.

That `RealWorld` argument looks much less cryptic when we consider the definition of `IO`, which is simply a `newtype`:

```
newtype IO a = IO
    (State# RealWorld -> (# State# RealWorld, a #))
```

So under the hood, IO actions are a lot like the state monad: a state of type `RealWorld` is carried over to the next step, though `RealWorld` is never constructed and it exists only at compile time.

We want operations to create, read, and of course compare-and-swap for our CAS arrays. The respective primitive functions on `MutableArray#` for our operations are:

```
newArray#
  :: Int# -> a
    -> State# s -> (# State# s, MutableArray# s a #)

readArray#
  :: MutableArray# s a-> Int#
    -> State# s -> (# State# s, a #)

casArray#
  :: MutableArray# s a -> Int# -> a -> a
    -> State# s-> (# State# s, Int#, a #)
```

We realize that, instead of using the monadic `IO` interface for threading `RealWorld`, we can also pass them manually and construct IO actions with the `IO` constructor. So, by just following the types, we devise the following definition for the create operation:

```
newCasArray :: Int -> a -> IO (CASArrayIO a)
newCasArray (I# n) a = IO $ \st0 ->
    let (# st1, arr #) = newArray# n a st0
        in (# st1, CASArrayIO arr #)
```

It's a bit noisy but still understandable. Read is shorter:

```
readCas :: CASArrayIO a -> Int -> IO a
readCas (CASArrayIO arr) (I# n) = IO $ readArray# arr n
```

But how about the `cas` operation? Quite involved:

```
cas :: Ord a => CASArrayIO a -> Int -> a -> IO a
cas (CASArrayIO arr) (I# n) a = IO $ \st0 ->
    let (# st1, c #) = readArray# arr n st0        -- 1
        a' = if a > c then a else c                -- 2
        (# st2, r, b #) = casArray# arr n c a' st1 -- 3
        in (# st2, b #)                            -- 4
```

Step by step, this works as follows:

1. Read the current value at the specified location into c.

2. Compare c and the specified new value, a, and determine which of them comes first; place that to a'.

3. Swap the value at the specified location with a'; if it still equals c, read in step.

4. Return the current value at the specified location.

The only problem with using primitives like this is that we need to take care of threading the state correctly at every primitive operation. This produces a lot of noise, like in the cas function. Fortunately, a lot of this can be abstracted with the help of the primitive package. The primitive package defines a type class PrimMonad along with instances for IO, ST, and monad transformers from the transformers package:

```
class Monad m => PrimMonad m where
  type PrimState m
  primitive
    :: (State# (PrimState m) → (# State# (PrimState m), a #))
       → m a
```

The associated type PrimState in PrimMonad is just RealWorld for anything IO-based, and for ST s it is the s. The primitive function is merely a generalization of the IO constructor we used previously. Rewriting our cas function with primitives, we import Control.Monad.Primitive and then define:

```
cas' :: Ord a => CASArrayIO a -> Int -> a -> IO a
cas' (CASArrayIO arr) (I# n) a = do
    c <- primitive $ readArray# arr n
    let a' = if a > c then a else c
    primitive $ \st →
        let (# st', _, b #) = casArray# arr n c a' st
            in (# st', b #)
```

Control inlining

The inliner in GHC is pretty well optimized for lots of different situations, but sometimes a bit more control over inlining is desired. GHC supports a number of pragmas and options for controlling inlining:

- INLINE and NOINLINE: Respectively, always or never inline a definition.

- INLINABLE: Consider the definition for inlining despite its size. Normally, GHC might mark some definitions as no-inline because of their big size.

Inlining is simply replacing a term in the caller-site with that term's definition itself. In general, this increases code size when a term is used more than once, but the GHC inliner is optimized to keep the increase to a minimum. In practice, the only situation where use of NOINLINE is justified is when unsafePerformIO is used to build top-level shared variables, if you're really desperate for smaller code size in, for example, embedded systems or tweaking rewrite rules.

An explicit INLINE makes the most sense for large definitions that really should be inlined for performance reasons. For example, a huge vector transformation would likely benefit from further fusion when inlined. An explicit INLINE might be required for such huge computation.

Some special quirks are related to inlining. Firstly, GHC only inlines a definition when it is fully applied to its arguments. Consider these seemingly identical definitions:

```
{-# INLINE s #-}
s x y z = x z (y z)

{-# INLINE s' #-}
s' x y = \z → x z (y z)
```

The first one would inline only after being applied to three arguments. The second one inlines when applied to two.

Using rewrite rules

Another powerful optimization step along with inlining is rule-based rewriting. Rewrite systems are what enable speed in Haskell lists and libraries such as vector, text, and bytestring.

Rules tell the GHC optimizer to rewrite certain code fragments with something else. Rules allow us to write things like this:

```
-- file: lem-rewrite.hs
lem x = x || not x
{-# RULES "lem/tautology" forall a. lem a = True #-}
```

The name of the rule is mandatory and comes after RULES. But there is a problem with such a rule. If we attempt to compile it, we'll get a warning:

```
lem-rewrite.hs:3:11: Warning:
    Rule "lem/tautology" may never fire
      because 'lem' might inline first
    Probable fix: add an INLINE[n] or NOINLINE[n] pragma on 'lem'
```

This gets us right into the fragile nature of rewrite rules. Rules interact with inlining so that getting rules to fire correctly is tricky. The suggestion is to add either `INLINE` or `NOINLINE` pragma (with a phase control number), which seems odd; why would an `INLINE` pragma change the inlining behavior of such a small function? It gets inlined anyway, right?

Where `INLINE` further enhances a small definition is that it tells GHC to at least retain a copy of the definition as we wrote it (its RHS). Without an `INLINE` pragma, a definition that isn't exported is completely erased early on in compilation. The `INLINABLE` pragma works similarly to `INLINE` in this case, retaining both the optimized and original RHS.

In this case, it would actually be enough to export `lem` by adding a module signature such as module `Main (lem) where`. The default module definition when none is given is `module Main (main) where`. The other (better) option is to use an explicit `INLINE` or `NOINLINE` pragma.

Specializing definitions

Overloading a function via a type-class enforces a level of indirection in the form of a lookup dictionary. If some of the overloaded versions are heavily used, it might make sense to specialize that version of the function at the expense of slightly increased code size.

GHC can be asked to create specialized versions of type-class overloaded definitions with `SPECIALIZE` pragmas. Given an overloaded function such as:

```
lookup :: Ord key => [(key, v)] → key → v
```

We can ask GHC to create a version of lookup for `(Int,Int)` valued keys with:

```
{-# SPECIALIZE lookup :: [((Int,Int), v)] → v → (Int,Int) → v #-}
```

In effect, a specialized version is copied from the original definition at compile time and rewrite rules are generated that ensure usages where the key type is decidedly always `(Int,Int)` are specialized. Those rules can also fire after inlining and other rewrites have taken place.

It's also possible to write rewrite rules that specialize a generic function with some completely different user-defined function (from a different module even). For example, we might have a `UserKey` type, for which comparisons via `Ord` are particularly inefficient when doing a lookup. So we have devised a custom function for doing lookups based on `UserKey`:

```
lookupByUser :: [(UserKey, v)] → v → UserKey → v
```

Now instead of replacing every instance of lookup with our `lookupByUser` in the code base, we could provide a rewrite rule that does it for us. This has the added effect of hiding the implementation detail. The rule itself looks like this:

```
{-# RULES "lookup/lookupByUser" lookup = lookupByUser #-}
```

This rule fires when types match in the call-site.

 To inspect which rules fired, compile with `-ddump-rule-firings`. To see which rules were defined in the compiled modules, compile with `-ddump-rules`.

Phase control

The part in GHC that performs optimizations based on inlines, rewrites, and specializations, among others, is known as the *simplifier*. The simplifier consists of a number of phases and each phase consists of multiple iterations. By default, there are three phases numbered 2, 1, and 0. The phase number decreases between runs. In a single phase, optimizations associated with that phase are run repeatedly until a *fixed point*.

All of the `INLINE` pragmas, `RULES`, and `SPECIALIZE` pragmas support phase control in the form of a `[N]` or `[~N]` suffix, where N is some phase number (0, 1, 2). The first form means the simplification is in effect in phase N and onwards. The second form with a tilde means the simplification is active up to, but not including, phase N.

Restricting simplifications to certain phases makes sense mainly in two situations. The first one is to prevent inlining from happening before certain rule rewrites take place. The second, when a rewrite in an earlier phase, which might subject the definition for fusion, if not fused results in slower code than the unfused version. To counter this, we can add a rule that fires only at the last phase, and which undoes the first rewrite. (The first rewrite should also be restricted to earlier phases.)

Trivia at type-level

The more expressive the types are, the more safety we can ensure at compile-time. What's more, expressive types serve as documentation that is always up-to-date.

Phantom types

A type that has type variables on the left-hand side that do not appear on the right-hand-side at all is called a *phantom type*. Such type variables are a cheap, in fact free, technique to guarantee correctness in multiple situations. An example from base is `Data.Fixed`, in which the precision of fixed-precision arithmetic is encoded in a phantom type.

An extremely useful class of phantom types is obtained in conjunction with **Generalized Algebraic Data Types (GADT)**. As a little silly example, consider:

```
-- file: gadts.hs
{-# LANGUAGE GADTs #-}

data Value a where
    Boolean :: Bool -> Value Bool
    Not     :: Value Bool -> Value Bool
    Numeric :: Num a => a -> Value a
    Sum     :: Num a => Value a -> Value a -> Value a
```

The first two constructors allow us to build values that contain single Booleans or Boolean values, but not, for example, negations of numeric values. The last two constructors allow single numbers as numeric values and sums of numeric values, but not sums of Booleans, or a Boolean and a number.

In effect, we can express any value as `a forall a. Value a`: Boolean values as `Value Bool`, numeric values as `Num a => Value a`, floating point values as `Float a => Value a`, and so on.

A common pattern is to define custom types with no inhabitants and use those as type arguments for phantom types.

Functional dependencies

Although functional dependencies (fundeps) are nowadays subsumed by associated types, fundeps might be a bit easier to grasp. So let's learn by example what fundeps are all about!

Say we are working with textual data: Strings, Text, and ByteStrings. But we would really like to not care about the actual datatype when we are indexing, for example. To solve this problem, we come up with a type class that provides a single overloaded function, index, that knows how to index into any container. So the code we write looks like this:

```
-- file: fundeps.hs
{-# LANGUAGE MultiParamTypeClasses #-}
{-# LANGUAGE FlexibleInstances #-}
```

```
{-# LANGUAGE FunctionalDependencies #-}

import qualified Data.Text as T
import qualified Data.ByteString as BS
import Data.Word (Word8)

class Index container index elem where
    index :: container -> index -> elem

instance Index String Int Char where
    index = (!!)

instance Index T.Text Int Char where
    index = T.index

instance Index BS.ByteString Int Word8 where
    index = BS.index
```

We load this up in GHCi and confirm that it works. But when we get into actually using our new shiny Index class, we bump into lots of ambiguous type errors!

```
> index ("foo" :: String) 0
```

```
<interactive>:74:1:
    Could not deduce (Num index0)
    from the context (Num index, Index String index elem)
      bound by the inferred type for 'it':
                (Num index, Index String index elem) => elem
      at <interactive>:74:1-26
    The type variable 'index0' is ambiguous
```

And GHC is completely right here. Although we hadn't given any instances other than Index String Int Char for String-containers, we cannot be sure that someone won't do that in some other module, for example.

With functional dependencies, we can rule out some instances and thus improve type inference. For our Index, the container type decides the type of its elements, so we would augment the class head with | container → elem. Thus we have:

```
class Index container index elem | container -> elem where
    index :: container -> index -> elem
```

We could also, if desired, have written `container → elem index` to say that the `container` decides both element and index types, or `container index → elem` for `container` and `index` together deciding the type of element. The latter would be useful to allow instances such as `Index String (Int, Int) String`, that is, using a range as the `index` to return a substring.

Type families and associated types

An associated type can be used everywhere a functional dependency can be used. An implementation of our `Index` class using an associated type for the element is:

```haskell
-- file: associated.hs
{-# LANGUAGE MultiParamTypeClasses #-}
{-# LANGUAGE FlexibleInstances #-}
{-# LANGUAGE TypeFamilies #-}

import qualified Data.Text as T
import qualified Data.ByteString as BS
import Data.Word (Word8)

class Index container index where
    type Elem container
    index :: container -> index -> Elem container

instance Index String Int where
    type Elem String = Char
    index = (!!)

instance Index T.Text Int where
    type Elem T.Text = Char
    index = T.index

instance Index BS.ByteString Int where
    type Elem BS.ByteString = Word8
    index = BS.index
```

Note that the element is no longer a type parameter, like in the fundep case, but an associated type delimited by `Elem`. `Elem` can be thought of as a type-level function; when we say type `Elem` container, we mean that instances of this class must define a type into which container maps. The result of that type is denoted by `Elem` container.

The idea of type-level functions applies to type families as well, of which associated types are just a special case. The `Elem` type could be expressed as a standalone type family:

```
-- file: datafamilies.hs
type family Elem container
type instance Elem String = Char
type instance Elem T.Text = Char
```

The **type families** considered so far have actually been type synonym families. Data families are also supported, both associated and standalone. For data families, the right-hand side is not a synonym but an actual datatype declaration. For example, we could define a `type` function that maps tuples to their strict representations:

```
-- file: datafamilies-closed.hs
data family TStrict a

data instance TStrict (a, b) = TStrict2 !a !b
data instance TStrict (a, b, c) = TStrict3 !a !b !c
[...]
```

The main advantage of data families versus type synonym families is that data families are always injective. In our example, each strict tuple is thus associated with exactly one tuple. Injectivity allows us to recover type information for better type inference and more importantly allows some programs not possible with type synonym families.

The final quirk regarding standalone type and data families is that a data family is either open or closed. In an open type family, new instances can be defined wherever the family is in scope, and also in different modules. But all instances of a closed type family must be specified in a where clause right after declaring the family. Strict tuples as a closed type family would look like this:

```
data family TStrict a where
    TStrict (a, b) = TStrict2 !a !b
    TStrict (a, b, c) = TStrict3 !a !b !c
    [...]
```

Useful GHC extensions

We have already used a number of extensions available in GHC, such as **MultiParamTypeClasses**, **TypeFamilies**, **FlexibleInstances**, and so on. The nice thing about most extensions in GHC is that, if you accidentally try to use a language feature that is behind an extension, GHC gives you a hint about which extension you forgot.

In this last section, we'll look at some more useful extensions available in reasonably modern GHC. There are other extensions, of course, and this is just a glimpse. For an exhaustive list of currently supported extensions, see the `Language.Haskell.Extension` module from the `Cabal` library.

Monomorphism Restriction

Some of the most confusing type errors originate from the **monomorphism restriction (MR)**. Consider this program:

```
-- file: mr.hs
main = do
    let f = (1 +)
    print $ f (6   :: Int)
    print $ f (0.1 :: Double)
```

The most general type for `f` would be `Num a => a → a`. But due to MR, the inferred type is monomorphic in `a`. The error message we get if we attempt to compile the program is "**Couldn't match expected type 'Int' with actual type 'Double'**". Monomorphic type is inferred from context. In our case, `f` gets type `Int → Int`, because that is its first usage. If the type cannot be inferred from the context, then the monomorphic type is chosen in line with the type defaulting rules.

Strangely enough, if we instead let `f x = (1 + x)`, then MR won't kick in and the program compiles just fine. In this regard, function syntax is very much different from pattern syntax (`f = \x → 1 + x`).

 Monomorphism restriction has been on by default in compiled code, and off in GHCi, since GHC 7.8.1.

The motivation for MR is that in some cases it prevents a computation from being performed twice. Consider this:

```
let len = Data.List.genericLength [1..1000]
print (len, len)
```

With MR, `len` gets the monomorphic type `Num a => a` with `a` instantiated to Integer. This is ideal as `len` gets memoized. However, if MR didn't monomorphize the type, `len` would have the polymorphic type `Num a => a`, meaning that evaluating `len` requires passing in a dictionary for `a`, preventing memoization.

If requiring a type signature for polymorphic bindings is not desirable, MR can be disabled with the **NoMonomorphismRestriction** language extension.

Extensions for patterns and guards

The GHC extension **ViewPatterns** allows arbitrary functions (views) in patterns. The advantage of view patterns over guards is more concise code in some cases. Consider this `funky` function:

```
funky xs | 0 <- length xs = "Empty list!"
         | 4 <- last   xs = "Ends in four!"
         | n <- sum    xs = "Sum is " ++ show n
```

We can write this more clearly with view patterns:

```
-- file: viewpatterns.hs
{-# LANGUAGE ViewPatterns #-}

funky (length -> 0) = "Empty list!"
funky (last   -> 4) = "Ends in four!"
funky (sum    -> n) = "Sum is " ++ show n
```

Note that we didn't need to bind the argument (`xs`) to a variable at all.

Our definition of `funky`, which uses pattern matching inside guards, was originally enabled by an extension known as **PatternGuards**, nowadays turned on by default.

A relatively new extension related to patterns is **PatternSynonyms** (available in GHC 7.8 and later). Like the name suggests, with PatternSynonyms we can make synonyms for patterns. Pattern matching on a pattern synonym works just like pattern matching on a real constructor.

Pattern synonyms are declared using a new top-level pattern keyword. For example, consider a program that extensively uses structures of type (`Bool`, `Bool`, `Bool`, `Bool`) to represent bit arrays of length 4, and that we rarely need to look at more than one bit at a time. So, instead of laying out the whole structure every time:

```
fun bits | (b1,b2,b3,b4) <- bits = ...
```

We can define pattern synonyms that extract specific bits from the structure:

```
-- file: patternsynonyms.hs
{-# LANGUAGE PatternSynonyms #-}

pattern B1 a <- (a,_,_,_)
pattern B2 a <- (_,a,_,_)
pattern B3 a <- (_,_,a,_)
pattern B4 a <- (_,_,_,a)
```

These synonyms can be used like this:

```
fun (B1 True) = 1
fun (B2 True) = 2
fun (B3 True) = 3
fun (B4 True) = 4
```

Pattern synonyms are identifiers just like types and constructors, meaning that they can occur in export and import lists.

The final pattern-related extension we shall consider is **ScopedTypeVariables**. Normally in Haskell, all type variables in a type signature are instantiated fresh, meaning that all type variables will be implicitly for-alled.

Scoped type variables are useful when we would like to write explicit type signatures for polymorphic function bindings within another polymorphic function. In the following function, it is impossible to give go a type signature without scoped type variables.

```
-- file: scoped-type-variables.hs
{-# LANGUAGE ScopedTypeVariables #-}

fun :: forall a b. (a -> b) -> [a] -> [a] -> ([b], [b])
fun f xs ys = let go :: [a] -> [b]
                  go = map f
              in (go xs, go ys)
```

Note that explicit forall; without it, type variables a and b would still be in scope only in the signature for fun.

Strict-by-default Haskell

Two of the new features added in GHC 8.0.1 are the Strict and StrictData extensions, that change Haskell from a lazy-by-default language into a strict-by-default language (on a per-module basis).

When **StrictData** is in effect, fields in the data declaration are considered as if they had a strictness annotation (!) in front, unless the field is explicitly set to lazy with the laziness annotation (~):

```
data S = S a    -- 1
data S = S !a   -- 2
data S = S ~a   -- 3
```

Under normal circumstances, (1) is interpreted as (3), but under StrictData it is interpreted as (2). Writing laziness annotations is not allowed unless StrictData is enabled.

On the other hand, the Strict extension adds a bang to all pattern bindings everywhere in the module. With Strict in effect, normal irrefutable patterns, ~(x,y), become just lazy patterns. Irrefutable patterns can be recovered with ~(~(x,y)).

Summary

We began this chapter by looking at what Haskell projects usually consist of and how Cabal and stack are used to manage project complexity and dependencies. We glanced at the basic usage of main test libraries and frameworks for Haskell and how they can be integrated into a cabalized project. We learned how to handle errors and exceptions. Even more importantly, we learned how to not do errors; why prefer throwIO over error (or throw)? Why are asynchronous errors so vicious in lazy semantics?

In the latter part of this chapter, we explored some Haskell trivia and techniques specific to GHC: lazy patterns, coding with GHC primitives (the magic hash), inlining, writing rewrite rules, using phantom types, fundeps, type families, the monomorphism restriction, and some useful GHC extensions. Now you should be able to both read and write cabal files, devise test suites with test libraries (QuickCheck, SmallCheck, and HUnit) and test frameworks (Hspec, Tasty), and throw and catch exceptions correctly; you should also have absorbed some trivia about Haskell and GHC.

In the next chapter, we will look at parallelization and RePa, a Haskell library for high-performance parallel array programming.

5
Parallelize for Performance

Nowadays, as single processor cores are not getting much faster, CPU manufacturers instead keep increasing the number of cores in processors, implying that high-performance programs must accordingly exploit more and more parallelism to keep up with this breadth-wise hardware development.

Turns out, one of Haskell's strongest aspects, referential transparency, is very valuable for parallelization. Automatically knowing that some distinct expressions won't interact with each other means they are safe to execute simultaneously. Note that parallelism is very different from concurrency, which usually refers to interacting processes (they aren't necessarily executed in parallel).

In this chapter, we will cover what the Haskell ecosystem currently has to offer for parallelism: a powerful parallel runtime system, fairly high-level abstractions for parallel evaluation, data parallel programming, and diagnostic tools for parallel programs. The learning objectives for this chapter are to have an overview of the parallel runtime system, parallelizing Haskell programs and profiling them:

- Parallelizing plain Haskell programs using either Eval strategies or par schedules
- Learning about the parallel runtime system and sparks
- Using RePa for data parallel programming
- Inspecting parallel performance using ThreadScope

Primitive parallelism and the Runtime System

In Haskell, parallel execution (of pure values) boils down to evaluating thunks into WHNF simultaneously. The GHC primitive we can use to annotate parallelism is called par, exported from the `Control.Parallel` module in the `parallel` package:

```
par :: a → b → b
```

Note that par has exactly the same type as seq, which is used to control strictness. So whereas a `seq` b ensures that a is evaluated when b is evaluated, a `par` b evaluates a in parallel with b.

Let's start with a simple example. Everyone's favorite naive Fibonacci function appears again. This time, however, we will be calculating multiple Fibonacci numbers simultaneously. The following program prints Fibonacci numbers between 37 and 40:

```
-- file: fib.hs
fib :: Int -> Int
fib n
  | n <= 1 = 1
  | otherwise = let a = fib (n - 1)
                    b = fib (n - 2)
                in a + b

main = print $
  let x = fib 37
      y = fib 38
      z = fib 39
      w = fib 40
      in (x,y,z,w)
```

Note that there are no parallelism annotations yet, just plain lazily evaluated expressions. Compiling with the normal non-parallel runtime, we'll get the following performance:

```
$ ghc -O2 -with-rtsopts="-s" parallel-fib.hs
$ ./parallel-fib


  Total    time    4.285s  (  4.285s elapsed)
```

The threaded runtime is enabled by passing the `-threaded` flag to GHC. The Runtime System flag `-N<n>` controls how many system threads the Runtime System uses. We test the performance on a machine with four cores:

```
$ ghc -O2 -threaded -with-rtsopts="-s -N4" fib.hs
$ ./fib
  Total    time    11.204s  (  3.892s elapsed)
  Productivity  99.7% of total user, 287.2% of total elapsed
```

What we see here is that the elapsed time, also known as wall-clock time, perhaps got a bit smaller, but the user time, CPU time, almost tripled. Also note `287.2%` `of total elapsed`; if your program had utilized all four cores to the max, that percentage will have been closer to 400%. And, actually, if we execute the program multiple times we would sometimes observe this behavior and on other occasions the same behavior as with the non-parallel version. This is because of subtle things that happen inside the parallel runtime system.

It's unlikely that the threaded runtime would have actually parallelized our thunks of `fib` expressions. In general, it is impossible to know whether it is actually beneficial to evaluate thunks in parallel, because expressions can share subexpressions, and moving data between threads is expensive.

To tell GHC to evaluate our `fib` thunks in parallel, we can use `par` and `pseq`, which is semantically like `seq` but is subtly different when it comes to parallelism. The parallelized program looks like this:

```
let x = fib 37
    y = fib 38
    z = fib 39
    w = fib 40
in x `par` y `par` z `par` w `pseq` (x, y, z, w)
```

With this our program now performs better on four cores:

```
Total    time    6.698s  (  1.739s elapsed)
Productivity  99.9% of total user, 384.7% of total elapsed
```

That's roughly 2.5 times faster with four cores as opposed to with just one core. However, we were running four cores; why wasn't the speed four times greater?

Remember that the naive Fibonacci algorithm grows exponentially in time, so the largest evaluation actually dominates the runtime of our program. We didn't parallelize the calculation itself, and calculating the 40th Fibonacci number takes about 1.7 sec, which is the best we could hope for when each individual Fibonacci number is still calculated sequentially.

Spark away

The technique used in the parallel runtime to distribute work between processors works via units of work called *sparks*. The Runtime System contains a spark pool, from which it distributes work to vacant processor cores. What happens in `par x y` is that a pointer to x is pushed into the spark pool.

The `-s` statistics show for our naive Fibonacci the following line:

```
SPARKS: 3 (3 converted, 0 overflowed, 0 dud, 0 GC'd, 0 fizzled)
```

This says that our program generated three sparks (from three calls to `par`), the evaluation of which was entirely initiated from the spark pool by the Runtime System (`converted`). Other things that can happen for a spark in a spark pool include:

- **Overflowed**: The spark was not added into the spark pool, because the pool was at its maximum capacity.

- **Dud**: When the argument to `par` is already evaluated, it's counted as dud. The spark pool is not touched at all.

- **GC'd**: Before the spark got evaluated, it was garbage-collected and removed from the spark pool.

- **Fizzled**: Evaluation was triggered by the program; that is, the work was not distributed directly by the Runtime System.

Sparking is relatively cheap, as it's only a pointer assignment. However, it's not free. Consider parallelizing the naive Fibonacci by calculating each recursive call in parallel:

```
let a = fib (n - 1)
    b = fib (n - 2)
    in a `par` b `par` a + b
```

This hurts performance, because we now create millions of sparks mostly of small pieces of work. But if we limit sparking to larger recursive calls where $n > 25$, we get a finer work distribution but not too many sparks:

```
fib n
  | n <= 1 = 1
  | n <= 25 = fib (n - 1) + fib (n - 2)
  | otherwise = let a = fib (n - 1)
                    b = fib (n - 2)
                    in a `par` b `par` a + b
```

This reduces the runtime to about 1.4 sec, which is a bit over three times faster than the one-core version. Considering overheads and other load on my machine, that's a pretty good speedup.

Chapter 5

Subtle evaluation – pseq

Remember that pseq we used a little while ago? This is different from the earlier seq in that pseq is strict only its first argument, whereas seq is strict in its both arguments. In normal usage, this doesn't make a difference.

However, the strictness analyzer in GHC infers from a `seq` b that it doesn't make any difference whether a is evaluated before b or vice versa; therefore it is possible that the expression becomes b `seq` a `seq` b. This would be a problem with parallelism. Consider this, for example:

```
(a `par` b) `seq` (a + b)
```

GHC might turn this into:

```
(a + b) `seq` (a `par` b) `seq` (a + b)
```

Here, parallelism would be destroyed. Using pseq instead of seq prevents GHC from inferring this.

When in doubt, use the force

In our Fibonacci examples, we were parallelizing computations that returned Ints. Such basic structures are completely evaluated by seq. par always evaluates its first argument to WHNF, although we often want to evaluate bigger structures in parallel. The cleanest way to evaluate structures completely is to use force from the deepseq package:

```
Control.DeepSeq.force :: NFData a => a → a
```

The force function evaluates (sequentially) its argument to **Normal Form (NF)**.

Note, however, that there is a great difference between these expressions:

```
a `par` b `pseq` (a, b)
force (a, b) `par` (a, b)
```

The first one evaluates a in parallel with b, whereas the second one would evaluate a and b sequentially.

Now that we are familiar with sparks and the two parallelization primitives, par and pseq, we can start building abstractions to help us be more expressive about parallelism in our programs.

The Eval monad and strategies

The first abstraction we will look at is the `Control.Parallel.Strategies` module from the `parallel` package. The core Strategy API consists of the following:

```
data Eval a
instance Monad Eval

type Strategy a = a → Eval a

runEval :: Eval a → a

using :: a → Strategy a → a

rseq :: Strategy a
rdeepseq :: NFData a => Strategy a
rpar :: Strategy a
```

The principle is to use `using` or `runEval` to evaluate a lazy data structure in parallel, using some strategy. Essentially we have separated the algorithm (a lazy data structure) from the parallel evaluation (a strategy).

As a simple example, consider calculating the minimum and maximum elements of many lists in parallel. We write an algorithm, which doesn't encode any parallelism, called `minmax`:

```
-- file: rows.hs
import Control.Parallel.Strategies
minmax :: [Int] -> (Int, Int)
minmax xs = (minimum xs, maximum xs)
```

Then we have a list of lists (matrix) and a list of minimums and maximums (`minmaxes`):

```
matrix = [ [1..1000001], [2..2000002], [3..2000003]
         , [4..2000004], [5..2000005], [6..2000006]
         , [7..2000007] ]
minmaxes = map minmax matrix
```

Then, when we are about to evaluate the results, we apply a strategy to parallelize the evaluation:

```
print (minmaxes `using` parTraversable rdeepseq)
```

What happens here is that:

- We used `parTraversable` to evaluate the elements of a list in parallel
- In every parallel evaluation, we use the `rdeepseq` strategy to evaluate the element fully

Strategies work in conjunction with lazy data structures. The level of granularity at which a strategy can define parallelism is limited by the data structure. Arbitrary complex lazy data structures can have similarly complex strategies completely separated from the algorithm that builds the structure. However, data dependencies in the algorithm limit the possible benefits of applying parallel strategies, because copying data between threads is not free.

Directly using the `Eval` monad, we can express arbitrarily complex strategies. Consider these three strategies for evaluating a two-tuple:

```
strat1 (a, b) = do
  x ← rpar a
  y ← rpar b
  return (x, y)
```

This variant creates sparks for both elements and returns immediately. The elements might get evaluated by some thread:

```
strat2 (a, b) = do
  x ← rpar a
  y ← rseq b
  return (x, y)
```

This variant creates a spark for the first element and evaluates the second element before returning. The first element might or might not be evaluated by then (by some other thread):

```
strat3 (a, b) = do
  x ← rpar a
  y ← rseq b
  rseq a
  return (x, y)
```

This third variant creates a spark for the first element, evaluates the second element, and before returning also ensures that the first element has been evaluated. If it wasn't evaluated between sparking it and evaluating the second element, it is evaluated sequentially here.

Though it is possible to interleave the algorithm with an `Eval` computation, it is usually clearer to annotate parallelism with `using` and or other combinators within the algorithm, not the other way around. There useful strategy combinators in `Control.Parallel.Strategies` to encourage this.

One such function is `parListChunk`, which splits a list into chunks of a given size and evaluates those chunks in parallel. This is usually called static partitioning. Often it is better to divide the work into smaller units and leave the hard job of assigning the work to the scheduler in the Runtime System. We already used this tactic in the naive Fibonacci case, where we created lots of sparks and let the Runtime System scheduler decide on which cores the work happens.

The benefit from avoiding static partitioning is that programs with granular (but not too granular) sparks scale to multiple cores and thus require less fine-tuning by the programmer. The challenge is to aim for small units of work in sparks, but not too small, so that overhead from the spark pool is kept to minimum.

Composing strategies

The encouraged pattern for using strategies is to compose them by parameterization. Most strategies take other strategies as arguments, such as:

```
evalList :: Strategy a → Strategy [a]
parList :: Strategy a → Strategy [a]

evalTuple2 :: Strategy a → Strategy b → Strategy (a, b)
```

All strategy combinators also have `eval` and `par` variants, the first of which evaluates the parts of a structure sequentially, and the second in parallel. The parameters define strategies with which to evaluate the parts.

The composition of strategies analogous to function composition is `dot`:

```
dot :: Strategy a → Strategy a → Strategy a
```

As one could guess, the strategy `s2` `dot` `s1` first applies the strategy `s1` and then strategy `s2`.

How do we write a strategy that evaluates elements of a list in parallel, but returns only after all elements have been fully evaluated? The solution is:

```
rdeepseq `dot` parList rdeepseq
```

When writing strategies for custom data types, a most useful combinator is `rparWith`:

```
rparWith :: Strategy a → Strategy a
```

This is like (rpar `dot`), except more efficient. In essence, it combines a given strategy with an rpar so that the parameter strategy is applied within the parallel evaluation. For a custom two-tuple, we could write the following strategy combinatory, which evaluates the two parts in parallel according to some strategies:

```
-- file: tuple-par.hs
data T a b = T !a !b

parT :: Strategy a -> Strategy b -> Strategy (T a b)
parT sa sb (T a b) = do
  a' <- rparWith sa a
  b' <- rparWith sb b
  return (T a' b')
```

When writing strategies, it's important to understand how the lazy evaluation model works in order to not shoot yourself in the foot. It's not too hard to write incorrect strategies that don't retain references correctly. Particular things to keep in mind are as follows:

- rpar (f x): not binding the result and using it later is very bad (the newly-created thunk just gets garbage-collected). Always bind and use the result!
- rpar x: not binding the result is OK, as long as x is used later on.
- rparWith strat x: This is also OK, as long as x is used later on.

For big custom data types, it might not be feasible or desired to write custom strategy combinators. In such cases, building the structure inside Eval can be the most elegant solution. Especially if elements of the computation are not dependent on each other, writing the computation in applicative style is very concise. For example:

```
data A = A Int Bool [Double] String

buildPar :: A
buildPar = runEval $
  Record <$> rpar toInt
         <*> rpar toBool
         <*> evalList rpar toList
         <*> rpar toString
```

Here all fields and even the elements of the list are all evaluated in parallel. The parallelization is completely transparent to the caller of buildPar.

Fine-tune granularity with chunking and buffering

As we have seen, creating sparks in slightly excessive amounts produces good results, because the runtime can assign work to free cores at a finer granularity. However, we also witnessed that too much granularity will hurt performance because of overheads. So often, a problem in parallelizing boils down to limiting granularity.

In general, dividing the problem space into chunks and parallelizing the evaluation of chunks instead of single problems is the classic strategy to reduce granularity. A convenient combinator in `Control.Parallel.Strategies` does just this for lists. It's called `parListChunk`:

```
parListChunk :: Int → Strategy a → Strategy [a]
```

The first argument defines the chunk size. Its use is straightforward:

```
[ fib n | n ← [1..30] ] `using` parListChunk 6 rseq
```

This evaluates chunks of six consecutive elements sequentially, and all chunks in parallel.

But what about when a list is used as a stream? We wouldn't want to sacrifice the nice streaming property of lazy lists when parallelizing its evaluation. We want to buffer the list up to some depth in parallel, consume some portion from the start, and then continue evaluation further.

Such a rolling buffer is implemented by the `evalBuffer` and `parBuffer` strategies in `Control.Parallel.Strategies`, the former for sequential buffering and the latter for parallel. These strategies work nicely even with infinite lists. Consider this list:

```
xs = [ fib n | n ← [1..] ] `using` parBuffer 6 rseq
```

Here, evaluating `xs` to Weak Head Normal Form triggers the parallel evaluation of elements up to the 7th element. Evaluating the second element triggers the evaluation of the 8th element, the third the 9th, ad infinitum.

The Par monad and schedules

The `parallel` package restricts us to expressing our computations as lazy data structures. Moreover, such computations must always be pure, so no parallel IO is possible. Sometimes this isn't feasible and we would like to express more control. Somewhat inherently, more control implies less expressiveness. This trade-off is made in the `monad-par` package.

The core interface in `Control.Monad.Par` consists of:

```
data Par a   -- instance Monad
runPar :: Par a → a
fork :: Par () → Par ()
```

The `monad-par` library defines its own context for computations, namely `Par`. The second important operation, next to executing the computation via `runPar`, is `fork`, which forks a computation so it happens in parallel.

Communication between computations in `Par` happens via `IVar`:

```
data IVar a
new :: Par (IVar a)
get :: IVar a → Par a
put :: NFData a => IVar a → a → Par ()
```

To run two computations, `c1` and `c2`, in parallel and return their results in a tuple, we would write:

```
-- file: ivar-testing.hs
import Control.Monad.Par

f :: (NFData a, NFData b) => a -> b -> (a, b)
f c1 c2 = runPar $ do
  i1 <- new
  i2 <- new
  fork $ put i1 c1
  fork $ put i2 c2
  r1 <- get i1
  r2 <- get i2
  return (r1, r2)
```

What happens here is:

- We create two empty Ivars, `i1`, and `i2` (`new`)
- We fork two computations that put their results into corresponding Ivars (`fork $ put ...`)
- We wait for both results (`get`) and then return them

Note that, once an IVar has been filled (with put), it may not be emptied nor its contents swapped. So the computation model in Par is similar to the lazy evaluation in Haskell itself: a reduction graph, directed and acyclic. This time however, we are reducing IVars and not Haskell values (thunks), which gives us a little better control over evaluation.

With IVars, we are being more explicit about when evaluation happens. Calls to put guarantee that all values in IVars are evaluated to normal form. However, we still can't control the flow exactly; a forked `Par` action may be executed anywhere between the call to fork and `get`, which requires a value from a forked `Par`. But with pure values, the result is always deterministic.

The dataflow-style of parallel programming that `monad-par` encourages is better suited for some applications, whereas the strategy-style parallel evaluation of lazy data structures is better for others.

spawn for futures and promises

You might be familiar with the concept of a future or promise from other programming languages. In essence, we can think of IVar as a future or promise that the value will be calculated at the latest when it is required.

The `monad-par` package supports future- or promise-style parallel programming via the `spawn` function. The `spawn` function takes a computation and immediately returns the result wrapped in `IVar`:

```
spawn :: NFData a => Par a → Par (IVar a)
```

For the moment, consider a situation where we have four computations **A**, **B**, **C**, and **D**. Some of them depend on the result of others, conforming to this graph:

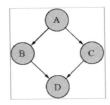

We see that **B** and **C** could execute in parallel. To express this in the `Par` monad, we can write:

```
-- file: spawn.hs
computation :: A -> (A -> B) -> (A -> C) -> (B -> C -> D) -> Par D
computation fa fb fc fd = do
  av <- newFull fa              -- (1)
  bv <- spawn $ do fb <$> get av -- (2)

  cv <- spawn $ do fc <$> get av -- (3)

  b <- get bv                   -- (4)
  c <- get cv
  return (fd b c)               -- (5)
```

- First, at (1) we make sure that the first computation A is fully performed. newFull creates IVar and fills it with a fully evaluated value.

- At (2) and (3), we have spawned two computations to run in parallel. One calculates B and the other C.

- At (4), we now wait for both B and C to complete.

- Finally, at (5) we perform the last computation D.

Non-deterministic parallelism with ParIO

What if the computations A, B, C, and D involved IO? The IO module from monad-par, Control.Monad.Par.IO, provides another monad for parallel IO: ParIO.

ParIO is largely similar to Par, except that it allows lifting IO operations into it. IO also brings with it some non-determinism over pure Par.

With ParIO, we cannot use the same functions that worked with pure Par. We need to use the overloaded API from the abstract-par package. The function names stay the same with the overloaded API, so it's no big deal – really a drop-in replacement (for pure Par too).

Let's see how we would write our A, B, C, D computation in terms of IO actions. The required imports change from one import to three:

```
import Control.Monad.IO.Class
import Control.Monad.Par.IO
import Control.Monad.Par.Class
```

From the first module, we need only liftIO to perform IO actions in ParIO. The second module gives us the ParIO type. The last one is the overloaded Par API.

The computation itself doesn't change much:

```
-- file: spawnio.hs
computationIO
  :: IO A -> (A -> IO B) -> (A -> IO C) -> (B -> C -> IO D)
  -> ParIO D
computationIO fa fb fc fd = do
  av <- newFull =<< liftIO fa
  bv <- spawn $ liftIO . fb =<< get av

  cv <- spawn $ liftIO . Fc =<< get av

  b <- get bv
  c <- get cv
  liftIO (fd b c)
```

Basically we just plugged in some liftIO here and there. Bear in mind that the only order enforced on IO actions is due to calls to put and get; an IO action may be performed whenever all IVar data dependencies before it have been met. So when doing impure parallelism, ensure that I/O actions interact with each other only via IVars to prevent unexpected behavior.

Diagnosing parallelism – ThreadScope

Next we will look at a program visualization tool, ThreadScope. Install the threadscope executable with:

```
stack install threadscope
```

To extract the eventlog that ThreadScope uses from a Haskell program, we need to compile with -eventlog and execute with the -l Runtime System option. Running the program then generates a program.eventlog file, which ThreadScope reads. In a convenient single recipe, we lay out these commands:

```
ghc -O2 -threaded -eventlog -with-rtsopts="-N -l" program.hs
```

```
./program
```

```
threadscope program.eventlog
```

ThreadScope provides a graphical user interface. The opening view shows processor core utilization. An example view from some eventlog is:

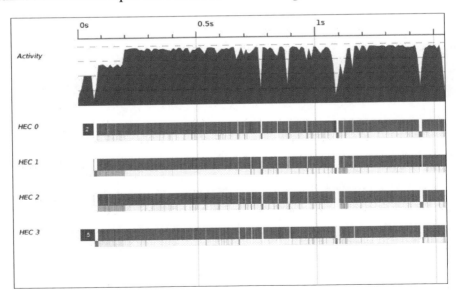

Along with total utilization, we can see the work split on all processors (four in this case). What we also see in this graph, below each core utilization, is that there is GC activity. The program actually pauses quite often just to do GC for a split second. Sometimes such scenarios might require further investigation. In this case, the application in question is the parallelized naive Fibonacci program from before and this GC activity was to be expected.

Other things that ThreadScope shows us include the spark pool sizes over the program's lifetime. For example:

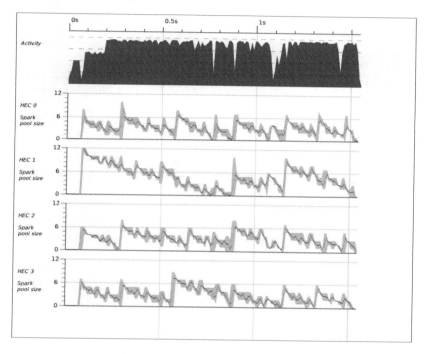

This is again data from the naive Fibonacci program. Most of the time there's some work available for all cores, which is good. The graph is rather rough because of the exponential nature of the algorithm, so this is about as good a spark rate as we can reasonably expect.

Data parallel programming – Repa

Repa (regular parallel) is a Haskell library providing regular parallel arrays. Repa performs very well in image processing, for example. Doing computations on large data structures in parallel is Repa's specialty. Repa is installed with:

```
stack install repa
```

The parts on Repa in this chapter are written for version 3.4.0.2 of the Repa library. The main interface is exported by the Data.Array.Repa module.

At first glance, the library perhaps looks a bit complex. For instance, the parallel sum function has this daunting type signature:

```
sumAllP
   :: (Shape sh, Source r a, Elt a, Unbox a, Num a, Monad m)
   => Array r sh a -> m a
```

Repa uses a lot of classes to overload functionality over different types of array. The type of immutable arrays in Repa contains three type variables:

```
data Array r sh e
```

Here, r defines representation, sh defines shape, and e defines the array elements' type. For example, a one-dimensional array of unboxed Int is given by:

```
Array U DIM1 Int
```

Mutable arrays in Repa can be represented by another type, MVec r e. The difference with immutable arrays is that mutable arrays don't have a defined shape; they're always linear or one-dimensional. But rarely is it necessary to use explicitly mutable arrays thanks to Repa's fusion system.

Playing with Repa in GHCi

Let's fire up GHCi to get the hang of the Repa library. A one-dimensional array of unboxed Ints is constructed from a list with the fromListUnboxed function:

```
> import Data.Array.Repa as Repa
> let x = fromListUnboxed (ix1 3) [0, 1, 2 :: Int]
> :t x
x :: Array U DIM1 Int
```

Many definitions from Repa overlap with definitions from Prelude, so we want a shorthand qualifier for the Repa library. Then, when building a list, note that we had to provide fromListUnboxed with the exact size or shape of the resulting array. The recommended way to construct shape definitions is with the ix1, ix2, and ix3 functions.

Repa arrays are shape-polymorphic, but not shape-agnostic; Repa is actually quite strict about aligning shapes correctly in computations. On the type level, we are guaranteed that the number of dimensions will match or else there will be a type error. Constructing two-dimensional arrays is straightforward:

```
> let y = fromListUnboxed (ix2 2 2) [1, 1, 1, 0 :: Int]
> y
AUnboxed ((Z :. 2) :. 2) [1,1,1,0]
```

Here, we witness the show instance for unboxed arrays. Conforming read instances are of course also provided. The specialized data type under the array abstraction leaks a little, in a sense. AUnboxed is the concrete data type for unboxed vectors whereas array r sh e is in fact an (associated) type family, or in clearer terms just a function on the type level. So although array is not really a data type itself, in practice it can be thought of as one.

We can retrieve the shape of any Repa array as a value with the extent function:

```
> extent y
(Z :. 2) :. 2
```

Indexing into Repa arrays happens with the (!) operator. The index is given as a shape of the same type as the array's extent. For instance:

```
> y ! ix2 1 0
1
```

Mapping and delayed arrays

We can map over the elements in the functor style with Repa.map:

```
map :: (Shape sh, Source r a) → (a → b) → Array r sh a → Array D
    sh b
```

Looking at the type of map, we see that, whatever representation the argument array uses, the representation of the resulting array is always D for delayed. In the delayed array representation, each element is given as a function in a sense. Indexing works normally for delayed arrays (the work related to calculating the element is done on-demand):

```
> Repa.map (+10) x ! ix1 1
11
```

There aren't show/read instances for delayed arrays, however. The advantages of explicitly delayed evaluation are mostly related to fusing workers in optimization.

To evaluate a delayed array such as `Repa.map` returns, we use either `computeP` or `computeS`. The former evaluates elements in parallel and the latter sequentially:

```
computeP :: Monad m => Array r1 sh e → m (Array r2 sh e)
computeS :: Array r1 sh e → Array r2 sh e
```

Type classes were omitted for clarity. What we see is that the parallel `computeP` has to execute in some monad. `computeP` ensures parallel evaluation has been completed at a certain point of monadic computation. In effect, nested data parallelism is not supported by `Repa`.

As for the monad to use with `computeP`, it really does not matter that much, as long as it conforms to the monad laws of course. We can ditch the monad after finishing computation:

```
> let [r] = computeP (Repa.map (+10) x) :: [Array U DIM1 Int]
> r
AUnboxed (Z :. 3) [10,11,12]
```

Here we used the list monad, but could have used IO or ST as well.

Reduction via folding

Many array reductions are easily expressed as a fold. The `foldS`/`foldP` functions are used for sequential and parallel folding over the innermost dimension. The resulting dimension is one rank lower:

```
> :t foldP
foldP
  :: (Monad m, Shape sh, Source r a, Unbox a, Elt a) =>
     (a -> a -> a) -> a -> Array r (sh :. Int) a ->
     m (Array U sh a)
> foldP (+) 0 y
AUnboxed (Z :. 2) [2,1]
```

To reduce all dimensions flat into a single scalar, use the `foldAllS`/`foldAllP` functions. The parallel sum of all elements could be implemented as `foldAllP (+) 0`. Take care that, if using parallel folding, the combiner function is associative and the starting element is neutral; for a parallel fold to be parallel, `Repa` needs to use the starting element multiple times to calculate sub-folds in different threads.

To fold over other dimensions, we should first transform the array's shape so that the foldable dimension is lowest. In `Repa`, reshaping arrays is usually done in place by index-space transformations. To swap the lowest two dimensions around without copying, the convenience function `transpose` is provided:

```
transpose
  :: (Shape sh, Source r e) =>
```

```
          Array r ((sh :. Int) :. Int) e -> Array D ((sh :. Int) :. Int) e
> foldP (+) 0 (transpose y)
AUnboxed (Z :. 2) [2,1]
```

Swapping arbitrary dimensions or indeed arbitrarily mapping indices is called backpermuting in Repa. For instance, swapping the highest dimension with the lowest dimension of a three-dimensional array can be done like this:

```
> let z = fromListUnboxed (ix3 3 2 1) [1, 2, 3, 4, 5, 6 :: Int]
> let z' = backpermute (ix3 1 2 3) (\(Z :. a :. b :. c) -> ix3 c b a)
z
> computeS z' :: Array U DIM3 Int
AUnboxed (((Z :. 1) :. 2) :. 3) [1,3,5,2,4,6]
```

A couple of specialized folds are provided, namely for sum (sumS/sumP/sumAllS/sumAllP) and element equality (equalsP/equalsS).

Manifest representations

So far, we have met unboxed and delayed array representations. Unboxed arrays belong to something called manifest representations. Representations are where the array is stored as if it is in memory, that is, not ad-hoc via mapping functions, which delayed arrays are.

If the array elements cannot be unboxed, then we would have to use boxed arrays (V) that present a level of indirection. Boxed arrays perform worse than unboxed, so unboxed arrays should always be preferred if possible.

> When working with arrays, boxed or not, the deepSeqArray function may come in handy to ensure complete evaluation of an array data structure. An easy trap is when a call to computeP is deferred so that its evaluation is triggered by another computeP later. Attempting to evaluate multiple computeP at the same time produces a runtime error. Best practice would be to evaluate all computeP in the same monad.

The third manifest representation in Repa is B for strict ByteStrings. The advantage of Array B sh Word8 over Array U sh Word is that B-arrays can be turned into ByteStrings and vice versa in O(1). The conversion functions can be found separately in the Data.Array.Repa.Repr.ByteString module, not exported by Data.Array.Repa:

```
module Data.Array.Repa.Repr.ByteString
fromByteString :: Shape sh => sh → ByteString → Array B sh Word8
toByteString :: Array B sh Word8 → ByteString
```

The ByteString representation can be used to manipulate textual data in tabular form efficiently. But remember to ensure that you only need to consider 8-bit characters. ByteString is not really a textual representation.

The fourth and final manifest representation, F, considers foreign memory buffers in the C heap just like ByteStrings do, but generalized for other values besides Word8. This representation is only relevant if your code interfaces with foreign code.

Delayed representation and fusion

Along with manifest representations are delayed representations. The first delayed representation, D, presents elements as functions from indices to elements. Most combinators in Repa return arrays in a delayed representation. This is because we can eliminate a lot of intermediate arrays, for instance, mapping twice like in:

```
computeS . Repa.map (+ 1) . Repa.map (* 2)
```

Like we would expect from other fusion frameworks, this fuses into a tight loop. The intermediate delayed array is certainly eliminated when compiling. In a way, the fusion framework in Repa gives us more control over when fusion happens. This is nice because it makes it easy to predict the performance of Repa programs. Although our code looks like we are operating on immutable arrays, constructing them over and over again, in practice correctly written Repa programs will optimize very nicely into fast code.

 Using computeS/computeP quite often requires an explicit type signature, because the target array is polymorphic in its representation (either unboxed array, boxed array, or foreign buffer). Usually unboxed array is the desired choice, for which more specific functions, computeUnboxedP and computeUnboxedS, provide specialized type readily.

Indices, slicing, and extending arrays

Index types in Repa are defined as:

```
data Z
data tail :. head = !tail :. !head
```

Convenient type synonyms and smart constructors are provided for dimensions up to five:

```
type DIM0 = Z
type DIM1 = DIM0 :. Int
```

```
...
type DIM5 = DIM4 :. Int

ix1 :: Int → DIM1
...
ix5 :: Int → Int → Int → Int → Int → DIM5
```

However, Repa has full support for arrays of an arbitrary but finite number of dimensions, if there's ever need for such arrays.

The `Shape` type class captures properties of an array's extent and its dimensions. For instance, the number of dimensions of a shape can be retrieved with the `rank` function and the overall count of elements with the `size` function. See the `Data.Array.Repa.Shape` module for all supported operations.

Index space transformations readily defined include imposing a new shape on an array element regardless of its original shape with reshape, appending two arrays by appending their lowest dimensions together with (++), and transposing dimensions with `transpose`. We can extract a sub-range with the `extract` function:

```
> y
AUnboxed ((Z :. 2) :. 2) [1,1,1,0]

> computeS $ extract (ix2 1 1) (ix2 1 1) y :: Array U DIM2 Int
AUnboxed ((Z :. 1) :. 1) [0]
```

The `extend` and `slice` functions involve some type families in their type signatures. At first these look complicated:

```
> :t extend
  :: (Slice sl, Shape (SliceShape sl), Shape (FullShape sl),
     Source r e) =>
     sl -> Array r (SliceShape sl) e -> Array D (FullShape sl) e

> :t slice
slice
  :: (Slice sl, Shape (FullShape sl), Shape (SliceShape sl),
     Source r e) =>
     Array r (FullShape sl) e -> sl -> Array D (SliceShape sl) e
```

Ouch, how do you read these things? Let's write signatures for extend and slice without all the details:

```
extend :: sl → Array r (SliceShape sl) e → Array D
  (FullShape sl) e
slice :: Array r (FullShape sl) e → sl → Array D (SliceShape sl) e
```

Now concentrate on that `sl` type variable; both `extend` and `slice` take such a type as one of their two arguments, the other one being an array. Then we have two type-level functions (type families): `FullShape` and `SliceShape`.

Now things are a little clearer. extend takes a slice of an array (of shape `SliceShape sl`) and produces a full array (of shape `FullShape sl`); for slice, the shapes are the other way around.

Then the `sl` thing? It's called slice specification. Intuitively, the end result depends on how we are slicing the array (or extending a slice, in the case of extend). `SliceShape` is the (type-level) function that tells us the shape based on the slice specification. `FullShape` gives the original array's shape (result array in the case of extend).

Recall that Repa defines dimensions inductively with the (`:.`) type constructor. So the shape of three-dimensional arrays is:

```
DIM3 ~ (((Z :. Int) :. Int) :. Int)
```

The slice and full shapes are given as type families with these instances:

```
type instance FullShape (sl :. All) = FullShape sl :. Int
type instance FullShape (sl :. Int) = FullShape sl :. Int
type instance FullShape (Any sh) = sh
type instance FullShape Z = Z

type instance SliceShape (sl :. All) = SliceShape sl :. Int
type instance SliceShape (sl :. Int) = SliceShape sl
type instance SliceShape (Any sh) = sh
type instance SliceShape Z = Z
```

There are two new data types: `Any` and `All`. These are both *nullary* constructors. Now, for a slice specification to be sensible its `FullShape` and `SliceShape` should be of the form `Z :. Int … :. Int`. Clearly, all shapes are also slice specifications. The slice shape of `DIM3` reduces as follows:

```
Z :. Int :. Int :. Int    -- SliceShape (sl :. Int) = SliceShape sl
Z :. Int :. Int
Z :. Int                  -- SliceShape Z = Z
Z
```

The `FullShape` function is just the identity.

This slice retains the structure of all other dimensions but the lowest; for the lowest dimension, it takes the first index and ignores all others. Thus its `SliceShape` is one rank lower.

```
Any :. (0 :: Int)
```

This one slices along the second lowest dimension:

```
Any :. (0 :: Int) :. All
```

For instance:

```
> z
AUnboxed (((Z :. 3) :. 2) :. 1) [1,2,3,4,5,6]
> computeS $ slice z (Any :. (0 :: Int) :. All) :: Array U DIM2
  Int
AUnboxed ((Z :. 3) :. 1) [1,3,5]
```

When writing the slice specification, first consider the lowest dimension. Should all elements be included, or just the element at one index? If all, the last constructor is All. If a certain index, write an Int. Then consider the next lowest dimension: should all indices (All) or just a certain index be considered? That's the second last constructor. The highest dimensions that should be preserved should be written off with a single Any constructor.

Whereas in slicing All and Any preserve the structure and indices drill-down, in extending All and Any still preserve the structure but each index number defines a new dimension at the position where it appears. The new dimensions replicate the contents of the supplied array:

```
> x
AUnboxed (Z :. 3) [0,1,2]
> computeS $ extend (Any :. (2::Int)) x :: Array U DIM2 Int
AUnboxed ((Z :. 3) :. 2) [0,0,1,1,2,2]
> computeS $ extend (Any :. (2::Int) :. All) x :: Array U DIM2 Int
AUnboxed ((Z :. 2) :. 3) [0,1,2,0,1,2]
> computeS $ extend (Any :. (2::Int) :. (2::Int)) x :: Array U
  DIM3 Int
AUnboxed (((Z :. 3) :. 2) :. 2) [0,0,0,0,1,1,1,1,2,2,2,2]
```

Convolution with stencils

In image processing, among other applications, the convolution operation (*) is used. Discrete convolution is defined by:

$(A * K)(x, y) = sum\_i\ sum\_j\ A(x + i, y + j)\ K(i, j)$

Here A is the array (image) and K is a stencil, basically a small matrix.

Let's consider a simple example. A 5x5 grayscale image is given by this matrix:

```
1 1 1 1 1
0 0 1 0 0
1 1 1 1 1
0 0 1 0 0
0 0 1 0 0
```

And the following stencil extracts the feature of horizontal lines:

```
0 0 0
1 1 1
0 0 0
```

To represent the stencil in Repa, we'll use a quasi-quoter that comes with Repa, [stencil2|...|]. We will need these imports:

```
-- file: stencil.hs
{-# LANGUAGE QuasiQuotes #-}

import Data.Array.Repa as Repa
import Data.Array.Repa.Stencil
import Data.Array.Repa.Stencil.Dim2
```

For now, we'll build the image from a function with fromFunction:

```
image :: Array D DIM2 Double
image = fromFunction (ix2 5 5) $
    \(Z :. x :. y) -> if x == 2 || y == 2 then 1 else 0
```

As for the stencil, we can use the ready stencil framework present in Repa and construct something with type Stencil:

```
stencil :: Stencil DIM2 Double
stencil = [stencil2| 0   0   0
                     1   1   1
                     0   0   0 |]
```

The convolution operation simply overlays the stencil over each pixel in the image and produces a new value for that pixel by calculating sum of the elementwise product with the stencil. The mapStencil2 function does exactly this:

```
mapStencil2
  :: Source r a =>
    Boundary a -> Stencil DIM2 a -> Array r DIM2 a ->
      Array PC5 DIM2 a
```

The `Boundary` argument defines what happens at pixels on the edges, where the stencil goes over the boundaries of the image. Three popular options are available:

```
data Boundary a = BoundFixed !a
                | BoundConst !a
                | BoundClamp
```

`BoundClamp` assigns edge pixels the same values as in the original image, `BoundConst` treats points outside the image as having been given a constant value, and `BoundFixed` assigns a fixed value where the stencil cannot be fully applied.

The representation of the result array, PC5, is also delayed in nature. It is something called a *partitioned array*. Although it is a detail that we don't need to worry about, the compute functions understand it. The convolution is then produced by:

```
computeP $ mapStencil2 (BoundConst 0) stencil image
    :: IO (Array U DIM2 Double)
```

This produces an array that looks like this:

```
3 3 3 3 3
0 1 1 1 0
3 3 3 3 3
0 1 1 1 0
0 1 1 1 0
```

Now if we applied a filter, like this:

```
Repa.map (\x -> if x >= 3 then 1 else 0)
```

The resulting image would contain only the horizontal line in the input image:

```
1 1 1 1 1
0 0 0 0 0
1 1 1 1 1
0 0 0 0 0
0 0 0 0 0
```

This is the basic idea behind edge detection. And what's more, it scales to larger images performantly and will automatically scale to however many processors are available.

Cursored and partitioned arrays

Although we just concluded it isn't necessary to acknowledge the existence of the PC5 array representation that the stencil transformation produced, that isn't completely correct. The distinction between bare delayed (D) and cursored/partitioned (C, P) representations makes a difference in certain applications.

To see the need for exposing this difference in the API, let's continue with our convolution example by extending it with one more edge detector. Can you guess what kind of a pattern this stencil detects?

```
stencil' :: Stencil DIM2 Double
stencil' = [stencil2| -1  1 -1
                      -2  1 -2
                      -1  1 -1 |]
```

Yes, it detects vertical lines not intersected by anything.

Applying this and our previous stencil separately with some appropriate normalizing thresholds we get:

```
st1, st2 :: Array D DIM2 Double
st1 = Repa.map (\x -> if x >= 3 then 1 else 0) $
        mapStencil2 BoundClamp stencil image

st2 = Repa.map (\x -> if x >= 1 then 1 else 0) $
        mapStencil2 BoundClamp stencil' image
```

Both of these have the same shape and type: `Array D DIM2 Double`. Combining these to one image and computing the result look like this:

```
> import Data.Bits ((.|.))
> computeUnboxedP (zipWith (.|.) st1 st2)
```

The result is this:

```
1 1 1 1 1
0 0 0 0 0
1 1 1 1 1
0 0 1 0 0
0 0 1 0 0
```

Now, looking at `Repa.map` again, we note that it always produces a delayed array, which wraps every element into its own function. This is suboptimal when we have partitioned our array such that sets of indices share computations (the Repa stencils did that).

To open up more possibilities for compile-time optimizations, we should use structured versions of **smap** and **szipWith**. These functions preserve the partitioning and cursoring and let us benefit from index sharing. With these changes, the types change a little, but not much:

```
st1, st2 :: Array PC5 DIM2 Int
st1 = smap (\x -> if x >= 3 then 1 else 0) $
```

```
        mapStencil2 BoundClamp stencil image

st2 = smap (\x -> if x >= 1 then 1 else 0) $
        mapStencil2 BoundClamp stencil' image

> print $ computeUnboxedS $ szipWith (.|.) st1 st2
```

Writing fast Repa code

There are numerous tricks for writing fast and well-parallelizing code with Repa.
Enumerating from most important to least important, we have:

- **Vectorize:** Work the algorithm such that as much as possible is done with
  array operations. Use unboxed arrays unless you have a good reason not to.

- **Compute only where necessary:** The more delayed arrays there are, the
  more fusion will likely take place and the produced code will be faster.
  Unless not evaluating would take up too much memory, it is usually best to
  defer it further. Computation usually creates a new manifest array.

- **Parallelize with optimal granularity:** Using parallel `computeP`, `foldP`,
  and others is faster on bigger arrays or with a bigger bunch of work; for
  little work, `computeS` and `foldS` have less overhead. The lack of nested
  parallelism encourages us to lift parallelism to the top level for best effect.

- **Compile with optimizations, threaded and with LLVM:** A good base set
  of flags for Repa programs in production is `-Odph -threaded -rtsopts`
  `-fllvm -fno-liberate-case -optlo-O3`.

- **Bang everything:** All lazy arguments and data type fields should be strict.

- **Inline extensively:** The fusion system relies heavily on worker functions
  getting inlined. Instead of cluttering your code with `INLINE` pragmas,
  consider compiling with these flags `-funfolding-use-threshold1000`
  `-funfolding-keenness-factor1000`. They tell GHC to inline everything.
  This might increase binary sizes considerably, so these flags should probably
  be enabled on a per-module basis (using the `OPTIONS_GHC` pragma).

- **Use unsafe versions of Repa functions:** The function `unsafeIndex` and
  others from `Data.Array.Repa.Unsafe` should be preferred when correctness
  is guaranteed. These unsafe variants don't do bounds-checking and cause
  undefined behavior if used incorrectly. Therefore, unsafe functions shouldn't
  be used when developing or testing code.

Additional libraries

There are a number of libraries that complement Repa:

- `repa-devil`: Load and write arrays as image files. Apparently this has been deprecated in favor of the `friday` and `friday-devil` libraries.

- `repa-io`: Load and write arrays in bitmap, binary, ASCII matrix, and vector formats.

- `repa-algorithms`: Quite performant implementations of algorithms for matrix operations, Fourier transform, randomized arrays, and more flexible convolution functions.

- `repa-stream` and `repa-flow`: Data-parallel streaming libraries built on top of Repa.

Example from image processing

We'll conclude this chapter with a full-blown example of image processing with Repa. We will do letter recognition from images with convolution. For the sake of demonstration, we'll restrict ourselves to well-defined black-and-white images with text in a pixel-correct font that is assumed to be known. The image we will try to read letters from is this:

To simplify things even further, we'll assume that the text is oriented exactly horizontally.

Next, we will proceed to load the image from the file, identifying letters and then text. Then we will test and evaluate the performance and see if we can squeeze in some optimizations.

To follow along, write the code into a Haskell source code file by copying as we go forward. First, these are a bunch of imports we will be using:

```
-- file: letterrec.hs
{-# LANGUAGE QuasiQuotes #-}

import Data.Array.Repa as Repa
import Data.Array.Repa.Algorithms.Convolve
import Data.Array.Repa.IO.BMP
```

Loading the image from file

We have a few options for how to read an image file into a Repa array. One is the `repa-devil` library (which has now been deprecated in favor of `friday/friday-devil`). Here we will operate on just BMP images using the `repa-io` library. So make sure that library is installed:

```
stack install repa-io
```

We'll represent pixels as single Doubles that represent luminance:

```
type Image r = Array r DIM2 Double
```

Reading in an image is simple. In addition, we'll have to convert RGB values to luminance. Luckily, this problem is solved by `Pixel.doubleLuminanceOfRGB8`. The final problem is that `readImageFromBMP` from `repa-io` builds the array so that the lowest pixels are at the top of the array. This is fixed by a mirror function. Our read action becomes:

```
readImage :: FilePath -> IO (Image U)
readImage fp = do
  result <- BMP.readImageFromBMP fp
  return $! computeS $ mirror $ case result of
    Left err -> error "readImage: Failed to load image from
      file"
    Right array -> Repa.map Pixel.doubleLuminanceOfRGB8 array

mirror :: Image D -> Image D
mirror img = backpermute (extent img)
  (\(Z :. x :. y) -> ix2 (mx - 1 - x) y) img
  where Z :. mx :. _ = extent img
```

Note that I used ($!) instead of ($). This way, if the image file was faulty, we get an error before `readImage` IO action completes. With lazy return, the error would be silently propagated to wherever the returned `Image D` thunk is next requested.

We computed the result here instead of returning a delayed array because the convolution operation we'll be using expects an unboxed array as input.

Identifying letters with convolution

Next for the convolution. We'll implement recognition for three letters: a, b, and c. We make stencils for each letter. But using the stencils in the `repa` library is not an option this time, because letter b is larger than 7x7 in our font, which is the upper bound on stencil size in `Data.Array.Repa.Stencil`.

To represent larger than 7x7 stencils, we'll again resort to repa-algorithms, specifically the `Data.Array.Repa.Algorithms.Convolve` module. The function we'll be using is `convolveP`. Specialized for our `Image` type, we have:

```
convoleP
   :: Monad m =>
      (DIM2 → Double) → Image U → Image U → m (Image U)
```

This convolution represents the stencil as an unboxed array too. The first argument is used to decide what happens at the edges.

The stencils for letters a, b, and c in our font are therefore:

```
sta, stb, stc :: Image U
sta = fromListUnboxed (ix2 6 5)
      [ -1,   1,   1,   1,  -1
      , -1,  -1,  -1,  -1,   1
      , -1,   1,   1,   1,   1
      ,  1,  -1,  -1,  -1,   1
      ,  1,  -1,  -1,  -1,   1
      , -1,   1,   1,   1,   1 ]

stb = fromListUnboxed (ix2 8 5)
      [  1,  -1,  -1,  -1,  -1
      ,  1,  -1,  -1,  -1,  -1
      ,  1,   1,   1,   1,  -1
      ,  1,  -1,  -1,  -1,   1
      ,  1,  -1,  -1,  -1,   1
      ,  1,  -1,  -1,  -1,   1
      ,  1,  -1,  -1,  -1,   1
      ,  1,   1,   1,   1,  -1 ]

stc = fromListUnboxed (ix2 6 5)
      [ -1,   1,   1,   1,  -1
      ,  1,  -1,  -1,  -1,   1
      ,  1,  -1,  -1,  -1,  -1
      ,  1,  -1,  -1,  -1,  -1
      ,  1,  -1,  -1,  -1,   1
      , -1,   1,   1,   1,  -1 ]
```

To use these to recognize letters, for each letter and corresponding stencil we apply convolution and read from the result where the stencil matched exactly. Matching exactly means that, for every 1, there is a 1 in the input image and, for every -1, there is a 0 in the input image.

The following function takes a letter stencil and input image and creates a two-dimensional character array of found matches with the size the same as the input image:

```
match
  :: Monad m => Char -> Image U -> Image U -> m (Array D DIM2
    Char)
match char stencil image = do
  let
    threshold = sumAllS (Repa.map (max 0) stencil) - 0.1

  res <- convolveP (const 0) stencil image
  return $! Repa.map
    (\x -> if x > threshold then char else '\NUL') res
```

First we calculated the threshold value from the stencil. The `0.1` is there to accommodate for inaccuracy from the bitmap (white pixels aren't exactly 1).

Next we apply convolution. Finally, we convert elements that are above the threshold into characters. Others are set to null characters. We return this (delayed) array.

At this point, we can fire up GHCi and see if we match letters:

```
> :load letterrec.hs
> img <- readImage "image.bmp"
> res <- match 'a' sta img
> filter (/= '\NUL') $ toList $ computeUnboxedS res
"aa"
```

Yep, seems to work correctly. Repeat for other characters to verify further, if you wish.

Let's add one more letter, d. We note that d is exactly a flipped b in our font, so we can get away with just this:

```
std :: Image U
std = computeUnboxedS . transpose . mirror $ transpose stb
```

Extracting strings from an image

Now for the final feature: combining letter recognizers into a complete string recognizer.

The recognizer takes an image as input, so:

```
recognize :: Monad m => Image U -> m String
recognize img = do
```

Then we execute matches for all letters we recognize:

```
let recs = [ match c st img
  | (c, st) ←[ ('a', sta), ('b', stb),
    ('c', stc), ('d', std) ] ]

  letters <- sequence recs
```

Here, `recs` is a list of computations that produce arrays. To execute them, we used sequence. Now letters is a list of arrays. Then, to combine them, we'll just apply an element-wise maximum over them all:

```
combined <- computeUnboxedP $ foldl1 (Repa.zipWith max)
  letters
```

Then, to also accommodate for line-endings, we turn all left-most elements into newline characters. This is safe, because those are always NUL characters (our convolution always sets edges to zero). The final step is to convert the array into a list and, strip nulls and excess line endings; then recognition is complete!

```
let Z :. _ :. my = extent combined

  lineEnds = Repa.traverse combined id $ \f ix@(Z :. _ :. y)
    ->
  if y == my - 1 then '\n' else f ix

    return $! unlines . words $ filter (/= '\NUL') $ toList
      lineEnds
```

The very last thing to do is test it. Here's a `main` that does this:

```
main = do
  img <- readImage "image.bmp"
  str <- recognize img
  putStr str
```

And a quick testing at GHCi makes it clear that our recognizer works:

```
> :load letterrec.hs
[1 of 1] Compiling Main          ( letterrec.hs, interpreted )
Ok, modules loaded: Main.
> main
bcdc
abca
```

Testing and evaluating performance

Now it's time to see how our recognizer performs. For testing purposes, I tiled our test image 5,000 times into a single image (size 3550x2100 pixels, 21.3 MB).

The first try was with a non-threaded runtime and no special optimizations:

```
ghc -rtsopts -O3 letterrec.hs
./letterrec +RTS -s
  7,323,831,024 bytes allocated in the heap
  4,803,680 bytes copied during GC
  268,385,496 bytes maximum residency (9 sample(s))
  4,978,072 bytes maximum slop
  342 MB total memory in use (27 MB lost due to fragmentation)
```

```
    Tot time (elapsed)  Avg pause  Max pause
  Gen  0      13281 colls,      0 par    0.045s   0.044s     0.0000s  0.0001s
  Gen  1          9 colls,      0 par    0.016s   0.016s     0.0018s  0.0146s
```

```
  INIT    time    0.000s  (  0.000s elapsed)
  MUT     time    9.158s  (  9.172s elapsed)
  GC      time    0.061s  (  0.059s elapsed)
  EXIT    time    0.015s  (  0.015s elapsed)
  Total   time    9.238s  (  9.246s elapsed)

  %GC     time       0.7%  (0.6% elapsed)

  Alloc rate    799,722,664 bytes per MUT second

  Productivity  99.3% of total user, 99.3% of total elapsed
```

Now we have a baseline from which we can try to get faster. Next, let's see how well parallelization affects the results. Compile with a threaded runtime and run on three system cores:

```
ghc -rtsopts -threaded -O3 letterrec.hs
./letterrec +RTS -N4 -s
```

The main differences from a non-threaded runtime were: elapsed time reduced to 4.4s (speedup by a factor of 2) and the memory footprint went up a little, due to more work being done simultaneously.

Let's next add LLVM into the mix. With LLVM, we should use `-Odph` instead, because it enables better optimizations for Repa and LLVM code:

```
ghc -rtsopts -threaded -Odph -fllvm -optlo-O3 -fno-liberate-case
   -funfolding-use-threshold1000 -funfolding-keeness-factor1000
./letterrec +RTS -N4 -s
```

This cuts down runtime to about 3.8s (speedup factor of 2.5).

Last, let's see if we could still have added some code-level optimizations. There are a few things we could do. But most of the time is spent in `convolveP`, which is largely out of our control. Anyway, we could:

- Add bangs to all function arguments and use explicit `INLINE` pragmas
- Use `unsafeTraverse` and `unsafeBackpermute` instead of `traverse` and `backpermute`

Together, these account for about 3%-better performance in our program. If we had implemented more of the labor and not just handed all the heavy lifting to `convolveP`, inlining and unsafe functions would make for a bigger difference.

A better alternative to blindly cluttering code with bangs and pragmas is as usual to profile the program to find the bottlenecks. For instance, the ThreadScope profile of our program looks like this:

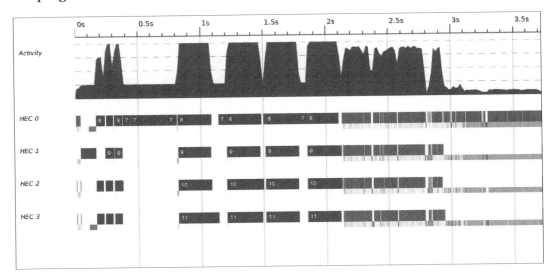

What we see in the middle are the four convolution passes. Together they make up about 1.5 seconds or 45% of the total runtime.

The first 0.8 seconds are spent in loading and processing the input image. Much of it is sequential. With the extra-large image, it seems like our program could benefit from using `computeP` in `readImage` instead of `computeS`.

That one second after convolution passes is probably spent combining the character arrays into one. Even though we simply fold sequentially, Repa manages to squeeze in a lot of parallel processing when we just wrapped the thing in `computeP`. We didn't even need to use a real parallel fold (for lists).

Finally, the last 0.8 seconds are spent in constructing the output string... Er, I mean it's spent doing GC. Once again a linked list performs badly. For better performance, we should switch to a more memory-friendly representation instead.

Summary

Now we have crammed in how parallelism is done in Haskell and an overview of the threaded runtime. We parallelized pure and lazy data structures with strategies and `Eval` (the `parallel` package). For more control and parallelism in IO, we had to resort to schedules and Par (the `monad-par` package). We dived into data-parallel programming with Repa and even wrote a string recognition program with it.

We learned to use the event log and ThreadScope to diagnose the parallel performance of Haskell programs. Things to keep in mind when parallelizing programs are: use good granularity, not too much overhead but not too much sequential processing either; compile with flags optimized for parallelism, especially with Repa; and profile and diagnose before applying transformations at the code level.

In the next chapter, we will look at stream processing in Haskell: I/O, networking, and streaming libraries such as conduits and pipes. Lazy I/O, combined with interacting with networks, produces nightmarish bugs and sadly it's not easy to get right every time. And the consumer and producer types in some libraries we will look at are scary for sure – but this is just to prevent you from writing incorrect programs!

6
I/O and Streaming

I/O in Haskell is a source of confusion for many. The I/O functions in the base library are lazy and allow the interleaving of I/O side effects with pure code. This produces weird errors at runtime or, even worse, just incorrect behavior without errors. On the other hand, interleaved side-effects allow easy file processing in constant space, among other things. Fortunately, more robust alternatives for streaming have been proposed and implemented as libraries.

In this chapter, we will learn to use some of the most popular streaming libraries. But before that, we will tear down problems with lazy I/O, because it's still often the easiest and most elegant way to do I/O. We will also consider an alternative to lazy I/O, strict I/O.

The I/O we do in this chapter consists of standard input and output, file handles, and network sockets. These cover almost all I/O that's possible in Haskell (we don't do foreign interfaces in this chapter). Resource management is closely related to I/O and so that will be covered too. We will also cover perhaps the most widely seen specific kind of data output ever: writing logs and log files from applications. We will look at the following topics:

- Working with lazy I/O: recognizing and avoiding problems
- Taking care of freeing resources and using **ResourceT**
- Working with streaming libraries: `io-streams`, `pipes`, and `conduit`
- Adding logging abilities to Haskell applications: fast-logger and monad-logger

Reading, writing, and handling resources

Although it's a common joke that because Haskell is a pure language, we couldn't observe its effects, Haskell actually has very powerful and sophisticated facilities for interacting with the outside world. Besides reading and writing to files and network sockets, I/O affiliates to managing resources that provide for input and output.

In this section, we will first point out laziness in Haskell I/O, doing networking with low-level sockets, and consider managing handles and resources.

Traps of lazy I/O

Lazy I/O allows pure functions to be interleaved with I/O actions arbitrarily. It is important to know when an I/O action defers its action part for later. To demonstrate how easy it is to fall prey to lazy I/O, consider this innocent-looking file manipulation procedure:

```
-- file: readwrite.hs

main = do
    writeFile "file.txt" "old"
    old <- readFile "file.txt"
    writeFile "file.txt" "new"
    putStrLn old
```

However, running this code produces an error at runtime:

```
readwrite.hs: file.txt: openFile: resource busy (file is locked)
```

The culprit is `readFile`, which is lazy in its return value: reading the file begins only when we demand the results. That would happen on the last line. But `readFile` does set a lock on the file in the Runtime System immediately, leading to `writeFile` failing.

Here's another example, using `withFile` from `System.IO` to manage the file resource as a file handle:

```
-- file: readwithfile.hs

import System.IO

main = do
    old <- withFile "file.txt" ReadWriteMode hGetContents
    putStrLn old
```

This time, the runtime error message has more information, as it is associated with a handle instead of a file:

```
readwithfile.hs: file.txt: hGetContents: illegal operation (delayed read
on closed handle)
```

What's worse, because I/O operations in the base library work with strings, it wouldn't even be enough to seq the result. We would have to do something like seq (last string).

On the other hand, lazy IO and strings allow us to program input and output streams in a similar way to streaming with pure lists. For example, the echo program in Haskell is simply:

```
-- file: echo.hs

main = getContents >>= putStr
```

Or using the interact combinator:

```
main = interact id
```

File handles, buffering, and encoding

The Handle data type is used by Runtime System to manage reading and writing from and to filesystem objects. Standard input, output, and error channels are also handles. These handles are exported in System.IO as stdin, stdout, and stderr, respectively. For convenience, basic reading, writing, and appending functions are defined that hide handle opening and closing under the hood. These functions correctly close the handle or Handle? make consistent globally even when exceptions are raised.

When working with Handles directly, you are responsible for closing every handle you open. Best practice is to use utility functions, such as withFile, that correctly close handles even in the case of exceptions. With openFile, you are responsible to call hClose on the Handle that openFile returns, preferably using finally or bracket from the Control.Exception module. An example use of bracket is in the withFile combinator, which we could equally implement ourselves as:

```
-- file: bracket.hs

import Control.Exception
import System.IO hiding (withFile)

withFile :: FilePath -> IOMode -> (Handle -> IO r) -> IO r
withFile file mode go = bracket (openFile file mode) hClose go
```

Buffering is also controlled via Handles. The preferable buffering mode depends on the application. Three different buffering modes are supported:

- **BlockBuffering**: This is the fastest buffering mode with least overhead, best suited for high-bandwidth applications.
- **LineBuffering**: Input and output is handled one line at a time. Best-suited for terminal applications.
- **NoBuffering**: Input and output is handled one word or character at a time. This is the only choice for highly interactive terminal programs, for example. The overhead is very big when processing large amounts of data with no buffering.

Basic I/O operations don't bother defining standard buffering modes and instead depend on default buffering of the operating system.

Most of the time the defaults are reasonably sane, such as block-buffering for files and line-buffering for terminal applications. But this isn't always the case: if your application depends on a specific buffering mode, you should set it yourselves with hSetBuffering. For example, to ensure that a terminal application uses line-buffering for both input and output in all cases, we should do something like the following:

```
-- file: interact.hs
import Data.Char (toUpper)
import System.IO

main = do
    hSetBuffering stdin LineBuffering
    hSetBuffering stdout LineBuffering
    interact (map toUpper)
```

Alongside buffering, text encoding is also a property of handles in text mode. By default, files are always in text-mode and only opened in non-text or binary mode with openBinaryFile. Encoding is controlled with hSetEncoding (from System. IO) and, just like with buffering modes, the default encoding depends on the underlaying system's configuration. To set standard input encoding to utf-8, use:

```
hSetEncoding stdin utf8 :: IO ()
```

Binary I/O

Using handles in binary mode with functions from System.IO is slightly cumbersome because the interface is low-level, based on pointers (Ptr a). The bytestring package is usually a better option for binary I/O.

Recall that ByteStrings came in two flavors: strict and lazy. Both have their own I/O interfaces using respective `ByteString` variants. The I/O interface with `bytestring` is named consistently with the `string IO` interface, using exactly the same names, such as `getLine`, `getContents`, `interact`, `readFile`, `writeFile`, and so on.

Before we do I/O with `ByteStrings` though, we should ensure that the handle we are using is in binary mode. Functions such as `withBinaryFile` and `openBinaryFile` take care of this for us. But `stdin`, `stdout`, and `stderr` are by default in text-mode and should be set to binary mode with `hSetBinaryMode`. This ensures that no special encoding takes place and no newline translation is performed.

Recall the `echo` program (`echo.hs`) we wrote a few pages ago? There is a small problem with that implementation: with binary files, end-of-line and end-of-file characters could clutter output in the case of non-textual data. So in a correct `echo` program, we should set both `stdin` and `stdout` to binary mode at startup.

The strict `ByteString` from `Data.ByteString` is always a single, fully evaluated, strict byte array. This is to be expected from a strict data structure. But what is not so obvious is that I/O operations with strict ByteStrings are also strict. So the write-read-write program that failed with lazy string or String? make consistent globally IO will work fine with strict `ByteString IO`:

```
-- file: readwrite-bs.hs
{-# LANGUAGE OverloadedStrings #-}

import qualified Data.ByteString as B

main = do
    B.writeFile "file.txt" "old"
    old <- B.readFile "file.txt"
    B.writeFile "file.txt" "new"
    B.putStr old
```

Note that if you are relying on ASCII encoding with ByteStrings then, as usual, you should probably be using the Text data type instead. However, the `Data.ByteString.Char8` module provides functions for interpreting ByteStrings as ASCII. Functions such as `hPutStrLn` (relies on newline character) belong strictly to the `Char8` module.

As a consequence of strictness, it's not possible to stream with strict ByteStrings like it is with lazy strings. Fortunately, lazy ByteString works much the same way as String. The API is very similar too.

Implementing the `echo` program correctly with lazy ByteStrings, we write:

```
-- file: echo-lbs.hs

import System.IO
import qualified Data.ByteString.Lazy as L

main = do
    hSetBinaryMode stdin True
    hSetBinaryMode stdout True
    L.getContents >>= L.putStr
```

Note that for lazy ByteStrings, there's also a corresponding lazy `Char8` module, `Data.ByteString.Lazy.Char8` for ASCII-dependent functions.

Textual I/O

Although String is a perfectly fine datatype to use in non-critical applications and for small strings, they're horribly space-inefficient for large strings and not completely Unicode-correct. The Text data types, strict and lazy, from the `text` package are a lot better datatypes for larger strings.

The IO functions for Texts are again named just like IO functions for Strings and ByteStrings, but for some reason IO functions are in their own modules named `Data.Text.IO` and `Data.Text.Lazy.IO`.

I/O performance with filesystem objects

Let's for a moment consider the performance impact of using different datatypes for I/O: String, strict and lazy ByteString, and strict and lazy Text. We'll benchmark by processing 512 MB of zeroes with different implementations of `echo`. All programs were compiled with **-O3**. The tests were run as:

```
dd if=/dev/zero of=/dev/stdout bs=1M count=512 | ./echo +RTS -s
```

The results are tabled as:

Datatype	Time taken	Heap allocations	Copied in GC	Memory in use
String	18.4 seconds	22, 000 MB	1, 000, 000 kB	1 MB
ByteString (lazy)	7 seconds	550 MB	110 kB	2 MB
ByteString (strict)	8 seconds	1, 000 MB	6, 100 kB	1,100 MB

Datatype	Time taken	Heap allocations	Copied in GC	Memory in use
Text (lazy)	17 seconds	32, 000 MB	31, 000 kB	1 MB
Text (strict)	21 seconds	33, 000 MB	56, 000 kB	2,900 MB

In terms of time taken, String isn't too bad. But GC traffic is orders of magnitude larger than with any other datatype. Not surprisingly, the most efficient representations are ByteStrings. Also notable is that there is a considerable memory overhead in producing a large strict Text, but the lazy Text is clearly a better option than String overall.

Sockets and networking

The `Network.Socket` module from the `network` package exposes the C socket API unclear?. The more recent `socket` package takes a more type-safe approach than the `network` package. Using either package is straightforward when there is knowledge of network programming in general; the interested reader might consider picking up a favorite networking book, as this isn't one.

Acting as a TCP/IP client

Using the `network` package, the function `connectTo` can be used to open a Handle to a remote endpoint:

```
connectTo :: HostName → PortID → IO Handle
```

For example, we could make a HTTP request directly with a TCP socket in GHCi:

```
> import System.IO
> import Network

> h <- connectTo "google.com" (PortNumber 80)
> hPutStr h "GET / HTTP/1.1\nHost: www.google.com\n\n"
> hGetContents h

"HTTP/1.1 200 OK\r\nDate: Sat, 07 May 2016 13:19:47 GMT\r\nExpires:
-1\r\nCache-Control: private, max-age=0\r\nContent-Type: text/html;
charset=ISO-8859 …
```

Note that, because `connectTo` returns a handle, we could just as well use `hPutStr` and other handle functions from `bytestring` or `text` libraries. The same points about buffering discussed previously in Handle's apply here as well: for interactive applications, you should probably set the Handle to line-buffering (the default is block-buffering).

Unfortunately, the `network` package is potentially confusing to navigate: while the C socket API is exported as is in `Network.Socket`, the `Network` module exports a slightly higher-level but much restricted API that supports only TCP/IP.

Using the `Network.Socket` module is more laborious and error-prone than using the higher-level `Network` module. Instead of `connectTo`, we would create a socket with correct parameters and then bind an address to it. The `connectTo` from previous example becomes then:

```
> import Network.Socket

> s <- socket AF_INET Stream defaultProtocol
> addrInfos <- getAddrInfo Nothing (Just "google.com") (Just "80")
> connect s (addrAddress (head addrInfos))
```

To read and write to such an opened socket, we could call `socketToHandle` on s to obtain a Handle on the `Socket` and use it with `System.IO`, `bytestring`, or `text`. Alternatively, we could use the `send` and `recv` functions directly on the `Socket`. Those use Strings, however. A third similarly fast option is the `Network.Socket.ByteString` module that provides `send` and `recv` functions for ByteStrings. (There are actually two modules: one for strict and other for lazy ByteString socket IO.)

Acting as a TCP server (Unix domain sockets)

How about being at the other endpoint of a TCP connection, that is, accepting requests instead of making them? With the easy Network API, we would create a `Socket` with `listenOn` and then accept requests

```
listenOn :: PortID → IO Socket
accept :: Socket → IO (Handle, HostName, PortNumber)
```

However, for more control, we should use the slightly lower-level `Socket` interface.

Let's take an example of **Inter-process Communication (IPC)** using Unix domain sockets. The following therefore applies only on Unices, but is easy to adapt to others by using the `AF_INET` socket family.

This server program opens a Unix domain socket `./echo.socket` and echoes back everything it receives:

```
-- file: socket-echo.hs

import Control.Exception
import Network.Socket

server = bracket
```

```
    (socket AF_UNIX Stream defaultProtocol)
    close
    (\s -> do
        bind s (SockAddrUnix "./echo.socket")
        listen s 1
        (conn, _) <- accept s
        talk conn)
where
  talk s = do r <- recv s 1024
              putStrLn r
              send s r
              talk s
```

There are quite a few steps in this simple socket server:

1. Create a socket (Socket) with the correct family (AF_UNIX), type (Stream) and protocol number (defaultProtocol = 0).
2. Bind an address ("./echo.socket") to the socket.
3. Start listening for incoming connections.
4. Accept a connection and bind it to a variable (conn :: Socket).
5. Communicate with the new connection (talk).

This program only serves the first inbound client. In a real application, we would likely want to serve multiple clients simultaneously. This would mean to forkIO a new thread for every new connection from accept.

Also note that, for demonstration, I've excluded all error handling, except freeing the socket at the end of program. Almost all of the socket functions might throw errors, though not all recoverable.

 Unix domain sockets are not automatically removed. On the server, one would probably want to try deleting the socket file at startup if it exists.

The corresponding client program is similar except simpler (here I've omitted even closing the socket, assuming that the socket will persist over the lifetime of the client):

```
client = do
    s <- socket AF_UNIX Stream defaultProtocol
    connect s (SockAddrUnix "./echo.socket")
    send s "ping"
    pong <- recv s 1024
    putStrLn pong
```

When running server and client in separate terminals, they both print **ping** and exit.

Raw UDP traffic

So far we have used exclusively the `network` package and TCP. To demonstrate UDP, we'll switch to the `socket` package. The main difference between these libraries lies in the socket datatype. The `socket` library's socket has three additional type variables to encode the family, type, and protocol of the socket:

```
data Socket family type protocol
```

Also the `socket` function now takes no arguments but we should encode information in an explicit type signature. So, to create a UDP socket we would write:

```
socket :: IO (Socket Inet Datagram UDP)
```

Some function names have changed in version 0.6 of socket relative to earlier versions. The following applies for version 0.6 of the `socket` library.

Because of the extensible design of the `socket` library, it is split into multiple smaller modules. The unfortunate consequence of this is that we need quite a few imports for even small programs. For a UDP echo server-client pair, we'll use this preamble:

```
-- file: socket-udp.hs
{-# LANGUAGE OverloadedStrings #-}

import Control.Monad (forever)
import System.Socket
import System.Socket.Protocol.UDP (UDP)
import System.Socket.Type.Datagram (Datagram)
import System.Socket.Family.Inet
      (Inet, SocketAddress(..), inetLoopback)
```

UDP is a simpler protocol than TCP, namely we don't need to listen to and accept requests, and so the server program is considerably simpler:

```
server = do
    s <- socket :: IO (Socket Inet Datagram UDP)
    bind s (SocketAddressInet inetLoopback 3003)
    forever $ do
        (msg, addr) <- receiveFrom s 1024 mempty
        sendTo s msg mempty addr
```

Note that I've again excluded all error handling; at least the socket should be freed after use (with `close` and `bracket`). Otherwise the socket will leak memory!

The client program is also simplified somewhat in UDP:

```
client = do
    s <- socket :: IO (Socket Inet Datagram UDP)
    connect s (SocketAddressInet inetLoopback 3003)
    send s "ping" mempty
    receive s 1024 mempty >>= print
```

Note that it wouldn't be mandatory to connect; we could instead specify the destination in sendTo just like we needed to in the server program. This is all due to the stateless nature of UDP.

Networking above the transport layer

Instead of working directly in the lower levels of abstraction like TCP, higher-level interfaces are provided by numerous libraries.

The network-transport library defines an abstract API for endpoint-to-endpoint communication. Additional libraries implement the API for different transports: network-transport-tcp for TCP and network-transport-zeromq for ZeroMQ transports.

For networking in the application level, there are many specialized libraries; search for them in Hackage by application name or refer to *Chapter 14, Library Recommendations*.

Managing resources with ResourceT

Remember when we were creating sockets, it was important to always close them after use (so that they wouldn't leak memory)? So far we have usually wrapped every socket, or resource, in a bracket (except when we were just lazy and testing). In larger applications, there are larger amounts of resources that should be free at some point. It quickly becomes cumbersome to always bracket everything.

As usual with Haskell, abstracting resource handling with a monad (transformer) turns out to work quite well. One such monad transformer is ResourceT m a from the resourcet package.

With ResourceT, we are no longer required to nest resource allocations with brackets. Instead, we can perform allocate in ResourceT to obtain a resource and register a release action for it that will be performed last when the ResourceT finishes. allocate has the following type:

```
allocate
    :: MonadResource m => IO a → (a → IO ()) → m (ReleaseKey, a)
```

Now consider allocating two resources, two file handles: one to read from and another to write to. We could write two nested brackets as such:

```
import Control.Exception
import System.IO

copy_bracket :: IO ()
copy_bracket =
    bracket (openFile "read.txt" ReadMode) hClose $ \f1 →
    bracket (openFile "write.txt" WriteMode) hClose $ \f2 →
        hGetContents f1 >>= hPutStr f2
```

We can rewrite this using ResourceT as:

```
-- file: resourcet.hs

import Control.Monad.IO.Class (liftIO)
import Control.Monad.Trans.Resource
import System.IO

copy_resourcet :: ResIO ()
copy_resourcet = do
    (_, f1) <- allocate (openFile "read.txt" ReadMode) hClose
    (_, f2) <- allocate (openFile "write.txt" WriteMode) hClose
    liftIO $ hGetContents f1 >>= hPutStr f2
```

ResIO is just a synonym for ResourceT I/O. Note that there is less nesting and more monadic binding in this version, which is better for composability. To execute a ResIO, we need to use run ResourceT to convert it into an I/O:

```
main = runResourceT copy_resourcet
```

The first element in return tuple of allocate is of type ReleaseKey. We can use this to deallocate the resource early, using release :: MonadIO m => ReleaseKey → m ().

Bottom line is that ResourceT greatly simplifies composing resource-allocating and -deallocating actions (by adding a monadic allocation interface) and also makes it easy to interleave resource allocation with effects from other monads (by being a transformer).

Streaming with side-effects

Lists are pure, but the streaming property is still useful also in impure I/O settings. Although lazy I/O has its share of problems, it isn't the only streaming I/O technique in Haskell. It's fully possible to use explicit buffers, for example, to read and process iteratively using the low-level functions in `System.IO`. This program uses a pointer to an integer to stream random numbers from `

```
-- file: ptr.hs

import System.IO
import Foreign.Ptr (Ptr)
import Foreign.Storable (Storable(sizeOf, peek))
import Foreign.Marshal (alloca)

main = withBinaryFile "/dev/random" ReadMode $ alloca . process
  where
    process :: Handle -> Ptr Int -> IO ()
    process h ptr = go where
      go = do
          count <- hGetBuf h ptr (sizeOf (undefined :: Int))
          if count > 0
              then do num <- peek ptr
                      print num
                      go
              else return ()
```

As can be seen, this program is pretty verbose. The same program could perhaps be written in C more concisely, and that's because Haskell isn't designed for fiddling with pointers and memory areas – though it's fully possible. Put more favorably, Haskell encourages thinking more (and more) in the abstract.

That's all about Foreign modules for now (we'll meet them again in more depth in the FFI chapter). From now on, we'll focus on streaming abstractions other than lazy I/O, of which there are many.

Choosing a streaming library

Streaming frameworks in Haskell have come a long way along the years, starting with lazy I/O. The problem with lazy I/O is foremost unpredictable resource handling, and that there is little control over when given effects happen precisely, because effects are interleaved with pure code. This allows for elegant code in small scale, but it becomes hard to control effects in larger scale.

In the 00s, work by Oleg Kiselyov initiated a surge of streaming libraries. Some of the first ones published on Hackage were `iteratee`, `enumerator`, and `iterIO` at the turn of 2010. Instead of imperatively using buffers for streaming data, `iteratee`-based I/O abstracts such patterns in composable monadic actions. Unlike lazy I/O, `iteratee` based I/O is strict (in I/O, at least).

Nowadays, the libraries most seen in use with new code include `pipes`, `conduit`, and `io-streams`. `pipes` and `conduit` evolved simultaneously and hence they have a lot of overlap in their feature sets. Later versions of conduit actually featured a heavy internal redesign largely influenced by `pipes`. For those interested in such things, it's worth mentioning that the types and most functions in pipes have been checked using Coq (a theorem proving system) to ensure that the implementation is a law-abiding category.

An unfortunate feature of both `conduit` and `pipes` is their type framework: the types are hard to wrap one's head around even for a seasoned Haskeller. On the other hand, `io-streams` library has its focus on user-friendliness with its simple types (and is restricted to I/O).

Both `pipes` and `conduits` are very flexible, but if you're really sure you need even more control and more abstractions over your streams in the form of networked stream transducers, perhaps you should take a look at the `machines` library by Edward Kmett.

In this section, we'll first introduce `io-streams` and then `pipes` and `conduits`.

Simple streaming using io-streams

The `io-streams` package defines two data types dubbed "smart handles" to represent streams:

```
data InputStream c
data OutputStream c
```

There are exactly three primitive functions on smart handles. They are:

```
read   :: InputStream c → IO (Maybe c)
unRead :: c → InputStream c → IO ()
write  :: Maybe c → OutputStream c → IO ()
```

In other words, we can read elements from an `InputStream` or push items back into an `InputStream`; or we can write an element into an `OutputStream`. A `Nothing` is used to signal end-of-file in both read and write.

This set of three primitives is both powerful and easy to grasp. Though the `io-streams` package provides lots of useful combinators, they're all implemented in terms of the primitives. Using higher-level combinators often makes code more concise, of course, but it isn't mandatory.

Let's see what we can accomplish with `io-streams`. But first: how to construct streams? There are two such functions, one for input and other for output streams:

```
makeInputStream  :: IO (Maybe a)       → IO (InputStream a)
makeOutputStream :: (Maybe a → IO ()) → IO (OutputStream a)
```

Here again, `Nothing` represents end-of-file. New input streams can be built from an IO action that is performed to generate next element and output streams are built from a consuming IO action that takes the input element as argument.

Creating input streams

Now we are ready to build some streams. The first stream we build will be one that generates random numbers. First things first, here are some imports we'll use in this example:

```
-- file: io-streams.hs

import Data.IORef (newIORef, readIORef, writeIORef)
import Control.Monad.IO.Class (liftIO)
import System.Random (randomIO)

import System.IO.Streams (Generator, InputStream, OutputStream)
import qualified System.IO.Streams as S
```

If we were to use `makeInputStream`, we see that there's no built-in way to store state between yielded elements. This means we have to resort to imperative state, such as `IORef`. Here's an implementation of a random stream using an `IORef` to store the count of numbers left to produce:

```
randomInputStreamRef :: Int -> IO (InputStream Double)
randomInputStreamRef count = do
    ref <- newIORef count
    S.makeInputStream $ do
        n <- readIORef ref
        if n <= 0
            then return Nothing
            else do writeIORef ref $! n - 1
                    r <- randomIO
                    return (Just r)
```

Unfortunately, this is quite verbose, but this is Haskell. Surely we could do better, right? Of course! One option is to use the `Generator` monad, which provides a `yield` operation and `MonadIO` instance. This stream is equivalent to our IORef-based stream:

```
randomInputStreamGen :: Int -> IO (InputStream Double)
randomInputStreamGen count = S.fromGenerator (go count)
    where
        go :: Int -> Generator Double ()
        go 0 = return ()
        go n = liftIO randomIO >>= S.yield >> go (n - 1)
```

Or, if it suits your fancy, we could write a stream as an anamorphism, known also as unfold. The relevant `io-stream` combinator is:

```
unfoldM :: (b → IO (Maybe (a, b))) → b → IO (InputStream a)
```

With the `unfoldM` combinator, we get yet another way of expressing a random stream:

```
randomInputStreamAna :: Int -> IO (InputStream Double)
randomInputStreamAna count = S.unfoldM go count
    where
        go 0 = return Nothing
        go n = randomIO >>= \r -> return (Just (r, n - 1))
```

However, note that there is a slight overhead in these abstractions. In a quick and controversial benchmark, I observed that timewise the differences are negligible (with $n = 500, 000$), though some differences in heap usage were observable:

- The Generator-based random stream used about 6% more heap than the IORef-based stream
- The anamorphism/unfold-based stream used about 12% more heap than the IORef-based stream

It isn't strictly necessary to create IO actions that yield next values to create input streams. Input (and output) streams can be generated via various other methods, including:

- From a list: `S.fromList :: [c] → IO (InputStream c)`
- From files (see module `System.IO.Streams.File`)
- From ByteStrings (see module `System.IO.Streams.ByteString`)
- From Vectors (see module `System.IO.Streams.Vector`)
- From Handles (see module `System.IO.Streams.Handle`)

- From Sockets (see module `System.IO.Streams.Network`)
- From output of external processes (see module `System.IO.Streams.Process`)

Using combinators and output streams

The `toList` function can be used to convert any input stream into a list. Testing our random streams, we fire up GHCi:

```
> :load io-streams.hs
> randomInputStreamAna 3 >>= S.toList
> [0.1745076027065504,0.9856406364162231,0.653112050978402]
```

Mapping is a basic stream transformation:

```
> randomInputStreamAna 3 >>= S.map (*10) >>= S.toList
[6.09571320125644,5.815660274344739,0.23496022064959265]
```

With the `fold` function from `io-streams` we can fold over an input stream, producing a single value:

```
> randomInputStreamAna 3 >>= S.fold (+) 0
1.6587768967308916
```

Handling exceptions and resources in streams

Handling exceptions when using `io-streams` is exceptionally simple: just handle them normally in I/O with machinery from `Control.Exception`. It's important to catch exceptions where it makes sense, that is, whether inside a computation of an input stream or an exception from stream creation action (`IO (InputStream a)`).

As an example of the former scenario, catching within a stream computation, we'll create a stream which produces output by performing element-wise division on two input streams. Division by zero is not well defined, so we'll want to omit such results from the output stream. Here's the combinator:

```
-- file: io-streams-exceptions.hs

import Control.Exception
import System.IO.Streams (Generator, InputStream, OutputStream)
import qualified System.IO.Streams as S

divideBy :: InputStream Int -> InputStream Int
        -> IO (InputStream Int)
divideBy as bs = S.makeInputStream go
```

```
    where
      go = do
          ma <- S.read as
          mb <- S.read bs
          case (ma, mb) of
              (Just a, Just b) ->
                  (return $! Just $! div a b)
                  `catch`
                  (const go :: ArithException -> IO (Maybe Int))
              _ -> return Nothing
```

So we read one element from each stream, divide them, and return the result, except when the division raises an exception, which we'll catch and proceed to reading the next two elements, without producing any output yet.

Note that it's important we fully evaluate the result Int on the right-hand side of catch – otherwise the error would propagate to wherever we demand that Int (which can be practically anywhere, or nowhere if it's never needed).

We can test that our stream works correctly with:

```
main = do x <- S.fromList [0..4]
          y <- S.fromList [1,0,0,2]
          divideBy x y >>= S.toList >>= print
```

This prints [0,1].

The other strategy to error handling is to intentionally propagate the error up to what will call read on the stream. In this scenario, it's also important to raise the exception in the IO monad, not deferring it in a yielded thunk. For example, this is not good:

```
> s <- S.makeInputStream (return (Just undefined))
```

Calling read on such a stream won't fail, that is, this won't catch the exception:

```
> S.read s `catch` (\(e::SomeException) -> print "catched" >>
  return Nothing)
Just *** Exception: Prelude.undefined
```

Note that extra care needs to be taken because results are wrapped in Maybe's. Even these won't fail within the yielding computation:

```
S.makeInputStream (return $! Just undefined)
S.makeInputStream (return (Just $! undefined))
```

But this one does fail at first read:

```
S.makeInputStream (return $! Just $! undefined)
```

This demonstration is slightly contrived: as usual with exceptions, it's almost always better to use `throwIO` instead of error/undefined when failing in the IO monad.

What comes to the `Generator` monad? Unfortunately, exceptions cannot be caught there. The most important consequence is that resources should never be allocated in that of the `Generator`. Of course, singular IO actions that both acquire and free resources are excluded from this, as well as IO actions that catch exceptions from within themselves.

An example of parsing using io-streams and attoparsec

As an example of both `io-streams` and the parsing library `attoparsec` for which `io-streams` provide bindings, in this section we'll build a chat log parser that works over streams. The log file format we shall consider looks like:

```
-- file: messages.log

[00:50] <Seneca> It is the power of the mind to be unconquerable
[05:03] <Leibniz> The monad here is nothing but a simple substance
which enters into compounds
=== Erin enters the chat
[00:01] <Erin> Warriors should suffer their pain silently
```

Though the content itself is quite arbitrary, the log file is line-based and on each line there is either a message or a notification. Notifications start with `===`, and messages follow the general format: `[time] <person> message`.

The first thing we'll need (after some imports) is some datatypes to express the content. We write the following:

```haskell
-- file: io-streams-parser.hs

{-# LANGUAGE OverloadedStrings #-}

import Data.Monoid ((<>))
import Control.Applicative ((<|>))
import Data.ByteString (ByteString)
import Data.Attoparsec.ByteString.Char8 as PC8

import System.IO.Streams (Generator, InputStream, OutputStream)
import qualified System.IO.Streams as S
import System.IO.Streams.File (withFileAsInput)
```

```
import System.IO.Streams.Attoparsec (parserToInputStream)

data Line = Notification ByteString
          | Message Time User ByteString deriving Show

type Time = ByteString
type User = ByteString
```

Self-explanatory so far! Now for the parser, or parsers. We'll start with simple ones: parsers for timestamps and persons or users. Using applicative syntax, we can write these concisely as:

```
timeParser :: Parser Time
timeParser = char '[' *> takeWhile1 (/= ']') <* char ']'
    <* PC8.takeWhile (== ' ')

userParser :: Parser User
userParser = char '<' *> takeWhile1 (/= '>') <* char '>'
    <* PC8.takeWhile (== ' ')
```

The (p *> q) combinator simply applies parser p, discards its results, and proceeds to apply parser q. The (<*) combinator is like (*>) but takes results only from the first argument instead. The parser primitives char and takeWhile come from the attoparsec library. Both (*>) and (<*) are infixl, meaning they associate to the left and so the whole parser can be read from left to right. The final result is where a (*>) is followed by a (<*).

Parser for a line is slightly more involved:

```
lineParser, messageParser, notificationParser :: Parser Line

lineParser = messageParser <|> notificationParser

notificationParser = string "=== "
    *> (Notification <$> PC8.takeWhile (/= '\n'))

messageParser = Message <$> timeParser
                        <*> userParser
                        <*> PC8.takeWhile (/= '\n')
```

The (p <|> q) combinator tries to apply parser p, and if it fails, proceeds with q.

We can verify that our parsers work, in GHCi:

```
> :load io-streams-parser.hs

> > parseOnly lineParser "[time] <user> a message"
```

```
Right (Message "time" "user" "a message")

> parseOnly lineParser "=== notification"
Right (Notification "notification")
```

Now that we have our parser, we should hook it up into a stream. The input stream we'll be using comes from a file. Our output stream will print messages into standard output, discarding everything else.

As is customary in `io-streams`, Nothing values represent end-of-file. So we need one last parser. One that tries reading a next line, returning nothing when reaching the end-of-file:

```
logParser :: Parser (Maybe Line)
logParser = (endOfInput *> pure Nothing) <|>
    (fmap Just lineParser <* PC8.takeWhile (== '\n'))
```

Then the output stream: this time, we'll use the `OutputStream` type and some funny operators:

```
lineOutputStream :: IO (OutputStream Line)
lineOutputStream = S.contramapMaybe f =<< S.ignoreEof S.stdout
  where
    f (Message _ _ msg) = Just (msg <> "\n")
    f _                 = Nothing
```

The two funny operators here are `S.contramapMaybe` and `S.ignoreEof`. The first one maps a function (`f`) over the values before feeding them into the output stream, discarding Nothings (like `mapMaybe` from `Data.Maybe`). The `S.ignoreEof` on `S.stdout` prevents `io-streams` from closing standard output when a `Nothing` is encountered. Normally `io-streams` closes Handles in output streams when a `Nothing` is encountered in the stream.

Now we can write the main program itself:

```
main = withFileAsInput "messages.log" $ \is -> do
    lines <- parserToInputStream logParser is
    outs <- lineOutputStream
    S.connect lines outs
```

The `parserToInputStream` function builds an input stream from repeatedly applying our `logParser` parser. The `S.connect` is a utility function which combines an input stream with an output stream. We can confirm our program does what we intended:

```
> :load io-streams-parser.hs
> main
```

```
It is the power of the mind to be unconquerable
The monad here is nothing but a simple substance which enters into
compounds
Warriors should suffer their pain silently
```

Streaming using pipes

The next streaming library we'll consider is `pipes`. Now we have only one stream type compared to two types in `io-streams`, but that is a considerably more complicated type:

```
data Proxy a' a b' b m r
```

Now skim your eyes for a while and unsee `a'` and `b'`. Then `Proxy` would be something that takes in values of type `a` and produces output values of another type `b` while performing effects in some monad `m`. The `r` type variable is just the result type of the monad.

The `a'` and `b'` exist for bidirectional communication along pipelines and aren't often needed. For convenience, `pipes` provides some type synonyms that simplify pipes types a lot. Three most used of those are:

```
type Producer' b m r
type Consumer' a m r
type Pipe a b m r
```

`Type` variables correspond to variables in `Proxy`. Omitted type variables are not relevant here now.

The primitives in (unidirectional) pipes are reduced to two, contrary to three, for `io-streams`. They're called `await` and `yield`:

```
await :: Monad m => Consumer' a m a
yield :: Monad m => b -> Producer' b m ()
```

The types actually tell precisely what these functions do. `await` returns a value that was yielded from the input-side of a pipe in the monad (the first and last type variables are unified). `yield` takes as argument a value of type that is unified with the output-side's type and passes it forward in the stream.

We can say that consumers await whereas producers yield. Now note that `Pipe` is a strictly more general type than consumers or producers. So pipes can both `yield` and `await`.

Here is one example of each, producer, consumer and pipe:

```
-- file: pipes.hs

import Control.Monad
import System.Random (randomIO)
import Pipes

randoms :: Producer' Int IO ()
randoms = forever (liftIO randomIO >>= yield)

taking :: Monad m => Int -> Pipe a a m ()
taking 0 = return ()
taking n = await >>= yield >> taking (n - 1)

printing :: Show a => Consumer' a IO ()
printing = forever (await >>= liftIO . print)
```

Composing and executing pipes

There's one more type synonym of `Proxy` we'll need to introduce. It's a pipe that neither yields nor awaits, called `Effect`:

```
type Effect' m r
```

We need this to understand how to execute `pipes`. The relevant function is:

```
runEffect :: Monad m => Effect m r → m r
```

Combining a producer with a consumer using the (`>->`) operator yields an `Effect`. Here's an `effect` combining our previous examples:

```
effect :: Effect IO ()
effect = randoms >-> taking 5 >-> printing
```

We can run this `effect` with `runEffect`:

```
> :load pipes.hs
> runEffect effect
4486626397489119841
571690255473717323
-8556621642364119471
-1668223325432668307
-4935317933637218898
```

For loops and category theory in pipes

The (>->) combinator is really more general than this and works with almost any two instances of Proxy:

```
(>->)
  :: Monad m =>
     Proxy a' a () b m r
  -> Proxy () b c' c m r -> Proxy a' a c' c m r
```

This looks really similar to normal function composition, (.), if we just forget about other type variables than a, b, and c:

```
(.) :: (b → c) → (a → b) → (a → c)
```

Indeed, (>->) even forms a category with the identity pipe cat, like (.) forms a category with the identity function id. A category must satisfy the category laws, identity, and associativity:

```
     id . f = f                cat >-> f = f
     f . id = f                f >-> cat = f
(f . g) . h = f . (g . h)   (f >-> g) >-> h = f >-> (g >-> h)
```

This is relevant mostly because pipes draw its elegance from category theory. Though by no means is it required from the programmer using the library to know category theory.

pipes provides a combinator for, which can be used to transform producers:

```
randomsPositive :: Producer' Int IO ()
randomsPositive = for randoms (\r → when (r > 0) (yield r))
```

There's also a synonym for for: (~>). for too forms a category, with yield as the identity.

```
randoms ~> (\r → when (r > 0) (yield r))
```

Then we have the (>~) combinator. Note the symmetry with (~>). Whereas (~>) transformed yields, (>~) transforms awaits. It's useful to supply the same expression to a consumer:

```
> runEffect $ lift getLine >~ taking 5 >-> printing
```

(>~) forms a category together with await.

Handling exceptions in pipes

Similar to `io-streams`, it isn't possible to catch exceptions in a Proxy. However, `pipes` is polymorphic in the base (m) monad, so within a lifted computation, exceptions can be caught even "outside" IO if using `lifted-base`. If the base monad is IO, then normal machinery from the `exceptions` package would be sufficient to catch exceptions.

A useful idiom is to wrap the lifted computation in a `try`, effectively "lifting" the exception to the pipeline as an `Either`:

```
-- file: pipes-exceptions.hs

import Control.Exception
import Pipes
import GHC.IO.Exception (IOException(..))

tolerantStdinLn :: Producer' String IO ()
tolerantStdinLn = do
    x <- lift $ try readLn
    case x of
        Left e@IOError{} -> return ()
        Right ln -> yield ln >> tolerantStdinLn
```

Strengths and weaknesses of pipes

The `pipes` philosophy is pretty much elegance first, as we have witnessed in its category-theory-inspired operators. There's also one relatively new feature in `pipes` that we haven't touched (and won't): bidirectional flow. This is related to the additional type variables in the Proxy type. With bidirectional flow, `pipes` admits for `generator` and `iteratee` design patterns, making requests and responses in addition to normal data flow.

Unlike `io-streams` that worked over IO, `pipes` works over arbitrary monads, which is definitely a plus. However, exceptions must be caught within computations in the inner monad. For one, in `io-streams`, we could resume a stream from where it left after handling exceptions raised from a stream, but with `pipes`, it isn't possible to resume a pipeline. On the other hand, `pipes` is declarative and doesn't require an IO action to build a pipeline.

Streaming using conduits

Starting with conduit version 1.0.0.0, the core library design is just like that of the `pipes` Proxy type with bidirectional flow removed. The core conduit type is called `ConduitM`:

```
data ConduitM i o m r
```

What comes to conduit's type synonyms compared to pipes synonyms: producers are now sources, pipes are conduits and consumers are sinks:

```
type Source    m o
type Conduit i m o
type Sink      i m   r
```

The operator that chains conduits together is (`=$=`). The (`$$`) operator connects source with sink, evaluating the conduit, along with side-effects:

```
(=$=) :: Monad m
      => Conduit a m b → ConduitM b c m r → ConduitM a c m r
($$)  :: Monad m
      => Source m a → Sink a m b → m b
```

There's considerably less noise in conduit type signatures because of the absence of bidirectional flow.

 In conduit versions before 1.0.0.0, there were different datatypes for sources, conduits, and sinks. In this design, two more operators were needed for connecting ((`$=`) and (`=$`)). These are no longer necessary.

Here's a simple conduit program. This implements the exact same randoms program from the `pipes` section:

```
-- file conduit.hs

import Control.Monad
import Control.Monad.IO.Class (liftIO)
import Data.Conduit
import System.Random (randomIO)

randoms :: Source IO Int
randoms = forever (liftIO randomIO >>= yield)

taking :: Monad m => Int -> Conduit a m a
taking 0 = return ()
taking n = do x <- await
```

```
                 case x of
                     Nothing -> return ()
                     Just y -> yield y >> taking (n - 1)

printing :: Show a => Sink a IO ()
printing = do x <- await
                 case x of
                     Nothing -> return ()
                     Just y -> liftIO (print y) >> printing

main :: IO ()
main = randoms =$= taking 5 $$ printing
```

This is substantially longer because the `await` primitive of conduits returns its result wrapped in `Maybe`, as in `io-streams`. Instead of writing every conduit program with the primitives, it is best practice to utilize functions from additional `conduit` modules (and libraries) beyond `Data.Conduit`, such as the following:

- `Data.Conduit.List` (conduit) provides list-like combinators for conduits
- `Data.Conduit.Combinators` (conduit-combinators) replaces the functionality of `Data.Conduit.List` and enforces conduit best practices
- The `conduit-extra` package provides additional modules for textual and binary data, parsing, and so on, similar to `io-streams`
- `Conduit` (conduit-combinators) is a convenience module which re-exports lots of useful conduit-related machinery

Handling resources and exceptions in conduits

The main advantage of `conduits` over `pipes` is that handling resources and exceptions is built into the `ConduitM` type.

Resource handling is generalized via ResourceT. This instance allows us to use ResourceT machinery within any conduit whose inner monad allows it to:

```
instance MonadResource m => MonadResource (ConduitM i o m)
```

Exception handling is lifted to conduits using the extensible `extensions` library:

```
instance MonadThrow m => MonadThrow (ConduitM i o m)
instance MonadCatch m => MonadCatch (ConduitM i o m)
```

With `conduits`, we have combinators such as bracket lifted to `conduits`:

```
bracketP :: MonadResource m
    => IO a → (a → IO ()) → (a → ConduitM i o m r)
    → ConduitM i o m r
```

And also `catch` lifted to `conduits`:

```
catchC :: (MonadBaseControl IO m, Exception e)
    => ConduitM i o m r → (e → ConduitM i o m r) → ConduitM i o m r
```

Resuming conduits

It is possible to feed some source into a sink, using the ($$+), process, until the sink has finished and then save the source at where it left, turning `Source` into a `ResumableSource`. `ResumableSources` can be passed around freely and used almost like normal sources later with ($$++):

```
($$+)  :: Monad m
        => Source m a -> Sink a m b
        -> m (ResumableSource m a, b)

($$++) :: Monad m
        => ResumableSource m a -> Sink a m b
        -> m (ResumableSource m a, b)
```

For an example, consider this `Source` which yields consecutive numbers from zero:

```
counter :: Source IO Int
counter = go 0
  where go n = yield n >> go (n + 1)
```

With ResumableSources, we can use this as a source of unique identifiers, for example. Here's an illustrating GHCi session:

```
> (resume,_) <- counter $$+ taking 5 =$= printing
0
1
2
3
4
> resume $$++ taking 3 =$= printing
5
6
7
```

ResumableSources can also be converted into normal sources with `unwrapResumable`. ResumableSources give us back the nice feature that was built into `io-streams` and that was lost in pipes, namely first-class streams. But one thing is still missing which is related to exceptions.

When an exception was raised inside an `io-stream` stream, it would propagate upward, but leave the stream in the state it was at before raising the exception. To copy this behavior in conduits, we would catch exceptions in `conduit/sink` and end computation. Then, as the pipeline stops accepting input, use (`$$+`) to convert the source into an `ResumableStream`.

Logging in Haskell

A final thing we'll consider is more related to I/O than streaming: logging in Haskell applications. Logging is important in any sufficiently important application.

In a small scale, a list- or DList-based `WriterT` monad is often all that is needed: it's simple and potentially pure (if the underlying monad is pure). However, on a bigger scale it doesn't make sense to store messages in an internal pure data structure. Instead, it's most efficient to write them to disk (or over a network) immediately (likely still using a buffer, though).

Furthermore, it would be nice if the logging functionality could be decoupled from other application code, even reused between different applications.

A popular solution which provides just that kind of decoupling is the `monad-logger` library. It uses a library called `Fastlogger`, which provides logging that scales in multicore environments. Most notoriously, `FastLogger` is used in the **Web Application Interface (WAI)** package used by many high-performance Haskell web frameworks and applications.

Logging with FastLogger

The core datatype in `FastLogger` is `LoggerSet`, whose constructors are not exposed. Internally, it holds multiple loggers, one for each OS thread (`-N<x>`). A `LoggerSet` is built with one of the smart constructors:

```
newFileLoggerSet   :: BufSize -> FilePath -> IO LoggerSet
newStdoutLoggerSet :: BufSize -> IO LoggerSet
newStderrLoggerSet :: BufSize -> IO LoggerSet
```

Log messages are written to that of a `LoggerSet` using `pushLogStr(Ln)`:

```
pushLogStr :: LoggerSet → LogStr → IO ()
```

The `LogStr` datatype is also abstract (constructors not exposed). `LogStr` construction is overloaded via type class `ToLogStr`, provided with default instances for textual data:

```
class ToLogStr msg where
     toLogStr :: msg → LogStr

instance ToLogStr String
instance ToLogStr ByteString
instance ToLogStr Text
instance toLogStr LogStr
```

Here's a GHCi session to demonstrate usage:

```
> import System.Log.FastLogger
> logger <- newStdoutLoggerSet defaultBufSize
> pushLogStr logger (toLogStr "a log message")
a log message
```

It's encouraged to create your own log message datatype and write custom instances for `ToLogStr` (inductively utilizing existing instances). For performance reasons, it's better to specialize your logging functions to avoid `ToLogStr` dictionary-passing, as in `pushLogStr`.

Note that `FastLogger` provides the bare minimum needed for efficient logging: monomorphic file and stream loggers and a simple overloaded interface for building log messages. On top of this, it's easy to build other mechanisms, such as custom log messages and logging functions.

More abstract loggers

Version 2.4.4 of `FastLogger` had some new functionality. Among others, a new type alias was introduced: when we partially apply `pushLogStr` with a `LoggerSet`, we get the extremely simple yet powerful `FastLogger` function:

```
type FastLogger = LogStr → IO ()
```

Now, instead of using `LoggerSet`s directly, we can step up abstractions one notch. The `withFastLogger` function takes an argument of type `LogType`, with which we can build many kinds of loggers:

```
withFastLogger :: LogType → IO (FastLogger → IO a) → IO a
```

This function takes care of closing the `LoggerSet` correctly, so you don't need to worry about leaking loggers. The second argument is a callback which can make use of the logger function. The different constructors of `LogType` initialize different kinds of loggers. In addition to `stdout`, `stderr`, and file logging, it becomes trivial to create file-rotating loggers:

```
data LogType
  = LogNone
  | LogStdout BufSize
  | LogStderr BufSize
  | LogFileNoRotate FilePath BufSize
  | LogFile FileLogSpec BufSize
  | LogCallback FastLogger (IO ())
```

Timed log messages

It's often very useful to have timestamps in log messages. However, in high-performance applications with high-frequency logging, date rendering becomes a bottleneck, unless we cache rendered dates. Fortunately, `FastLogger` (versions later than 2.4.4) comes with a solution for date caching that only renders dates at most once per second. Timed `FastLoggers` have the type:

```
type TimedFastLogger = (FormattedTime → LogStr) → IO ()
```

Timed loggers are created with the `withTimedFastLogger` function:

```
withTimedFastLogger
  :: IO FormattedTime -> LogType -> (TimedFastLogger -> IO a) ->
     IO a
```

The first argument requires an IO action to return formatted time (ByteString), which we should build with `newTimeCache`:

```
newTimeCache :: TimeFormat -> IO (IO FormattedTime)
```

Just an IO action within an IO action. This is used as in:

```
> getTimeStamp <- newTimeCache "%Y-%m-%d %H:%M"
> getTimeStamp
"2016-05-11 15:02"
```

To attach timestamps into log messages, we need a log function which formats the timestamp. Here's one for logging events of type `String`:

```
logFormat :: String -> FormattedTime -> LogStr
logFormat msg time = toLogStr time <> ": " <> toLogStr msg
```

Now let's put everything together into a complete program that logs something nonsensical (yet true). Let's try a top to bottom approach. We wish to write log messages with a simple IO action taking only our log message (String) as its argument. This is easily expressed as:

```
-- file: fastlogger.hs
{-# LANGUAGE OverloadedStrings #-}

import Data.Monoid
import System.Log.FastLogger

type MyLogger = String -> IO ()

app :: MyLogger -> IO ()
app log = do
    log "Haskell is fun"
    log "and logging is fun too!"
```

Now we only need the `main` that executes our application, supplying it with an appropriate logger. There is nothing new in the function body that follows – I have just combined everything we discussed so far about (timed) logging and formatting:

```
main = do
    getTimeStamp <- newTimeCache "%Y-%m-%d %H:%M"
    withTimedFastLogger getTimeStamp (LogStdout defaultBufSize) $
        \logger -> app (logger . logFormat)

logFormat :: String -> FormattedTime -> LogStr
logFormat msg time = toLogStr time <> ": " <> toLogStr msg <> "\n"
```

Just to confirm everything works as it should:

```
> :load fastlogger.hs
[1 of 1] Compiling Main                ( fastlogger.hs, interpreted )
Ok, modules loaded: Main.
> main
2016-05-11 16:20: Haskell is fun
2016-05-11 16:20: and logging is fun too!
```

So what did we gain from using `FastLogger`? We wrote about four lines, but in those four lines we got all these:

- Timestamped log messages with a timestamp cache.
- Custom timestamp and log message formatting.

- Completely decoupled setup and configuration of logging from the application code.
- If you wanted to, the log function could be hidden in a Reader monad and write a log action, thus eliminating the need to pass the log function around. In fact, this pattern is already captured in the monad-logger library.

Monadic logging

In MonadLogger, logging functions are polymorphic in the MonadLogger class. You can either define an instance for your application monad, or use the add-on LoggingT transformer:

```
class Monad m => MonadLogger m where
    monadLoggerLog :: ToLogStr msg => Loc → LogSource → LogLevel

instance MonadIO m => MonadLogger (LoggingT m)
[...]
```

Instances for transformer stacks from mtl/transformers, conduits, and pipes are also provided out of the box for MonadLogger.

Here's an example monadic logger program, that does nothing else but logs 500,000 lines (for no particular reason):

```
-- file: logging-t.hs

{-# LANGUAGE TemplateHaskell #-}

import Data.Text (pack)
import Control.Monad
import Control.Monad.Logger

app :: LoggingT IO ()
app = replicateM_ 500000 ($(logInfo) (pack "msg"))

main = runStdoutLoggingT app
```

See that, with help from LoggingT, we got rid of a lot more boiler-plate than with using **fast-logger**. What's nice is that we actually got a new feature: the template Haskell function $(logInfo) logs the code file and line number the log message originated from! This is very valuable in debugging.

Customizing monadic loggers

If the default log message format of `MonadLogger` is not enough, it is fully customizable via the `monadLoggerLog` class method. As an illustration, let's add timestamps to our log messages using monadic logging. `MonadLogger` really works only with monads, so we need to create one. Actually, let's make one from scratch: we only need access to a logger function in our monad, so this `App` monad will suffice:

```
-- file: monadlogger.hs
{-# LANGUAGE OverloadedStrings #-}
{-# LANGUAGE DeriveFunctor #-}

import Control.Monad.Logger
import Data.Monoid
import System.Log.FastLogger

type MyLogger = LogStr -> IO ()

newtype App a = App { unApp :: MyLogger -> IO a }
              deriving (Functor)
```

This will actually turn out to be an exercise in writing `Functor-Applicative-Monad` instances (neither `Applicative` nor `Monad` can be derived in this case). If you'd like a challenge, try writing the instances yourself now! Or just read on:

```
instance Applicative App where
    pure x = App $ \_ -> pure x
    App f <*> (App g) = App $ \log -> f log <*> g log

instance Monad App where
    App f >>= g = App $ \log -> do r <- f log
                                   unApp (g r) log
```

Now, we're not really interested in source file positions in our log messages, because it simplifies the `MonadLogger` instance a bit, as can be seen:

```
instance MonadLogger App where
    monadLoggerLog _ _ _ msg = App $ \log -> log (toLogStr msg)
```

Now we need a test application and a `main` (and a timestamped log message formatting function). With slight alterations, we reuse those we defined in our FastLogger example:

```
app :: App ()
app = do
```

```
        logInfoN "Haskell is fun"
        logInfoN "and logging is fun too!"

    logFormat :: LogStr -> FormattedTime -> LogStr
    logFormat msg time = toLogStr time <> ": " <> msg <> "\n"

    main = do
        getTimeStamp <- newTimeCache "%Y-%M-%d %H:%m"
        withTimedFastLogger getTimeStamp (LogStdout defaultBufSize) $
            \logger -> unApp app (logger . LogFormat)
```

All that is left to do is testing, so here we go:

```
> :load monadlogger.hs
[1 of 1] Compiling Main    ( monadlogger.hs, interpreted )
Ok, modules loaded: Main.

> main
2016-05-11 16:10: Haskell is fun
2016-05-11 16:10: and logging is fun too!
```

Now we can conclude our application does what we expected it to do. Logging in Haskell is indeed fun and easy.

Summary

In this chapter we have covered the advantages and disadvantages of lazy I/O and its alternatives: strict I/O and some streaming solutions. We learned to connect to remote network endpoints as clients and to write own network servers in Haskell. We also learned that acquired I/O resources such as handles and sockets must always be freed. For this, we considered two main solutions: functions such as `bracket` and the `ResourceT` monad transformer.

After reading this chapter you should now understand and be able to use lazy I/O without surprising memory leaks and correctly release all acquired resources as well as exceptions. You know and can use three streaming libraries: rudimentary `io-streams`, elegant `pipes`, and industrial `conduits`. You are also bound to enjoy doing logging from your Haskell programs with FastLogger and monads with `monad-logger`.

In the next chapter, we will focus on concurrent programming in Haskell. Light-Lightweight GHC threads give a lot of flexibility for the concurrent programmer, and software transactional memory provides an easy-to-use framework for handling critical sections in a more abstract fashion.

7
Concurrency and Performance

Writing concurrent programs that are correct is hard: subtle race conditions, resources blocked by another thread, asynchronous exceptions, and so on. Basically, a lot can go wrong. Remember that, whereas parallelism points to execution model (multiple threads running simultaneously), concurrency is more like a paradigm: multiple threads working together, intertwined. However, concurrent threads are often run in parallel for responsiveness and performance reasons.

In this chapter, we will write concurrent Haskell programs making use of light-weight threads and type-safe concurrency primitives like **MVars**. For complex programs, we will learn to build atomic transactions with **Software Transactional Memory (STM)**.

We will consider some models for concurrent programming: asynchronous workers and actors. And although asynchronous exceptions are usually to be avoided (like those from calls to error/undefined), asynchronous exceptions are useful for notifying one thread from another. Finally, we'll look at working with lifted concurrency operations to other monads besides IO, which can be extremely convenient sometimes.

We will cover:

- Becoming familiar with light-weight threads, primitive concurrency functions, and mutable variables
- Building complex atomic transactions using Software Transactional Memory
- Using the Async API for concise asynchronous processing
- Lifting concurrency operations and exception handling using `MonadBase` and `MonadBaseControl`

Threads and concurrency primitives

One of the basic forms of concurrent programming involves sharing read-write data between threads. Usually data is shared via references. From fastest to most flexible, the three types of mutable references in Haskell are IORef, MVar, and STM. All three can be used, at least to some extent, in a thread-safe manner. We start our concurrent journey with a simple reference, IORef, and work our way to arbitrarily complex transactions using STM.

Threads and mutable references

The most basic reference type in Haskell is IORef. The core IORef API is compact, one datatype and a few atomic operations:

```
module Data.IORef

data IORef a

newIORef :: a → IO (IORef a)
readIORef :: IORef a → IO a
writeIORef :: IORef a → a → IO ()
modifyIORef :: IORef a → (a → a) → IO ()
atomicModifyIORef :: IORef a → (a → (a, b)) → IO b
```

IORef is always *full*, that is, there is always a value to be read without blocking. They're just simple mutable references. IORef is very fast. They're the fastest option when all you need is a single mutable reference and no locking. If you need more complexity than that, you shouldn't be using an IORef.

Now that we have shared memory (IORef), we need ways to program interleaved threads that can use the shared memory. The most important module for working with threads in Haskell is Control.Concurrent, and the most important function is forkIO:

```
forkIO :: IO () → IO ThreadId
```

A thread is simply an IO () action, like the main program is an IO (). With forkIO, we can make any IO () execute in its own thread. Calls to forkIO return immediately and give us a ThreadID that identifies the newly forked thread.

The following program illustrates forking and mutable references. It prints multiple instances of a and b in some order for a split second:

```
-- ioref.hs

import Data.IORef
```

```
import Control.Concurrent

fun ref c = do
    x <- readIORef ref
    writeIORef ref c
    putStr x
    fun ref c

main = do
    ref <- newIORef "a"
    forkIO $ fun ref "a"
    forkIO $ fun ref "b"
    threadDelay 5000
```

We can run this via `runhaskell ioref.hs`. The output pattern looks like
`aababababababa` and so on and is around 200 characters long. Note carefully that we
didn't bother killing the child threads; in Haskell, when the main thread exits, all
child threads will die too. However, we did use `threadDelay`, which blocks the
current thread for a given number of microseconds.

While our program was multi-threaded, we were actually running it in a single
Operating System (OS) thread. The single-threaded Runtime System always uses
just one OS thread, but features a scheduler of its own for light-weight threads.

Light-weight threads are cheaper than OS threads: a smaller memory footprint, very
cheap to create and destroy, and they share the same heap objects with other light-
weight threads in the same Haskell program.

Actually `runhaskell` didn't bother compiling our program, but merely interpreted
it. If we compile the program and run the compiled version, still in a single
OS thread, the output would look like `abaaaaaaaaaaaaaaa...`, with the `b` thread
sometimes not getting a second chance to execute at all within the split second.

In a compiled single-threaded program, the runtime tries to avoid excess context-
switching. The interpreted version executed more like one step at a time, using a
different scheduler. Because of this, it is often insufficient to test concurrent programs
only interactively (in GHCi or via `runhaskell`), because scheduler semantics are
different to compiled programs.

Avoid accumulating thunks

Even mutable references are not safe from the unfortunate consequences of lazy evaluation; it's deceptively easy to accidentally accumulate a big chain of unreferenced thunks in an `IORef`, because `modifyIORef` is not strict in its second argument. A classic example is using `IORef` as a counter:

```
import Control.Monad (replicateM_)
import Data.IORef

main = do
    counter <- newIORef 0
    replicateM_ 10000000 (modifyIORef counter (+1))
    print =<< readIORef counter
```

This will probably finish cleanly, but requires almost 1 gigabyte of memory.

It's up to you to ensure that you don't leak memory in values you write into `IORef`. Depending on the datatype, if evaluation to Weak Head Normal Form is enough then the strict version of `modifyIORef`, `modifyIORef'`, is a clean and concise option.

Atomic operations with IORefs

All of the operations for `IORef` are atomic as such, but it's hard if not impossible to make combinations of atomic operations on IORefs remain atomic. One atomic operation on IORefs, however, provides a little more flexibility than others:

```
atomicModifyIORef :: IORef a → (a → (a, b)) → IO b
```

Essentially, `atomicModifyIORef` allows us to read the value of an `IORef` and write a new value based on the old value, ensuring that no other thread could read or write the value in between. A strict variant is also available: `atomicModifyIORef'`.

An example use case would be a unique identifier supply. When drawing a new identifier from a `IORef Int`, we need to fetch the current one and then atomically update the supply. The `newUID` function below is thread-safe:

```
-- file: ioref-supply.hs

import Data.IORef

type Supply = IORef Int

createSupply :: IO Supply
createSupply = newIORef 0

newUID :: Supply -> IO Int
newUID supply = atomicModifyIORef' supply $ \uid -> (uid + 1, uid)
```

This is about as far as we can reasonably get atomically using plain `IORef`. Next we'll look at a more practical concurrency primitive, `MVar`.

MVar

Mvar is a box that may be full or empty. It supports the atomic operations `takeMVar` and `putMVar`, which empty and fill the box, respectively. The core API is referenced here. Many utility functions are omitted:

```
module Control.Concurrent.MVar

data MVar a

newMVar :: a → IO (MVar a)
takeMVar :: MVar a → IO a
putMVar :: MVar a → a → IO ()
```

MVar is slightly slower than IORef, but more flexible. For instance, it's trivial to reserve a shared resource to be used only by one thread at a time:

```
-- file: mvar-reserve.hs

import Control.Exception (bracket)
import Control.Concurrent (forkIO)
import Control.Concurrent.MVar

printing lock str =
    bracket (takeMVar lock)(\i -> putMVar lock $! i+1)(\_ -> print
str)

main = do
    lock <- newMVar () :: IO (MVar ())
    forkIO $ printing lock "output a"
    forkIO $ printing lock "output b"
    forkIO $ printing lock "output c"
    takeMVar lock >>= print
```

The preceding program prints three lines from three different threads and finally outputs the number of printed lines. By taking the contents lock `MVar` each time before printing, and putting something back after each `print`, we ensure that printing is never inlined:

```
"output a"
"output b"
"output c"
4
```

Without the lock, we would very likely witness output like:

```
"outpu"t"o ouaut"tp
puutt bc""
```

Notice that we used `bracket` to ensure that we don't reserve the lock indefinitely in case an exception is thrown. This function takes three arguments. The first argument acquires a resource (`takeMVar`), the second releases it (`putMVar`) and the third does something with the resource between acquire and release. `bracket` ensures that the resource is released if an exception is raised.

The Runtime System is smart enough that, in simple cases, it can recognize when the program is waiting indefinitely and kill the thread with a thread blocked indefinitely in an `MVar` operation exception. But if you have many threads, it is possible to deadlock your program with an empty `MVar`. Also a full `MVar` can block, because `putMVar` will wait until the `MVar` is empty before filling it.

Like `IORef`, `MVar` is lazy in its contents and it's important to ensure that no thunk chain in an `MVar` clutters the heap of your program.

MVars are fair

`MVar` has some nice properties. For instance, it's guaranteed that when multiple threads are sleeping, blocked on same `MVar`, none of the threads can be blocked indefinitely. In practice, the threads are woken up in the order they are blocked. The wakeup and taking of the `MVar` is a single atomic operation.

Another feature of `MVar` is that it's not susceptible to reordering by the underlying processor architecture; for `IORef`, it's possible that reads get moved to be performed before writes:

```
writeIORef ref1 True
x <- readIORef ref2
```

These lines would probably get swapped around on an x86 system, where loads (read) can move ahead of stores (write). This is problematic when references are used from multiple threads. `MVar` is thus a more suitable synchronization primitive than `IORef`.

For what it's worth, the `atomicModifyIORef` and `atomicWriteIORef` operations resist described reordering.

MVar as a building block

Many concurrent data structures in base and elsewhere use MVar as their building blocks. For instance, semaphores (Control.Concurrent.QSem) and channels (Control.Concurrent.Chan) are built with MVars.

Building your own data structures with MVar isn't hard. Let's build an unbounded FIFO queue with non-blocking enqueue and dequeue operations. This is like the Chan type in Control.Concurrent.Chan, but more inefficient.

We'll represent our FIFO as two lists. The first list represents the head of the queue, with the head element being the next element to read. The second list represents the tail of the queue, the head element being the newest enqueued element:

```
ioref-counter.hs
-- file: mvar-queue.hs

import Control.Concurrent.MVar

data Queue a = Queue (MVar [a]) (MVar [a])

newQueue :: IO (Queue a)
newQueue = Queue <$> newMVar [] <*> newMVar []
```

The enqueue operation is straightforward: we just need to cons (:) an element to the second list:

```
enqueue :: Queue a -> a -> IO ()
enqueue (Queue _ ys_var) x = modifyMVar_ ys_var (return . (x :))
```

I've used the modifyMVar_ utility function, which puts the original contents back to the MVar in the case of an exception:

```
modifyMVar_ :: MVar a → (a → IO a) → IO ()
```

We can also return a result with the modifyMVar function, which we'll use shortly too:

```
modifyMVar :: MVar a → (a → IO (a, b)) → IO b
```

Dequeueing is more complex. Now we uncons the first list. If that list is empty, we need to reverse the second list and insert it into the first list, at the same time emptying the second list. In the code, we have:

```
dequeue :: Queue a -> IO (Maybe a)
dequeue (Queue xs_var ys_var) = modifyMVar xs_var $ \xs_q ->
    case xs_q of
        x : xs -> return (xs, Just x)
         [] -> modifyMVar ys_var $ \ys_q ->
```

```
return $ case reverse ys_q of
    [] -> ([], ([], Nothing))
    x : xs -> ([], (xs, Just x))
```

Usually we only take the first MVar. If we need to reverse the tail, we take the second list too, momentarily locking both MVars.

We can now witness that our queue works as it should:

```
> q <- newQueue :: IO (Queue Int)
> enqueue q 1
> enqueue q 2
> enqueue q 3
> enqueue q 4
> dequeue q
Just 1
> dequeue q
Just 2
> dequeue q
Just 3
> dequeue q
Just 4
> dequeue q
Nothing
```

A better FIFO implementation is already provided by the Control.Concurrent. Chan module, which also supports channel duplication. Next we'll have multiple actors reading and writing from each other via a broadcast channel.

Broadcasting with Chan

The Chan datatype resembles our queue a lot. The core API is:

```
module Control.Concurrent.Chan

data Chan a

newChan :: IO (Chan a)
writeChan :: Chan a → a → IO ()
readChan :: Chan a → IO a
dupChan :: Chan a → IO (Chan a)
```

The only addition is dupChan, which creates a copy of the channel such that reads and writes to either the original or the copy appear in both. The duplicated channel starts empty, though.

The `client` function that follows takes its integer identifier and a read-and-write channel. It responds to messages of the form `request <myid>` with a `response <myid>` in the same channel:

```
-- file: chan-actors.hs

import Control.Monad
import Control.Concurrent
import Control.Concurrent.Chan

client :: Int -> Chan String -> IO ()
client i chan = go where
    go = do input <- readChan chan
            if input == ("request " ++ show i)
                then writeChan chan ("response " ++ show i)
                else return ()
            go
```

The following `main`, written compactly with monad utility functions, forks three clients with different identifiers. A single channel is duplicated for each client, so that every client receives all messages:

```
main = do
    chan <- newChan
    chans <- replicateM 3 (dupChan chan)
    zipWithM_ (\i c -> forkIO $ client i c) [1..] chans

    forM_ [1..3] $ writeChan chan . ("request " ++) . show
    getChanContents chan >>= mapM_ print . filter (isPrefixOf
"response")
```

The `getChanContents` function turns the channel contents into a lazy streaming list. Unlike `hGetContents`, which returns a finite list when the file handle returns EOF, `getChanContents` builds a really infinite list. When we run this program, we see the following output:

```
"response 1"
"response 3"
"response 2"
chan-actors: thread blocked indefinitely in an MVar operation
```

The "thread blocked indefinitely in an `MVar` operation" exception above comes from one of the client threads. The Runtime System detects that after call to `getChanContents`, all threads are waiting on the same `Chan` and throws anexception. It isn't possible to close a `Chan`; it will remain open forever.

Software Transactional Memory

Software Transactional Memory (STM) is the highest-level general concurrency abstraction we will consider. STM provides composable atomic transactions, meaning we can combine reads, writes, and other operations in multiple memory locations into single atomic operations. Transactions can be aborted or retried.

An STM transaction lives in the STM monad:

```
data STM a
instance Monad STM
```

Transactions are performed with the `atomically` function:

```
atomically :: STM a → IO a
```

Another important primitive is the `retry` function, which aborts the current transaction and retries it when some of its dependencies have changed (in some other transaction in another thread):

```
retry :: STM a
```

Basic transactional variables are provided by the STM package itself. Advanced structures are provided by additional packages. The following are provided in `stm:Control.Concurrent.STM`:

- `TVar`: A shared memory location analogous to `IORef`, but transactional
- `TMVar`: Mutable variable analogous to `IORef`
- `TChan`: Channels analogous to `Chan` from base
- `TQueue`: Faster channels without support channel duplication
- `TBQueue`: Bounded and non-duplicable channels
- `TArray`: Transactional arrays analogous to arrays from the `array` package

Some more transactional datatypes are provided by the `stm-containers` and `stm-chans` packages.

STM example – Bank accounts

We can represent account balance as a `TVar`:

```
-- file: tvar-account.hs

import Control.Concurrent.STM
```

```
type Balance = Int
type Account = TVar Balance

createAccount :: Balance -> STM Account
createAccount = newTVar
```

The basic operations that can be done on accounts are `withdraw` and `deposit`. Implemented as STM transactions, we get the following transactions:

```
withdraw account amount = do
    balance <- readTVar account
    if balance - amount < 0
        then retry
        else writeTVar account $! balance - amount

deposit account amount = do
        balance <- readTVar account
        writeTVar account $! balance + amount
```

Our accounts can't go negative. Therefore, withdrawals will wait until the balance becomes available. Retrying inside a transaction will restart the STM transaction at the beginning, but only after the variable (`account`) has been touched by some other transaction. It won't wait in a busy loop or anything.

We can compose `withdrawal` and `deposit` to create a `transfer` transaction, which transfers a given amount from one account to another:

```
transfer from to n = do
    withdraw from n
    deposit to n
```

Note how easily we composed two atomic operations into one atomic operation. STM makes sure that all modifications made in an incomplete transaction are discarded. Furthermore, because of atomicity, it is guaranteed that nothing else could update the contents of any variable that is used during the transaction.

This is guaranteed to execute atomically, no matter how many threads try to `withdraw` from the `account` in one moment. For an example of usage, here we transfer from one account to another:

```
acc1 <- atomically $ createAccount 5
acc2 <- atomically $ createAccount 3
atomically $ transfer acc1 acc2 2
atomically (readTVar acc1) >>= print
atomically (readTVar acc2) >>= print
```

There is a small overhead in using `TVar` or `TMVar` instead of `MVar`, so if performance is critical and no complex logic is involved, an `MVar` (or even `IORef`) might be more suitable than `STM`.

But there are also two even more important caveats that `TMVar` have over `MVar`. One is that `TMVar` isn't fair; it might take an indefinite time for some thread to unblock on a contended `TMVar`. Another caveat is due to overhead from `STM`, a simple `takeTMVar` might not be single-wakeup like a `takeMVar` is, which is a big penalty for highly-contended mutable variables.

Alternative transactions

There is an operation that allows us to combine transactions, such that if the first one does not yield a result but would wait, we can try another transaction. The operation is `orElse`:

```
orElse :: STM a → STM a → STM a
```

This is exactly the (`<|>`) operation from `Alternative` class, which `STM` implements.

For instance, to withdraw from a fallback account if the primary one doesn't have enough balance, we have the following transaction:

```
import Control.Applicative

withdraw' :: Account -> Account -> Balance -> STM ()
withdraw' primary secondary amount =
    withdraw primary amount <|> withdraw secondary amount
```

Exceptions in STM

Because `STM` is not I/O nor are I/O actions liftable to `STM`, we cannot use `throwIO` to throw exceptions within an `STM` transaction. We could use `throw` or `error`, but those are asynchronous and don't guarantee ordering respective to other STM operations, like `throwIO` does for IO.

The correct way to throw exceptions from `STM` is `throwSTM`:

```
throwSTM :: Exception e => e → STM a
```

And to catch exceptions within `STM`, we can use `catchSTM`:

```
catchSTM :: Exception e => STM a → (e → STM a) → STM a
```

Alternatively, the `MonadThrow`/`MonadCatch` classes from the `exceptions` package capture correct `throw` and `catch` functions for `STM` among other monads.

Runtime System and threads

The **GHC Runtime System** comes in two flavors: threaded and non-threaded. For truly single-threaded applications, it's usually better to use the default non-threaded runtime, because there's more overhead in the threaded one. The non-threaded runtime features a scheduler for light-weight GHC threads (created via `forkIO`), providing for single-threaded concurrent programming.

Usually though, a concurrent program benefits from being multi-threaded – that is, using multiple CPU capabilities triggered via the `-N<n>` RTS flag when compiled with `-threaded`. The Runtime System creates one system thread for every capability and schedules light-weight threads to run in parallel on its system threads.

An important caveat with the non-threaded runtime is that if a light-weight thread has blocked a system call, the whole program will block. On the threaded runtime, GHC can schedule light-weight threads to run on other system threads while the other thread is blocked on a system call.

In Haskell, threads are identified by their ThreadId. One is returned by `forkIO` to the main thread, and the current ThreadId can be retrieved with `myThreadId`. We can use this `ThreadId` to throw exceptions from any thread to any other thread asynchronously, using `throwTo`:

```
throwTo :: Exception e => ThreadId → e → IO ()
```

The `killThread` function throws a `ThreadKilled` exception to the target thread. The `forkIO` function discards the `ThreadKilled` exception (also the exceptions `BlockedIndefinitelyOnMVar` and `BlockedIndefinitelyOnSTM`):

```
-- file: forking.hs
-- outputs nothing
test1 = do
    tid <- forkIO $ threadDelay 100000000
    killThread tid

-- outputs exception: Prelude.undefined
test2 = do
    tid <- forkIO $ undefined
    killThread tid
```

If you need to catch all exceptions from a thread, use `forkFinally`:

```
forkFinally :: IO a → (Either SomeException a → IO ()) → IO ThreadId
```

In Haskell, when the main thread exits, all child threads are killed as well. Often it's useful to wait for all threads to exit, or inform some other thread when a thread dies. For this, forkFinally is the perfect utility:

```
-- waits for the child thread to exit
test3 = do
    mvar <- newEmptyMVar
    tid <- threadDelay 5000000 `forkFinally` \_ -> putMVar mvar ()
    takeMVar mvar
```

Masking asynchronous exceptions

It's possible to mask asynchronous exceptions for a short period of time using Control.Concurrent.mask. When a thread is in a masked state, no asynchronous exception will be raised as long as the thread does not block, or is uninterruptible. In principle, atomic operations such as operations on IORef, operations on MVar that don't block, and STM transactions that don't use retry won't be interruptible. The masked IO action is provided with a restore function, which restores the masked state to what it was outside the mask:

```
mask :: ((forall a. IO a → IO a) → IO b) → IO b
```

The restore function is the only way to restore to an unmasked state in a current thread. If mask is called from an already masked context, then its restore function won't unmask exceptions. Furthermore, new threads created via forkIO inherit the masked state of their parent, though it's possible to use forkIOWithUnmask to create a new thread with a restore function that unmasks exceptions in the child thread:

```
forkIOWithUnmask :: ((forall a. IO a → IO a) → IO ()) → IO ThreadId
```

To ensure that, in a new thread, an exception handler is established and executed despite asynchronous exceptions in a masked state while the main body is executed in an unmasked state, the pattern we would use is:

```
mask_ $ forkIOWithUnmask $ \unmask →
    catch (unmask main_body) exception_handler
```

The mask_ function is like mask but without a restore function.

Note that this is subtly different from using forkFinally, because forkFinally does not unmask exceptions in the main body if they were masked in the main thread.

If you cannot be sure of the enclosing masking state, use forkIOWithUnmask (usual in library code).

If you need to mask exceptions around an interruptible operation, then this can be done with `uninterruptibleMask`. Be warned though, it's easy to render your program unkillable if the masked operation blocks for whatever reason.

Asynchronous processing

Executing asynchronously involves forking a computation to execute in another thread and right after continuing to do other things. In interactive applications, it is often useful to execute things in the background, in order not to block the user interface for too long. Usually we want to use the results from the asynchronous worker thread once it has finished. Sometimes we wish to cancel a long-running asynchronous computation, in order not to leave unwanted jobs lying around.

Although it is totally possible to create asynchronous jobs with waits and cancels using `MVar` and perhaps `STM`, the Async API in the `async` package provides much nicer solutions.

But first, to be convinced there's nothing magical in the Async API abstraction, we'll build something with just `MVar` and `STM`. So, forking multiple asynchronous threads and waiting for their results is trivial with a few instances of `MVar`: just create an `MVar` for every worker and make the workers put their results into one of the `MVar` locations. Then, in the main thread, take each of the result `MVar`:

```
-- file: mvar-async.hs

import Control.Concurrent

doAsync :: MVar a -> IO a -> IO ThreadId
doAsync mvar job = forkIO $ do
    r <- job
    putMVar mvar r

main = do
    mvars <- sequence [newEmptyMVar, newEmptyMVar]
    sequence [ doAsync mvar getLine | mvar <- mvars ]
    results <- mapM takeMVar mvars
    print results
```

This works, but only as long as the asynchronous job does not throw an error. If the thread errors then the MVar is left empty, leading to our program failing with a BlockedIndefinitelyOnMVar exception. To fix this, we need to install an exception handler that puts something into the MVar before the worker thread exits. This improved version handles that:

```
doAsyncSafe :: MVar (Either SomeException a) -> IO a -> IO ThreadId
doAsyncSafe mvar job = mask_ $ forkIOWithUnmask $ \unmask ->
    do { r <- unmask job; putMVar mvar (Right r) }
    `catch` \e -> putMVar mvar (Left e)
```

This also ensures that the worker thread isn't disrupted by asynchronous exceptions at any point, except for the asynchronous job itself, by using forkIOWithUnmask.

Let's take another case: waiting for either one of two jobs to complete. One solution would be to use just one MVar and the tryPutMVar function in order to not block if the other thread already filled the MVar.

Another solution involves STM. The obvious benefit to using STM is that this solution composes seamlessly with other STM transactions. The following implementation of eitherOr utilizes the STM primitive orElse to obtain a result when either of two jobs return:

```
-- file: stm-either.hs

import Control.Concurrent
import Control.Concurrent.STM

eitherOr :: IO a -> IO b -> IO (Either a b)
eitherOr job_a job_b = do
    a <- doAsyncSTM job_a
    b <- doAsyncSTM job_b
    atomically $ fmap Left (takeTMVar a) `orElse` fmap Right (
    takeTMVar b)

doAsyncSTM :: IO a -> IO (TMVar a)
doAsyncSTM job = do
    tmvar <- newEmptyTMVarIO
    forkIO $ do r <- job
            atomically $ putTMVar tmvar r
    return tmvar
```

I have omitted exception handling for clarity. Basically we just wait for one of two `TMVar` variables to fill. But what if we would like to cancel one computation once the other finishes? After all, it's not good to leave threads lying around, as running threads cannot be garbage-collected. We would need to throw a `ThreadKilled` exception (using `killThread`) or something similar to cancel a job.

Using the Async API

Instead of explicitly keeping track of and managing all our asynchronous threads, we can utilize the Async API to do the hard lifting for us. For instance, the `withAsync` combinator provides automatic cancellation:

```
withAsync :: IO a → (Async a → IO b) → IO b
```

In `withAsync action (\a -> inner)`, the asynchronous job `action` is coupled with the computation `inner` such that if `inner` finishes (with an exception or otherwise), the asynchronous thread is killed if it is still running.

The `Async` type represents an asynchronous job. It encapsulates the `ThreadId` and means to wait or poll the job's result (or a raised exception). To create an `Async` without automatic cancellation, use `async`:

```
async :: IO a → IO (Async a)
```

One of the simplest operations on an `Async` is to wait for its result:

```
wait :: Async a → IO a
```

But we can also do more, like wait for one of multiple `Async` to complete, and automatically cancelling all others when one finishes, by using `waitAnyCancel`:

```
waitAnyCancel :: [Async a] → IO (Async a, a)
```

We can also wait for `Async` within an `STM` transaction using `waitSTM :: Async a → STM a`.

Async example – Timeouts

Let's take a concrete example using the Async API. Say we need to write a command-line interface that reads lines of user input, but times out if the user hasn't finished the line within five seconds. After the timeout, the prompt is reset.

One way to write this program is using `withAsync`, as follows:

```
-- file: async-cli.hs

import Control.Monad (forever)
import Control.Concurrent
import Control.Concurrent.Async

main = forever $
    withAsync getLine $ \userInput ->
    withAsync (threadDelay 5000000) $ \timeOut -> do
        res <- waitEither userInput timeOut
        case res of
            Left input -> print input
            Right _ -> putStrLn "Timeout!"
```

We use `waitEither` to wait for either of two `Async`s to complete. If a line was received, then we print the line; and if a timeout was reached instead, we print `Timeout!`. Finally, the other `Async` is cancelled.

Note that in this case what we do after one of the `Async`s has completed executes fast (just print a line). But if it was something more complex, like if we wanted to continue to some other part of the program, we should cancel the other `Async` before continuing there. Instead of cancelling manually, we can rewrite our program such that we exit both `withAsync` actions before processing the result. This ensures that neither `Async` is left running:

```
main2 = forever $ do
    res <- withAsync getLine $ \userInput ->
           withAsync (threadDelay 5000000) $ \timeOut ->
           waitEither userInput timeOut
    case res of
        Left input -> print input
        Right _ -> putStrLn "Timeout!"
```

It turns out our `res` computation is already captured by the `race` combinator in the `async` library:

```
race :: IO a → IO b → IO (Either a b)
```

We can rewrite our program using `race`, yielding very concise code:

```
main3 = forever $ do
res <- getLine `race` threadDelay 5000000
case res of
Left input -> print input
Right _ -> putStrLn "Timeout!"
```

The `race` combinator is not only more concise but quite a bit faster too; `Async` relies on `STM` to provide the flexibility, but `race` can be (and is) implemented using `MVar` and `throwTo`. As an exercise for the reader, consider how you would implement race using `MVar` and `throwTo`, such that the other computation gets killed when the first finishes.

Composing with Concurrently

The `async` library provides two types: the `Async` type we have already met and a type called `Concurrently`:

```
newtype Concurrently a = Concurrently { runConcurrently :: IO a }
instance Applicative Concurrently
instance Alternative Concurrently
instance Monoid a => Monoid (Concurrently a) -- since 2.1.0
```

Values of type `Concurrently` are built simply by wrapping an `IO` action with the exposed constructor. The magic of `Concurrently` lies in its `Applicative`, `Alternative`, and `Monoid` instances. These instances allow composing actions concurrently by either waiting for results from all actions (`Applicative`, `Monoid`) or either of multiple options (`Alternative`).

So, to compose either of two alternatives, use (`<|>`):

```
-- file: concurrently.hs

import Control.Applicative
import Control.Concurrent
import Control.Concurrent.Async

lineOrTimeOut :: Concurrently (Either String ())
lineOrTimeOut =
    Concurrently (fmap Left getLine) <|>
    Concurrently (fmap Right (threadDelay 5000000))
```

And to compose many into one, use (`<*>`) and (fmap/(`<$>`)):

```
threeLines :: Concurrently (String, String, String)
threeLines = (,,)
    <$> Concurrently getLine
    <*> Concurrently getLine
    <*> Concurrently getLine
```

To get the result of `Concurrently`, apply `runConcurrently` and execute the resulting IO action:

```
> runConcurrently lineOrTimeOut
Right ()
```

The number of concurrent threads can be determined from the number of `Concurrently` constructors there are. Wrapping and composing IO actions this way using `Concurrently` has many nice properties:

- There is no need for any special combinators, just the full power of the `Functor`, `Applicative`, and `Alternative` classes

- Composition using the `Alternative` instance ensures that unused actions get cancelled

- Composition using `Applicative` instance ensures that all results are waited for before returning, and makes it hard to forget about concurrent jobs

Lifting up from I/O

In real-world applications, it's quite usual for much of the code base to live in monads or monad stacks. In such situations, concurrency operations from `Control.Concurrent` become challenging, because they all are monomorphic in `IO`. Sometimes this isn't much of a problem, because we can use `liftIO` from the `MonadIO` class to lift arbitrary IO actions.

But `MonadIO` leaves two important cases uncovered. The first one is about other base monads besides `IO`, such as `STM`. Though more limited in its use cases, it's sometimes desired to have a monad stack on top of `STM`. The other case is about exception handling, for which `MonadIO` is quite insufficient; all of `Control.Exception` is monomorphic in `IO`, meaning a lot of plumbing if they are used within a monad stack.

In this chapter, we'll look at some solutions to both cases. Another thing that's often desired, and which we'll cover first, is top-level mutable references. In some languages these are called `globals`, and though they're often shunned, Haskell kind of supports them but in a way that's more useful.

Top-level mutable references

All references (`IORef`, `MVar`, `TVar`) are created in the `IO` or `STM` monad. It is possible to escape `IO` using `unsafePerformIO`, and it's safe to do so when used correctly. One such safe use is at top-level accompanied with a `NOINLINE` pragma:

```
-- file: top-level.hso
import Data.IORef
import System.IO.Unsafe (unsafePerformIO)

globalVariable :: IORef String
globalVariable = unsafePerformIO (newIORef "")
{-# NOINLINE globalVariable #-}
```

It's important to set the variable to non-inlinable, because if it inlines, a new `IORef` might get created on reference. Equally important is to ensure the top-level variable has a monomorphic type. For instance, this is bad:

```
globalVar :: Num a => IORef a
globalVar = unsafePerformIO (newIORef 0)
```

Even if `globalVar` is not inlined, it now represents a function (with an implicit class dictionary parameter). Effectively this means that a new `IORef` is created every time we reference `globalVar`.

When it comes to transactional variables in `STM`, it should be noted that `atomically` cannot be used inside `unsafePerformIO` (weird things will happen). Instead, the `IO` variations should be used, such as `newTVarIO` which lives in `IO` and can be used with `unsafePerformIO`. The same considerations about inlining and monomorphic typing apply for transactional top-level variables as well.

Lifting from a base monad

The `transformers` library provides the `MonadIO` class to lift from base `IO`. With base we mean the bottom monad of a monad transformer stack. The `transformers-base`, library, on the other hand, provides a `MonadBase` class to lift from an arbitrary base:

```
class MonadBase b m | m -> b where
    liftBase :: b a -> m a
```

Type variable `b` represents the base (for example, `IO`) and `m` is the monad to lift operations to. For `MonadBase IO`, `liftBase` is equivalent to `liftIO`. The benefits of `MonadBase` are mostly in its other base instances, such as `STM` or `ST`. For instance, if we were writing complex `STM` transactions and wanted to wrap some common data with a `Reader` monad on top of `STM`:

```
-- file: transactionm.hs

import Control.Monad.Base
import Control.Monad.Trans.Reader
import Control.Concurrent.STM

type TransactionM a = ReaderT String STM a
```

To lift STM transactions to `TransactionM`, we could use `Control.Monad.Trans.lift`. But if the stack was bigger, we would end up doing `lift . lift . lift` or similar, and if we instead had our `TransactionM` be a `newtype`, it would be impossible to lift STM operations into it using `lift`. By using `liftBase`, we can circumvent both of these restrictions, because a single `liftBase` will lift through an arbitrary stack as long as the base monad is sitting at the bottom.

The `newtype` case is straightforward; we can derive the instance for `MonadBase`:

```
{-# LANGUAGE GeneralizedNewtypeDeriving #-}

newtype TransactionM' a = TransactionM' (ReaderT String STM a)
    deriving ( Functor, Applicative, Monad
             , MonadReader String, MonadBase STM )
```

If on the other hand you don't need the full power of STM, then the `stm-lifted` library provides basic atomic operations such as `readTVarIO`, `dupTChanIO`, and so forth on transactional variables lifted into `MonadIO`.

Lifting base with exception handling

Lifting operations using `MonadBase` was very similar to `MonadIO`, just more general in the base monad. But lifting operations from `Control.Concurrent` is trickier. For instance, how do we lift `forkIO` into, say, `WriterT Int IO`? We have to decide what happens with the added state from the transformers. In the case of `forkIO`, that's simple: just duplicate the current state into the new thread. But how about an exception handler of `catch`?

```
catch :: Exception e => IO a → (e → IO a) → IO a
```

A generalized version of `catch` provided by the `lifted-base` package has this signature:

```
module Control.Exception.Lifted

catch :: (MonadBaseControl IO m, Exception e)
    => m a → (e → m a) → m a
```

Like `MonadBase`, `MonadBaseControl` is a `type` class that allows lifting operations from the base monad. As the name implies, `MonadBaseControl` adds something extra to the lifting. The `type` class definition is also entirely different from `MonadBase`:

```
class MonadBase b m => MonadBaseControl b m | m → b where
  type StM m a :: *
  liftBaseWith :: (RunInBase m b → b a) → m a
  restoreM :: StM m a → m a
```

Fortunately, it isn't necessary to understand how this class works in order to use MonadBaseControl; in terms of user interface, it looks just like MonadBase (or indeed MonadIO).

But what is useful to understand is the main implication of MonadBaseControl, namely that it saves the added monadic state (as a value of associated type StM m a) and uses this saved state to run computations such as the exception handler in catch. This means that the computation in an exception handler is executed using the monadic state before calling catch. What's more, the monadic state from a computation that throws an exception is also discarded.

Apart from generalizing Control.Concurrent and Control.Exception with module names suffixed with Lifted, in the lifted-base library there are generalized versions of some other modules in base as well, including, for example, Data.IORef.Lifted. Some functions generalize well with just MonadBase IO, and those are left as such. Others that require monadic state controlling are marked with MonadBaseControl in their type signatures.

Because of the associated type in MonadBaseControl class, making an instance for a newtype is substantially harder than MonadBase. Sadly, GHC won't derive any instances for classes with associated types, and the higher-order class functions sure aren't making our lives any easier.

For reference, here's an example of a manually-written derived instance for a newtyped monad stack:

```
-- file: newtype-monadbasecontrol.hs

newtype Handler a = Handler
    { unHandler :: LoggingT (StateT HandlerState (ReaderT Config IO))
a
    } deriving ( ... )

instance MonadBaseControl IO Handler where
    type StM Handler a = StM
      (LoggingT (StateT HandlerState (ReaderT Config IO))) a

    liftBaseWith f = Handler $ liftBaseWith $ \q -> f (q . unHandler)

    restoreM = Handler . RestoreM
```

Summary

In this chapter, we started by looking at light-weight threads and `forkIO`. Closely related to this, we looked at mutable references `IORef` and `MVar` in concurrent settings. Atomic operations on those reference types were quite limited, which is why we next dived into `STM` for arbitrarily complex transactions. Then we considered a nice higher-level abstraction over an asynchronous program, the Async API. One of the main benefits of using `Async` is easy and automatic cancellation of asynchronous jobs. Finally, we lifted concurrency operations into complex monad stacks.

In the next chapter, we will take a deeper look at the Runtime System, scheduling, and garbage collection. We will look at what options there are to tweak both the compiler and the Runtime System. We will learn how the GHC compilation pipeline works and how to read the intermediate core language that GHC produces just enough to spot possibly missed optimizations.

8
Tweaking the Compiler and Runtime System (GHC)

In the previous chapter, we got programmed concurrent applications and used the related powerful features of GHC. Next we concentrate on tuning GHC and its Runtime System. For the best performance, it's necessary to tune the compiler and Runtime System according to the application's specific needs. For instance, heavy number crunching benefits greatly from a different compilation path using LLVM, at the expense of longer compilation times and portability. There are lots of useful options, tricks, and tweaks available in GHC that we will look at in this chapter.

This chapter attempts to highlight the most important flags and options in GHC and RTS. It's not meant to be a substitute for GHC UserGuide, which is much more comprehensive. Instead, we cover options in a systematic and easy-to-follow way, starting with compiler options and proceeding with Runtime System options.

At the end of this chapter, the reader will understand the big picture of compiler phases in GHC and the most important options that affect compilation, optimization, code generations, linking, and preprocessing in GHC. The reader will be familiar with the Runtime System, its scheduler, green threads, memory management, and the garbage collector. We will mention some important configuration options that affect Runtime System performance or enable tracing features.

An additional Haskell feature more or less related to GHC is **Safe Haskell**, which helps programmers in trusting libraries to do what they promise. In essence, Safe Haskell enforces referential transparency: a Safe Haskell module cannot use `unsafePerformIO`, for example. In this chapter, we will learn how Safe Haskell can help in trusting code and validating it We will take a look at the following topics:.

- Compiling and linking with GHC
- Configuring and tuning GHC and the Runtime System

- Compiling safely with Safe Haskell
- Understanding memory management, GC, and scheduler in Runtime System

Using GHC like a pro

The Glasgow Haskell Compiler is a mighty beast. It's a product of almost three decades of active development and innovation. The lead developers have, for a long time, been Simon Peyton Jones and Simon Marlow. The compiler is written in Haskell itself, though the Runtime System is written in C and C--. GHC is open source and licensed under a permissive three-clause BSD license.

To be able to effectively use the compiler, it's necessary to understand the big steps GHC performs when compiling Haskell code. GHC consists of a front end, back end and something that goes in-between.

The GHC front end performs type-checking and type inference, after which Haskell code is transformed into an intermediate language called **Core**. Core is like Haskell but syntactically simpler. Much of GHC's magic happens as code transformations from Core to Core: strictness analysis, optimization, rewrite rules, inlining, automatic unboxing of arguments, and so on.

The GHC backend takes Core code and turns it into machine code. Core is first transformed into another intermediate language called **STG** (short for **Spineless Tagless G-machine**) which is essentially a language for expressing graph reduction. Then, STG is transformed into C--. Finally, C-- is either directly converted into machine code using GHC's native code generator, converted to LLVM code for compilation with LLVM, or printed as C code to be compiled with GCC. However, the C route is generally deprecated and is not included in usual builds of GHC (it may still be used for cross-compiling).

Next, we will consider the most important GHC flags and common use cases. For a complete overview, consult the GHC UserGuide.

Operating GHC

There are a few ways GHC can be invoked.

The most basic form is `ghc program.hs`. This compiles a single-module Haskell program. To compile a multi-module program, that is, one that consists of multiple .hs files, use `ghc --make Main.hs`. The `--make` flag tells GHC to automatically resolve dependent source files from module declarations and to compile them.

```
module A where
import B
import C
```

```
# files: A.hs, B.hs, C. hs
ghc --make A.hs
```

The multi-module mode of GHC has advantages as opposed to a hand-crafted `Makefile`: automatic dependency resolution, cached compilation and parallel compilation using the `-j<n>` flag. Most of the time though `Cabal` and `cabal-install` are used in developing multi-module projects, which takes care of calling GHC with `--make` and possibly `-j`.

Other GHC modes of operation are interactive, expression evaluation, and `runghc`. The interactive mode (flag `-i`) is exactly just GHCi, while expression evaluation (flag `-e <expr>`) is like the interactive mode, but executes just one Haskell expression given as a command-line argument. The `runghc` executable that ships with GHC evaluates a whole Haskell module in the interactive mode:

```
$ runghc <<<'main = putStrLn "Hello World"'
Hello World
```

Multiple options that affect GHC's behavior can be useful in Haskell development. For instance, in some cases GHC doesn't automatically detect that something that affects the resulting program has changed, and GHC doesn't trigger recompilation as it should. Experimenting with different optimization flags is one such scenario. In such cases, the flag `-fforce-recomp` is useful. It forces recompilation of target modules.

When doing type-error-driven development, some people prefer seeing the top-most error first. By default, GHC prints errors in the order it encounters them, leading to the latest printed error being bottom-most. The `-freverse-errors` flag reverses this order.

Flags related to a warning that GHC produces are especially useful. It's good practice to always develop with `-Wall` to get warned about a lot of possible problems in code, such as unused variables, inexhaustive case matches, and more.

Use `-Werror` to turn all warnings into errors. This flag is useful for addressing all warnings in a large codebase, but it isn't advisable to use `-Werror` by default because it can unnecessarily break builds with different tool or library versions. Combine `-Werror` with `-fforce-recomp` to not silently suppress warnings with cached module builds.

If using stack, the `--pedantic` option executes GHC with `-Wall -Werror`.

Circular dependencies

Without doubt, every Haskell programmer has bumped into a circular dependency problem. Circular dependencies are not directly supported by GHC, due to the way the Haskell module system works. There is limited support for mutually recursive modules in GHC, but they should be avoided if at all possible. There is no support for mutually recursive packages, which means that mutually recursive modules make it impossible to reasonably split a project into separate packages later.

To demonstrate that mutually recursive modules are possible, consider these cyclic modules:

```
module B where
    import A (a)
    b = a ++ "b"

module A where
    import B (b)

    a = "a"
    main = print b
```

Attempting to compile this is futile:

```
$ ghc --make A.hs
Module imports form a cycle:
        module 'A' (A.hs)
        imports 'B' (./B.hs)
  which imports 'A' (A.hs)
```

However, with a few additions we can make this cycle compile. First, we need to create a B.hs-boot file which holds an abbreviated version of module B. Essentially, we need to lay out exposed data types and function signatures. We don't need to give function definitions:

```
-- file: B.hs-boot

module B where
    b :: String
```

Then we need to break the cycle by adding a SOURCE pragma to where we import B, in module A:

```
module A where
    import {-# SOURCE #-} B (b)
    ...
```

In big projects with a lot of isolation in modules, it might become painfully hard to design module dependencies so that there are no cycles. Fortunately, most of the time that extra work will pay off as better design.

Adjusting optimizations and transformations

A big section of GHC's Haskell compilation pipeline is code transformations from Core to Core. GHC performs strictness analysis on Core to compile functions with strict arguments more efficiently, because, for instance, strict arguments can be safely unboxed. The inliner reduces indirection in the program, and GHC's inliner is quite aggressive. A plethora of individual optimizations are performed if enabled. Rewrite rules written by library authors express algebraic properties that help the compiler to identify and eliminate expensive identities.

GHC does not try to optimize your code unless a -O[<n>] flag is specified. There are two good reasons for this default. Firstly, compilation with optimizations takes considerably longer, which makes it less suitable for fast iteration. Secondly, code transformations are not always benign; if the sophisticated heuristics guess wrong, the result is slower or even incorrect code. Even supposedly benign optimizations enabled by -O might produce slowdown in some corner cases, though such cases are rare. First observing performance without optimizations gives a baseline from which to start optimizing.

The state hack

Some optimizations jeopardize performance more easily than others. One particularly nasty effect is observed when the heuristics of an optimization called state hack makes a bad guess. In state hack, GHC attempts to optimize "stateful" computations such as IO or ST that carry a state token by eta-expansion; by assuming that an IO () computation is only performed once, we can transform (representing IO with RealWorld → (RealWorld, a)) the following:

```
foo a = let b = … in
  \w1 -> let (w2, ()) = action1 b w1
             (w3, ()) = action2 w2
         in (w3, ())
```

The following version uses just one function call, instead of a nested lambda. This is a much faster call:

```
foo a w1 = let b = …
               (w2, ()) = action1 b w1
               (w3, ()) = action2 w2
           in  (w3, ())
```

However, if we are executing an action (`foo a`) multiple times, where `a` is fixed, and computing `b` is expensive, the latter version will exhibit a massive slowdown due to calculating `b` again every time!

The state hack heuristics are quite good in newer GHCs and it's hard to find a case where a slowdown is perceived. However, if you think that state hack is slowing down your code, give it a try and compile with `-O -fno-state-hack`.

Floating lets in and out

Other optimizations that interact with let bindings are `-ffloat-in` and `-ffull-laziness`, the latter of which would perhaps be better described as "float-out Both are enabled by `-O`. Floating lets bindings nearer their use site and possibly eliminates unnecessary allocations when the code branches, so that the binding ends up never being used. On the other hand, floating outwards with what is called full-laziness transformation tries to increase sharing and so might also increase memory residency.

Full laziness does not compose well with `unsafePerformIO` tricks. For a while now, imagine this `unsafeVar` in scope:

```
-- file: full-laziness.hs

import Control.Monad
import Control.Concurrent.MVar
import System.IO.Unsafe

unsafeVar :: a -> MVar a
unsafeVar i = unsafePerformIO (newMVar i)
{-# NOINLINE unsafeVar #-}
```

These are both bad, that is, they produce only a single `MVar`:

```
let xs = replicate 10 (unsafeVar 1)
xs ← replicateM 10 (return (unsafeVar 1))
```

But by using `forM` and compiling with `-O0`, this one produces `10` distinct MVars:

```
xs <- forM [1..10] $ \_ -> return (unsafeVar 1)
```

The preceding however breaks under `-O`, because the `unsafeVar` is floated up, producing code like this:

```
xs <- let x = return (unsafeVar 1) in forM [1..10] $ \_ -> x
```

Turning off full laziness via `-fno-full-laziness` will make this code correct again. Another way to circumvent full laziness is to artificially force a call to `unsafePerformIO` to depend on the inner context. In our example, we could do this:

```
xs <- forM [1..10] $ \i -> return (unsafeVar' i 1)


unsafeVar' :: b -> a -> MVar a
unsafeVar' _ i = unsafePerformIO (newMVar i)
{-# NOINLINE unsafeVar' #-}
```

However, this kind of code, using `unsafePerformIO` for no real reason, shouldn't be written unless there is a real reason for masquerading `IO` computations as pure values.

Eliminating common subexpressions

Here's another thing to be wary of with unsafe tricks: the **Common Subexpression Elimination** optimization (CSE). Take this code:

```
-- file: cse.hs
main = do
    let a = unsafeVar 5
        b = unsafeVar 5
    takeMVar a
    takeMVar b
```

Again, all is well under `-O0`. But with `-O`, which enables `-fcse`, GHC will infer that a = b, producing code akin to:

```
main = do
    let a = unsafeVar 5
    takeMVar a
    takeMVar a
```

With the `-fno-cse` flag, we can make this work. Note that CSE is not beneficial in general. We might end up retaining a big thunk for long periods, whereas without CSE it could be allocated anew once needed. However, a much bigger concern for CSE is inductive datatypes such as linked lists. For instance, with too eager CSE, this program would blow up in memory (lists get floated out into a single list, retained between calls to sum):

```
main = do
  print $ sum [1..10000000]
  print $ sum [1..10000000]
```

Liberate-case duplicates code

Liberate-case is one of those transformations that generates more code. Actually, in unfortunate cases, it can cause an explosion in code size. That is because liberate-case always creates new code. For instance, consider this function:

```
-- file: liberate-case.hs

option = ('a', 'b')

fun x = case option of
            (a, _) -> a : fun x
```

If this recursive function is compiled without `liberate-case` optimization, then `fun` ends up doing a pattern match on every recursive evaluation. Because `option` occurs free in `fun`, it would be enough to pattern match it only once because its value wouldn't change from one recursive iteration to the next. Liberate-case would unroll the definition of the recursive function `fun` once and eliminate free terms, producing code equivalent to:

```
fun x = case option of
            (a, _) -> a : (let f x' = a : f x' in f x)
```

Although liberate-case was useful in this simple example, sometimes we just don't want it. Notably, the liberate-case transformation does not interact too well with a rules-based fusion. It can lead to lots of duplicated code, especially when combined with keen inlining. A lot of duplication in Core implies a harder time for other optimizations, thus hurting performance. For instance, the authors of the `Repa` library suggest using `-fno-liberate-case`.

Compiling via the LLVM route

The LLVM compilation route should be preferred over the default native code generator when performance matters. LLVM is an intermediate representation at the level of assembly code. LLVM is more recent and provides more opportunities for optimizations at the lowest level.

Generated LLVM code from GHC is in practice always at least as fast as, and usually faster than, whatever the native code generator produces. The main downside of LLVM is that it's slower to compile than using the native code generator, which makes a big difference in slowing down development cycles.

To choose the LLVM route, say `-fllvm` to GHC. Because LLVM has its own optimization flags that are different from GHC's, it makes sense to pass `-optlo-O3` to GHC, which in turn passes `-O3` to LLVM , which enables some optimizations in LLVM's intermediate representation.

GHC has rough support for **Single Instruction, Multiple Data (SIMD)** instructions in the form of GHC primitives defined in GHC.Prim module. They only work if using the LLVM backend. As of now, the representation is quite limited and their use cases questionable. However, in principle, substantial work libraries such as vector could in the future be made to use SIMD instructions. For the time being, SIMD is not explicitly used in the Haskell ecosystem, though intermediate LLVM might incorporate some optimizations that use SIMD.

Linking and building shared libraries

By default, GHC statically links Haskell libraries to executables it produces. This means that an executable built with GHC is usually compatible in a similar environment which has no Haskell-specific libraries installed. It is possible to link Haskell libraries dynamically using the -dynamic flag to save disk space.

GHC is also able to produce regular shared objects with the -shared flag to be used from C, for instance. For shared objects, it's also best to give a GHC flag -fPIC, to generate position-independent code.

While Haskell libraries are normally linked statically, non-Haskell libraries are usually linked dynamically. GHC uses the system linker to link with non-Haskell libraries, and we can pass it arguments via GHC with the -optl prefix. So the GHC option -optl-static will link other non-Haskell libraries statically. Static linking may help with portability.

The GHC Runtime System, which is necessary to execute Haskell programs built with GHC, is configured at linking time. Multiple flags control the Runtime System that gets linked into an executable: -threaded links with the multi-core version of Runtime System that can run on multiple OS threads; -with-rtsopts=<opts> specifies RTS flags at link time; -debug enables additional debug event output from RTS (configured further via RTS flags); and -eventlog enables event tracing (for **ThreadScope**).

The -rtsopts={none,some,all} linker flag controls which Runtime System flags can be given for the executable itself via +RTS. By default this is some, which enables some safe options. Simple -rtsopts enables all configurable options (the exact set of options depend on the given GHC flags), identical to -rtopts=all.

Preprocessing Haskell source code

GHC supports using the **C preprocessor (CPP)** on Haskell source files. CPP is a simple macro language which enables conditional computation and macros. It is not enabled by default but is behind the language extension -XCPP. It is advisable to only use the C preprocessor for conditional compilation, that is, do not define constants using CPP.

The problem with CPP is that it is not type-checked and that it understands C, but not Haskell. CPP easily messes up Haskell code by expanding macros in string literals and comments, changing significant whitespace and identifiers containing ' or # characters. In particular, multi-line string literals almost certainly won't work with most C preprocessors.

Acceptable use cases for CPP in Haskell are:

- Compiling differently for different operating systems
- Compiling for different versions of libraries for backwards-compatibility
- Disabling or enabling some features in production versus development versions

CPP is used with GHC just like it is used with C. Macros can be defined from the command-line using -D and undefined using -U flags for GHC, just like with C. For example, the following program only prints when -DDEVELOPMENT is given for GHC:

```
-- file: cpp.hs

{-# LANGUAGE CPP #-}

main = do
#ifdef DEVELOPMENT
    print "just debugging"
#endif
    return ()
```

CPP flags can be hidden behind Cabal flags in a **cabal** file, using the ghc-options field to conditionally pass CPP options:

```
flag development
  description: Turn on development settings
  default: False

library
  if flag(development)
    ghc-options: -DDEVELOPMENT
```

GHC also supports arbitrary custom preprocessors. Use the `-F` flag to tell GHC to preprocess and `-pgmF=<executable>` to tell it which program to use as the preprocessor. Preprocessing can be enabled on a per-module basis using the `{-# OPTIONS_GHC -F #-}` pragma. The preprocessor program itself could be defined, for example, in a cabal file.

Enforcing type-safety using Safe Haskell

Safe Haskell is an effort to help running untrusted code safely. It's a pretty unique thing, though it is still bit rough around the edges. The main purposes of Safe Haskell include to machine-check untrusted code, define a safe subset of Haskell that cannot use unsafe functions, call foreign C, or hang the system.

Safe Haskell contains language extensions (`-XSafe`, `-XTrustworthy`, and `-XUnsafe`) and the compiler flag `-fpackage-trust`. Safe Haskell marks every module either **Safe, Trustworthy, Unsafe,** or **Safe-Inferred**. Only modules that are either Safe or Safe-Inferred are machine-checked to use only safe language. However, safe modules may still use modules that don't fit to only safe language. This leads us to transitive trust, which we will look at in a moment.

Any module can be marked Trustworthy, which is essentially the library author promising that the exposed API is safe, although internally it might not be. It's now up to the user to decide whether to trust the author and thus the library.

Enabling any of the Safe Haskell extensions enables one new language feature, the `safe import` keyword:

```
{-# LANGUAGE Unsafe #-}
import safe qualified Data.List as List
```

A module imported with safe guarantees that the imported module is trusted at compile-time. Trust is determined differently, whether the `-fpackage-trust` flag is in effect or not. For "safe" imports, it holds that:

- `-fno-package-trust`: Module is trusted if it is not marked unsafe.

- `-fpackage-trust`: Module is trusted if it's marked Safe or Safe-Inferred, or Trustworthy with the module's package trusted in the package `db`. All transitive dependencies must also be trusted.

These points hold for all imports for a module that is `-XSafe`. For such modules, the language is restricted: everything unsafe is banned. Some surprising things are considered unsafe in Safe Haskell, including generalized newtype deriving, template Haskell, overlapping instances, rewrite rules, and Typeable.

If a library author wants to use unsafe language features but still make the library available to Safe Haskell, she/he marks the library as Trustworthy. This doesn't restrict the language, but gives the library user an option to trust. Local packages are marked trusted using `ghc-pkg trust <package>-<version>`.

Safe Haskell does not protect from malicious code being run at compile-time. For example arbitrary executables could be called during compilation as custom preprocessors. Safe Haskell does not even aim to protect from compile-time issues. The solution for that is to build with isolated privileges.

Tuning GHC's Runtime System

GHC's Runtime System is not something that could be called elegant, consisting of 50,000 lines of C and C-- (a C-like language) code that does a lot of managerial things to execute compiled Haskell programs. The RTS is responsible for managing exceptions, implementing GHC's primitive functions (those suffixed with a magic hash), and scheduling light-weight threads. Memory management, profiling facilities, and STM are all implemented in RTS, and more.

How is this relevant to a Haskell programmer? Knowing the scope and limitations of the RTS is one thing. Also, the RTS isn't so much a black box; it can provide useful feedback about running programs, such as memory usage, garbage-collection statistics, profiling information, and so forth. Many aspects of the RTS are configurable via flags, whose optimization is necessary to max out performance. Different applications utilize the RTS in wildly different ways.

Runtime System flags are set at program startup:

```
./program +RTS opts -RTS
```

Using `-RTS` is optional, marking the end of Runtime System options and the continuation normal program arguments.

One thing that rarely crosses one's mind is that, because GHC is built with GHC itself, all discussions about the Runtime System apply to GHC itself. You can pass Runtime System options to the compiler with `+RTS` just like to any normal Haskell program.

If you wish to specify RTS options to the program being compiled, use the GHC flag `--with-rtsopts`.

Scheduler and green threads

GHC implements light-weight threads, commonly known as **green threads**. These threads use less memory than traditional operating system threads and are thus lighter to schedule. Threads are represented by **Thread State Objects (TSOs)**. In Haskell, `ThreadId` corresponds to a TSO:

```
data ThreadId
    -- instance Eq, Ord, Show
```

Each TSO has a stack allocated with it. The default stack size is 1 kilobyte (controlled via the RTS flag `-ki`). TSOs are garbage-collected. Usually, TSOs are retained by a capability's run queue. Capability is a GHC name for an operating system thread the RTS is running. Each capability has its own run queue. In other situations, TSOs are retained in waiting lists on a concurrency variable such as an `MVar`.

Most of the memory overhead in a green thread comes from the stack size (1k). Reducing this to smaller values via the `-ki` RTS option might improve performance when spawning a lot of very small threads frequently. Conversely, lots of fat threads may benefit from bigger values.

When using the threaded runtime, the most important RTS option is `-N<n>`. This option controls the number of capabilities in use, loosely corresponding to the number of cores. On systems with more than two cores, it's rarely useful to set `-N` even to the number of cores on the system, because there are likely other programs running on your system that may hinder the RTS scheduler's performance. The number of capabilities can also be changed from code using `setNumCapabilities`.

Sparks and spark pool

Remember how we used `Control.Parallel.par` for requesting parallel evaluation? What the `par` operator actually does is that it allocates a spark in a capability's spark pool. Sparks are really cheap, because they're just pointers in a circular buffer. Valid sparks are pointers to unevaluated thunks – work that could be performed.

A spark is turned into a green thread when there are no threads in the run queue. Also, the scheduler tries to share sparks with other idle capabilities. This is important, because usually sparks are added to the spark pool of the currently executing capability which might be reserved for a long time. It is more efficient for each capability to have their own spark pool than a global spark pool, because a global pool would require acquiring a lock before adding sparks.

Bounded threads and affinity

Normal green threads (created with `forkIO`) may get transferred at almost any time from one capability to another. Usually, this is not a problem. In fact, most of the time automatic migration results in very good performance. There are, however, two special cases where `forkIO` might be insufficient.

The first case is merely an optimization: sometimes it may be possible to get better performance by fixing threads to capabilities; for example, you are sure that threads interact in such ways that they shouldn't migrate between capabilities. These should be extremely rare cases; carelessly fixing capabilities can result in degraded performance. Nonetheless, using `forkOn` it's possible to fix a thread's capability:

```
forkOn :: Int → IO () → IO ThreadId
```

Another case that's more common is related to foreign calls to or from C. Some foreign calls depend on `OS-thread-local` state. This means that a thread that's interfacing with a C library which depends on thread-local state (OpenGL, for example), should use the `forkOS` function instead. A thread forked with `forkOS` is bounded to an operating system thread – a bounded thread:

```
forkOS :: IO () → IO ThreadId
```

In particular, the main program is always a bounded thread. Unbounded threads usually yield better concurrency performance than bounded threads, which is why it's discouraged to do lots of work in the main thread in a concurrent program. Instead, fork worker threads using `forkIO` or use `runInUnboundThread` (a `runInBoundThread` exists, too).

Indefinite blocking and weak references

The `BlockedIndefinitely` family of exceptions come with a detail that's not immediately apparent. In principle, a thread will not receive an exception of the blocked indefinitely kind as long as some other thread is holding a reference that could be used to unblock the thread. In the case of `BlockedIndefinitelyOnMVar`, one such reference is the MVar itself; we can unblock a `takeMVar` with a `putMVar` in another thread (or the other way around).

The nitty-gritty detail is, however, that just a reference to a `ThreadId` is enough to prevent *blocked indefinitely* exceptions from being thrown. After all, we could throw arbitrary asynchronous exceptions (including `ThreadKilled`) to the blocked thread using `throwTo`.

To keep a reference to a `ThreadId` and still allow that thread to receive `blocked indefinitely` exceptions, we can make a weak reference to the `ThreadId` instead of a direct reference. The following program doesn't retain a reference to the `ThreadId` but just a **Weak ThreadId**, resulting in the child thread dying:

```
-- file: weak-threadid.hs

import Control.Concurrent
import Control.Concurrent.MVar

main = do
    tid <- forkFinally (do { var <- newEmptyMVar
                           ; takeMVar (var :: MVar ())
                           }) print >>= mkWeakThreadId
    threadDelay 10000000
    print =<< deRefWeak tid
```

This outputs thread blocked indefinitely in an MVar operation, perhaps surprisingly followed by a Just value. The `doRefWeak` function de-references a weak reference, returning nothing if the value had been GC'd, or otherwise the value wrapped in **Just**. In this case, the garbage-collector hadn't yet collected the unnecessary `ThreadId`.

Heap, stack, and memory management

Due to immutability, Haskell programs produce lots of memory traffic. Or, in garbage-collection terms, a lot of garbage is produced. However, immutability greatly simplifies garbage collector implementation and enhances its performance. The key trick used by memory management in Haskell is from the following observation: a value can never refer to values newer than itself, nor can it refer later because values are immutable.

GHC's GC is generational. Newer data is subject to garbage collection in the first generation. If data survives the first GC generation, it's retained in the second generation. By default there are two generations. New data is first allocated in the allocation area (default size 512 KB). When the allocation area is filled, the first generation of GC is performed (minor GC). Only live data is kept and retained in the main memory. Everything else just gets removed.

Almost all Haskell data lives in the heap: data constructors and fields, functions, thunks, mutable and transactional variables (STM), TSOs, and so on. Types that can be inhabited by bottom (_|_), undefined, must be represented by a pointer. Such types are called *lifted*. In general, types that are represented by pointers are called *boxed types*. Boxed unlifted types exist too.

We can control minimum and maximum heap size with the RTS options -H and -M, for example,-H1G. The Runtime System will allocate more space for the heap as it grows in size (as long as it doesn't grow over the maximum size specified by -M, which is unlimited by default). The benefit of specifying a larger starting size for the heap is that there's less need for re-allocation. If the program's memory usage varies a lot over time, it improves overall performance to specify a bigger base heap size.

Heap usage is profilable, as discussed in the previous chapter on profiling. There's a technical overhead in heap profiling that's accumulated in every heap object as some extra fields. Profiling tooling subtracts that memory overhead exactly in reporting, but some programs' performance might be drastically degraded under heap profiling.

Evaluation stack in Haskell

In traditional, eagerly-evaluated languages, when an exception occurs often, a call stack is printed, which shows the stack of functions or methods that were called to produce the error. In Haskell, with lazy evaluation, there's no need to keep track of a call stack (though in newer versions of GHC there's some support for call stacks to help debugging partial functions).

There is, however, something called stacks in the Runtime System. Instead of functions or methods, these stacks hold pattern matches; they're sort of evaluation stacks. When a thread is evaluating a thunk, there's a stack associated with the evaluation. This is where stack overflows occur in Haskell, for example, in a non-strict left-fold. In a less dramatic, more common case, a stack is filled with a lot of case expressions, just to be collapsed later on – a classic space leak.

Noticing space leaks in the stack is a tricky business. Often big stacks are evaluated before being exhausted, but still consume unnecessary amounts of resources. It's possible to limit the maximum size of one thread's stack using the RTS option -K, for instance,-K1k. The default limit is 80% of physical memory. Often big stacks are perfectly valid, which is why this approach doesn't always work.

Tuning the garbage collector

Along with memory management in Haskell comes the garbage collector. It's multi-threaded (when using the threaded runtime) and generational. Lots of GC options are tunable. It is also in the GHC developer's interests to experiment with different GC settings, to see what works best in a lazy and pure language.

Generational garbage collectors sort live objects into different generations, from newest to oldest. Newer generations get collected more frequently than older generations. Because Haskell is pure, generational garbage collection is easy to implement. In fact, GHC implements multi-generational GC, and the number of generations is fully configurable using the RTS option `-G<n>`. The default number of generations is 2. A maximum number that's still sensible is around 4; otherwise, oldest generations practically never get collected.

Some of the most useful GC flags are `-A<size>` and `-n<size>`. The former controls allocation area size, and the latter divides the allocation area into chunks of a specified size. The advantage of chunking the allocation area is evident in multi-core environments. By default, there's no chunking and the first core to fill its allocation area triggers GC over all cores, even if the other cores still have plenty of allocation area left. With chunking, the core is given a new chunk instead.

For instance, to set the allocation area to 64 megabits and chunk it into sizes of 4 megabits, set `-A64m -n4m`. Remember that chunking is only advantageous when running in parallel.

The garbage collector copies by default, which means that data is copied from the allocation area to some fresh memory block. It is possible to instead enable the compacting algorithm for the oldest generation with the `-c` flag. The compacting algorithm is most useful when there's a good ratio (say 30%) of live data to heap size.

Parallel GC

GC options related to parallelism are `-qg<gen>` and `-qb<gen>`. The former enables parallel GC in generations `gen` and higher (default: 0). The latter enables load-balancing in generations higher than `gen` (default: 1). Omitting `gen` turns off parallel GC or load balancing completely.

Even if your program is completely sequential, it might benefit from parallel GC depending on heap size and GC utilization. For a sequential program, it's probably a good idea to use parallel GC only in generations 1 and higher, because generation 0 is highly sequential anyway, so extra overhead hurts performance.

Parallel GC load balancing is, by default, enabled only for generations 1 and higher. Migrating GC work from one core to another requires data copying, which hurts locality in a fast-paced generation 0. For a parallel program where threads don't interact much with each other (that is, a web server), it might be beneficial to disable load balancing altogether (using `-qb`).

Profiling and tracing options

We have already used many of the profiling and tracing options in RTS. Most extensively, we've used the -s[<file>] statistics summary flag to get a nice summary about bytes allocated, bytes copied during GC, maximum residency, and so forth. The uppercase variant -S[<file>] prints more information, giving information about every GC event as they happen:

Alloc bytes	Copied bytes	Live bytes	GC user	GC elap	TOT user	TOT elap	Page	Flts
521128 (Gen: 0)	161784	161776	0.000	0.000	0.005	0.001	0	1
523608 (Gen: 0)	322720	322864	0.001	0.001	0.006	0.003	0	0
523608 (Gen: 1)	483888	483864	0.001	0.001	0.007	0.004	0	0
523600 (Gen: 0)	322280	645000	0.000	0.000	0.008	0.005	0	0

. . .

This (-S) is probably way too much detail though.

And if even -s is too much, if you'd like to see just a one-line summary at program termination, use -t[<file>]:

```
<<ghc: 1532385248 bytes, 2925 GCs, 76266654/408929240 avg/max bytes
residency (17 samples), 860M in use, 0.000 INIT (0.000 elapsed), 0.901
MUT (0.901 elapsed), 3.265 GC (3.268 elapsed) :ghc>>
```

Using -t in combination with --machine-readable produces a nice map-like structure that's easy to read using Prelude.read or similar. The following is an example output from a program run with +RTS -t --machine-readable:

```
 [("bytes allocated", "1532385248")
 ,("num_GCs", "2925")
 ,("average_bytes_used", "76266654")
 ,("max_bytes_used", "408929240")
 ,("num_byte_usage_samples", "17")
 ,("peak_megabytes_allocated", "860")
 ,("init_cpu_seconds", "0.000")
 ,("init_wall_seconds", "0.000")
 ,("mutator_cpu_seconds", "0.898")
 ,("mutator_wall_seconds", "0.898")
```

```
,("GC_cpu_seconds", "3.269")
,("GC_wall_seconds", "3.272")
]
```

Finally, the -T flag makes statistics accessible using methods from the GHC.Stats module. We used this flag in *Chapter 3, Profile and Benchmark to Your Heart's Content*, where we hooked the ekg performance monitoring library to our program.

Tracing using eventlog

The eventlog contains information about scheduler events, GC events, sparks, and user-defined events. To generate an eventlog from a program, compile it with -eventlog and supply -l<flags> for the RTS. The flags are optional– refer to the GHC UserGuide for what is configurable. The eventlog is written to the program. eventlog file in binary format. The tool that you'll most likely want to inspect the eventlog with is **ThreadScope**, as discussed in *Chapter 3, Profile and Benchmark to Your Heart's Content*.

The eventlog is used for performance profiling. It's possible to emit your own events from code. Using the eventlog for event messaging, instead of plain trace debugging, means that the eventlog can show more information about which processor cores thunks were evaluated or actions performed with. Use Debug.Trace.traceEvent and traceEventIO to emit eventlog events.

Options for profiling and debugging

Profiling and options for profiling have been discussed extensively in *Chapter 3, Profile and Benchmark to Your Heart's Content*. Most options require compiling with profiling support, except one, which generates a very basic heap profile in file program.hp: -hT. Use hp2ps to render the report as a nice PostScript graph.

For profiling and debugging multithreaded programs, the RTS clock interval option -V<secs> is of special interest. Setting -V0 effectively makes the scheduler deterministic. The RTS will be doing a lot more context-switching, but everything is deterministic. Eliminating non-determinism is really useful for debugging concurrent applications. For instance, determinism ensures reads and writes in concurrent threads are always performed in the same order.

Summary of useful GHC options

The last part of this chapter collects options for GHC and the Runtime System into a concise reference. Let's start off with GHC.

Basic usage

These are some of the most often used general flags related to compilation with GHC:

- `--make`: Compile a multi-module program
- `-j<n>`: Parallel compilation
- `-i`, `-e`, `runghc`: Interactive and evaluation modes
- `-fforce-recomp`: Force recompilation
- `-Wall`: Turn on all code-level warnings
- `-Werror`: Turn all warnings into errors
- `-freverse-errors`: Print top-most error last

The LLVM backend

The LLVM route is the preferred compilation path for numeric code. It requires the LLVM libraries and a compatible system. The flags used to enable LLVM are:

- `-fllvm`: Compile via LLVM
- `-optlo-O3`: Enable optimizations in the LLVM backend

Turn optimizations on and off

GHC has a sophisticated optimization pipeline. Every optimization can be turned on and off separately, but that's rarely necessary. Good default sets of optimizations are enabled with the `-O` family of flags:

- `-O`: Standard set of benign optimizations (same as `-O1`)
- `-Odph`, `-O2`, `-O3`: Enable more optimizations
- `-fno-state-hack`: Disable the state hack optimization
- `-ffloat-in`, `-ffull-laziness`: Let-floating in and out
- `-fno-cse`: Disable common subexpression elimination (CSE) optimization

Configuring the Runtime System (compile-time)

The following flags affect the Runtime System that is linked to the program. The Runtime System has configurable flags of its own, discussed later on:

- `-threaded`: Link with threaded Runtime System
- `-with-rtsopts=<opts>`: Specify RTS flags at link time
- `-debug`: Enable additional RTS debug events
- `-eventlog`: Enable event tracing for ThreadScope
- `-rtsopts={none,some,all}`: Enable configuring `RTSoptions` via `./program +RTS`
- `-static`, `-dynamic`: Link Haskell libraries statically or dynamically (default: `-static`)
- `-shared -fPIC`: Build a shared object
- `-optl-static`: Link non-Haskell libraries statically

Safe Haskell

These are flags for controlling Safe Haskell compilation:

- `-XSafe`, `-XTrustworthy`, `-XUnsafe`: Enable Safe Haskell extensions
- `-fpackage-trust`: Refuse compiling untrusted code

Summary of useful RTS options

The following sections describe flags for controlling the Runtime System's behavior. The exact set of flags available depend on how the Runtime System was configured (via GHC flags).

Scheduler flags

The number of capabilities (OS threads) to use is controlled with `N<n>:`. This can be changed with `setNumCapabilities`. (default: 1)

Memory management

These are flags for controlling used heap and stack size:

- `-H<size>`: Minimum heap size (default: `0`)
- `-M<size>`: Maximum heap size (default: unlimited)
- `-ki<size>`: Minimum stack size (default: `512k`)
- `-K<size>`: Maximum stack size (default: 80% system memory)

Garbage collection

These are flags for controlling the generational garbage collector:

- `-G<n>`: Number of GC generations (default: 2)
- `-qg<gen>`: Minimum generation to apply parallel GC to (default: 0)
- `-qb<gen>`: Minimum generation in parallel GC to apply load-balancing (default: 1)
- `-c`: Enable compacting algorithm for oldest generation

Runtime System statistics

These are flags for collecting statistics from GHC Stats and the eventlog:

- `-t[<file>]`, `-s[<file>]`, `-S[<file>]`: Output to file or `stderr`
- `-T`: Enable statistics collection via `GHC.Stats`
- `-t[<file>] --machine-readable`: Output summary in machine-readable format
- `-l<flags>`: Gather an eventlog (for ThreadScope)

Profiling and debugging

These are flags to generate the heap profile from Haskell programs:

- `-hT`: Basic heap profile; render using hp2ps
- `-h*`: Heap profiling options (require compiling with profiling support)
- `-V0`: Eliminate non-determinism in parallel programs

Summary

In this chapter, we have discussed the easiest way to increase GHC Haskell's performance: tweaking compiler and Runtime System flags. Enabling optimizations, compiling via LLVM, and enabling LLVM optimizations is a quick route to a usually very respectable performance. Although most of the time GHC's sophisticated, heuristic optimizations produce faster code, this is not always the case. Some optimizations produce slow and even incorrect code under certain situations. Unsafe functions in particular interact badly with many optimizations. Furthermore, eager inlining may produce very big binaries.

We discussed features in the Runtime System and how to enable and configure them. Light-weight (green) threads were cheap, scheduled by RTS, and enabled easy concurrent evaluation via sparks, but were limited with regard to foreign system calls. The parallel and generational garbage collector also had multiple tunable parameters to experiment with.

In the next chapter, we will learn to read GHC's intermediate language, Core. It allows us to observe whether the optimizer did the right thing. For example, unboxing is explicit in Core.

9

GHC Internals and Code Generation

In the previous chapter, we learned to tweak options in GHC and Runtime System. In this chapter, we will dive into GHC's internal language, Core. We will learn to read Core and to spot possible problems in Core. Such problems arise when, for instance, the strictness analyzer left an argument lazy and boxed, while it would have been a lot more performant to make it strict and unboxed. We can basically just read such situations from Core, because strictness is explicit and unboxed arguments are always output with hashes.

Recall that the hash suffix is referred to as the magic hash in Haskell. Magic hashes mark primitive functions and types (those provided by GHC itself). We call these **primops**. In this chapter, we will learn to program with primops directly. Sometimes raw primop programming is an easy way to get reliably good performance. Also, a lesser-known fact is that GHC supports some SIMD operations via the LLVM backend. As of now, SIMD support is not complete and not as powerful as it could be, but still useful at a small scale. We'll use SIMD as an example of primop programming.

Our third main topic is meta-programming using **Template Haskell** and datatype generic programming using GHC Generics. Generic programming in Haskell is quite pleasant and, what's even better, in principle comes with a zero runtime overhead. Template Haskell is really powerful, albeit slightly verbose. Like, with great power comes great responsibilities, meta-programming should always be the last resort!

In this chapter, we will cover the following topics:

- Making sense of the Core language
- Programming with GHC primitives
- Using GHC Generics to write data-type-generic code
- Meta-programming with Template Haskell

Interpreting GHC's internal representations

The first internal representation in GHC is Core, the second one is **STG**, and the third one **Cmm**. Both Core and STG are very functional, while Cmm is an imperative language which resembles C a lot. In this section we will learn to read GHC Core and to spot possible performance problems that might otherwise be hard to spot.

Reading GHC Core

Core is the intermediate language within GHC. Nearly all optimizations GHC does are only program transformations from Core to Core. Reading Core is pretty straightforward for anyone who has read Haskell. For the most part, Core is just let bindings, pattern matches, and function applications. The challenge is in naming conventions, because Core can be quite a noisy code. Following this is a (recursive) function definition in Core (with added line numbering):

```
1 Rec {
2 foo_rjH
3 foo_rjH =
4   \ ds_d1ya ->
5     case ds_d1ya of wild_X5 { I# ds1_d1yb ->
6     case ds1_d1yb of _ {
7       __DEFAULT ->
8         * $fNumIntwild_X5 (foo_rjH (- $fNumIntwild_X5 (I#
1)));
9       1 -> I# 1
10     }
11   }
12 end Rec }
```

The Haskell function definition from which this Core was generated is given in the following code block. Core can be inspected by giving the GHC flag `-ddump-simpl`, and optionally also `-dsuppress-all`. The flag `-dsuppress-all` discards parts of Core that are usually just extra noise:

```
foo :: Int -> Int
foo 1 = 1
foo n = n * foo (n - 1)
```

We note a few things about Core:

- Recursive bindings are *explicit*. Top-level recursive definitions are wrapped inside a `Rec` block, as seen earlier.
- Names of functions have added identifiers in them, while variable names are some generated gibberish.
- Function arguments are desugared into lambdas and all function application is prefix (no infix). Look at, for instance, the applications of `*` and `-`.
- Pattern matches are desugared into simple case expressions.
- Boxing is explicit, note, for example, the usage of Int's constructor `I#`.

Recursive bindings are defined via a `letrec` block, which actually corresponds to Haskell's `let` block. That is because all Haskell `let` blocks are by default recursive; that is, the name on the left-hand side is in scope in its right-hand side.

Some identifiers in Core are named anew (`ds_d1ya` instead of the original n), others have added suffixes (`foo_rjH` instead of `foo`) and finally there are some totally new identifiers from optimization transformations in Core that weren't visible in the original Haskell code. But all in all, the correspondence between Haskell and Core is usually easy to see.

Let's look at some more complex Core next. The following Haskell `main` function is simple and straightforward:

```
main = do
    line <- getLine
    print $ foo (read line)
```

Its unsuppressed Core is printed as follows:

```
main :: IO ()
[GblId, Str=DmdType]
main =
  >>=
    @ IO
    GHC.Base.$fMonadIO
```

```
            @ String
            @ ()
            getLine
              (\ (line_aqk :: String) ->
                  print
                      @ Int
                      GHC.Show.$fShowInt
                      (foo_rjH (read @ Int GHC.Read.$fReadIntline_aqk)))

:Main.main :: IO ()
[GblId, Str=DmdType]
:Main.main = GHC.TopHandler.runMainIO @ () main
```

Firstly, we note that our `main` using `do` notation was desugared to use just monadic bind (`>>=`). Now, recall that the general type signature of monadic bind is:

```
(>>=) :: Monad m => m a -> (a -> m b) -> m b
```

There are three type variables (in order of occurrence): `m`, `a` and `b`. We can read from Core what we saw earlier that `m` is specialized to `IO`, `a` to `String` and `b` to `()`, as expected. Type specializations are notated using the `@` symbol:

```
>>=
    @ IO
    GHC.Base.$fMonadIO
    @ String
    @ ()
```

Some GHC-internal implementation details also "leak" into the Core dump, like `GHC.Base.$fMonadIO`. Usually these are not relevant to the programmer. This particular term (`$fMonadIO`) is the monad type-class dictionary for the `IO` type. In Core, the type-class dictionaries are represented in the same way that normal function arguments are.

We see also that there are two top-level definitions of something `main`. The lower one is an actual entry point, namely `:Main.main` (the default module name is `Main`, when none is given in the Haskell file).

Between the functions' type signatures and the definitions between brackets, there is a set of flags assigned by GHC for that definition. These flags are used to control various optimizations.

Spineless tagless G-machine

STG is the representation after Core and before Cmm. It is simpler than Core and functional. GHC dumps STG by flag `-ddump-stg`. Our `foo` function corresponds to the following STG syntax:

```
foo_rjH =
    sat-only \r srt:SRT:[rjH :-> foo_rjH, rlI :-> $fNumInt]
      [ds_s1yw]
        case ds_s1yw of wild_s1yx {
          I# ds1_s1yy ->
              case ds1_s1yy of _ {
                __DEFAULT ->
                  let {
                    sat_s1yC =
                        \u srt:SRT:[rjH :->foo_rjH, rlI :->
                          $fNumInt] []
                        let {
                          sat_s1yB =
                              \u srt:SRT:[rlI :-> $fNumInt] []
                              let { sat_s1yA = NO_CCS
                                I#! [1];
                              } in  - $fNumIntwild_s1yx
                                sat_s1yA;
                          } in  foo_rjH sat_s1yB;
                    } in  * $fNumIntwild_s1yxsat_s1yC;
                1 -> I# [1];
              };
        };
```

STG is quite different from Haskell syntactically. Lambdas have the unconventional form:

```
\r srt:SRT:[rjH :->foo_rjH, rlI :-> $fNumInt] [ds_s1yw]
```

After the backhash, you can see that there is one of the three flags: re-entrant (r), updatable (u), or single-entry (s). The arguments to the lambda are at the very end between brackets using normal list syntax.

Updatable lambdas are such that, after evaluation, their contents can be rewritten by the results. The thunks correspond to updatable lambdas. The lambdas that take arguments are usually re-entrant, meaning their results can't be memorized similarly.

In STG, constructor applications such as `I# [1]` are always written fully saturated. A saturated application means that all arguments are given in the argument list. The partial constructor applications are converted into lambdas in STG.

Now, because we didn't compile with optimizations, GHC didn't bother with a strictness analysis and thus our `foo` is suboptimal. There is unnecessary boxing, which is not too hard to see from this cleaned version of `foo` function's STG:

```
foo_rjH = \r [ds_s1yw] =
    case ds_s1yw of wild_s1yx {
        GHC.Types.I# ds1_s1yy ->
            case ds1_s1yy of _ {
                __DEFAULT ->
                    let {
                      sat_s1yC = \u []
                          let {
                              sat_s1yB = \u []
                                  let {
                                      sat_s1yA = I#! [1];
                                  } in  - wild_s1yxsat_s1yA;
                              } in foo_rjHsat_s1yB;
                          } in * wild_s1yxsat_s1yC;
                1 ->GHC.Types.I# [1];
            };
    };
```

Here, we can see that arguments to * always get fully evaluated. But GHC pedantically creates thunks for both arguments. The second argument, `sat_s1yC`, which corresponds to `foo (n-1)` is a thunk and so is `sat_s1yB`, which corresponds to the expression *(n-1)*.

Compiling with optimizations (`-o`) the generated STG is much simpler:

```
$wfoo =
    \r srt:SRT:[] [ww_s4wx]
        case ww_s4wx of ds_s4wy {
            __DEFAULT ->
                case -# [ds_s4wy 1] of sat_s4wz {
                    __DEFAULT ->
                        case $wfoosat_s4wz of ww1_s4wA {
                            __DEFAULT -> *# [ds_s4wyww1_s4wA];
                        };
                };
            1 -> 1;
        };
```

This version of `foo` doesn't generate any intermediate thunks. In fact, look at the new name: `$wfoo`. This indicates that `foo` now operates on unboxed values. Indeed, there is no unwrapping or wrapping of `I#` values.

Primitive GHC-specific features

All strictly GHC-specific functionality is contained in GHC.* module. The GHC.Exts module is of particular interest. The GHC.Prim module (re-exported by GHC.Exts) exports core primitives in GHC.

For a while now, GHC has shipped with primitives for SIMD processor instructions. These are available when compiling via the LLVM backend (-fllvm).

SIMD stands for **Single Instruction, Multiple Data**. It basically means performing the same operation on a whole vector of machine numbers at the cost of performing that operation on just one number. SIMD vector types can be found in the GHC.Prim module. The specialized vectors are named like Int8X16#, which stands for an Int8 vector of length 16. DoubleX8# stands for a vector of eight double precision values:

```
data Int8X16#
data DoubleX8#
```

These types are primitive and there are no exposed constructors.

To create vectors that can be used with SIMD instructions, we have two basic options. The first one is to use one of the broadcast functions like:

```
broadcastDoubleX8# :: Double# → DoubleX8#
```

These broadcast functions create vectors with all elements initialized to the given value.

The other option is to pack the vectors from unboxed tuples:

```
packDoubleX4# :: (#Double#, Double#, Double#, Double##) ->DoubleX4#
```

There also exist unpack functions that go the other way around, from SIMD vectors to unboxed tuples.

Because the SIMD types are unlifted (marked with a #), we cannot have polymorphic functions over them. So, there is a function for every pair of operation and SIMD vector types. Fortunately, these functions are named predictably. Operations that are supported for SIMD vectors are:

```
packSXN#   :: (# ... #) ->SXN#
unpackSXN# :: SXN# -> (# S, ... #)

insertSXN# :: SXN# -> S# -> Int# ->SXN#

negateSXN# :: SXN# ->SXN#
plusSXN#   :: SXN# ->SXN# ->SXN#
```

```
minusSXN#   ::  SXN# ->SXN# ->SXN#
timesSXN#   ::  SXN# ->SXN# ->SXN#

divideSXN#  ::  SXN# ->SXN# ->SXN#
quotSXN#    ::  SXN# ->SXN# ->SXN#
remSXN#     ::  SXN# ->SXN# ->SXN#
```

Basic arithmetic operations are therefore supported. All operations are element-wise. In addition to those shown previously, operations are provided to read and write SIMD vectors from primitive arrays (ByteArray# and MutableByteArray#) and addresses (Addr#).

The GHC primitive SIMD interface is a bit cumbersome because it is given on top of the primitives. However, if one is desperate to speed up that manual SIMD vectorization, one would usually require total control over strictness and the program flow.

Kinds encode type representation

Kinds are like types for types. For instance, lifted inhabitable types have the kind *, like:

```
'c' :: Char :: *
Just 1 :: Maybe Int :: *
```

Type constructors, on the other hand, contain the arrow symbol. The following example will help clear things out:

```
Maybe :: * -> *
Either :: * -> * -> *
```

Unlifted types are of the # kind:

```
'c'# :: Char# :: #
```

Starting with GHC 8, types and kinds have been unified. There's now a single indexed type of types:

```
data TYPE a :: RuntimeRep -> *
```

Datatype generic programming

GHC Generics provide a nice interface for datatype generic programming. The core idea is that every datatype is representable as a sum of products. The GHC.Generics module defines a small sufficient set of datatypes. The unit type represents constructors with no arguments:

```
data U1 p = U1 -- unit
```

The V1 datatype, on the other hand, represents types with no constructors (empty):

```
data V1 p -- empty
```

Sums and products are represented respectively by the following types:

```
(:+:) f g p = L1 (f p) | R1 (g p) -- sum
(:*:) f g p = f p :*: g p          -- product
```

The sum types with more than two constructors are represented by the recursive application of (:+:), and it's a similar case for the product types.

The K1 datatype acts as a container for values (of type c):

```
newtype K1 i c p = K1 { unK1 :: c } -- container
```

The final datatype is a metadata wrapper:

```
newtype M1 i t f p = M1 { unM1 :: f p }   -- metadata wrapper
```

The Generic type class glues arbitrary Haskell datatypes to their representations with the types that were mentioned earlier. The (associated) type family Rep maps datatypes to their generic representations:

```
class Generic a
  type Rep a :: * -> *
  from :: a -> Rep a x
  to :: Rep a x -> a
```

For example, the instance for Either boils down roughly to the following:

```
type instance Rep (Either a b) = K1 R a :+: K1 R b
```

However, since there is metadata attached to subexpressions, the real instance is, in fact can be seen here:

```
type instance Rep (Either a b)
  = M1 D D1Either
      (M1 C C1_0Either (M1 S NoSelector (K1 R a))
       :+:
      M1 C C1_1Either (M1 S NoSelector (K1 R b)))
```

Furthermore, GHC.Generics defines type synonyms D1 = M1 D, C1 = M1 C, and S1 = M1 S, which ultimately helps a bit with readability.

At first glance, it isn't obvious how class functions from and to are useful. The key is to exploit the fact that these represent something and are supposed to be some constructions of the building blocks—V1, U1, (:*:), (:+:), K1, M1—and nothing else, except some other types wrapped within K1's. This fact now enables us to create fully datatype generic functions—just overload it over the six generic constructors.

Working example – A generic sum

For the sake of an example, let's create a generic numeric sum traversal function and call it gsum. We will accomplish this via two type classes, GSum and GSum':

```
-- file: gsum.hs

{-# LANGUAGE DefaultSignatures #-}
{-# LANGUAGE FlexibleContexts #-}
{-# LANGUAGE TypeOperators #-}

import GHC.Generics

class GSum' f where
    gsum' :: f p -> Double

class GSum a where
    gsum :: a -> Double

    default gsum :: (Generic a, GSum' (Rep a)) => a -> Double
    gsum = gsum' . from
```

GSum' will handle calculating the sum in the case of the GHC.Generics representation, while GSum will handle the any cases of other types. The magic that will help us save a lot of boilerplate is the highlighted default implementation for GSum. Its type is restricted so that the argument must have a Generic instance, which is auto-derivable for all Haskell types, and also a GSum' instance for the type's representation in Generics.

Let's first add some base cases for numeric values:

```
instance GSum Double where
    gsum = id
```

```
instance GSum Int where
    gsum = fromIntegral
```

```
instance GSum Integer where
    gsum = fromInteger
```

`Double`, `Int`, and `Integer` are now the atoms that add to the sum. Next, we will make GSum work over any data structure that consists of these atoms at "leaves". We will achieve this by adding `GSum'` instances for the types of Generic's representation: `V1`, `U1`, `(:*:)`, `(:+:)`, `K1`, and `M1`.

The `GSum'` instance for the empty datatype (`V1`) is trivial; there are no values of the `empty` type, so this case is not actually usually even reached:

```
instance GSum' V1 where
    gsum' _ = undefined
```

The nullary case is also easy. There are no numbers contained in nullary leaves. So a `0` is appropriate, as in the following code block:

```
instance GSum' U1 where
    gsum' U1 = 0
```

Next, we take a look at some interesting cases: sums and products. For sum types we just branch out and apply `gsum'` inductively. For products we apply `gsum'` to both, and sum the results into the following code block:

```
instance (GSum' f, GSum' g) => GSum' (f :+: g) where
    gsum' (L1 x) = gsum' x
    gsum' (R1 y) = gsum' y
```

```
instance (GSum' f, GSum' g) =>GSum' (f :*: g) where
    gsum' (x :*: y) = gsum' x + gsum' y
```

In the container (`K1`) or our leaf case, we need more information than `GSum'` can give us. We need to convert the contained value into a Double. These are the base cases we defined instances of GSum for, so we apply `gsum` (instead of `gsum'`) to the contained value at leaves:

```
instance GSum c => GSum' (K1 i c) where
    gsum' (K1 x) = gsum x
```

Finally, the metadata (`M1`) case is just an unwrapping that discards metadata information:

```
instance GSum' f => GSum' (M1 i t f) where
    gsum' (M1 x) = gsum' x
```

With all this in place, it's now trivial to add instances of GSum for any Haskell type that is also an instance of Generic.

For our own types, we can derive both Generic and GSum. This requires enabling the DeriveGeneric and DeriveAnyClass extensions. For instance:

```
{-# LANGUAGE DeriveGeneric #-}
{-# LANGUAGE DeriveAnyClass #-}

data T a b = TA a | TB b | TAB a b
          deriving (Generic, GSum)
```

For the existing datatypes, we can enable the StandaloneDeriving extension and list the instances we want:

```
{-# LANGUAGE StandaloneDeriving #-}

deriving instance (GSum a, GSum b) =>GSum (Either a b)
deriving instance (GSum a, GSum b) =>GSum (a, b)
```

Let's load our code into GHCi and test that gsum works as we intended it to:

```
> :load gsum.hs
>gsum 5
5.0
>gsum ( (TAB 1 2, TAB 5 8) )
16.0
>gsum (TA 42 :: T Int Int)
42.0
```

With quite minimal boilerplate, we managed to create an extendable datatype generic sum function. Everything we did was safe and checked by the type checker at compile time; there was no need for any kind of dynamic typing.

The runtime cost of the GHC Generic representation is 0: there is usually no overhead for GHC Generics, because the Rep type representation is erased at compile time, unlike the reflection in Java, which has a considerable runtime cost.

Generating Haskell with Haskell

If the power of GHC Generics is not enough, that is, you really need to generate code that isn't derivable from the structure of datatypes, the solution you're looking for is Template Haskell (TH). TH is much more sophisticated than the C preprocessor. With TH, one basically has the full power of Haskell at one's disposal for code-generation. Like Haskell, Template Haskell will not compile unless it produces at least syntactically correct code.

Code generation should be used sparingly. It is easy to write highly unmaintainable code using Template Haskell. On the other hand, code generation can be an easy route for incorporating non-trivial domain-specific optimizations into a Haskell program. Most often though, Template Haskell is used mostly to replace boilerplate code by code that generates that boilerplate.

Template Haskell code lives in the Q monad. Take a look at the following code block:

```
-- module Language.Haskell.TH

data Q a

-- instances include: Monad, MonadFail, Quasi
```

In the `Language.Haskell.TH` module, the core algebraic datatypes that are able to represent Haskell syntax tree are also defined—declarations (`Dec`), expressions (`Exp`), patterns (`Pat`), and types (`Typ`). These are the four top-level terms that can be constructed and plugged in as source code for the compiler to process.

Interpolating template values is called splicing. The splicable expression must live in the Q monad and return a top-level term of correct type. The correct term type depends on the splicing context. Following this is an example each of an expression, declaration, pattern, and type expressed as template values:

```
module MySplices where

-- Expression: literal 1
myExp :: Exp
myExp = LitE (IntegerL 1)

-- Declaration: n = 1
myDec :: Dec
myDec = ValD (VarP (mkName"n")) (NormalBmyExp) []

-- Pattern: (1, 2)
myPat :: Pat
```

```
myPat = TupP [LitP (IntegerL 1), LitP (IntegerL 2)]

-- Type: Maybe Int
myType :: Type
myType = AppT (ConT (mkName"Maybe")) (ConT (mkName"Int"))
```

The `Language.Haskell.TH` module documentation conveniently gives examples for each constructor and their meaning. The constructor naming convention is also convenient; all constructors of `Exp` end in `E`, for example (`LitE` for literals, `VarE` for variables, `LamE` for lambdas, and so forth).

Splicing with $(...)

Now that we know how to write expressions using the algebraic datatypes, we can use the `$ (...)` splice operator to insert these values into our source code. We also need to lift pure terms into the `Q` monad using `pure`. Here are examples of contexts where splicing is applicable:

```
-- file splice-testing.hs
{-# LANGUAGE TemplateHaskell #-}

import MySplices

two :: Int
two = $(pure myExp) + $(pure myExp)

-- n = 1
$(pure [myDec])

f :: (Int, Int) -> String
f $(pure myPat) = "1 and 1"
f _             = "something else"

mint :: $(pure myType)
mint = Just two
```

A few points to note:

- It is a type error trying to splice expression `Q Exp` where a pattern `Q Pat` splice is expected.
- For convenience, top-level `Dec` splices are actually required to be a list of definitions or `Q [Dec]`. That's why we wrapped `myDec` into a singleton list.

- We intentionally defined our terms (myExp, myDec, myPat, and myType) in a separate module than to where we spliced them into. This is strictly necessary due to GHC's stage restriction: only definitions imported from other modules can be used inside a splice expression.

If you are wondering what GHC spliced, you can use the -ddump-splices flag when compiling:

```
$ ghc --make -ddump-splices splice-testing.hs
[1 of 2] Compiling MySplices        ( MySplices.hs, MySplices.o )
[2 of 2] Compiling Main             ( splice-testing.hs, splice-
testing.o )
splice-testing.hs:7:9-18: Splicing expression

    pure myExp ======> 1
splice-testing.hs:7:25-34: Splicing expression

    pure myExp ======> 1
splice-testing.hs:10:3-14: Splicing declarations

    pure [myDec] ======> n = 1
splice-testing.hs:16:11-21: Splicing type

    pure myType ======> Maybe Int
splice-testing.hs:13:5-14: Splicing pattern

    pure myPat ======> (1, 2)
```

Names in templates

In our declaration, we used the mkName :: String → Name function to create a Haskell identifier:

```
myDec = ValD (VarP (mkName "n")) (NormalB myExp) []
```

The mkName function sort of lifts the given string into a variable name in the meta program. The name is dynamic in the sense that the value it references to when spliced is the closest in scope. Names from mkName are resolved like any other Haskell bindings. This illustrates mkName:

```
n = 5
main = print $ (pure $ VarE $ mkName "n")
    where n = 1
```

This prints 1, because the where clause is closer to the splice.

Often it is convenient to have uncapturable names. For this, there is function
newName:

```
newName :: String -> Q Name
```

This one now lives in the Q monad, unlike mkName which was pure. Every name's generated with newName is uncapturable. For example, this program won't compile because the newName is not in scope:

```
main = print $(fmap VarE (newName "n"))
  where n = 1
```

Another way to generate names is to lift them from Haskell-land. Single-quote prefix lifts names for values:

```
right, left, pi' :: Name
right = 'Right
left  = 'Left
pi' = 'pi
```

Double-single quotes lift type names instead:

```
either :: Name
either = ''Either
```

The reason we need to use different quote-styles for values and types is because in Haskell, types and values, including type constructors, have their own namespaces. We need to somehow indicate to which namespace we are referring.

Smart template constructors

For every datatype constructor (LitE, ValD, and others) there is a "smart" constructor (litE, valD, and others) whose result and (most) arguments have been lifted to the Q monad. This is often convenient, because sub-expressions don't then need to be explicitly sequenced with monadic bind.

```
ValD :: Pat -> Body -> [Dec] -> Dec
valD :: PatQ -> BodyQ -> [DecQ] -> DecQ
```

PatQ is just a synonym for Q Pat.

The constN function

The normal `const` function takes two arguments and returns the first while ignoring a second argument. Now, we would like to have a set of `constN` functions for many N, which take *N+1* arguments, return the first argument and ignore all the others. The type signatures should look like the following:

```
const1 :: a -> b -> a
const2 :: a -> b -> c -> a
const3 :: a -> b -> c -> d -> a
...
```

The `constN` function here creates a definition for such `const` variant for given *N*:

```
module ConstSplices where

import Language.Haskell.TH

constN :: Int -> Q Dec
constN nth = do
    expr<- constExp nth
    let name = mkName $ "const" ++ show nth
    return $ FunD name [ Clause [] (NormalB expr) [] ]

constExp :: Int -> Q Exp
constExp nth = do
    a <- newName"a"
    return $ LamE (VarP a : replicate nth WildP) (VarE a)
```

A few things to note:

- We use `mkName` to create a capturable name for `const1`, `const2`, and so on.
- The `constExp` splice uses `newName` instead to name the first argument (a) of a lambda. Effectively, this turns into \a _ ... _ -> a.

To generate function declarations `constN` for *N* upto 15, we would write at top-level:

```
$(forM [1..15] constN)
```

But we could also generate them on demand using `constExp`:

```
putStrLn $ $(constExp 2) "Hello!" () 42
```

Lifting Haskell code to Q with quotation brackets

Whereas `$(...)` splices Q along with values into a source code, it's dual `[|...|]` (Oxford brackets) turns source code into Q values:

```
idExp :: Q Exp
idExp = [| \x -> x |]
```

Note that:

```
$( [| e |] ) == e
```

There are different brackets for quoting expressions `[e|...|]`, patterns `[p|...|]`, declarations `[d|...|]`, and type `[t|...|]`. A `[|...|]` is equal to writing `[e|...|]`.

It's perfectly fine to splice within a quotation:

```
$([| $(constExp 2) 'a' |]) 'b' 'c'
```

Launching missiles during compilation

It's possible to embed arbitrary IO actions into the Q monad using `runIO`:

```
runIO :: IO a -> Q a
```

An IO action could be used to embed a compilation timestamp as a constant or to source another file. For example, the source for a program written in an embedded **domain specific language (DSL)** could be read in at compile time and the corresponding Haskell code generated.

Although contrived, you could even read a line from standard input during splicing:

```
$(fmap (LitE . StringL) $ runIOgetLine)
```

Reifying Haskell data into template objects

Given a name, we can retrieve some information about the term itself using `reify`.

```
reify :: Name -> Q Info
```

Because type and constructor names may overlap, it is advised to use `reify` in conjunction with `lookupTypeName` or `lookupValueName` which lookup identifiers in correct namespaces:

```
lookupTypeName  :: String -> Q (Maybe Name)
lookupValueName :: String -> Q (Maybe Name)
```

Or, if you're certain that the name is (or should be) in scope, use the single quote notation:

```
reify 'value
reify ''Type
```

Reification is very useful, for instance, base code generation on a datatype. It's much like GHC Generics but with more flexibility. Common use cases are: defining class instances or completely new boilerplate functions for the datatype. For example, the lens library provides TH splices to generate lenses (a generalization of getters and setters) for user-defined datatypes.

Deriving setters with Template Haskell

When you declare a record in Haskell, the only way to update one of the fields then is to use the record syntax. For instance, we have the following user datatype:

```
data User = User
    { firstName :: String
    , lastName  :: String
    , age       :: Int
    } deriving Show
```

To update the age field of the user, we would write:

```
let user' = user { age = newAge }
```

But if we wanted to, we could write a setter function for a field:

```
age' :: User -> Int -> User
age' u newAge = u { age = newAge }

let user' = age' user newAge
```

Writing a setter for every field of every type would be laborious to say the least. Fortunately, we can automate the process by using a little Template Haskell.

```
setterDec :: Name -> Q Dec
setterDec nm = do
    let nmD = mkName $ nameBase nm ++ "'"-- (2)

    nmV<- newName"val"
    nmP<- newName"p"

    let pat  = [VarPnmV, VarPnmP]                        -- (3)
        body = NormalB $ RecUpdE (VarEnmP) [ (nm, VarEnmV) ] -- (4)

    return $ FunDnmD [ Clause pat body [] ]               --(1)
```

At (1), we build a function definition (FunD) named `field'` for a given field. The name is specified at (2) using mkName from the field name that is given as an argument to our setterDec template function. Note that a function may have multiple definitions with different patterns, therefore the second argument to FunD is a list of clauses.

In lines (3) and (4), we have defined arguments to our setter function (new field value and the object itself). The arguments val and p are given new unique names using newName. The record update itself is encoded in a record update expression using the RecUpdE constructor.

To create setters for every field of a datatype at once, we can write another template function:

```
deriveSetters :: Name -> Q [Dec]
deriveSetters nm = do
    TyConItyCon<- reify nm                                  -- (1)
    case tyCon of
        DataD _ nm tyVarscs _ -> do                         -- (2)
            let fieldsTypes = nub (concatMaprecFieldscs)  -- (3)
            forMfieldsTypes $
                \(nm, ty) ->setterDec nm                    -- (5)
    where                                                   -- (4)
      recFields (RecC _ xs) =
          map (\(var,_,ty) -> (var, ty)) xs
```

Here we now use reify to fetch information about the identifier. We are assuming that the identifier points to a type constructor, TyConI (1). Further, it should be a datatype, a DataD (2), as opposed to a newtype or type synonym for instance.

The magic of this template function happens at (3) when we get a list of record field names and their types that appear in the datatype. The list of fields in a single record (RecC) is retrieved at (4). A datatype can have multiple constructors with differing record fields, so we need to concatenate them all into a list and then remove duplicates with nub.

Finally at (5), we loop over unique record field names and create a setter definition for each record field using our setterDec template function.

Testing this out for our user datatype, we would use this splice at top-level:

```
deriveSetters ''User
```

Using `-ddump-splices`, we can confirm that the generated code is as we intended it to be:

```
$ ghc -ddump-splices reify-example.hs

[2 of 2] Compiling Main                    ( reify-example.hs, reify-
example.o )

reify-example.hs:13:1-20: Splicing declarations

    deriveSetters''User

  ======>

    firstName'val_a450p_a451 = p_a451 {firstName = val_a450}

    lastName'val_a452p_a453 = p_a453 {lastName = val_a452}

    age'val_a454p_a455 = p_a455 {age = val_a454}
```

There are three setter functions, as expected!

Note that, in this case we used about two dozen lines for two template functions in exchange of three one-liners. This isn't exactly what one could call good pay-off; much more the opposite. However, if we had tens of record fields as opposed to just three, which would often be the case, then the template solution starts to look viable.

Quasi-quoting for DSLs

One last feature of GHC closely related to Template Haskell is *quasi-quoted expressions*. Recall that the Oxford bracket notation `[e|...|]` enabled us to "un-quote" Haskell expressions into their object representation in the template datatypes (`Exp`, `Dec`, and so on).

This "un-quoting" of Haskell expressions is extendable to arbitrary syntax inside the brackets. More formally this is called quasi-quoting and quasi-quoters are defined as `QuasiQuoter`:

```
data QuasiQuoter = QuasiQuoter
    { quoteExp  :: String → Q Exp
    , quotePat  :: String → Q Pat
    , quoteType :: String → Q Type
    , quoteDec  :: String → Q Dec
    }
```

That is, depending on the splicing context quasi-quoter is a function from `String` to a syntax tree.

Quasi-quoters are generally used together with the datatype class and utility functions such as `dataToExpQ` (GHC 7), or the little more convenient `liftData` (starting with GHC 8):

```
dataToExpQ :: Data a => (Data b => b → Maybe (Q Exp)) → a → Q Exp
liftData :: Data a => a → Q Exp
```

The `liftData` function is equivalent to `dataToExpQ` applied to (const `Nothing`) – the first argument is there just to provide an option to override some constructor's representation.

Data is a derivable class when using the `DeriveDataTypeable` GHC extension. Thus, essentially, if we have a parser for an arbitrary datatype, and so we can convert it to a quasi-quoter with almost no effort. Shown here is a really quick illustration of a quasi-quoter for matrices `[[Double]]`:

```
module MatrixSplice where

import Language.Haskell.TH.Quote

matrix :: QuasiQuoter
matrix = QuasiQuoter { quoteExp = dataToExpQ (\_ -> Nothing) .
parse }

parse :: String -> [[Double]]
parse = map (map read . words) . filter (/= "") . lines
```

Now we can write matrices with minimum syntax directly into a Haskell source file. Here are some examples:

```
-- file compact-matrix.hs
{-# LANGUAGE QuasiQuotes #-}
import MatrixSplice

m1, m2 :: [[Double]]

m1 = [matrix|
  1 2
  2 1
|]

m2 = [matrix|
  1.5 4.2 5
  5.5 4.1 4
  4.5 4 1 6
|]
```

Note that `parse` could produce values of any type, as long as the value has a data instance. Quasi-quoting makes Haskell an even more friendly platform for embedded domain-specific languages, because it allows the seamless integration of the actual syntax of a custom language with the host language.

Summary

We started this chapter from GHC internal representation Core. We looked at the differences in Core syntax as opposed to Haskell syntax, among them explicit boxing, recursive bindings, explicit specialization and the passing of class dictionaries. Next, we took a glance at STG, the next internal representation after Core that's even simpler. Then we considered how GHC exposes its primitives: magic hash, unlifted types, and the unlifted kind.

Our second subject was code generation with GHC using GHC Generics. The essential idea with Generics is to represent every datatype as a sum of products using a handful of indexed datatypes (`:+:`, `:*:`, and so on). It then becomes easy to write general functions over all datatypes by converting to or from the general sum-of-products representation. Then we looked at full-blown code generation using Template Haskell, which enabled us to generate code, declarations and expressions by directly manipulating the program's abstract syntax tree.

In the next chapter we will be interacting with other languages from within Haskell, and interacting with Haskell from within other languages. It turns out that Haskell is surprisingly mature in this respect: the C foreign function interface is very robust and tooling is good. Going the other way around, GHC is able to compile Haskell into a shared object callable from other languages.

10
Foreign Function Interface

In the previous chapter, we learned how the GHC code generator works and how to dig deeper into the compiler pipeline when necessary. In this chapter we will learn to interface with C from Haskell, and with Haskell functions from C. The **foreign function interface** (**FFI**) is part of the Haskell language report. The tooling for binding into shared libraries and also for compiling Haskell into shared libraries is quite mature. In this chapter we will cover the fundamentals of the FFI: importing and exporting functions, marshalling data, invoking the Haskell runtime from C, and building shared libraries with Haskell.

One of Haskell's strongest points compared to many languages is in fact the FFI: it's relatively easy to integrate parts written in Haskell to programs written in C or the other way around. By extension, integrating Haskell with other languages by going through the C level is also not too hard. Building a shared library (a shared object or a DLL) with Haskell and GHC is quite easy:

- Calling C functions from Haskell and Haskell functions from C
- Using Haskell to build a shared library and using the library from C
- Marshalling pointers and data through the FFI between C and Haskell

From Haskell to C and C to Haskell

A classic usage of the FFI is calling C functions from Haskell. So let's start with that. Consider that you wrote a function in C, for instance the recursive n^{th} Fibonacci number like the fib.c file here:

```
/* file: fib.c */

int fib_c(int num)
{
  if (num <= 2)
```

```
      {
        return 1;
      }
      else
      {
        return(fib_c(num - 1) + fib_c(num - 2));
      }
}
```

Although naive, this implementation is still faster than the Haskell equivalent.

Now, to call this fast naive `fib_c` function from Haskell, at its simplest we could just add the following line to a Haskell source file and then we would have a `fib_c :: Int → Int` Haskell function:

```
-- file: ffi-fib.hs

foreign import ccall
  fib_c :: Int -> Int

main = print $ fib_c 20
```

The only FFI-specific thing here is `foreign import`. Note that, with some earlier versions of GHC, it was necessary to explicitly enable the FFI with `-XForeignFunctionInterface`.

To compile this program, we should give both the Haskell and C source file to GHC:

```
$ ghc ffi-fib.hs fib.c
[1 of 1] Compiling Main          ( ffi-fib.hs, ffi-fib.o )
Linking ffi-fib ...

$ ./ffi-fib
6765
```

Common types in Haskell and C

However, there's one problem in our binding: the Haskell `Int` type isn't guaranteed to match C's `int` type. In general, the types could have different sizes. The FFI specification explicitly addresses this problem by requiring Haskell implementations to provide a set of Haskell types that correspond to C types.

Haskell wrappers for common C types are defined in `Foreign.C.Types`. For instance, the `int` C type is `CInt` in Haskell, unsigned long in C is `CULong` in Haskell, and so on.

So to ensure correctness on all architectures, we should have written this instead:

```
foreign import ccall fib_c :: CInt -> CInt
```

A common pattern that is often used in Haskell bindings is to use C types in internal bindings and then expose wrappers that convert between C and Haskell types (such as `fromIntegral` for converting between `Int` and `CInt`).

Conversely, common Haskell types have corresponding C types defined in the header file `HsFFI.h`, which is distributed along with GHC. For instance, the Haskell `Int` type corresponds to `HsInt` in C, and the Haskell type `Ptr` is represented by `HsPtr` in C.

Using the Haskell types on the C side is also an option. We just need to include the Haskell FFI header file to use them:

```c
/* file: hs-fib.c */

#include <HsFFI.h>

int fib_c(HsInt num)
{
...
}
```

Importing static functions and addresses

The complete syntax for importing C definitions to Haskell-land is:

```
foreign import <callconv> [safe/unsafe] "<impent>"
    <variable> :: <type>
```

Let's see this syntax in more detail:

- For C binding, the calling convention `<callconv>` should be set to `ccall`, as we did in our previous example. Other calling conventions include `stdcall` for Win32 API bindings, and `cplusplus` for C++ calling convention.

- By default foreign calls are marked safe. Marking an import unsafe reduces the overhead of calling an external entity, but unsafe calls cannot call back to the Haskell system. Such callbacks are rather rare, so unsafe imports are used often.

- In the `impent` we define what we wish to import from the C side. If omitted, it defaults to `<variable>`. For instance, our `fib_c` function from earlier corresponds to impent `"fib_c"`.

- `<variable> :: <type>` just defines how the import looks in Haskell. Note that GHC does zero sanity checking on what you give it as a type. If the Haskell type doesn't align with the C-side definition, a segmentation fault awaits. The types don't need to match exactly though: for instance a `Bool` is a perfectly fine `int`.

The `impent` is actually a bit more complex. The complete syntax is given by:

```
impent → "[static] [chname] [&] [cid]" | "dynamic" | "wrapper"
```

There are three main alternatives: `static`, `dynamic`, or `wrapper`. Static function import (`"static [cid]"`) is the default behavior. To import a static address, the identifier `cid` should be preceded with an ampersand (`&`). Typing `static` in the `impent` is only necessary when importing C identifiers named `dynamic` or `wrapper`. Optionally, we can specify the exact header file `chname` from which the identifier to import (`cid`) is searched for.

Consider this C source file, defining a static function called `update` and a static address named `c_var`:

```
/* file: c_var.c */

int c_var = 0;

void update() {
  c_var = 42;
}
```

To use these two identifiers from Haskell, we import the variable with type `Ptr CInt` and update with type `IO ()`. Note that any static function can be imported either as a pure function or as an `IO` action. It is left up to the binding author to choose how to import a definition, because there is no systematic way to know whether a given C function is pure or not!

```
-- file: ffi-c-var.hs

import Foreign.C (CInt)
import Foreign.Ptr (Ptr)
import Foreign.Storable (peek)

foreign import ccall unsafe "&" c_var :: Ptr CInt
foreign import ccall unsafe update :: IO ()

main = do peek c_var >>= print
          update
          peek c_var >>= print
```

Let's compile this program and verify it works correctly:

```
$ ghc ffi-c-var.hs c_var.c
[1 of 1] Compiling Main              ( ffi-c-var.hs, ffi-c-var.o )
Linking ffi-c-var …

$ ./ffi-c-var
0
42
```

Now we know how to import static functions and variables that we have defined by ourselves in C source files.

To import a definition from an arbitrary header file, we should specify the header in the foreign import statement. For instance, to import the `sin` function from the `math.h` library:

```
-- file: ffi-math-h.hs
foreign import ccall unsafe "math.h sin"
    csin :: Double -> Double

foreign export ccall
    fun :: Int -> Int -> Int
```

This is really all that is required to import identifiers from system-wide C library headers. Such a definition can be compiled with just `ghc source.hs`.

Exporting Haskell functions

Exporting Haskell functions for use in C is as easy as importing functions from C. Here is a simple example that exports the Haskell function `fun`:

```
-- file: FunExport.hs
module FunExport where

foreign export ccall
    fun :: Int -> Int -> Int

fun :: Int -> Int -> Int
fun a b = a ^ 2 + b
```

Compiling this in GHC:

```
$ ghc -c FunExport.hs
```

GHC generates an object file `FunExport.o` and a header file `FunExport_stub.h`, effectively with the contents:

```
extern HsInt fun(HsInt a1, HsInt a2);
```

To call Haskell directly from C means that we need a `main` function in C. Then we need to initialize the Haskell system by ourselves using `hs_init()`. Here is an example C program that does that and then calls our Haskell `fun` function:

```
/* file: fun_export.c */

#include <stdio.h>
#include "FunExport_stub.h"

int main(int argc, char *argv[]) {
  hs_init(&argc, &argv);
  printf("%d\n", fun(1, 2));
  hs_exit();
}
```

To compile this C program we should not use a C compiler directly; instead we use GHC. The reason for this is that GHC is more knowledgeable about how the program should be linked, specifically the Haskell parts of it. The following command line creates a dynamically linked executable named `fun_export`, with the Haskell parts linked statically.

```
$ ghc --make -no-hs-main fun_export.c FunExport.o -o fun_export

$ ./fun_export

3
```

It's important to call `hs_init()` before using any identifiers from Haskell-land, and to terminate it when no longer needed with `hs_exit()`. Otherwise the program will `segfault`.

 Remember to enable optimizations for both Haskell and C when compiling for production! In our preceding example we would have used, for example, `ghc -c -O2 FunExport.hs` for the first and `ghc -optc-O ...` for the C second step.

Compiling a shared library

Given a Haskell source file, say `FunExport.hs`, we can create a shared library `libfunexport.so` with the following GHC command line:

```
ghc --make -dynamic -shared -fPIC FunExport.hs -o libfunexport.so
```

All flags, except perhaps -fPIC, are necessary to successfully build a shared library (at least with GHC 7 series and GHC 8.0.1). The most important flag is -shared, which specifies that we want to build a shared library. Unfortunately, GHC does not as yet support building the base libraries with -fPIC, which is a requirement for embedding into a shared object. Thus we need to link the shared object dynamically with -dynamic.

A similar command on a Windows machine can be used to build a DLL instead of a .so file. Just replace the .so suffix with .dll.

To compile and link a (C) program that uses the shared library, we need to jump through some extra hoops. A complete command line that takes a C source file (fun_export.c) that uses identifiers from the header file (FunExport_stub.h), links against a shared library (libfunexport.so), and uses GCC to compile a dynamically linked executable could look like the following:

```
gcc fun_export.c -o main \
-I /usr/lib/ghc-7.10.3/include \
-L. -L/usr/lib/ghc-7.10.3/rts \
-lHSrts-ghc7.10.3 -lfunexport \
-Wl,-rpath=/usr/lib/ghc-7.10.3/rts -Wl,-rpath='$ORIGIN'
```

The first line is self-explanatory. The -I flag specifies where to find the HsFFI.h header file. The -L flags specify where the Haskell Runtime System library and our own shared library are located. With the -l flags we are linking against the RTS and our own library.

On the last lines, the -Wl,-rpath=... flags specify additional runtime search paths for the executable. These are necessary so that the libraries can be found when the executable is to be run if they are located in non-standard paths. Special $ORIGIN refers to the directory name of the executable.

It's also possible to dynamically load (as opposed to link) a shared library from program code. The following is an example of a dynamic loading library funexport in C:

```
/* file: dyn_fun_export.c */

#include <stdio.h>
#include <dlfcn.h>

int main(intargc, char *argv[]) {
  void *dl = dlopen("./libfunexport.so", RTLD_LAZY);

  void (*hs_init)(int *argc, char **argv[]) = dlsym(dl,
    "hs_init");
```

```
    hs_init(&argc, &argv);

    int (*fun)(int a, int b) = dlsym(dl, "fun");
    printf("%d\n", fun(1, 2));
}
```

When compiling this, we only need to link against dl to gain access to dynamic loading:

gcc dyn_fun_export.c -o main -ldl

We also need to slightly modify our Haskell shared library to make it suitable for dynamic loading. The problem is that we still need the Haskell Runtime System, but by default it is not linked to a Haskell shared library. We need to specifically request that when building the shared library with -lHSrts-ghc7.10.3.

ghc --make -dynamic -shared -fPIC FunExport.hs -o libfunexport.so -lHSrts-ghc7.10.3

With this, the shared library is pretty much self-contained and can be loaded dynamically.

Function pointers and wrappers

Importing static functions was easy, but how about dynamic functions and function pointers? In Haskell, function pointers are represented by the datatype FunPtr. To import a function pointer into Haskell-land, we do the following:

```
-- file: ffi-funptr.hs

import Foreign.Ptr (FunPtr)

foreign import ccall"math.h & cos"
    p_cos :: FunPtr (Double -> Double)
```

We need the ampersand and a FunPtr return type. It's also possible for a C function to return a function pointer, in which case we could leave the ampersand out and import the function statically. In any case the result is a FunPtr return type in Haskell-land.

To convert a FunPtr return type into a Haskell function to call it, we need to jump through an extra hoop. Specifically, we must ask the FFI to generate a call routine for our specific function type using the dynamic impent. In this case that type is Double -> Double, so we write:

```
foreign import ccall "dynamic"
    mkF :: FunPtr (Double -> Double) -> (Double -> Double)
```

The `impent` is purely semantic: there is no need to define anything else to generate the call routine. Now we can apply `mkF` to our function pointer and get an ordinary Haskell function:

```
ghci> (mkF p_cos) pi
-1.0
```

The `"dual"` of dynamic is `wrapper`. Wrappers turn Haskell functions into `FunPtr` to be passed into the **foreign** side:

```
foreign import ccall "wrapper"
    toF :: (Double -> Double) -> IO (FunPtr (Double -> Double))
```

Note that creating a foreign function pointer from a Haskell function must be an `IO` action. The types for `dynamic` and `wrapper` types must conform to the general formulas (for some Haskell function `f`):

```
dynamic: FunPtr f -> f
wrapper: f -> IO (FunPtr f)
```

Haskell callbacks from C

Using FFI `wrappers` and `function` pointers we can easily pass Haskell functions as callbacks to foreign functions. Consider wanting to call this C function, which takes a function pointer as its first argument:

```c
/* file: callbacks-procedure.c */

void procedure(void (*callback)(double), double n) {
  callback(n * 3);
}
```

Here is an example Haskell program that calls `procedure`:

```haskell
-- file: callbacks.hs

import Foreign.Ptr (FunPtr)

foreign import ccall safe      -- (1)
procedure :: FunPtr (Double -> IO ()) -> Double -> IO ()

foreign import ccall"wrapper" -- (2)
toCallback :: (Double -> IO ()) -> IO (FunPtr
  (Double -> IO ()))

printRes :: Double -> IO ()      -- (3)
```

```
printRes x = putStrLn $ "Result: " ++ show x

main = do
cont <- toCallback printRes    -- (4)
procedure cont 5               -- (5)
procedure cont 8               --
```

Tearing this down, we have:

- At (1) we import the procedure as a normal FFI function. Note that we must import it `safe` – if it is imported `unsafe`, our program will crash at runtime with the helpful error message:

  callbacks: schedule: re-entered unsafely.

  Perhaps a 'foreign import unsafe' should be 'safe'?

- At (2) we create the `wrapper` to wrap a Haskell function as a function pointer that can be passed to procedure.

- At (3) we use the pure Haskell callback function (`printRes`). In this case, it is an I/O action with `()` `result type`; `IO ()` corresponding to `void *` on the C side.

- At (4) we wrap our callback into a function pointer.

- At (5) are two example calls for `procedure` from Haskell `main`.

So, using arbitrary Haskell functions as callbacks to foreign calls is very easy. The only necessary boilerplate is creating an FFI wrapper corresponding to the callback function's type, and wrapping callbacks as function pointers before passing them to the procedure.

Data marshal and stable pointers

The Haskell types `Ptr a` and `FunPtr a` represent pointers in foreign, raw memory (outside the Haskell heap). Relevant operations on foreign pointers are provided by the `Storable` type class, which has instances for primitive marshallable data types. A third pointer type is `StablePtr a`, which is a pointer to an object in the Haskell heap.

On top of passing primitive values and pointers through the FFI, almost arbitrary data can be marshalled between Haskell and C (and by extension other languages) relatively easily.

Allocating memory outside the heap

A centric type-class in marshalling is `Foreign.Storable.Storable`. Storable types must provide a length, byte alignment, and the methods `peek` and `poke`:

```
class Storable a where
  sizeOf :: a ->Int
  alignment :: a ->Int
  peek :: Ptr a -> IO a
  poke :: Ptr a -> a -> IO ()
  ...
```

Primitive allocation routines are located in the `Foreign.Marshal.Alloc` module. Normal dynamic allocations are provided for using `malloc` and also `alloca`, which allocates a block of memory used locally. Using `alloca` we don't need to take care of freeing allocated memory, because the combinator does it for us once the local computation finishes:

```
malloc :: Storable a => IO (Ptr a)
alloca :: Storable a => (Ptr a → IO b) → IO b
```

Haskell lists are usually represented as arrays in C. To convert between a linked list in Haskell and an array in C, we can use the `Foreign.Marshal.Array` module. Methods are once again overloaded over `Storable`, as in:

```
newArray :: Storable a => [a] → IO (Ptr a)
peekArray :: Storable a => Int → Ptr a → IO [a]
```

Strings in Haskell are also linked lists, but in C they're null-terminated consecutive blocks of memory. Convenience routines for working with this translation are located in the `Foreign.C.String` module.

Pointing to objects in the heap

Haskell values in foreign code are represented by stable pointers, `StablePtr a`. A special pointer type is needed for values in Haskell due to GC: normally GC could and does collect or move objects in the heap, changing their memory location. But values pointed to by stable pointers don't get collected or relocated. Thus, stable pointers are ideal for passing Haskell values into C and back.

Stable pointers support these operations: `create`, `de-ref` and `free`. From the type signatures we can infer that a `StablePtr` pointer can really point to Haskell values of any (concrete) type:

```
newStablePtr    :: a -> IO (StablePtr a)
deRefStablePtr :: StablePtr a -> IO a
freeStablePtr  :: StablePtr a -> IO ()
```

On the C side very little can be done with a `StablePtr` pointer. The `HsStablePtr` pointer is merely guaranteed to be a valid pointer, within the Haskell runtime, that is once derefenced with `deRefStablePtr`. The pointed value will be retained by GC at least until `freeStablePtr` is called.

Marshalling abstract datatypes

Any Haskell datatype can be made marshallable by giving it a `Storable` instance. Instead of writing the instance by hand, accommodating for correct alignment in the corresponding C structs and so forth, we can automate a lot of the process using the hsc2hs tool.

For instance, consider having the following C header file and custom `struct`:

```
// file: struct-marshal-c.h

typedefstruct {
    int a;
    double b;
} Some;
```

The corresponding Haskell datatype and (pseudo-)Haskell source file that will contain the `Storable` instance starts with:

```
-- file: struct-marshal.hsc

#include <struct-marshal-c.h>

import Foreign.Storable

data Some = Some { a :: Int, b :: Double }
```

Note the `.hsc` extension and an `#include` directive. We are going to preprocess this file with hsc2hs, which calculates size and alignments for the marshal.

A quick note before going forward: on GHC 8 the following macro is already present in `hsc2hs`, but for the GHC 7 series we need to define the `alignment` macro by ourselves. On GHC 8 the following is unnecessary:

```
#let alignment t = "%lu", (unsigned long)offsetof(struct {char
  x__; t (y__); }, y__)
```

Now we can write the `Storable` instance:

```
instance Storable Some where
    sizeOf _ = (#size Some)
    alignment _ = (#alignment Some)
    peek ptr = Some <$> (#peek Some, a) ptr
                     <*> (#peek Some, b) ptr
    poke ptr some = do
        (#poke Some, a) ptr (a some)
        (#poke Some, b) ptr (b some)
```

Note the use of # macros. These will be expanded by running `hsc2hs`:

`hsc2hs -I. struct-marshal.hsc`

`hsc2hs` generates a `struct-marshal.hs` file that is now valid Haskell and can be fed into GHC.

Using a pre-processor is highly recommended when creating Haskell bindings to C libraries. In addition to hsc2hs there is another preprocessor called c2hs. These have many overlapping features but each has some unique characteristics as well.

Marshalling in standard libraries

The core Haskell container libraries (`bytestring`, `vector`, `text`, and others) include good support for efficient marshalling of their datatypes through the FFI.

All ByteString values are actually already stored outside the Haskell heap, which means that foreign code can read and write a ByteString with zero copying needed. However, such interoperability is deemed unsafe because it easily breaks referential transparency. That is why these fast marshalling functions are placed in the `Data.ByteString.Unsafe` module. Slower but safer marshal alternatives are in the `Data.ByteString` module.

The `vector` package deals with marshalling by providing custom vector types with storable instances in the `Data.Vector.Storable` package. This representation is slightly slower than using pure unboxed vectors, but is the `vector` type of choice if marshallability is required.

Finally, the text package contains a `Data.Text.Foreign` module which provides conversion functions. Marshalling unicode-correct text between C is not trivial in every case, so Text marshal is a bit more complicated.

Summary

In this chapter we have imported C functions as Haskell functions, exported Haskell functions as C functions, passed pointers (both foreign and stable) and data through the FFI, built a shared library with Haskell, and used hsc2hsto to write a `Storable` instance for a custom datatype. You have learned to invoke the FFI from both the C and the Haskell side and to manage memory in both the Haskell heap and the lower-level memory area also used by C.

The next chapter will be about another implementation-level concept like the FFI: GPU-programming using Haskell. Graphics processors are much better suited for highly parallel number-crunching applications, which is the reason for the GPU's popularity in high-performance numeric computing. An excellent Haskell library, `Accelerate`, defines a language that greatly simplifies usually mundane and hard GPU programming. In addition, `Accelerate` is backend-agnostic: the same code could run on any hardware solution (CPU/LLVM, CUDA, OpenCL, and others) given a suitable backend implementation.

11
Programming for the GPU with Accelerate

In recent years, **Graphics Processing Units (GPUs)** have become prominent hardware in areas other than just plain graphics applications. This practice is known as **General-Purpose Computing On Graphics Processing Units (GPGPU)**. Due to their ability to perform highly parallel computations much more efficiently compared to a CPU, the GPU is often utilized, for instance, in machine-learning applications. The GPU is specialized to perform certain kinds of vectorized computations extremely efficiently. It's not nearly as flexible as a CPU is. Single cores in a GPU are far less powerful than CPU cores, but there are hundreds of smaller cores in a GPU.

Due to their parallel nature, GPUs use wildly different instruction sets than, say, the x86. The two dominant ways of writing programs that run on the GPU are Nvidia's proprietary **CUDA** platform and **OpenCL**, which is an open source framework and standard for writing programs that run on heterogeneous hardware (CPU, GPU, DSP, FPGA, and others). Both CUDA and OpenCL are designed to work with low-level imperative languages: CUDA for C, C++, and Fortran, while OpenCL defines its own C-like language.

The Haskell library Accelerate is a high-level EDSL for writing programs that execute on the GPU. Accelerate is fully backend-agnostic: the same Accelerate program can be turned into a CUDA application, executed using the reference interpreter on the CPU, and translated into an OpenCL application, a Repa application, an LLVM application, or indeed extended with your own backend. Currently, only the interpreter and CUDA backend are considered mature.

In this chapter, we will learn to write high-performance programs with Accelerate and to run them on the GPU. Although first we test our programs using the reference interpreter. The chapter will cover the following topics:

- Writing in the core Accelerate language, operations, and expressions
- Running on CUDA and writing efficient high-level GPU programs
- Using Accelerate's extra features: tuples, reductions, and backend foreign functions

Writing Accelerate programs

Accelerate arrays are indexed by similar data types with Repa arrays, in other words, snoc-style lists:

```
data Z
data tail :. head = tail :. head
```

Like Repa, `type` synonyms are provided for Accelerate indices:

```
type DIM0 = Z
type DIM1 = DIM0 :. Int
type DIM2 = DIM1 :. Int
...
```

The Accelerate array type is `Array sh e`. We can build accelerated arrays from lists with `fromList`:

```
> import Data.Array.Accelerate as A
> fromList (Z :. 5) [1..5]
Array (Z :. 5) [1,2,3,4,5]
```

Now let's try to do something with an `Array`: reverse it. Accelerate provides the function `reverse`, but it has this slightly daunting type signature:

```
reverse :: Elt e => Acc (Vector e) -> Acc (Vector e)
```

And if we try to apply `reverse` to an array directly, we are greeted with a type-mismatch error:

```
> A.reverse (fromList (Z :. 5) [1..] :: Array DIM1 Int)

<interactive>:24:12:
    Couldn't match expected type 'Acc (Vector e)'
                with actual type 'Array DIM1 Int'
```

The problem is that `reverse` expects its argument to be a vector wrapped within an accelerated computation: `Acc (Vector e)`. `Acc` type marks an accelerated computation that produces a value of the given type. Vector is just a synonym for a one-dimensional array. Accelerate provides a function to use bare arrays within computations, aptly named `use`:

```
use :: Arrays arrays => arrays -> Acc arrays
```

The `reverse` function also unsurprisingly returns `Acc`, an accelerated computation, so we need also some way to run such accelerated computation. One `run` function is provided by another module: `Data.Array.Accelerate.Interpreter`. Yet another `run` is provided by the `accelerate-cuda` package, which we'll meet shortly. For now let's use the interpreter:

```
Data.Array.Accelerate.Interpreter.run :: Arrays a => Acc a -> a
```

The `Arrays` type-class is used to overload over arrays and tuples of arrays.

Now we have all the pieces needed to reverse an accelerated array, so let's test it out:

```
>I.run $ A.reverse (use $ fromList (Z :. 5) [1..5]) :: Array DIM1 Int
Array (Z :. 5) [5,4,3,2,1]
```

Kernels – The motivation behind explicit use and run

Let's step back and think for a moment. Why did the `Accelerate` library designers decide that `reverse` and many other operations should take in and produce arrays inside some Acc context? In theory, the API could be completely transparent without exposing the internal Acc context at all.

The reason stems from how the GPU interacts with rest of the computer. The memory of a GPU is separate from the system RAM. This means that every array and indeed computation we wish to perform on the GPU must be loaded into the GPU memory from system memory. Loading stuff into or from the GPU is highly inefficient, so we would like to avoid doing it in excess.

In the lower-level (CUDA and OpenCL) frameworks, we would not only load data (arrays) explicitly but also define the computing kernels (computations) explicitly. In Accelerate, we load data explicitly but kernel-loading is largely abstracted away. The Acc datatype is in fact a sort of AST that is turned into code that is then compiled by an Accelerate backend (CUDA, for instance).

The trick that Accelerate employs is that its kernels are created on demand. In addition, for acceptable performance, it's necessary to memoize often-used kernels so that they're loaded only once. Memoization is the part where we as library users need to be conscious, because if we write code that doesn't reuse kernels enough, it really hurts performance. Arguably, solving this problem perfectly on the library side, even in Haskell, would be akin to solving the halting problem.

The rule of thumb for performance would be to always pass changing arguments inside accelerated arrays (Acc). Accelerate also provides some debugging tools to diagnose kernel-sharing problems. But for now we won't delve into optimizations and instead use Accelerate for getting things done.

Working with elements and scalars

The Accelerate API builds upon arrays: nearly everything is an array. This is understandable, because the GPU also operates on arrays. This doesn't mean we would need to throw away convenience of scalars. After all, scalars are just zero-dimensional arrays:

```
type Scalar e = Array DIM0 e
```

For convenience, Accelerate has its own expression language for manipulating scalars. An expression is represented by the abstract data type:

```
data Exp t
```

There's a plethora of related type-classes and instances for `Exp`. Most notably, if *t* is some Haskell numeric type, then `Exp` inherits its numeric nature via the classes `Num`, `Floating`, and `Fractional`.

To construct values in the expression language, we can use `lift`:

```
> lift (42 :: Int) :: Exp Int
42
```

If the value is truly constant (and an instance of the `Elt` type-class of array element types), `constant` is also an option:

```
constant :: Elt t => t -> Exp t
```

The expression language is closely tied to `Acc`. Once something is in `Exp`, we can't get it out without `run`. We can't evaluate `Exp` scalars directly. For that we need `unit`:

```
unit :: Elt e => Exp e -> Acc (Scalar e)
```

Once again, the GPU revolves around arrays so we needed a zero-dimensional array. So, all in all, the following conversions are possible:

```
> let a0 = 42          :: Int
> let a1 = lift a0     :: Exp Int
> let a2 = unit a1     :: Acc (Scalar Int)
> let a3 = run a2      :: Scalar Int
> indexArray a3 Z      :: Int
42
```

There's yet one more operation, the dual of `unit`, which turns an accelerated scalar array into an expression:

```
the :: Elt e => Acc (Scalar e) -> Exp e
```

The following figure sums up the transformations between the `Haskell`, `Exp`, and `Acc` worlds:

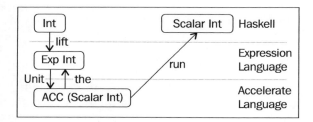

We can do basic arithmetic in the expression language:

```
> lift (1 :: Int) + lift (2 :: Int) :: Exp Int
3
```

`Exp` occurs where the Accelerate API expects or produces scalar values: indexing, mapping, array construction by element, and so forth. There is only a very small set of API operations that don't live in the `Acc` context. For instance, `indexArray` works on plain arrays, but not on arrays inside `Acc`. The (`!`) function does indexing within `Acc`, and produces an expression as opposed to a plain element:

```
(!) :: (Shape ix, Elt e) => Acc (Array ix e) -> Exp ix -> Exp e
```

Rudimentary array computations

Besides initializing accelerated arrays from Haskell lists using `fromList`, using the `generate` routine, we can initialize an array in parallel within an accelerated computation:

```
generate
  :: (Shape ix, Elt a) =>
     Exp ix -> (Exp ix -> Exp a) -> Acc (Array ix a)
```

Again, nearly everything is wrapped within an `Exp` or `Acc`. Note that functions cannot be expressions: we couldn't have an `Exp` (ix → a). And if we had just (ix → a), then for every element the Haskell runtime and thus CPU would need to be bothered, which is exactly what we want to avoid in GPU programming.

But how would we build a function of the required type `Exp ix -> Exp a`? Or more precisely, what can we do with a value, say, `Exp DIM2`? One thing we can do is index other arrays with it using (`!`). But what if we needed separate access to the components of the wrapped `DIM2`? We can't directly pattern-match, because `Exp` doesn't allow it. What we need is the `unlift` function:

```
unlift :: Unlift c e => c (Plain e) -> e
```

Contrary to its name, `unlift` is not exactly the dual of `lift`, which brings Haskell values into the `Exp` language. `unlift` can only bring back a small subset of values, specifically singleton types such as `Z` or (`:.`). Applied to an `Exp DIM2`, `unlift` gets specialized into the following:

```
unlift :: Exp DIM2 → Z :. Exp Int :. Exp Int
```

We can break up the dimensions of an `Exp DIM2`, but we cannot escape the expression language itself (without `run`). Usually this is exactly what you want, though, because most operations expect an `Exp` value anyways. The following code uses `generate` together with `unlift` to generate an array that is a combination of two arrays:

```
> let as = lift $ fromList (Z :. 3) [1..] :: Acc (Array DIM1 Int)
> let bs = lift $ fromList (Z :. 2) [100,100] :: Acc (Array DIM1 Int)

> run $ generate (index2 3 2)
    (\ix -> let Z :. x :. y = unlift ix
            in as A.!! x + bs A.!! y)
Array (Z :. 3 :. 2) [101,101,102,102,103,103]
```

Unsurprisingly, the `map` function on accelerated arrays operates on expressions:

```
A.map
  :: (Shape ix, Elt a, Elt b) =>
     (Exp a -> Exp b) -> Acc (Array ix a) -> Acc (Array ix b)
```

But a little crazy type won't stop us from doing simple things simply:

```
> run $ A.map (^2) as
Array (Z :. 3) [1,4,9]
```

Example – Matrix multiplication

Let's now use what we have learned so far and implement matrix multiplication with Accelerate. An approach which we will try first uses `generate` to produce the result matrix. So, let's start with a simple preamble:

```
-- file: matrix.hs

{-# LANGUAGE TypeOperators #-}

import Data.Array.Accelerate as A

type Matrix = Array DIM2 Double
```

The implementation with `generate` is relatively straightforward:

```
matProduct :: Acc Matrix -> Acc Matrix -> Acc Matrix
matProduct a b = let

    -- (1)
    Z :. mx :. _ = unlift (shape a) :: Z :. Exp Int :. Exp Int
    Z :. _ :. my = unlift (shape b) :: Z :. Exp Int :. Exp Int

    -- (2)
    in generate (index2 mx my) $ \ix ->
        let Z :. x :. y = unlift ix :: Z :. Exp Int :. Exp Int
            s1 = lift (Z :. x :. All)
            s2 = lift (Z :. All :. y)
            -- (3)
            in the $ A.sum $ A.zipWith (*) (slice a s1) (slice b s2)
```

At `(1)`, we get the size of the result matrix. At `(2)`, we would produce the matrix by mapping a function `(3)` over every individual index (in parallel). The function at `(3)` uses slice to get the row and column needed to compute a value at the given index. Then we use `A.sum` and to produce an expression.

But it turns out this implementation will not work.

The Haskell type-checks and compiles, but the Accelerate program will not work; we are greeted with an error message akin to the following:

```
*** Exception: Cyclic definition of a value of type 'Exp' (sa = 7)
```

This is one of Accelerate's ways of telling that you have (possibly) attempted to employ nested parallelism – which is not supported by Accelerate or the GPU.

Using the generate function, it's really easy to encode nested parallelism. The reason is that generate itself is parallel, so the supplied function must not be parallel. In our function, we are using the to produce an Exp from an accelerated computation, and then perform the computation in parallel; thus, we have nested parallelism.

To work around the limitations, we need to be clever. We can't express ourselves with generate. The goal should be to vectorize the algorithm altogether, because performing vectorized operations is what GPUs are extremely fast at. In general, we should avoid producing single scalar values (like generate function argument of generate) and operate on whole arrays instead.

A known vectorized version of matrix multiplication uses a third dimension to encode fold (sum). An implementation is given in the following section. Perhaps surprisingly, the vectorized version is more readable than the naive version. But it's not so easy to wrap one's head around:

```
matProduct :: Acc Matrix -> Acc Matrix -> Acc Matrix
matProduct a b = let

    Z :. mx :. _  = unlift (shape a)   :: Z :. Exp Int :. Exp Int
    Z :. _  :. my = unlift (shape b)   :: Z :. Exp Int :. Exp Int

    aRep = A.replicate (lift $ Z :. All :. my  :. All) a
    bRep = A.replicate (lift $ Z :. mx  :. All :. All) (A.transpose b)

    in A.fold (+) 0
        $ A.zipWith (*) aRep bRep
```

Note that A.zipWith zips element-wise in a linear fashion, while A.fold reduces the lowest dimension only. A.sum would be inappropriate here, because A.sum would produce a scalar. Indeed, a vectorized solution is not always imminent. But the benefit of vectorization is huge on highly parallel GPUs.

Flow control and conditional execution

In general, conditional `if-then-else` and similar constructs don't compose well with parallel execution. As a rule of thumb, conditionals should be kept to a minimum, but often some flow control is still needed.

In the `Exp` world, we have some unsurprising combinators. Here is the classic conditional, or `if-then-else`:

```
cond :: Elt t => Exp Bool -> Exp t -> Exp t -> Exp t
```

Here is its infix form:

```
(?) :: Elt t => Exp Bool -> (Exp t, Exp t) -> Exp t
```

This is a `while` construct:

```
while :: Elt e => (Exp e -> Exp Bool) -> (Exp e -> Exp e) -> Exp e
   -> Exp e
```

The `cond` and `while` operators also have variants lifted to the Acc world, named `acond` (infix (`?|`)) and `awhile`:

```
acond :: Arrays a => Exp Bool -> Acc a -> Acc a -> Acc a

(?|) :: Arrays a => Exp Bool -> (Acc a, Acc a) -> Acc a

awhile
  :: Arrays a =>
      (Acc a -> Acc (Scalar Bool)) -> (Acc a -> Acc a) -> Acc a -> Acc
a
```

Inspecting generated code

Accelerate programs are turned into an intermediate language, which is understood by Accelerate backends such as the interpreter or the CUDA backend. We can inspect the intermediate code easily via some handy `Show` instances in Accelerate. In particular, all `Acc arr` values can be shown. We can try that in GHCi:

```
> A.map (^2) (lift (fromList (Z:.3) [1..] :: Array DIM1 Int))

let a0 = use (Array (Z :. 3) [1,2,3])
in map (\x0 -> x0 * x0) a0
```

Exps are showable, and so are functions that take only `Acc` or `Exp` values as arguments:

```
> A.map (^2) :: Acc (Array DIM2 Int) -> Acc (Array DIM2 Int)

\a0 -> map (\x0 -> x0 * x0) a0
```

Looking at the generated code is one way of debugging Accelerate programs. If the generated code doesn't look right, the problem is likely in our code, not the backend. Even an attempt at showing can produce a runtime error, like sometimes happens when nested parallelism is encoded unintentionally.

Running with the CUDA backend

To compile using the CUDA backend, we should install the `accelerate-cuda` package from **Hackage**. Also required is the CUDA platform. Refer to the `accelerate-cuda` package documentation and CUDA platform documentation for further information:

```
cabal install accelerate-cuda -fdebug
```

The Haskell dependencies require some additional tools in scope, including `alex`, `happy`, and `c2hs`. Install those first if necessary. The `debug` flag gives our Accelerate CUDA programs some additional tools. There's no extra runtime cost versus no debug flag. The additional flags could interfere with the user program, though.

In principle, the only necessary code change for using the CUDA backend instead of the interpreter is to import the `run` function from `Data.Array.Accelerate.CUDA` instead of the `Interpreter` module:

```
import Data.Array.Accelerate.CUDA
```

The program below executes our matrix product of 100x100 matrices on the GPU using CUDA. Note that swapping back to the interpreter is a matter of swapping out CUDA for interpreter in the corresponding `import` statement. Indeed, with CPP, it is easy to put the choice behind a compile-time `cabal` flag as well:

```
-- file: matrix-cuda.hs

{-# LANGUAGE TypeOperators #-}

import Data.Array.Accelerate as A
import Data.Array.Accelerate.CUDA

type Matrix = Array DIM2 Double
```

```
matProduct = ...


main = let
    mat :: Matrix
    mat = fromList (Z :. 100 :. 100) [1..]

    res = run $ A.sum $ matProduct (lift mat) (lift mat)


    in print res
```

Assuming CUDA and the corresponding libraries are installed, we can compile the program like any other Haskell program. Note that all Accelerate programs must be linked with the threaded GHC runtime:

```
ghc -threaded -O2 matrix-cuda.hs
```

```
[1 of 1] Compiling Main        ( matrix-cuda.hs, matrix-cuda.o )
Linking matrix-cuda ...
```

We execute the resulting binary normally. The matrix product is calculated rather fast, using the GPU:

```
./matrix-cuda
Array (Z) [2.5088563200314e13]
```

Debugging CUDA programs

When `accelerate-cuda` is compiled with `-fdebug`, some extra options are available in compiled GPU programs. A full list is maintained in the `accelerate-cuda` package documentation. The following are a handful of useful flags:

- `-ddump-cc`: Dump information about CUDA kernel compilation and execution
- `-ddump-exec`: Dump CUDA kernels before execution
- `-fflush-cache`: Delete CUDA kernel disk cache

The additional output from our matrix product example program looks like the following:

```
./matrix-cuda -ddump-cc
0.09:cc: initialise kernel table
0.09:cc: persist/restore: 4 entries
0.09:cc: found/persistent
0.10:cc: found/persistent
```

```
0.10:cc: found/persistent
0.10:cc: entry function 'fold' used 40 registers, 0 bytes smem, 0 bytes
lmem, 0 bytes cmem
    ... multiprocessor occupancy 78.1% : 1600 threads over 50 warps in 25
blocks
0.10:cc: entry function 'foldAll' used 16 registers, 0 bytes smem, 0
bytes lmem, 0 bytes cmem
    ... multiprocessor occupancy 100.0% : 2048 threads over 64 warps in 2
blocks
0.10:cc: entry function 'foldAll' used 16 registers, 0 bytes smem, 0
bytes lmem, 0 bytes cmem
    ... multiprocessor occupancy 100.0% : 2048 threads over 64 warps in 2
blocks
```

Most of the time, we are executing with multiprocessor occupancy of 100%, which is really good. It's an indicator we are utilizing the full capabilities of the GPU.

Accelerate caches the CUDA kernels under a .accelerate directory under your home directory. When executing an Accelerate program for the first time, we spend a lot of time producing the kernels – in our small example, this accounted for about 1.5 extra seconds for just three kernels on my system. On consecutive executions, however, the kernels are pulled from the cache.

Use -fflush-cache to clear the cache before execution. To inspect only the executed kernels, pass -ddump-exec.

If the program is repeatedly producing new kernels when you think some previously used kernel could be reused, this can be spotted in the debug output.

More Accelerate concepts

So far, we have considered accelerated arrays and expressions. These are the primitives that Accelerate builds upon. On top, we have a bunch of functional machinery to help us express ourselves in accelerated computations: zips and unzips, reductions, permutations, stencils, and so forth. The complete API is documented in the accelerate package. In this section, we consider using some of the most useful parts of this machinery.

Working with tuples

GPUs don't allow array nesting or tuples as elements of an array. Nested arrays can be somewhat mimicked with higher-dimensional arrays. And it might not come as a surprise that Accelerate supports tuples as elements of an array. Internally, arrays with tupled elements are represented as tuples of arrays, but this is strictly an implementation detail. For the programmer, it really looks like we are working with tupled elements, which is sometimes very convenient.

With `zip` and `unzip`, we can (de)construct tupled elements within accelerated arrays with zero runtime cost. A tuple array could be used to represent an array of imaginary numbers, or instances.

The `lift` and `unlift` functions translate between tuple expressions and tuples of expressions. For instance, these are valid type specializations of `lift` and `unlift`:

```
lift :: (Exp Int, Exp Int) -> Exp (Int, Int)

unlift :: Exp (Int, Int) -> (Exp Int, Exp Int)
```

`lift` and `unlift` work with `Acc` in place of `Exp` too.

Regarding performance, it doesn't matter whether there is a tuple of expressions (`Exp`) or an expression of tuples. They have pretty much the same internal representation and will produce the same program.

Folding, reducing, and segmenting

Accelerate provides familiarly named `fold` and `fold1`, but unlike those versions of these functions in `Data.List`, the Accelerate ones fold over the innermost dimension only, so they can be used to reduce the rank of an array by one. To fold along all dimensions producing a scalar, functions like `foldAll` and `fold1All` can be used.

What's different versus `Data.List` style folds is that Accelerate's folds always proceed in parallel. This means that the folding function must be associative. To do sequential fold with Accelerate, we would need to use `sfoldl`, also from the `Accelerate` library. Note that `slfold` only reduces along the innermost slice:

```
sfoldl :: _ => (Exp a → Exp b → a)
    → Exp a
    → Exp sh
    → Acc (Array (sh :. Int) b)
    → Exp a
```

The slice is specified by an argument of type `Exp sh`. There is no ready-made solution for folding over a whole dimension or all dimensions sequentially. It is not a common need to fold a multi-dimensional array non-associatively, and a sequential fold of a big array isn't very efficient on a GPU due to the lack of parallelism.

One more folding variant provided by Accelerate operates on segments:

```
type Segments i = Vector i
```

Segments are how nested one-dimensional arrays can be represented in Accelerate: a segment array gives the lengths of successive logical sub-arrays within an array. The `foldSeg` and `fold1Seg` functions fold over each logical sub-array, producing an array with the same dimensionality but with the logical sub-arrays reduced.

Accelerated stencils

Stencils pop up in many applications. We have covered the basics of stencils in the *Chapter 5, Parallelize for Performance*. Now we will promptly consider how the stencil system present in Accelerate is used, and its limitations.

The `core` function stencil has a predictable signature:

```
stencil
  :: (Stencil ix a stencil, Elt b) =>
     (stencil -> Exp b)
     -> Boundary a -> Acc (Array ix a) -> Acc (Array ix b)
```

Note the `Stencil` type-class. It's multi-parameter with parameters for the shape, `element` type, and `stencil` type. For a one-dimensional array, the corresponding stencil is a tuple of its elements:

```
Stencil DIM1 e (Exp e, Exp e, Exp e)
```

For a two-dimensional array, we have tuples of tuples of elements; for instance, a 3x3 stencil would be as follows:

```
Stencil DIM2 e ( (Exp e, Exp e, Exp e)
, (Exp e, Exp e, Exp e)
, (Exp e, Exp e, Exp e))
```

We could nest tuples even further for higher-dimensional arrays. Provided `Stencil` instances are inductive on the array shape, so arbitrary ranks are supported. Furthermore supported are tuples of 3, 5, 7, and 9 elements.

The meat of a stencil application lies in the `stencil` function, that has the type (for some `Stencil` is a `stencil`):

```
stencil → Exp b
```

This is perhaps a more powerful way to represent stencils than Repa's element-wise multiplication. Nevertheless, expressing a 3x3 stencil that detects horizontal lines using a threshold of `0.5` is expressed easily:

```
stFun ( (x1, x2, x3)
      , (y1, y2, y3)
      , (z1, z2, z3) ) = y1 >* 0.5 &&*
                         y2 >* 0.5 &&*
                         y3 >* 0.5 ? (1, 0)
```

Accelerate also supports binary stencils, via the function `stencil2`. Binary stencils operate on two images, combining them neighborhood-wise. A binary `stencil` function would have the following type:

```
stencil :: stencil → stencil → Exp b
```

The `boundary` argument is very similar to how it is in Repa. The benefit of using Accelerate instead of Repa for stencils is, of course, higher parallelism. For bigger images or arrays, Accelerate can easily be many times faster on a GPU than Repa on a CPU.

Permutations in Accelerate

A permutation is an array transformation which reorders the elements, possibly replacing some with new elements and maybe altering the shape. Accelerate provides combinators for both forward and backward permutations. In a forward permutation, indices are mapped from the input array to the output array. Going backward, output array indices define input indices.

Reverse and transpose are examples of permutations. These two are provided by Accelerate by default. Generic forward permutation is called permute while backward permutation is `backpermute`.

Using the backend foreign function interface

Not every Accelerate backend is built even. Some backends provide routines that others don't that are a lot faster due to specialized hardware, for instance. Accelerate provides a thin layer for embedding backend-specific alternatives in accelerated computations. The FFI consists of two embedding functions (contexts omitted for clarity):

```
foreignAcc :: _ =>
    ff acc res → (Acc acc → Acc res) → Acc acc → Acc res

foreignExp :: _=>
    ff e res → (Exp e → Exp res) → Exp e → Exp res
```

The first argument in both `foreignAcc` and `Exp` is a value of a type defined by the backend. For instance, `accelerate-cuda` provides `CUDAForeignAcc` and `*Exp` datatypes that can be used to construct wrappers for CUDA-specific functions.

For example, CUDA has a fast float-specialized exponentiation `__expf`. We can easily access this faster primitive from Accelerate, although it's not provided by the Haskell library. What's nice is that by doing so we don't necessarily lock our program for CUDA only. The `foreignExp` wrapper expects a generic fallback as its second argument, which is expected to be slower, but works on any backend:

```
fexp :: Exp Float → Exp Float
fexp = foreignExp (CUDAForeignExp [] "__expf") exp
```

Summary

Now we have learned to write programs with Accelerate that run using the interpreter, and to compile and run them on CUDA-enabled GPUs. We know that Accelerate uses a code generator of its own internally. We understand it's crucial to write code that can efficiently reuse cached CUDA kernels, because their compilation is very expensive. We also learned that tuples are a free abstraction in Accelerate, although GPUs themselves don't directly support tupled elements.

In the next chapter, we will dive into Cloud Haskell and distributed programming using Haskell. It turns out Haskell is a pretty well-suited language for programming distributed systems. Cloud Haskell is an effort that streamlines building distributed applications, providing an abstraction over the network layer, among other things.

12
Scaling to the Cloud with Cloud Haskell

In this chapter, we will look at how distributed systems programming fits with Haskell. The motivation behind distributed systems is multifaceted. On one end, there is more computing power available with multiple physical machines. Then there are other resources besides computing power: storage space, network bandwidth, and other devices. Yet another advantage of proper distributed systems is resilience. With a growing number of machines, there are a growing number of failure points. A proper distributed system should be able to operate under arbitrary process failures.

Cloud Haskell is a relatively new but mature platform that's modelled from Erlang's wonderful execution model. Cloud Haskell brings distributed processes and process management to Haskell with modular network transport and fine-grained message and channel-based communication.

In this chapter, we will explore the Cloud Haskell platform. No deep knowledge about distributed systems is required. A general notion of a distributed system is enough. We will do basic message-passing, work with typed channels, and send and receive both data and closures of arbitrary data, including functions and procedures. We will look at the facilities for handling distributed failure in Cloud Haskell, that is, linking and monitoring processes. By the end of this chapter, you will be able to use Cloud Haskell to build your distributed system.

The chapter will cover the following topics:

- Launching Cloud Haskell nodes and processes
- Message-passing and typed channels
- Using closures to pass arbitrary data between machines
- Handling failure, linking processes together, and process monitoring

Processes and message-passing

The maze of packages around Cloud Haskell may seem daunting. But to get started, we really need just two packages: `distributed-process` and `distributed-process-simplelocalnet`. The former package implements the core features of Cloud Haskell: nodes, processes, serialization, and message-passing. In particular, it doesn't provide any implementation for communication between nodes. That's what the latter package is for.

Cloud Haskell is modular in its communication layer. The `distributed-process-simplelocalnet` package provides simple, zero-configuration networking for Cloud Haskell nodes. It uses UDP broadcasting for node discovery, which is adequate for our testing purposes in this section. So let's get started. At the time of writing, **distributed-process version 0.6.4** is the newest, so we'll be using that:

```
stack install --resolver lts-6.7 distributed-process distributed-process-simplelocalnet
```

The most important Cloud Haskell concept and type is `Process`:

```
data ProcessId

data Process
-- instance Monad, MonadIO, MonadMask
```

Cloud Haskell processes are lightweight threads that aren't necessarily executed on the local machine. `ProcessId` uniquely identifies a process across the distributed system, and `Process` in turn corresponds to a `ThreadId` on the machine it is executing on.

All code that somehow interacts with the Cloud Haskell API lives in the `Process` monad. It has a `MonadIO` instance as well as `MonadMask` (and `MonadThrow`/`MonadCatch`) instances, so `Process` can be used almost always where plain `IO` would be used.

Creating a message type

Let's now build a summer process that repeatedly takes in numbers from other processes, adds them to an internal counter, and responds to every number with the updated counter value. The first thing we need to write is a datatype that describes the messages that are passed in and out of such a summer process.

The basic API functions for message-passing in `Control.Distributed.Process` (from `distributed-process`) that we will be using are as follows:

```
send   :: Serializable a => ProcessId -> a -> Process ()
expect :: Serializable a => Process a
```

Messages are overloaded over the `Serializable` class. `Serializable` is implemented by every type with `Binary` and `Typeable` instances, in turn both of which are derivable. Still, we end up with quite a lot of code, because `Binary` is "derivable" only via **GHC Generics**:

```
import Data.Binary    (Binary)
import Data.Typeable  (Typeable)
import GHC.Generics   (Generic)

data SummerMsg = Add Int ProcessId
               | Value Int
               deriving (Show, Typeable, Generic)

instance Binary SummerMsg
```

Note that we included a `ProcessId` in the `Add` constructor. The idea is that the process which sends an `Add` message will include its own `ProcessId` in it so that the summer process knows where to send its `Value` reply.

Creating a Process

The next step is to write Process code for the summer. Using `expect` to get a message and `send` for replies, this is a straightforward task:

```
import Control.Distributed.Process

summerProc :: Process ()
summerProc = go 0
  where
    go s = do msg@(Add num from) <- expect
              say $ "received msg: " ++ show msg
              let s' = s + num
              send from (Value s')
              go s'
```

The `say` function is for debug purposes. By default, it outputs a string to standard error stream, but implementation varies depending on the Cloud Haskell transport layer used.

Spawning and closures

The `forkIO` equivalent for Cloud Haskell processes is spawn. Because a `Process` doesn't necessarily run on the machine or node that spawns it, `spawn` takes a `NodeId` as its argument:

```
spawn :: NodeId -> Closure (Process ()) -> Process ProcessId
```

A node is a machine or capability that is able to run Processes. If we just want to fork a Process to run on the local machine, we can get the local NodeId with `getSelfNode`.

Notice also that spawn takes a **Closure** type, not Process directly. This makes sense, because Process is akin to IO and we couldn't just transfer an arbitrary IO action from one machine to another. A `Closure` is a serializable form of arbitrary data or actions. To create closures, Cloud Haskell provides some Template Haskell magic that generates special remote tables for arbitrary serialization.

To make our `summerProc :: Process ()` spawnable, we create a remote table of it with the `remotable` TH splice:

```
remotable ['summerProc]
```

Among other things, `remotable` creates a new top-level definition `__remoteTable`. We'll need to provide this to the transport backend so that the backend can use it to map definitions to closures and back, and more. In general, a module that contains definitions should have one `remotable` splice, with all `remotable` definitions from that module listed.

To then create a closure, we use `mkStaticClosure`:

```
$(mkStaticClosure 'summerProc) :: Closure (Process ())
```

There is also `mkClosure`, which creates closures with one argument. Given f :: a → b, we have the following:

```
$(mkClosure 'f) :: a → Closure b
```

Now, for demonstration, we can create a process that spawns a summer process and interacts with it. Here we go:

```
[...]
import Control.Distributed.Process.Closure

summerTest :: Process ()
summerTest = do
    node<- getSelfNode
```

```
summerPid<- spawn node $(mkStaticClosure 'summerProc)

mypid<- getSelfPid

send summerPid (Add 5 mypid)
send summerPid (Add 7 mypid)

Value n <- expect
say $ "updated value: " ++ show n
Value n'<- expect
say $ "updated value: " ++ show n'
```

We use `getSelfNode` and `getSelfPid` to get the `NodeId` and `ProcessId` for the current process. We use `spawn` to create a new process from a closure, which gives us the `ProcessId` of the newly made process. We send messages to that, which in turn replies to us.

The final thing that's missing is the backend that initializes nodes and manages processes.

Running with the SimpleLocalNet backend

The `SimpleLocalNet` backend is easy to use, because it only requires a simple local network, something that all machines should have. Let's start with an example. Here's a `main` that executes the `summerTest` process from the previous section:

```
import Control.Distributed.Process.Node (initRemoteTable)
import Control.Distributed.Process.Backend.SimpleLocalnet
[...]

main :: IO ()
main = do
    backend<-initializeBackend "localhost" "9001"
        (__remoteTable initRemoteTable)
    startMaster backend $ \_ -> summerTest
```

There are two important functions: `initializeBackend` and `startMaster`. The former basically creates a new local node with some additional information (`backend :: Backend`). The `Backend` type is also part of the `SimpleLocalNet` backend.

The third argument to `initializeBackend` is of type `RemoteTable`: this is related to the `remotable` TH splice we saw previously. The `__remoteTable` definition that `remotable` generates is of type `RemoteTable → RemoteTable`. This is so that we can combine multiple remote tables with plain function composition. `initRemoteTable` is the "unit" of `RemoteTables` (an empty table).

The `startMaster` function is an auxiliary function which starts a process on a new node it creates in the network. There's also a `startSlave` function, which starts a slave node with no running processes yet. The second argument to `startMaster` is of the following type:

```
[NodeId] → Process ()
```

So, for convenience, `startMaster` automatically discovers every slave node in the network before starting the process. For now, we'll only use one node on our local machine (localhost) at port `9001`. Note that we could run multiple nodes on the same machine at the same port – Cloud Haskell backends should be considered as merely media where nodes live and communicate. From the application side, once we have a NodeId, it doesn't make a difference how the node is connected to the network. The backend used guarantees that messages flow between nodes.

Now let's compile and run our `main` and summer processes:

```
stack --resolver lts-6.7 ghc -- -threaded first-example.hs

./first-example

... pid://localhost:9001:0:11: received msg: Add 5
    pid://localhost:9001:0:10

... pid://localhost:9001:0:11: received msg: Add 7
    pid://localhost:9001:0:10

... pid://localhost:9001:0:10: updated value: 5

... pid://localhost:9001:0:10: updated value: 12
```

(Timestamps omitted for lack of space.)

Everything is as expected! Now we know how to create and execute processes using the simple `localnet` backend, and to send and receive messages between processes.

Using channels

While plain message-passing using `expect` and `send` works fine, it has some caveats. The biggest one is that all messages from all processes go to the same queue. This has two unfortunate implications. First, `expect` has to search the queue every time for a matching message. Second, we cannot know from which client the message came, or if it is even relevant anymore.

Cloud Haskell provides an abstraction called *typed channels* to overcome these difficulties. A channel consists of a `SendPort` and a `ReceivePort` that are connected to provide unidirectional communication using `sendChan` and `receiveChan`:

```
newChan :: (Typeable a, Binary a) => Process (SendPort a, ReceivePort
a)

receiveChan :: (Typeable a, Binary a) => ReceivePort a -> Process a

sendChan :: (Typeable a, Binary a) => SendPort a -> a -> Process ()
```

Because `SendPort` is `Serializable`, we can send them using send. This way, it is easy to establish bidirectional communication between a client and server, for instance. What's more, the channel is only valid through the lifetime of SendPort and corresponding ReceivePort. Messages can be put into the channel only after the channel's creation, unlike with plain messaging, where messages flow as long as the process is alive. Typed channels enable easy encapsulation.

Let's see a small example of using channels. We'll continue using a simple summer process just to emphasize Cloud Haskell features. First, a fairly minimal set of pragmas and imports:

```
-- file: client-server.hs
{-# LANGUAGE BangPatterns #-}

import Control.Monad
import Control.Distributed.Process
import Control.Distributed.Process.Node (initRemoteTable)
import Control.Distributed.Process.Backend.SimpleLocalnet
```

This time around, we will spawn clients that take a port to send numbers into. The `client` is a simple one-liner:

```
client :: SendPort Double -> Process ()
client sendport = forM_ [1..100] (sendChan sendport)
```

And here is the `master` process:

```
master :: Process ()
master = do
    ports<- replicateM 100 $ do                    -- (1)
        (sendport, recvport) <- newChan
        _pid <- spawnLocal (client sendport)
        return recvport

    port<- mergePortsRR ports                       -- (2)

    let loop !s = do                                -- (3)
```

```
        mn<- receiveChanTimeout 1000 port
        case mn of
            Just n  -> loop (s + n)
            Nothing -> do say $ "final: " ++ show s
                          terminate
    loop 0
```

First we spawn some clients and create a new channel for each (1). Then at (2), we merge all 100 ReceivePorts into one single ReceivePort using mergePortsRR:

```
mergePortsRR :: (Typeable a, Binary a) => [ReceivePort a] -> Process
(ReceivePort a)
```

That **RR** stands for **round-robin**, which gives each port an equal chance of being read under congestion. There is also mergePortsBiased, which favors the rightmost port.

At (3), we then repeatedly receive from the merged channel until there have been no messages for 1 millisecond. This timeout is built into receiveChanTimeout:

```
receiveChanTimeout :: (Typeable a, Binary a)
    => Int -> ReceivePort a -> Process (Maybe a)
```

When a timeout is reached, we print the final result and exit with terminate. Our main is the bare minimum:

```
main = do
    backend<- initializeBackend "localhost""9001" initRemoteTable
    startMaster backend (\_ -> master)
```

Running the program, we get the expected results:

```
./client-server
Thu Jul 14 21:32:05 UTC 2016 pid://localhost:9001:0:10: final: 505000.0
client-server: ProcessTerminationException
```

Establishing bidirectional channels

As mentioned earlier, only the sending endpoint of a channel is serializable. So it must always be the receiving end of a channel that creates it using newChan. To establish a bidirectional pair of channels between processes, they both create a channel and send the sendport to the other process.

In practice, this would look like the following:

```
-- file: bi-directional.hs

server :: Process ()
```

```
server = do
    pid<- getSelfPid
    (sendport', recvport) <- newChan
    _clientPid <- spawnLocal (client pid sendport')
    sendport<- expect

    sendChan sendport "ping"
    receiveChan recvport >>= say

client :: ProcessId -> SendPort String -> Process ()
client pid sendport = do
    (sendport', recvport) <- newChan
    send pid sendport'

    ping<- receiveChan recvport
    sendChan sendport ("pong: " ++ ping)
```

The relevant bits that establish the channels are highlighted. Note that these processes are not completely symmetrical, in that to run `client` we provide its master's process and upstream channel as arguments. But this isn't mandatory. With a bit more work, they both could establish channels via `send`/`expect`.

Calling a remote process

Previously, we used `spawn` to create new processes remotely. A common pattern is to spawn a process on a remote machine, wait for it to finish, and then collect the results. For this, Cloud Haskell provides a convenience operation, `call`:

```
call
    :: (Typeable a, Binary a) =>
       Static (SerializableDict a)
       -> NodeId -> Closure (Process a) -> Process a
```

There are two differences compared to `spawn`: the result type is `a` instead of `()` and there is a new argument, `Static (SerializableDict a)`. This is a reified `Serializable` dictionary for the process. Let's see `call` in action to understand it better:

```
rpc :: String -> Process Int
rpc str = return (length str)

remotable ['rpc]

foo :: Process ()
```

```
foo = do
    node<- getSelfNode
    str<- call $(functionTDict 'rpc) node ($(mkClosure 'rpc) "foo")
    say (show str)
```

Here are some points to note:

- We use mkClosure to turn rpc into a Closure. The one argument to rpc is passed normally outside the TH splice. This works only because rpc takes one monomorphic argument, String, and has a monomorphic result (Int). Also, remotable needs to have been called for rpc to create the static definitions.

- We use another TH splice, functionTDict, to get the serialization dictionary that is similar to the result type of rpc. There is also splice functionSDict, which gives the dictionary for the argument (source) type.

- If rpc threw an exception, this exception would be re-thrown at foo.

There is also a local version of call, named callLocal, which has a much simpler signature:

```
callLocal :: Process a → Process a
```

Though it seems like the identity function, it is not: the subprocess will get its own new ProcessId. This means that messages sent for the subprocess would be silently dropped when callLocal returns.

Handling failure

In a distributed system, it's customary to fail fast and let other processes deal with failure. This principle is encouraged in Erlang, from which Cloud Haskell is modelled. We should be prepared for an arbitrary process crashing, with its parent or monitoring process handling the failure (or propagating it further to a parent's parent).

There are two tactics to be noted about process failure in Cloud Haskell: linking and monitoring. The difference is that a linked process propagates exceptions to its parent, while an exception in a monitored process results in the monitoring process receiving a ProcessMonitorNotification message.

Firing up monitors

The basic monitoring API is the following:

```
monitor      :: ProcessId  → Process MonitorRef
monitorNode :: NodeId      → Process MonitorRef
monitorPort :: SendPort a → Process MonitorRef

unmonitor    :: MonitorRef → Process ()

withMonitor :: ProcessId  → Process a → Process a
```

We can start monitoring either a process, a node, or a channel. A `MonitorRef` is retained so that it's possible to `unmonitor` later. The `withMonitor` combinator combines `monitor` and `unmonitor`, by monitoring the process only when in the inner computation.

When a monitored process exits, a notification message is sent to the monitoring process. To catch the message along with other messages in the system, we need some additional machinery. Plain `expect` is not sufficient here, because it matches one type only.

Matching on the message queue

What we need to sensibly match on multiple message types at once is, unsurprisingly, provided by Cloud Haskell as a nice API. Details will follow, but the crux of it is here:

```
data Match b

receiveWait   :: [Match b] → Process b

match         :: Serializable a => (a → Process b) → Match b
matchUnknown :: Process b                          → Match b
matchChan    :: ReceivePort a     → (a → Process b) → Match b
```

The `match` API allows us to check for multiple types of message in the queue simultaneously. We can also interleave arbitrary ReceivePorts with the message queue with `matchChan`, or drop any messages with `matchUnknown`.

Here's an example of a combined receive operation:

```
receiveWait
    [ match $ \(n :: Int)    → …
    , match $ \(s :: String) → …
    , matchUnknown $          …
```

```
, matchChan recvport $ \x → …
]
```

It first tries for `Int` or `String` types in the message queue. If a message of neither type is available but instead there's some other message, we remove that from the queue. Otherwise, an attempt is made to read from channel `recvport`. If that's empty too, we start waiting until one of the `match` conditions is fulfilled.

The implementation of `Match` is based on STM, so the whole receive operation is atomic and it's efficient when waiting for events due to how STM works.

Linking processes together

Sometimes it's useful to handle failure at the level of a set of processes instead of a single process. Or maybe we want to ensure that a child process won't continue executing when its parent dies, as would happen when a process is merely monitored.

For the latter, Cloud Haskell provides a nice combinator, `spawnSupervised`:

```
spawnSupervised
:: NodeId → Closure (Process ()) → Process (ProcessId, MonitorRef)
```

This spawns a new process, starts monitoring it, and links the child to the parent. The link ensures that if the parent dies, the child dies too (or at the very least receives an asynchronous exception).

In case a supervised spawn doesn't fit your use case, there are more API functions for linking. Like monitoring, linking extends from processes to nodes and ports:

```
link, unlink          :: ProcessId  → Process ()
linkNode, unlinkNode :: NodeId      → Process ()
linkPort, unlinkPort :: SendPort a → Process ()
```

Links are always unidirectional, though it's possible to link processes to each other.

Message-passing performance

It's worth noting that message passing between processes normally goes between the network transport and undergoes serialization following deserialization. Serialization is not a free operation and it's inevitable between processes located on different nodes. However, processes on the same node don't necessarily need to do the relatively expensive serialization at all.

Cloud Haskell takes a conservative approach and doesn't by default optimize local node communication. The main reason is that skipping (de)serialization can possibly give different runtime semantics due to strictness. For instance, unnoticed bottoms can lurk in data that isn't fully forced. Messages sent over network must always be fully evaluated, so it's easier for the developer when such mistakes can be caught in early development.

People familiar with distributed systems know that communication and serialization is not cheap, and in production it doesn't make much sense to incur extra work in local communication. Luckily, Cloud Haskell does permit optimizing local communication. Unsafe `send` functions are provided in two places. The `Control.Distributed.Process.UnsafePrimitives` module replaces `send` functions from the main API, `Control.Distributed.Process`, while the main API provides unsafe variants with the `unsafe` prefix.

Using the unsafe variants is faster, but you will need to make sure you are not relying on evaluation-based asynchronous exceptions getting thrown in any process: an unsafe `send` can result in the exception being raised in the receiver instead of the sender.

Nodes and networking

Though Cloud Haskell processes communicate seamlessly together, they are completely oblivious to how they are connected. The transport layer provided by `Network.Transport` sits between the processes and a backend that implements the transport.

A Cloud Haskell backend provides on top of a transport layer some sort of peer discovery or allows for a predefined topology. A number of backends have been implemented and more are in development. At the time of writing, there are three well-supported backends available:

- SimpleLocalNet (`distributed-process-simplelocalnet`): Fully connected with optional client/slave configuration, TCP transport, and UDP multicast peer discovery

- P2P (`distributed-process-p2p`): TCP-transport with peer-to-peer discovery

- ZooKeeper (`distributed-process-zookeeper`): TCP transport that uses Apache ZooKeeper as naming registry

Each backend has its use cases. In first development phases, SimpleLocalNet is the easiest choice, but non-existent network topology configuration is not good in many applications. For a "truly" distributed system, in other words, one that doesn't have a central puppetmaster, a peer-to-peer transport is a good fit. And for a more managed system, a ZooKeeper-based solution is a strong option.

If none of the existing backend solutions is viable, it's not too hard to roll your own with the more various network-transport packages, for instance, a managed TCP transport with `network-transport-tcp` or using ZeroMQ and `network-transport-zeromq`.

All `Network.Transport.*` packages essentially provide ways to produce `Transports` that Cloud Haskell uses to launch nodes. The API in `Control.Distributed.Process.Node` is quite self-explanatory:

```
data LocalNode

newLocalNode    :: Transport → RemoteTable → IO LocalNode
closeLocalNode  :: LocalNode → IO ()

forkProcess     :: LocalNode → Process () → IO ProcessId
runProcess      :: LocalNode → Process () → IO ()

initRemoteTable :: RemoteTable

localNodeId     :: LocalNode → NodeId
```

So Cloud Haskell's `LocalNode` associates with a `NodeId`. Local node initialization requires a `Transport` and the `RemoteTable` for closure lookup. At least the first process is started by `forkProcess` or `runProcess`, after which `call` or `fork` can be used in the `Process` monad to spark more processes on local or remote nodes.

Cloud Haskell backends are just convenient wrappers over `network-transport`. It's not necessary to use a backend in itself.

Summary

In this chapter, we have learned to build distributed systems using the Cloud Haskell platform: launching nodes and processes, communicating via direct message passing between processes and with more flexible typed channels, passing remotely executed procedures in closures, and handling failure with process linking and monitoring. You now know how to build distributed systems with Cloud Haskell.

The next chapter will be about **Functional Reactive Programming (FRP)** and related Haskell libraries. Reactive programming, and especially FRP, challenges prevalent imperative control flow by a different notion of time. In imperative animation, for instance, timing is more or less implicit in the code, whereas in FRP, time would be just one more argument or input to an animation system. Reactive programming extends beyond just animation, though.

13
Functional Reactive Programming

Functional Reactive Programming (FRP) is an elegant way to express behaviors that change over time, such as user interfaces or animation. From a theoretical point of view, behaviors are time-varying values. Using simple behaviors as building blocks, we can build increasingly complex behaviors: complete programs, UIs, games, and so on. Behaviors compose very well and eliminate lots of tedious and error-prone work that's present in the traditional imperative approach with actions and callbacks.

Though FRP has simple semantics, efficient implementation is largely an open question. Existing FRP implementations take different approaches with different trade-offs. In semantics, FRP is continuous, in other words, functions of the real numbers. In practice, we are forced to make approximations, either via sampling, using discrete semantics or some hybrid of continuous and discrete. The more theoretically minded reader is encouraged to glance at the following FRP papers: *Functional Reactive Animation* (1997, Elliot and Hudak), *Push-Pull Functional Reactive Programming* (2009, Elliot).

In this chapter, we will not bother much with understanding the semantics exactly. Instead, we will work with simple but illustrative examples of FRP in practice using a few Haskell libraries that implement their own realizations of FRP: Elerea, Yampa, and Reactive-banana. Because there are so many examples, tutorials and additional libraries for hooking FRP logic into input and output sources, for example, graphics frameworks, we won't focus on that aspect of FRP. Instead, the focus is on the very core of FRP: elegant and powerful composition of behaviors and events.

This chapter will cover the following topics:

- Programming with three FRP frameworks: Elerea, Yampa, and Reactive-banana
- Pros and cons of discrete- and continuous-time signals, events and behaviors
- Coding recursion and mutual recursion in event networks
- Adding inputs and outputs to networks statically and dynamically

The tiny discrete-time Elerea

In order to not feel overwhelmed, we'll begin with one of the simplest formulations of FRP, Elerea. Elerea is a very minimalist implementation, which restricts itself to discrete-time semantics and sampling. There are no events and everything is computed on demand only. Furthermore, the API consists of high-level constructs so that it's exceedingly difficult to shoot yourself in the foot with this library.

Time-varying values of type a are represented as `Signal` a in Elerea:

```
data Signal a
-- instances incl. Monad, Eq
```

Signals can be thought of as functions Nat → a, though obviously they are represented differently.

Signals are made inside signal generators, `SignalGen a`:

```
data SignalGen a
-- instances incl. Monad, MonadFix, MonadIO
```

Signal generators have a `MonadFix` instance, which will later allow us to build mutually recursive signals.

The minimal API provides just a few signal building blocks. Excluding some trivial extensions, the core combinators are as follows:

```
delay     :: a → Signal a                      → SignalGen (Signal a)
snapshot  :: Signal a                          → SignalGen a
generator :: Signal (SignalGen a)              → SignalGen (Signal a)
memo      :: Signal a                          → SignalGen (Signal a)
till      :: Signal Bool                       → SignalGen (Signal Bool)

stateful  :: a → (a → a)                        → SignalGen (Sinal a)
transfer  :: a → (t → a → a) → Signal t → SignalGen (Signal a)

effectful :: IO a                              → SignalGen (Signal a)
```

We'll see some examples soon, but first we introduce `start`:

```
start :: SignalGen (Signal a) → IO (IO a)
```

This embeds a signal network built via the signal generator network into `IO`. Once the network is initialized, we get an IO action (`IO a`) that samples the network. We can think of `start` as a "start-the-world" action while the resulting action is a "sample-the-world" action. We define a `sigtest` function that performs 10 samplings and prints them as a list:

```
-- file: elerea-first-ex.hs

import Control.Monad
import FRP.Elerea.Simple

sigtest :: Show a => SignalGen (Signal a) -> IO ()
sigtest gen = start gen >>= replicateM 10 >>= print
```

Now, let's see some signals in action. First, we have `stateful` signals, similar to unfolding:

```
> sigtest (stateful 5 (+1))
[5,6,7,8,9,10,11,12,13,14]
```

Signals can be composed using general *Applicative* or *Monad* operations:

```
> sigtest $ do { a <- stateful 0 (+1)
              ; b <- stateful 0 (subtract 1)
              ; return ((+) <$> a <*> b)
              }
[0,0,0,0,0,0,0,0,0,0]
```

The `transfer` combinator "scans" values in the stream, producing a new stream:

```
> sigtest $ do { series <- stateful 5 (+1)
              ; transfer 1 (+) series
              }
[6,12,19,27,36,46,57,69,82,96]
```

This is analogous to the `scanl` function from Prelude:

```
> let series = iterate (+1) 5
> take 10 $ scanl (+) 1 series
[1,6,12,19,27,36,46,57,69,82]
```

Embedding arbitrary I/O actions as inputs is trivial with `effectful`:

```
> sigtest (effectful getLine)
hello
world
...
end
["hello","world",...,"end"]
```

Each combinator – `stateful`, `transfer`, and `effectful` – is simple and intuitive, but not always powerful enough in complex cases. We'll introduce the general building blocks delay, generator, and till with bigger examples next.

Mutually recursive signals

In a complex FRP application, we often need signals that depend mutually on each other. For instance, in a UI, actions depend on user input and available input depends on past actions. The Fibonacci series is one of simplest example programs that can be expressed as a combination of mutually recursive signals. In pseudo-code we have the following:

```
fib  <- 1 `cons` fib1
fib1 <- 1 `cons` fib2
let fib2 = fib + fib1
```

Here, `cons` is an operation that inserts one value to the *head* of the stream. But we can't quite directly translate this pseudo-code to SignalGen code, because the bindings are mutually recursive and a monadic bind is not recursive, though let bindings are.

Fortunately, we can utilize SignalGen's `MonadFix` instance, which will give us recursive bindings. In order to not bother with the details, we will use the `RecursiveDo` GHC language extension to yield recursive monadic bindings that look almost identical to normal monadic bindings:

```
{-# LANGUAGE RecursiveDo #-}
```

Now we can write a mutually recursive signal that produces the Fibonacci numbers:

```
fibonacci :: SignalGen (Signal Int)
fibonacci = do
    rec fib  <- delay 1 fib1
    fib1 <- delay 1 fib2
    let fib2 = (+) <$> fib <*> fib1
    return fib
```

The magic is in the new `rec` keyword introduced by `RecursiveDo`. It lets us introduce a mutually recursive group of bindings. The `delay` function is the `cons` operation on signals:

```
delay :: a -> Signal a -> SignalGen (Signal a)
```

Just to confirm our implementation works:

```
> sigtest fibonacci
[1,1,2,3,5,8,13,21,34,55]
```

RecursiveDo is really just syntactic sugar: all the magic happens in the `MonadFix` class and instance, which doesn't depend on any magic at all.

Signalling side-effects

With `effectful`, it's easy to turn IO effects into input signals in the network. To use signal output as a parameter to a side effect, we can use variants of `effectful` that take the signal to bind to as parameter:

```
effectful1 :: (t -> IO a) -> Signal t -> SignalGen (Signal a)

effectful2 :: (t1 -> t2 -> IO a)
-> Signal t1 -> Signal t2 -> SignalGen (Signal a)
```

In the following small program, on every line read outputs the sum of read numbers so far:

```
linesum :: SignalGen (Signal ())
linesum = do
    sigInputNumbers ← fmap read <$> effectful getLine
    sigSumNumbers   ← transfer (0::Int) (+) sigInputNumbers
    effectful1 (putStrLn . ("sum " ++) . show) sigSumNumbers
```

Or, without do notation we could write:

```
fmap (fmap read) (effectful getLine)
>>= transfer (0::Int) (+)
>>= effectful1 (putStrLn . ("sum: " ++) . show)
```

Here it is in action:

```
> sigtest linesum
5
sum: 5
10
sum: 15
```

```
3
sum: 18
```

This should demonstrate that it's really trivial to hook side effects to signals at any point of a network: beginning (with `effectful`), middle, or end (with `effectful1` or `effectful2` or `effectful3`, or `effectful4`). This is one of Elerea's strong points.

Dynamically changing signal networks

In Elerea, signal networks' structure is defined in the `SignalGen` monad. At first glance, this seems restrictive in that we couldn't alter the structure once the network is initialized. However, this is not true. Elerea provides a combinator called `generator`, which embeds a `SignalGen` producing signal into a signal:

```
generator :: Signal (SignalGen a) -> SignalGen (Signal a)
```

This is a powerful combinator that allows us to build very dynamic networks.

Let's take an example. Say we want to initiate a new countdown signal whenever a number is read from standard input. Empty lines decrease existing countdowns and when a countdown reaches zero, it is deleted. Our countdown signal is simple and self-explanatory:

```
countdown :: Int -> SignalGen (Signal Int)
countdown n = stateful n (subtract 1)
```

A signal of multiple countdown signals has type `Signal [Signal Int]`. A signal generator for such signal has the type of `readCountdowns` here:

```
readCountdowns :: SignalGen (Signal [Signal Int])
readCountdowns = do
    input <- effectful getLine                  -- (1)
    generator $ do                              -- (2)
        x <- input
        return $ case x of                      -- (3)
            "" -> return []
            _  -> return <$> countdown (read x)
```

This function is a mouthful, so let's break it down. At (1), we initialize a signal that reads lines from standard input. At (2), we apply `generator` to a value which has the following type: `Signal (SignalGen [Signal Int])`, that is, a signal which produces signals generators for lists of countdown signals. The signal itself takes a line and pattern-matches on its contents (3): an empty line doesn't produce any signals, while a line with one number produces a countdown that starts with the specified amount of time.

To drive a dynamic signal collection, we will save some trouble by utilizing the collection function with the following signature:

```
-- Implementation taken from Elerea's haddocks
collection :: Signal [Signal a] -> (a -> Bool) -> SignalGen
   (Signal [a])
collection source isAlive = …
```

Note that `collection` is not provided by the library, but its implementation is found from the documentation, under the section *A longer example*

With `collection`, we can easily combine a signal of new signals (`Signal [Signal a]`) and a filtering function (`a → Bool`) to upkeep a dynamic set of signals (`Signal [a]`). For the countdowns, the choice of filtering function is (`> 0`), that is, the countdown is deleted once it hits zero.

To drive a dynamically updating collection of countdowns, we write the following:

```
runCountdowns :: SignalGen (Signal [Int])
runCountdowns = do
    csig <- readCountdowns
    collection csig (> 0)
```

Very straightforward. Let's confirm it works:

```
> sigtest runCountdowns
5

5

5

5




10


[[5],[5,4],[5,4,3],[5,4,3,2],[4,3,2,1],[3,2,1],[2,1],[1],[10],[9]]
```

On every line, existing countdowns tick one down and new countdowns are added when a numeral is given, as intended. Now we know how to use `generator` to create dynamic signal networks in Elerea.

Performance and limitations in Elerea

The selling point in Elerea is its monadic interface that hides some implementation details and makes it trivial to compose signal generators and signals. As a consequence, plumbing signals and generators is somewhat restricting, although overall the interface is very powerful.

The biggest concern with Elerea is its eventless nature: every time, the signal network updates as a whole. It's not possible to update just a part of the network; on every tick, all signals are re-calculated. By using the memo primitive, we can memoize values within one update round, but this is always manual work. The library combinators memoize their values, but memoizing custom combinations is left to the library user.

Events and signal functions with Yampa

Yampa is an FRP framework that supports both continuous and discrete time. In Yampa, the most important concept is the signal function (SF). Signal functions are first-class transformations on signals, that is, time-dependent values:

```
data SF a b   -- think: Signal a → Signal b

-- instance Arrow, ArrowLoop, Category
```

Signal functions can be created and manipulated via the **Arrow** interface. For instance, a pure transformation (a → b) is turned into a signal function simply with arr from the Arrow class. Here's a signal function which squares values passed through it:

```
square :: SF Double Double
square = arr (^2)
```

The embed utility function can be used to test signal functions:

embed square (1, [(0, Just 2), (1, Just 3)])

[1.0,4.0,9.0]

The type signature of embed looks like this:

```
embed :: SF a b -> (a, [(DTime, Maybe a)]) -> [b]
```

The first argument is the signal function to sample from. The second is a tuple that consists of the initial input to the signal function and a list of sample times (DTime ~ Double), possibly accompanied by a new input value.

Because in Yampa we could theoretically sample the network represented by a signal function at any time (up to Double precision), we need to explicitly specify the times when new input is fed into the network. Note that embed is a pure utility; normally, the network is hooked to IO input and output using reactimate (introduced a bit later).

Signal functions are inherently pure: it's not possible to produce side effects within a signal function.

Besides creating signal functions from Haskell functions, we can combine existing SFs using general combinators from the Category, Arrow, and ArrowLoop classes. Here are the most important ones. For clarity, they are here specialized for SF:

```
arr   :: (b -> c) -> SF b c          -- lift pure function

(>>>) :: SF a b → SF b c → SF a c    -- like (.)
(<<<) :: SF b c → SF a b → SF a c    -- like flip (.)

(^<<) :: (c → d) → SF b c → SF b d   -- combine arr and (<<<)
(>>^) :: SF b c → (c → d) → SF b d   -- combine arr and (>>>)

(&&&) :: SF b c → SF b  c' → SF b     (c, c')
(***) :: SF b c → SF b' c' → SF (b, b') (c, c')

loop  :: SF (b, d) (c, d) -> SF b c  -- SF with feed-back
```

Adding state to signal functions

Signal functions in Yampa are continuous. State in a continuous setting is slightly different from the discrete case. Due to computational limitations, we can't express really continuous updates and need to use a discrete approximation. Then we need to make sure the state is always updated correctly no matter how often or rarely an evaluation occurs.

How would we implement a sum signal that works with continuous time? By using loop, we can get feedback of the sum so far. Effectively, loop ties a function's output to its input. That's not exactly what we want, however: we want to somehow specify the start value for the loop. Otherwise, we get an infinite loop where the output is fed as input indefinitely:

```
loop (arr go)
    where go (x,s) = let s' = x + s in (s', s')
    -- loops indefinitely
```

The solution here is to delay the feedback signal by one iteration. For this, Yampa provides a convenient combinator, `iPre`:

```
iPre :: a -> SF a a
```

`iPre` expects the initial value as argument (plain `pre` just leaves the initial argument undefined). With `iPre` we can delay the feedback signal for a `sum` signal with its initial value zero:

```
cSum :: SF Int Int
cSum = loop (second (iPre 0) >>^ go)
  where go (x,s) = let s' = x + s in (s', s')
```

Looping with an initial value is so common that Yampa provides a combinator `loopPre` that is a combination of `loop` and `iPre`.

Working with time

Many tasks, in games and simulation, for instance, must interact with time. We need to know how much time has passed since the beginning of evaluation or locally since the last iteration.

Yampa defines a signal that yields time since the beginning of signal function evaluation:

```
time :: SF a Time
> embed time ((), [(0.5, Nothing), (1, Nothing)])
[0.0,0.5,1.5]
```

We can build a `tick` function that gives the time passed since the last evaluation by us:

```
tick :: SF a Time
tick = time >>> loopPre 0 (arr (\(t, t') -> (t - t', t)))
> embed tick (0, [(1.3, Nothing), (2.2, Nothing)])
[0.0,1.3,2.2]
```

So it's easy to get the running time or a tick from the beginning of evaluation. But suppose we want to express a time from the beginning of some event? To get the start time of an animation, for instance. We need to use the discrete part of Yampa: events and switches.

Switching and discrete-time events

Yampa supports discrete-time FRP via events and switches. An event containing a value of type a is represented by Event a:

```
data Event a = Event a | NoEvent
-- instance Monad, Alternative, …
```

An event source is a signal function with some type SF a (Event b). Some example event sources are as follows:

```
never :: SF a (Event b)
now   :: b → SF a (Event b)
after :: Time → b → SF a (Event b)
```

Because event source is just a normal SF, we could yield events with arr. However, then we should take care that the event is emitted only once: because signal functions are continuous, unless the event is suppressed on subsequent samplings, it could occur more than once.

To react on events, we need switches. The basic one-time switch has the following type:

```
switch :: SF a (b, Event c) -- Default signal
       -> (c → SF a b)       -- Signal after event
       -> SF a b
```

The following signal yields the string foo for first 2 seconds, after which an event is fired and bar is yielded:

```
switchFooBar, switchFooBar' :: SF () String

switchFooBar  = switch  (constant "foo"&&& after 2 "bar") constant
switchFooBar' = dSwitch (constant "foo"&&& after 2 "bar") constant
```

Function dSwitch is identical to switch except that, at the time of the event, the previous signal is yielded one more time. The following shows the difference:

```
> embed switchFooBar ((), [(2, Nothing), (3, Nothing)])
["foo","bar","bar"]
> embed switchFooBar' ((), [(2, Nothing), (3, Nothing)])
["foo","foo","bar"]
```

This is a one-time switch: once the event occurs, we switch permanently to the new signal function. To switch on more events, we can apply `switch` recursively. For instance, this signal alternates between `foo` and `bar` every 2 seconds:

```
switchRec :: SF () String
switchRec = go (0, "foo", "bar")
  where
    go (t, x, y) =
         switch (constant x &&& after (t + 2) (t + 2, y, x)) go
```

Here, time for the after combinator is just threaded through as an argument. Note that the time signal and `Time` arguments are always relative to current evaluation context, irrespective of switching.

Another switch combinator is `rSwitch` (and its delayed version, `drSwitch`). This recurring switch accepts whole signal functions as events, and every time replaces the active SF with newly emitted SF. Take a look at its type:

```
rSwitch :: SF a b -> SF (a, Event (SF a b)) b
```

The first argument is the initial `SF a b`. Resulting SF expects an Event (`SF a b`) stream tupled with actual input `a`.

An example use of a recurring switch would be changing walk directions in a game, say between `foo` and `bar`. We can write this as follows:

```
swap :: SF Bool String
swap = rSwitch foo <<< identity &&& swapEv -- (1)
  where
    swapEv = edge >>> sscanPrim go True (Event foo) -- (2)

    go tag = event Nothing $ \_ -> -- (3)
        Just (not tag, Event $ if tag then bar else foo)

    foo = constant "foo"
    bar = constant "bar"
```

Here, `swap` is an SF that reads, for instance, a button press status as a Boolean. Its output alternates between `foo` and `bar`, so that every button press (from pressed to unpressed; `False` to `True`) triggers a switch. At (1), the Boolean input signal is tupled into the original signal and an `event` signal (`swapEv`), which is fed into `rSwitch`.

The `event` signal at (2) applies an edge detector transformation (`edge`) from the Yampa API. It yields an event every time an `edge` is detected in the input signal:

```
edge :: SF Bool (Event ())
```

In the second step, we scan over the Event signal with sscanPrim and on every triggered event yield an SF different from the previously active (foo or bar). The tag in (3) indicates which of the SFs is currently active. The combinators here are:

```
sscanPrim :: (c -> a -> Maybe (c, b)) -> c -> b -> SF a b

event     :: a -> (b -> a) -> Event b -> a
```

Confirm our swap works as intended:

```
> embed swap  (True, zip [1..] (map Just [False, False, True, False,
    True]))
["foo","foo","foo","bar","bar","foo"]
```

The third type of switch is perhaps the hardest to understand. It's called a *call-with-current-continuation* switch, kSwitch, or its delayed version, dkSwitch. Its type is:

```
kSwitch
  :: SF a b                      - initial SF
  -> SF (a, b) (Event c)         - event trigger
  -> (SF a b -> c -> SF a b)     - continuation SF
  -> SF a b
```

This switch allows access to the previous SF when deciding the continuation based on an event. We can choose to use the current SF in the new SF, for instance, as a pre- or post-processor. Like a normal switch, kSwitch switches only once. The difference is that deciding the continuation (third argument) is completely decoupled from the initial SF and event trigger. kSwitch composes a bit better than switch.

As a rather artificial example, we have the following SF:

```
withCC :: SF Int Int
withCC = kSwitch (arr (+1)) trigger cont
  where
    trigger = sscan f NoEvent

    f _ (inp,_) | inp > 1 && inp < 10 = Event (*inp)
                | otherwise = NoEvent

    cont f f' = f >>> arr f'
```

Initially, this SF adds 1 to every number in the stream. When a number larger than 1 and smaller than 10 is encountered, from that point onward the numbers are also multiplied by that number. Note how in deciding the continuation (cont), we don't know or care about the specifics of the initial SF, but we can use it as a part of the final SF.

Example run:

```
> embed withCC (1, zip [1..10] (map Just [10,2,10,3,10]))
[2,11,6,22,8,22]
```

Integrating to the real world

In all Yampa examples so far, we have simulated the pure signal functions with
embed. Signal functions are pure, so pure simulation is always possible. However, in
real applications, we want to integrate SF into a loop with the real world, IO. Because
signal functions store state, mere multiple calls to embed would be insufficient. We
need to preserve the state somehow.

For the simplest cases, Yampa provides a single combinator that guides us through
the integration. It's called reactimate and its type is:

```
reactimate
   :: IO a                           -- Init
   -> (Bool -> IO (DTime, Maybe a))  -- Get input
   -> (Bool -> b -> IO Bool)         -- Process output
   -> SF a b                         -- Signal function
   -> IO ()
```

Besides the SF to execute, we need to define three IO actions: one to supply the initial
input to the SF, one to sense input, and one to actuate output.

The sense function is informed via an argument whether it can block or not. The
sense result should be a tuple of time difference since the last iteration and new input
(if any).

The actuation is informed via an argument whether the output has changed since the
last actuation. When the actuation returns True, reactimation stops there.

However, in practice, reactimate always calls the sense function with False (no
block) and the actuation function with True (has changed). These arguments have
no effect in Yampa version 0.10.5 at least.

The following main reads numbers from standard input and adds them together
until hitting 42 or more, after which it exits:

```
main = reactimate init sense actuate sf
  where
    init = return "0"

    sense _ = do
      ln <- getLine
```

```
                 return (1, Just ln)

        actuate _ out = do
            putStrLn out
            return (out == "END")

    sf = arr read
        >>> sscan (+) 0
        >>> dSwitch (arr show &&& arr (filterE (>= 42) . Event))
            (\_ -> constant "END")
```

In complex applications, it isn't feasible to make `reactimate` the main loop of the program. The alternative is to use `reactInit` to yield a `ReactHandle` and react to feed input to it. Essentially these two functions decompose reactimate to two parts that allow for more flexibility.

Reactive-banana – Safe and simple semantics

The third and final approach to FRP we'll take a look at is Reactive-banana. Like Yampa, we have both continuous- and discrete-time semantics at our disposal. In Reactive-banana terminology, events describe discrete time, while behaviors describe continuous time. Behaviors in Reactive-banana are like signals in Elerea. Historically, the `names` event and behavior were the first to occur:

```
data Event a      -- instance Functor
data Behavior a   -- instance Functor, Applicative
```

Note that behavior is not Monad, unlike Elerea's signal, which did have a **Monad** instance. Instead, Reactive-banana supports **moments** as reactive computation contexts. There is a pure `Moment` monad, impure `MomentIO` monad and `MonadMoment` class that is used to overload moment context:

```
data Moment a      -- instance Monad, MonadFix, MonadMoment
data MomentIO a    -- instance ..., MonadIO

class Monad m => MonadMoment m where
    liftMoment :: Moment a -> m a

instance MonadMoment Moment
instance MonadMoment MomentIO
```

Example – First GUI application

The Reactive-banana framework is rather tightly tied with frameworks that provide the extra glue to drive reactive applications. Such frameworks exist for at least `wx` and `sdl` graphics libraries, in Haskell packages `reactive-banana-wx` and `reactive-banana-sdl2`. We'll be using the WX framework in this section:

```
cabal install reactive-banana-wx
```

In the `Reactive.Banana.Frameworks` module, there are the following data-types and functions that are used to execute any reactive network:

```
data EventNetwork

compile :: MomentIO () → IO EventNetwork

actuate :: EventNetwork → IO ()
pause   :: EventNetwork → IO ()
```

We express the reactive network as a `MomentIO ()`, compile that into an `EventNetwork` and use `actuate` to start it, pause to stop it.

Graphical display with wxWidgets

Our first example will be a counter with a very simple GUI: a display for the current counter value along with up and down buttons.

We start by defining the UI in the wxHaskell way, with a light preamble:

```
-- file: reactive-banana-counter.hs
{-# LANGUAGE ScopedTypeVariables #-}

import Graphics.UI.WX
import Reactive.Banana
import Reactive.Banana.WX

app :: IO ()
app = do
   f <- frame [ text := "App" ]
   up <- button f [ text := "Up" ]
   down <- button f [ text := "Down" ]
   res <- staticText f []
   set f
      [ layout := margin 10 (column 5
        [ widget res
        , row 5 [widget up, widget down]
        ])
      ]
   -- ...
```

There's nothing reactive here yet. We have defined a `frame` (window) of the application (`f :: Frame ()`), two buttons (`up` and `down`), and a text element (`res :: StaticText ()`), and set a layout for the frame.

Next, we use the `Reactive.Banana.WX` glue to build an event network that uses the two buttons as event sources and the text field as output. The relevant glue functions are:

```
event0
  :: w
  -> Graphics.UI.WX.Event w (IO ())
  -> MomentIO (Reactive.Banana.Event ())

sink
  :: w -> [Prop' w] -> MomentIO ()
```

Note that there are two distinct types called `Event` in `event0`: one from Reactive-banana and other from the `WX` library. Those `w` type variables stand for widgets, for instance, buttons (`up`, and `down`).

Here is the network description for our counter application:

```
-- ...
let network :: MomentIO ()
    network = do
       eup   <- event0 up command -- (1)
       edown <- event0 down command

       (counter :: Behavior Int)   -- (2)
          <- accumB 0 $ unions      -- (4)
             [ (+1) <$ eup
             , subtract 1 <$ edown
             ]

       sink res [ text :== show <$> counter ] -- (3)
-- ...
```

At (1), we bind commands (clicks) from the WX widgets `up` and `down` into Reactive-banana events `eup` and `edown`. At (2), we define the `counter` as a `Behavior Int`, that is, a time-varying integer. That integer then updates contents of the text box `res` at (3) by using `sink`.

At (4), we use two functions from Reactive-banana itself: accumB and unions. The applicative (a <$ ev) is used to replace event's ev emitted value with a. The two event sources of functions are merged with unions, which yields any of the events if available, and if events occur simultaneously, they are combined with function composition. The accumB combinator transforms a discrete signal of events into a continuous behavior:

```
accumB
  :: MonadMoment m =>
  a -> Reactive.Banana.Event (a -> a) -> m (Behavior a)
```

Now that we have a network description of type MomentIO (), we use compile to turn it into an EventNetwork and actuate to execute it:

```
-- ...
    evnet <- compile network
    actuate evnet

main = start app
```

The application is compiled normally with GHC:

```
ghc reactive-banana-counter.hs

[1 of 1] Compiling Main                    ( reactive-banana-counter.hs,
reactive-banana-counter.o )

Linking reactive-banana-counter …
```

We now have built a GUI in Haskell with Reactive-banana FRP and wxWidgets. Due to the portability of wxWidgets, the exact same reactive-banana-counter.hs file will compile and run under at least Linux, Mac, and Windows systems. I am using the 0.92.2.0 version of the wx Haskell library, which is compatible with wxWidgets 2.9 and 3.0. Here's a screenshot of the application under one Linux machine:

Combining events and behaviors

Events and behaviors are the core foundation of FRP in Reactive-banana. Behaviors
can be composed via the `Applicative` interface, but numerous other ways are also
provided by the Reactive-banana API. Some primitives are provided:

```
never :: Event a

unionWith
   :: (a -> a -> a) -> Event a  -> Event a -> Event a

filterE
   :: (a -> Bool) -> Event a -> Event a

apply
   :: Behavior (a -> b)  -> Event a -> Event b
```

It's apparent from the types what these functions do. `unionWith` combines two events
using the first argument to decide the result in case of simultaneous emits. `filterE`
suppresses events that don't match a predicate. `apply` applies a time-varying function
to events. Often `apply` is encountered in its infix form, (`<@>`).

A special case of `apply` is replacing events with time-varying values. The (`<@`)
combinator can be used in this case. For example, to turn every event from `etick`
into a random value sampled from behavior `brandom`, we write:

```
brandom <@ etick :: Event a
```

These primitives are stateless. To include state, for instance, accumulators, we need
the `Moment` context. `accumE` scans an event source of functions with an initial value,
similar to `scanl'`:

```
accumE
:: MonadMoment m =>
a -> Event (a -> a) -> m (Event a)
```

Note that `accumE` is subtly different from `accumB` we used in our example seen
before. The latter produces a behavior as opposed to an event. In fact, we can express
`accumB` in terms of `accumE` and another primitive `stepper`:

```
stepper
:: MonadMoment m => a -> Event a -> m (Behavior a)
```

Given an initial value and event stream, stepper yields a continuous behavior that uses always the latest value from the event stream (initial value if no event has fired yet). Writing accumB is then easy: accumulate events and memoize the latest value for the behavior:

```
accumB a ev = stepper a =<< accumE a ev
```

Switching events and behaviors

In Reactive-banana, we can switch in both discrete (Event) or continuous (Behavior) streams. There's only one switch type for each case:

```
switchE
  :: MonadMoment m =>
  Event (Event a) -> m (Event a)

switchB
  :: MonadMoment m =>
  Behavior a -> Event (Behavior a) -> m (Behavior a)
```

It's clear from the types how these switches work: switchE takes only one argument, an event of events. The effective event is always the latest one from the event event stream.

switchB takes two arguments: the initial behavior and an event of behaviors. The effective behavior is the latest from event or initial if no event has yet emitted.

Observing moments on demand

Almost always, there is only one MonadMoment computation in an application. That moment is what eventually gets turned to an EventNetwork.

In some special cases, it might be convenient to execute pure Moment computations on demand. The function that executes moments emitted in an event is called observeE:

```
observeE
  :: Event (Moment a) -> Event a
```

A useful combinator to use along with observeE is valueB, which samples a value of the Behavior:

```
valueB
  :: MonadMoment m => Behavior a -> m a
```

Essentially, observing allows executing "mini FRP networks" within the main network in a single step. When a `Moment` in a network is emitted, `observeE` immediately executes it and yields the result value. The network is discarded immediately. The only constraint is that the mini network has to be pure, that is, expressed as a Moment.

Nested networks probably have their uses. A small uncontrived example is hard to conceive, but one could be running a simulation that is expressed as an FRP network whenever an event occurs.

Recursion and semantics

Recursion is the final but certainly not the least important aspect of FRP we have yet to consider in Reactive-banana. Mutually recursive behaviors and events are the key for success in reasonably complex FRP networks.

Unlike the other frameworks (Elerea, Yampa) we have used in this chapter, Reactive-banana gives much simpler semantics with relation to recursive definitions. In general, recursion is always well defined as long as an event depends on itself only via a behavior, and vice versa.

In practice, this means that among other things, the second argument of `stepper` or (as a consequence of `stepper`) `accumB` can always safely depend on the result:

```
stepper :: MonadMoment a => a → Event a → Behavior a
accumB :: MonadMoment m => a -> Event (a -> a) -> m (Behavior a)
```

What about `accumE`? Feeding the result as an argument to `accumE` could at first glance look problematic. Consider:

```
ev <- accumE 1 ((+) <$> ev)
```

But this won't fail per se: instead, the event will just never occur! It won't enter an infinite loop or anything.

To make the preceding recursive definition do something sensible, we would need to supply an initial value for the event stream. This is only possible by using `apply` and expressing the event as a behavior – thus being perfectly valid.

In general, it's hard if not impossible to produce an infinite loop with the Reactive-banana API unless `valueB` is used.

One way to write the Fibonacci sequence implemented in Reactive-banana looks like this:

```
{-# LANGUAGE RecursiveDo #-}

fib :: Event () -> Moment (Behavior Int)
fib step = mdo
  fib1 <- stepper 1 (fib2 <@ step)
  fib2 <- accumB 1 ((+) <$> fib1 <@ step)
  return fib1
```

Basically, this is a combination of two mutually recursive behaviors: `fib1` and `fib2`. The first one starts at the head of the sequence, while `fib2` starts at the tail. At every step, the head (`fib1`) advances to the value of the tail, while the tail advances to the sum of current tail value.

Adding input and output

By now, you are familiar with the functions compile and actuate. Compile created from a network description (`MomentIO ()`), an EventNetwork in the `IO` monad, and actuate was used to execute the EventNetwork. In our GUI example, we used the `reactive-banana-wx` library as an aid to attach our network to the wxWidgets framework. What if we don't want to use wxWidgets or need to use some other input and output?

All the necessary glue for input and output is located in the `Reactive.Banana.Frameworks` module. In this section, we'll add input and output that are IO actions, and also see how to add dynamic input and output in the network.

Input via polling or handlers

The simplest way to add continuous input to a network is by using `fromPoll`:

```
fromPoll :: IO a → MomentIO (Behavior a)
```

`fromPoll` executes the `IO` action frequently, simulating a continuous `Behavior a`. It's clear that the `IO` action must be cheap so that the network isn't slowed down considerably.

An example use of `fromPoll` is a stream of random numbers:

```
fromPoll (randomRIO (0,1) :: IO Double)
:: MomentIO (Behavior Double)
```

The `Behavior` is updated every time the network processes an input event. In the case of a single random number, that means same random number is provided if it's used in multiple places. It makes sense, because semantically `Behavior` is a function of time: it doesn't get different values at the same time.

Pollers are sometimes useful. However, the preferred way to add input is via handlers. The **Handler** API is:

```
type Handler a = a → IO ()

newtype AddHandler a =
    AddHandler { register :: Handler a → IO (IO ()) }

newAddHandler  :: IO (AddHandler a, Handler a)

fromAddHandler ::     AddHandler a → MomentIO (Event a)
fromChanges    :: a → AddHandler a → MomentIO (Behavior a)
```

The idea is to use `newAddHandler` to create a pair of:

- `Handler a`: An `IO` action to push input of type `a` to the handler.
- `AddHandler a`: Event handler registration facility. `register addHandler myHandler` registers the handler `myHandler` to fire whenever an event is fired. The returned `IO` action can be used to unregister the handler.

Handlers are hooked to the network as either discrete (Event) or continuous (Behavior) input with `fromChanges` or `fromAddHandler`. Note that `fromChanges` is just a combination of `stepper` and `fromAddHandler`: `fromAddHandler >=> stepper x0`.

Reactimate output

Performing output from a network is simple by using `reactimate`:

```
reactimate :: Event (IO ()) → MomentIO ()
```

Essentially, we just express the output as an `IO` action event. Using the `Functor` instance for `Event`, it's easy to turn any event into an IO action.

So performing output on an event is easy. How about output based on behavior? Behaviors are continuous and we can't perform IO actions continuously. However, due to performance reasons, behaviors have rather sparse steps when they update. We can hook IO actions to these update steps or changes:

```
changes :: Behavior a → MomentIO (Event (Future a))
```

Changes of a behavior don't necessarily correspond to real changes in the value (there's not really a way to know whether the value has changed, as in not equal).

The new values are returned in events and wrapped inside the `Future` monad. The values are not immediately available, as the name future suggests. Instead, we access the new values via `reactimate'`:

```
reactimate' :: Event (Future (IO ())) → MomentIO ()
```

This works essentially just like `reactimate` except that it works with values from `changes`.

Input and output dynamically

It's possible to add and modify input and output dynamically in Reactive-banana. The function that allows this is called `execute` and has the following type:

```
execute :: Event (MomentIO a) → MomentIO (Event a)
```

`execute` turns events of `MomentIO` computations to events of their return values. This gives a lot of freedom: we can create new handlers (`liftIO newAddHandler`) or perform arbitrary `IO` or `MomentIO` code. However, there are no guarantees to execution order of the actions. This is why it's preferred to not use `execute` directly for output. You can call `reactimate` from within `execute` though.

For dynamic input, it's useful to combine `execute` with `switchE`. Yielding a new Event in the `MomentIO` monad (acquired via `newAddHandler`) in the argument for `execute` will yield an Event (`Event a`) – an event of events. Use `switchE` to turn that to an event that uses always the newest event as source.

Summary

In this chapter, we have worked with three different approaches to FRP: Elerea, with its safe monadic interface and discrete-only signals; Yampa and its first-class signal functions; and finally, Reactive-banana and its safe and simple hybrid semantics. Implementation differences are rather radical, but the theoretical FRP basis is still the same: model values as functions of time and include discrete events. It's also characteristic that interaction with the outside world, input and output, is more or less separated from application logic. Recursion is an important technique in FRP. For proper value recursion of monadically retrieved values in Haskell, the `MonadFix` class along with `mfix` or `RecursiveDo` is a must and often encountered in Haskell FRP code.

The next and final chapter will comprise a collection of robust, extensively tested and production-ready Haskell libraries for more different and less general use. It's an unfortunate fact in the Haskell ecosystem that even some of the very best libraries are poorly documented in their APIs. Hopefully, the recommendations in the next chapter of this book will give you some insight into the design and use of selected libraries.

14
Library Recommendations

This final chapter will list out generally useful Haskell libraries. As with any programming language ecosystem, libraries are a very important part of it. Good, modular, and extensible libraries are what really make for productive programming. The Haskell ecosystem has libraries of multiple varieties, from bad to outstanding. All of the libraries listed here are considered robust and safe and recommended for use in production.

It's an unfortunate fact that choosing a good Haskell library for your needs is no easy task. There are ways to compare and weigh libraries: When was the package last updated? Is its maintainer active? Is the library present in the newest Stackage snapshot? Still, it's easy to miss an excellent library for your specific use. Sometimes there might be a niche, not well-maintained library that fits just your need. Then use that, and refactor later if necessary. Haskell gives guarantees that make refactoring easy, so it's no big deal. If you like the library, it might be that maintaining the library yourself is not a big effort.

In this chapter, we will be covering the following topics:

- Lists of libraries sorted by use case structured in
- Overview of use cases, features, and robustness of mentioned libraries
- Examples for most libraries

Representing data

Libraries for storing text and binary, and arbitrary data in different containers:

- `vector`: High-performance fixed-size vectors with a powerful fusion framework. Supports unboxed (primitive) and boxed (arbitrary) elements with respective performance.

- `text`: Fast, memory-efficient, and unicode-correct text datatypes. Both strict and lazy variants. Orders of magnitude faster than `String` in many use cases (not all).

- `bytestring`: Extremely fast and efficient strict and lazy binary datatypes. Interfaces very well with the C FFI supporting marshalling in `O(1)`.

- `containers`: General-use immutable graph, map, set, sequence (a list with `O(1)` `cons` and `snoc`), tree structures for storing arbitrary (boxed) data.

- `unordered-containers`: Efficient, immutable hash maps (tables) and sets.

- `hashtables`: Efficient mutable hash maps and sets.

- `mutable-containers`: A library that abstracts over multiple mutable variable and container types.

Refer to *Chapter 2, Choose the Correct Data Structures* for use and discussion of these libraries and more about data representation.

Functional graphs

The best representation for a graph depends a little on the use case. The `Graph` type in containers uses an adjacency list and a few basic graph operations are provided.

One unique Haskell library, `fgl`, for **Functional Graph Library**, takes a different approach to programming with graphs, by considering graph as an inductive data-type.

One of the core ideas in `fgl` is contexts and decomposition. A context of a graph node is a triplet of the node's predecessors, successors, and the node itself. All graph manipulations can be expressed as inductive recursions over the contexts of a graph. Furthermore, it's surprisingly efficient.

For reference, here's a very, very small section of the fgl API:

```
-- module Data.Graph.Inductive.Graph

type Adj        b = [(b, Node)]

type Context  a b = (Adj b, Node, a, Adj b)

type Decomp g a b = (Mcontext a b, g a b)

empty :: Graph    gr => gr a b
match :: Graph    gr => Node → gr a b → Decomp gr a b
(&)   :: DynGraph gr => Context a b → gr a b → gr a b
```

The a and b type variables are for node and edge labels, respectively.

The API is overloaded over different representations of graphs (type variable gr). Different implementations are in distinct modules; for instance, one using a **patricia** tree is located in Data.Graph.Inductive.PatriciaTree module and called Gr a b.

Here's a small toy program which illustrates (de)composition using contexts. The build function creates a graph while sumNodes consumes one:

```
-- file: fgl.hs

import Data.Graph.Inductive.Graph
import Data.Graph.Inductive.PatriciaTree

build :: Int -> Gr Int ()
build 0 = empty
build n = (to, n, n, from) & build (n - 1)
  where
    to   = []
    from = [ ((), m) | m <- [n - 1, n - 2 .. 0] ]

sumNodes :: [Int] -> Gr Int () -> Int
sumNodes []       _  = 0
sumNodes (n:ns) gr = case mctx of
    Nothing            -> sumNodes ns gr
    Just (_,_,x,from) -> x + sumNodes
        (ns ++ [ m | (_,m) <- from ]) gr'
  where
    (mctx, gr') = match n gr
```

There are a lot of graph algorithms already implemented in fgl, as well as general combinators to help building your own special traversals. The feel in the library is very functional indeed: there's no need to drag along the graph or worry about keeping it consistent. In fgl, graphs are immutable, referentially transparent, while simultaneously not sacrificing speed.

Numeric data for special use

The libraries in this subsection are as follows:

- **base (module Data.Fixed)**: Standard fixed-precision arithmetic from the base. Precision decided at compile-time.
- **Decimal (module Data.Decimal)**: Fixed-precision Decimal type and some additional utility functions. Precision decided in runtime.

- **numbers (modules Data.Number.*)**: Constructive real numbers, multi-precision floats, fixed-precision decimals, and more. Precision decided at compile-time.

The Fixed datatype from `base` is good for fixed-precision arithmetic when you know the precision at compile-time. The precision is encoded as a phantom type, so it's not convenient to handle multiple precisions.

The `Decimal` library defines a more expressive `DecimalRaw` type and usually used `Decimal` synonym:

```
type Decimal = DecimalRaw Integer
data DecimalRaw I = Decimal
    { decimalPlaces :: !Word8, decimalMantissa :: !i }
```

The exponent is expressed as a `Word8`, giving at most 255 decimal places. The `Decimal` library automatically handles multiple precisions in the exponent. The result is always most precise (largest exponent). There are also utility functions such as `divide` and `allocate`, that distribute a single decimal into multiple parts or portions. The parts are guaranteed to always sum to the original decimal.

The `numbers` library implements some exotic number types. It features floating point numbers with arbitrary, user-defined precision decided at compile-time. Constructive real numbers (full-precision reals; computation may diverge). Automatic forward differentiated numbers, interval numbers and natural numbers.

Encoding and serialization

It's an extremely common need to convert data from one format to another. In Haskell, we often like working with Haskell values, because of guarantees of strong-typing and the expressivity of algebraic datatypes, though data must then be converted to and from Haskell values. Conversions should also be fast, because there could be a lot of data.

There are a lot of data formats for different use cases: binary serialization to disk for local storage, efficiently packed formats for transmission over network and formats for interfacing with other applications, even users, in APIs and the like. Next, we'll glance at some of the widely used binary and text serialization libraries.

Binary serialization of Haskell values

The libraries in this subsection are as follows:

- **binary, cereal**: Serialization using lazy ByteStrings using automatic or custom binary formats
- **store**: An even more direct and efficient serialization library from FPComplete

Efficiently serializing Haskell values into binary and back is crucial for performance in many applications. Fast serialization is important when handling lots of data, sending it over network or storing it on disk. For example, the performance of a disk cache system is highly dependent on the efficiency of serialization.

The binary package is a battle-tested, widely used library for serialization. It has a fast throughput and an easy API for adding new serialization instances. Usually, adding new instances by hand for custom types isn't necessary, because there are already generic serializations defined via GHC.Generics. If the format is important, however, it's necessary to create your own serialization instance.

The cereal package is more or less equivalent to binary. There are no major differences between these libraries, other than perhaps slightly different default serialization formats.

The store package is a newcomer in the serialization field from FPComplete. The library released in 2016 is in a couple of ways even faster than the already quite fast cereal and binary libraries. First, store avoids bit-swapping on x86: both binary and cereal use big endian for numbers while x86 uses little-endian. Store uses little endian. Second, store minimizes the number of allocations by allocating a correctly sized ByteString at once, instead of gradually allocating more space during serialization like is done in binary and cereal.

The store library has proved its competence benchmarks, showing as much as double the performance in encoding and decoding compared to binary and cereal. store isn't quite so portable as binary. In particular, older ARM processors are not supported.

Encoding to and from other formats

The libraries in this subsection are as follows:

- `cassava`: Parsing and encoding of CSV. Engineered for high-performance applications, with ease of use in mind.

- `aeson`: Parsing and encoding of JSON.

- `yaml`: Parsing and encoding of YAML files. Utilizes parsers and type-classes from `aeson`.

- `xml`: Simple encoding of XML values. See the *Parsing XML* section (covered later in the chapter) for parsing (possibly malformed) XML in Haskell.

- `json-autotype`: Generating Haskell types from JSON formatted examples.

There are a lot of common data formats. Haskell has libraries to serialize to and from all commonly used formats. Thanks to `GHC.Generics`, the necessary boilerplate is often minimized: just write a Haskell datatype that corresponds to the serialized format, derive `Generic`, serialization instance and that's it! This approach applies at least to `aeson` and `yaml`.

Both `aeson` and `yaml` use the same base serialization type classes (`ToJSON` and `FromJSON`). This means that the same instances can be used to serialize in both JSON and YAML formats. The classes are defined as:

```
class FromJSON a where
   parseJSON  :: Value → Parser a

   class ToJSON a where
   toJSON      :: a → Value
   toEncoding :: a → Encoding
```

That `Value` is a Haskell representation of JSON data. It's an algebraic datatype with constructors for objects, arrays, strings, numbers, booleans, and null.

JSON parsers are written in the `Parser` monad, which has `Alternative`, `MonadPlus`, and `MonadFail` instances, meaning there's no need for separate combinators needed to define parsers that accept multiple sources or to fail at any point in the parsing process. Most parsers can be written in applicative style, in other words, the following parses `{ "a":1, "b": 2 }`:

```
AB <$> v .: "a" v .: "b"
```

One "feature" of `aeson` is that it parses only well-formatted JSON: for instance, all keys of objects must be quoted with double quotes. So this is not valid and will not parse by `aeson`: `{ a:1, b:2 }`.

Finally, usually the generic deriving method should be preferred. If it's inconvenient to make the field names of your Haskell datatypes match exactly with keys in the JSON format, there is some configuration available in the generic derive method. Another configurable besides field names is **sum-type encoding**, for which there are a few strategies.

To go the other way around, from JSON data to Haskell types, for example, to generate bindings to an API, there exists a library called `json-autotype` which does exactly this. It uses heuristics to generate Haskell datatypes along with `ToJSON` and `FromJSON` instances that translate according to the example input JSON files.

CSV input and output

Comma-separated values (CSV) is a relatively simple data format. A simple parser is easy to write yourself from scratch, but in a high-performance setting, it's better to use an optimized library such as `cassava`.

The conversion API in `cassava` is similar to that in `aeson`, with `ToField` and `FromField` classes:

```
class FromField a where
    fromField :: Field → Parser a

class ToField a where
    toField :: a → Field
```

The **field** type is an alias for strict ByteString.

`cassava` supports an alternative interface using named records. The corresponding type-classes are `ToNamedRecord` and `FromNamedRecord`. Named records are represented as hashmaps from headers to values:

```
type NamedRecord = HashMap ByteString ByteString
```

The unnamed interface uses `Vectors` for records.

`cassava` utilizes high-performance data-structures such as ByteString, Vector, and HashMap to parse and generate CSV files. Although CSV is a simple format, there are a lot of subtle corner cases that should be handled accordingly, such as double-quote escaped fields, different newlines, and mapping names from a header to record fields. `cassava` takes care of the details nice and fast.

Persistent storage, SQL, and NoSQL

The libraries in this subsection are as follows:

- `acid-state` and `safecopy`: These libraries go hand in hand, giving a lightweight, disk-stored database of Haskell values with strong ACID guarantees and migrations.

- `persistent`: A by-product of the **Yesod** web framework, persistent is a backend-agnostic high-level query abstraction over SQL-like databases. Provides type-safe models with automatic schema migrations.

- `esqueleto`: Add type-safe SQL query EDSL that works with the persistent library and its models.

- HDBC: A SQL database abstraction layer similar to persistent except lower level. Provides transactions and marshalling of SQL values to Haskell values and the other way around.

- HDBC-odbc: Hook any ODBC-enabled database connection to HDBC.

- `persistent-odbc`: Hook any ODBC-enabled database connection to persistent via HDBC-odbc. Adds model and migration support.

acid-state and safecopy

The `acid-state` package provides a very good little database when the database can fit completely in memory. In short, `acid-state` uses a Haskell value as the database and user-defined transactions to query and update the database.

The database is stored in memory and on disk. The disk copy is very resistant to corruption, and call be rolled back to any earlier version assuming the event log and a checkpoint is still intact.

The `safecopy` package extends the `cereal binary` serialization package with version-controlled formats. It's relatively painless to change the serialization format even deep down in a hierarchy of datatypes.

The only downside is that both the old and new format must co-exist in code at least for the time of migrating. You are free to rename and move the old datatype freely, though. The only thing that matters is the version number, which must always increase when schema is changed.

persistent and esqueleto

The `persistent` library makes it almost trivial to work with SQL and also NoSQL
databases from Haskell. By defining your database models in the embedded model
language, `persistent` generates strongly typed model definitions that work with
`persistent` functions to insert, delete, and update rows. Lots of database adapters
are available of varying quality, most notably SQLite, PostgreSQL, and MongoDB are
well supported.

Here's how we would define a database schema in persistent, using
`TemplateHaskell` and quosi-quoting:

```
share [mkPersist sqlSettings, mkMigrate "migrateAll"]
     [persistLowerCase|
User
  username Text
  UniqueUsername username
Post
  author UserId
  content Text
|]
```

In this schema, we have two tables, `user` and `post`. Both will have fields named
`id` automatically. That `UniqueUsername` will turn into two things: a uniqueness
constraint in the database and a Haskell data-constructor with which we can query
unique rows from the table using `getBy` function of `persistent`.

To use this schema with say the SQLite in-memory backend, we could write the
following Haskell `main`:

```
main = runSqlite ":memory:" $ do        -- (1)
   runMigration migrateAll              -- (2)

   uid ← insert $ User "foobar"         -- (3)
   insert $ Post uid "First post"

   posts ← selectList [PostAuthor ==. uid] -- (4)
                  [Asc PostContent]
   liftIO $ print $ map (postContent . entityVal) posts
```

There is nothing that isn't type-safe in this example. At (1), the `runSqlite` function
initializes a connection to a database and runs an action in it. In case of exceptions,
the database is closed cleanly.

At (2), we perform database migrations if necessary. The **migrator** takes the schema definition as its target state, creating new tables and columns when necessary. Note that no destructive actions are taken automatically; dropping tables and columns must be done manually.

At (3), we perform a simple insertion to the database. The `insert` function returns the ID of the newly created row. We use this ID to consequently add a post entry to the database.

At (4), we use a simple `selectList` function of `persistent` to query some rows from the database. Note that `persistent` intentionally only deals with single tables: it doesn't do joins at all. Joins can be done either via raw SQL (automatic value interpolation is still provided in raw SQL queries) or with the **esqueleto DSL**.

Esqueleto is an add-on to persistent that brings complex database queries in a very type-safe embedded domain-specific language. Notably, table joins are supported, which is missing from `persistent` (unless manually crafting the query string). Queries in Esqueleto look a lot like queries in SQL, albeit with some extra noise from fancy operator names. A little noise is a small price to pay for compile-time checked queries.

For instance, here's an example query written in Esqueleto:

```
select $
from $ \(user `InnerJoin` post) → do
  on (user ^. UserId ==. post ^. PostAuthor)
    return (user, post)
```

This performs an inner join over tables `user` and `post`, returning all posts along with their author. It's equivalent to the following SQL:

```
SELECT user.* post.*
FROM user
INNER JOIN post ON user.id = post.author
```

HDBC and add-ons

HDBC is a library older than `persistent`, and is not as ambitious. HDBC aims to be merely an adapter between Haskell and SQL databases.

HDBC works with lots of databases, also including ODBC-compliant databases such as Microsoft SQL. `persistent` doesn't directly support ODBC, though there is an experimental library called `persistent-odbc` that adds ODBC compatibility to `persistent` via HDBC and HDBC-odbc.

HDBC is a better choice than `persistent` when you don't need automatic migrations, whole model support in Haskell or type-checked queries. HDBC gives just the bare minimum to conveniently interact with a SQL database from Haskell: connecting to a database, performing queries, and marshalling SQL values.

Networking and HTTP

The libraries in this subsection are as follows:

- `network (module Network)` and `network-uri`: Low-level networking on bare sockets
- `connection`: Easy-to-use abstraction on TCP connections. Supports TLS and HTTP or SOCKS proxies out of the box.

Basic low-level networking using the `network` package has been discussed in *Chapter 6, I/O and Streaming*.

For a bit higher-level TCP client communication, the `connection` package provides a nice little abstraction layer. Plus, `connection` supports SSL/TLS and SOCKS with minimal configuration. A connection is established primarily by defining a configuration value of type `ConnectionParams`, given by:

```
data ConnectionParams = ConnectionParams
  { connectionHostname  :: HostName
  , connectionPort      :: PortNumber
  , connectionUseSecure :: Maybe TLSSettings
  , connectionUseSocks  :: Maybe ProxySettings
  }
```

This is a simple yet effective API for all primitive TCP connections. The `get` and `put` operations use ByteString as data format. `connection` is the best library choice when you don't need much more but connect via TCP and transmit bytes, securely, possibly via a proxy.

HTTP clients and servers

The libraries in this subsection are as follows:

- `http-client`: Making HTTP requests. Does not support HTTPS.
- `http-client-tls`: Adds HTTPS support to `http-client`.
- `wreq`: Lens-based HTTP client library. Easy to use when basic knowledge of lenses is assumed. Supports HTTP and HTTPS.

- `wai`: Short form for **Web Application Interface**. Provides the bare minimum to receive and respond to client requests. Engineered for high-performance use

- `warp`: HTTP server for `wai`. Note that `warp` sits behind `wai` from the client's point of view.

For what it's worth, there is an old, minimally maintained library called `HTTP` that promises a simple interface for client-side HTTP requests. However, although fully functional, the `HTTP` library comes with a few unfortunate gotchas. HTTPS is not supported at all and the library can be too lazy in HTTP response values, which manifests as weird bugs.

In new code, it's recommended to use one of the newer HTTP client libraries, for instance, `http-client`, `http-client-tls`, or `wreq`. The first two use the connection library internally and provide a simple API. The `wreq` package takes abstraction even further, adding a lens-based API on top of `http-client` or `http-client-tls`.

It's worth mentioning that types generic for both server and client HTTP applications, such as status responses, headers, and URIs, can be found in a separate package, `http-types`. This is a dependency of many client and server-side libraries, and can be imported in library user's code if there's need for some URI manipulation.

For server-side HTTP programming without bells and whistles, the `warp` package is one high-performance option. It provides just enough to conveniently parse and respond to HTTP requests. `warp` has been proved to scale exceptionally well in multi-core environments, much thanks to the threaded Runtime System but just as much to wonderful engineering by its authors. Plus, `warp` provides support for HTTP/2.

Supplementary HTTP libraries

The libraries in this subsection are as follows:

- `json-rpc`: JSON Remote Procedure Call server and client. Engineered for high performance with ease of use in mind. Uses conduits.

- `websockets`: Simple web socket server and `client` library on top of network. Does not support secure (WSS) connections.

- `wai-websockets`: Uses `websockets` in a `wai` (`warp`) application. Also uses the `websockets` library. Use this if you already run a `wai` application and want to add `websocket` support to it.

- `REST`: Can be found on `silkapp.github.io/rest`. Defining REST APIs in Haskell, with autogeneration of JavaScript client code and documentation.

JSON remote procedure calls

Many web services provide **JSON-RPC** APIs that more or less conform to the official JSON-RPC specifications. Connecting to such a web service is relatively easy with any HTTP client. And if the API is too far from version 1 or 2 of the JSON-RPC spec, that might be an easier route than using the `json-rpc` library.

`json-rpc` works with all standard-conforming APIs. It adds its own logging (via `monad-logger`) and uses conduits to send and receive messages. Conforming to the spec, it tracks request IDs automatically. The biggest pain point of using `json-rpc` is that it uses conduits and its own monad transformer, the setup of which is non-trivial for those unfamiliar with either.

The `jsonRpcTcpClient`/`jsonRpcTcpServer` functions provide simple JSON-RPC client and server that don't necessitate knowing about conduits; however, the exposed configuration leaves more to be desired. For instance, it's not possible to override request or response headers, in which case one must drop to defining conduit source and sink for requests and responses manually.

It's worth noting that non-standard authentications in JSON-RPC, in other words, those that require an authorization key in the top-level JSON object, are not at all supported by `json-rpc` (without modifying the source) at least as of version 0.7.1.1 of the library.

Using WebSockets

The `websockets` package makes writing **WebSocket** applications, both client and server, in Haskell a breeze. The API is simple, and the internals are engineered for speed and ease of use. For instance, there are multiple variants of `receive` and `send` functions: for ByteString, Text, and user-defined serialization formats via type-class.

The `websockets` library is rather flexible, and can be used together with other interfaces. In particular, the `wai-websockets` library provides a compatibility layer between `websockets` and `wai` applications, such as the **warp HTTP server**. This makes it possible to support both HTTP and upgrading to web sockets in the same server application.

Programming a REST API

One of the most featureful ways to define REST APIs in Haskell is via the **Rest** framework developed by Silk. See the documentation at `http://silkapp.github.io/rest` for use. The killer features are automatic generation of documentation that's always up-to-date, client-code generation for Haskell and JavaScript clients, and API versioning.

Cryptography

The libraries in this subsection are as follows:

- `SHA` and `RSA`: Pure implementations of SHA routines and RSA encryption and signature algorithms. Not the fastest, but plain Haskell without any FFI. Created by Galois Inc.

- `HsOpenSSL`: Partial bindings to OpenSSL via FFI.

- `cryptonite`: Low-level cryptography primitives with varying API's and probably of varying quality.

- `skein`: Bindings to the skein family of fast and secure cryptographic hash functions.

For really robust, production-ready cryptography applications, one should look for bindings to existing cryptography libraries. For instance, the C implementation of the Skein hash function family has Haskell bindings in the similarly named library `skein`.

Although Haskell can be used to implement cryptographic algorithms, many of the algorithms rely on bit-twiddling for security in ways that GHC's code optimizations can potentially negate. This makes code vulnerable to side-channel attacks.

That said, some pure Haskell implementations of some algorithms exist. In particular, the `RSA` package is good and very suitable when external library dependencies are inconvenient. For what it's worth, the `RSA` package is developed at Galois Inc, a known US military contractor.

The `cryptonite` package provides miscellaneous cryptography building blocks. They are deemed relatively secure, but every use should be considered individually. There are not too many users or cryptography experts that will have thoroughly reviewed all of the library.

Web technologies

The libraries in this subsection are as follows:

- **Yesod framework**: Full-blown MVC web framework, with all the bells and whistles.

- **Snap / Happstack**: Also web frameworks, independent from each other. Comprises fewer features than Yesod, but still very useful.

- **blaze-html**: Blazingly fast combinator library for HTML templating. Uses ByteStrings and the builder pattern.

- **amazonka / AWS**: Bindings to the Amazon Web Service API. The `amazonka` bindings are autogenerated, full bindings, while `aws` is more user-friendly but partial.

Developing full-blown web applications in Haskell is easy, and there are multiple great libraries with overlapping features. In short, there are three major big frameworks: Yesod, Snap, and Happstack. Each of these provides basic things such as routing and templating. Yesod has most features of them, but also the steepest learning curve.

For just writing HTML in Haskell, one of the best options is `blaze-html`. `blaze-html` provides Haskell combinators for defining HTML. Internally it uses ByteString and builders, to quickly and incrementally generate web pages. There are also templating libraries for CSS and JavaScript as well, in particular the "Shakespearean templates" associated to Yesod.

For interfacing web services such as Amazon's, a few libraries exist. Amazon has at least two Haskell bindings: the autogenerated `amazonka` bindings and partial, more user-friendly `aws` library. There's also package `fb`, which provides bindings to the Facebook graph query language API.

Parsing and pretty-printing

The libraries in this subsection are as follows:

- `parsec`: Very featureful, general parser combinator library. Old and poorly maintained. Slower than `attoparsec`

- `attoparsec`: Simple and fast parser combinator library. Fewer features than Parsec

- `megaparsec`: A fork of Parsec, well maintained. Extremely flexible. Faster than Parsec but considerably slower than Attoparsec

- `happy` / `alex`: Parser combinator libraries aimed towards parsing (programming language) grammars.

- `pcre-heavy`: A reasonable regular-expression library.

Parsing is something that Haskell shines at. Applicative and monadic parser interfaces are really expressive. There are many awesome general-purpose parser libraries for Haskell. In general, the choice should be between Attoparsec and Megaparsec.

Attoparsec should be preferred as speed is critical; Megaparsec if features are more important. Attoparsec suits best for well-defined file formats, such as serialization. Megaparsec is a better choice when dealing with more arbitrarily formatted input.

The learning curve to all parser combinator libraries is rather steep. However, the general ideas are the same behind them all: using general `Applicative`/`Monad`/ `Alternative` interfaces to declare combinations and options.

Here are some examples of parsing using `Megaparsec`. First, imports:

```
> import Text.Megaparsec
> import Text.Megaparsec.String
```

Parsing in applicative style:

```
> let p = (,,) <$> digitChar
              <*> (char '.' *> digitChar)
              <*> (char '-' *> digitChar)

> parseTest p "2.4-6"
('2','4','6')
```

Alternatives between two parsers (using `Alternative`):

```
> parseTest (string "a"<|> string  "b") "b"
"b"
```

Parsing multiple occurrences of same parser:

```
> parseTest (many (string "a"<|> string  "b")) "aababb"
["a","a","b","a","b","b"]
```

Parsing with `lookAhead`:

```
> parseTest (manyTill (string "a") (string ";")) "aaaa;b"
["a","a","a","a"]
```

Lots of high-level parser combinators are available, but they are all just compositions of smaller parts. Such primitives are, for instance, `lookAhead`, which applies a parser without consuming input, and `try`, which turns any parser into a backtracking one that acts like it hadn't consumed input when failing.

The `Happy` and `Alex` parser libraries, on the other hand, are geared towards parsing grammars. They suit best for writing parsers for custom domain-specific languages.

Regular expressions in Haskell

Regular expressions (regex) are powerful, but they're pretty much write-only. It's an impossibility to reasonably maintain a sufficiently complex regex. Usually, it's a better idea to use a real parsing library, but regexes are still useful, mostly in one-off cases.

There are a few regex libraries for Haskell. One which has rather good reputation is `pcre-heavy`. It's an extension of `pcre-light`. Basically, `pcre-heavy` adds utility functions such as `substitions`, `splits`, and so forth. From the name, we can infer that `pcre-light` supports expressive **Perl 5 compatible regular expressions**. Both libraries are also pure Haskell for maximum portability.

`pcre-heavy` allows for writing regexes using a fine quasi-quoter, and takes in and returns any string type: String, Text, and ByteString are all supported without extra overheads.

Parsing XML

The library in this subsection `tagsoup` parses arbitrary XML and HTML documents.

A task that comes up from time to time is parsing XML or HTML documents. The unfortunate thing with many XML and HTML documents is that they're rarely well formatted: missing end tags are just one example of ill-formatted HTML.

`Tagsoup` is one solution for parsing arbitrary data from XML-formatted documents. To some extent, it supports ill-formatted XML as well. The API is overloaded over source representation data type, via a `StringLike` class. It supports all of String, strict and lazy ByteString and strict and lazy Text.

Pretty-printing and text formatting

The libraries in this subsection are as follows:

- `wl-pprint-*` packages: Pretty-printers based on Wadler/Leijen pretty-printers. Multiple implementations with different features are found in similarly named libraries.

- `text-format`: High-performance text formatting.

- `interpolateInterpolate`: Simple string interpolation using Template Haskell.

- `here`: Docs for Haskell using Template Haskell.

Pretty-printing is the process of turning data into user-friendly text format. Think, for instance, of printing a long string with appropriate line breaks, or printing Haskell values in a friendly way, in other words, commas at the beginning of lines and so on.

The Wadler/Leijen pretty-printer is a simple but powerful interface that has multiple implementations: nearly a dozen packages with `wl-pprint` in their name. Some add support for ANSI terminal colors, or terminfo support, annotations, one even using a free monad for documents. Unfortunately, no single implementation admits for all features.

For basic formatting in classic `printf`-style, there's of course `Text.Printf` in the base package that implements the "original" polyvariadic `printf` in Haskell. Unfortunately, it's not at all type-safe. Yet more, it uses the incredibly slow String.

For high-performance text-formatting, the `text-format` package brings a formatter for Text values. At core, we have the `format` function:

```
format :: Params ps => Format → ps → Text
```

The Format datatype has an `IsString` instance. Interpolations are marked by "{}". The `Params` type-class overloads specification styles for parameters. In particular, supported parameters are tuples and lists of parameters, plus others. Here's an example formatting:

```
> format "testing: {} {} {} {}" (1, 1.23, hex 254, "hello")

"testing: 1 1.23000 fe hello" :: Text
```

The type of `hex` is:

```
hex :: Integral a => a → Builder
```

The text `Builder` is also a valid parameter, which is convenient for controlling output format.

For really type-safe text formatting, there are a few interpolation libraries that use Template Haskell for convenience. For instance, the `interpolate` library has an almost ludicrously simple interface: one quasi-quoter "i" which is used in this fashion:

```
> :set -XQuasiQuotes
> import Data.String.Interpolate

> let world = "World!'

> putStrLn [i|Hello #{world} #{9 + 33}|]
"Hello World! 42"
```

However, bear in mind that interpolate uses String as the only possible representation. This can hurt performance with larger strings. The `Here` library is similar to interpolate, using different interpolation syntax (dollar instead of hash) and supporting whitespace trimming.

Control and utility libraries

The libraries in this subsection are as follows:

- `conduit`, `io-streams`, and `pipes`: General streaming libraries, that avoid problems with lazy IO

- `lens`: Solving the "nested record update" problem in a "batteries included" fashion

- `convertible`: Conversions between types using a single function without information loss

- `basic-prelude`, `classy-prelude`: `Prelude` alternatives that encourage best practices in modern Haskell

- `chunked-data`: Class abstractions to different builders, zipping, and reading and writing to files and handles

Streaming libraries are generally aimed at countering problems with lazy IO. Refer to *Chapter 6, I/O and Streaming*, for an in-depth discussion about problems with lazy IO and Haskell streaming libraries.

Using lenses

Lenses can be thought of as a generalization of getters and setters that compose well. A sore point of vanilla Haskell is nested record updates. The syntax is not very nice, for instance, this:

```
update rec new_c = rec { field_c = (field_c rec) { c = new_c } }
```

Here we update `field c` in `field field_c` of record `rec`. With lenses, we could have instead written the update as:

```
rec & field_c . c .~ new_c
```

(Assuming `field_c` and `c` are now lenses for renamed fields.)

In reality, lenses are a lot more than just setters. There are `travelsals`, `prisms`, and more. The lens rabbit hole goes very deep – but is for sure an eye-opening experience.

More beginner-friendly alternatives to monolithic and highly abstract lens library exist. The `data-lens` library provides vanilla Haskell 98 lenses. Library `fclabels` provides only the basics: get, set, and modify parts of a datatype.

Here's a complete example of the use of `fclabels`:

```
-- file: fclabels.hs

{-# LANGUAGE TemplateHaskell #-}

import Prelude hiding (id, (.))
import Control.Category
import Data.Label
```

At this point, notice that we have replaced function composition (`.`) and ID from Prelude with more general ones from `Category`. Fc-lables lenses compose as category, as opposed to lenses of `lens` library, that compose with function composition.

This is how we define lenses with `fc-labels`:

```
data Member = Member
            { _name :: String
            , _task :: String
            } deriving Show

data Team = Team
            { _leader :: Member
            , _memebrs :: [Member]
            } deriving Show

mkLabels [''Member, ''Team]
```

All the magic happens in the call to `mkLabels`. Actually, it's not much magic at all; all that happens is that from every field name that begins with an underscore, a lens is formed. The underscore is dropped.

Forming a lens is an entirely mechanical process of defining a getter and modifier. The getter is just `_field`, while the modifiers are more verbose:

```
\f rec → rec { field = f (field rec) }
```

Lenses are used with `get`, `set`, and `modify` functions. For instance:

```
> let john  = Member "John" "Test the software"
      peter = Member "Peter" "Lead team"
      team  = Team peter [john]

> get (name . leader) team
"Peter"
```

Here is an example of modifying a `record` field inside another record:

```
> modify (task . leader) (++ " and hire people") team
```

Consider using lenses if you have a lot of nested records and update them frequently.

Easily converting between types (convertible)

Another nuisance that comes up is conversions of values to other types, for instance, between different textual types, time types, numbers, and so on. The `convertible` package provides a solution to this in the form of a `Convertible` type-class:

```
class Convertible a b where
    safeConvert :: a → ConvertResult b
```

Because a conversion can be invalid, in other words, from an Int64 to Int32 can overflow, convertible doesn't allow the invalid conversion and instead results in an error. When you are sure that a conversion is safe, you can use the `convert` function in a safe manner:

```
convert :: Convertible a b => a → b
```

The only possible downside to using `convertible` is that it can hide expensive conversions, for instance, conversions back and forth between String and Text. The other possible problem is using it with other value polymorphic libraries, that can result in too ambiguous types, thus necessitating type annotations.

Using a custom Prelude

Relatively advanced Haskellers might find the exports of default Prelude lacking or even devastating: encouraging the use of String, asynchronous exceptions (error), and partial functions. Preferences vary from person to person, so in principle there could be as many Preludes as there are Haskellers.

Luckily, one doesn't have to start from scratch defining a custom Prelude, as some better starting points exist. The `basic-prelude` package provides one bare base for building a custom Prelude. The `classy-prelude` package is aimed at rather advanced programmers, who don't mind working with highly class-based functions.

Some of the convenience classes in `classy-prelude` come from other smaller packages. For one, the mono-traversable library abstracts over monomorphic containers. Essentially, it provides the classes `MonoFunctor`, `MonoFoldable`, `MonoTraversable`, and some others, that are just like `Functor`, `Foldable`, and `Traversable` except that they are monomorphic in the element values. Examples of such containers are Text (element Char) and ByteString (element Word8).

The element type is decided via an open type-family `Element`:

```
type family Element mono
```

Besides truly monomorphic elements, such as Char or Word8, the `Element` type-family allows for instances in which the element type is decided from a type variable in the container. For instance, we have:

```
type Element [a] = a
type Element (Either a b) = b
```

So the true meaning of "monomorphic" is in the classes, that are less generic than normal `Functor`/`Foldable`/`Traversable`. For instance, `omap` of `MonoFunctor` won't allow changing the element type unlike `fmap` would:

```
omap :: MonoFunctor mono
    => (Element mono → Element mono) → mono → mono
```

The motivation for using `mono-traversable` is that the classes allow for writing generic code that works with more container types, in particular using the same code for both monomorphic (Text, ByteString) and polymorphic (`[a]` and `Set a`) containers. There are also other type-classes present in the `mono-traversable` package; see the package documentation for details.

The `chunked-data` library was originally a part of `classy-prelude`, so reasonably it's re-exported there. It abstracts over a few things:

- Different builders, in particular `text` and `bytestring` builders, providing conversions to and from builders and their data representation
- Types that can be zipped together, in other words, `lists`, `vectors`, `trees`, `sequences`, and even `IntMaps`
- The `IOData` class abstracts over reading and writing Handles

Working with monads and transformers

The libraries in this subsection are as follows:

- `lifted-base`, `stm-lifted`: Lifting IO operations to arbitrary monad stacks
- `monad-control`: Lifting general control operations to any monad (provides `liftBaseWith`)
- `monad-logger`: Adding high-performance and flexible logging facilities to any monad
- `LogicT`: A backtracking logic programming monad
- `monad-unlift`: Provides more reliable state-saving in monad transformer stacks for a subset of transformers (specifically, monad morphisms)
- `monad-loops`: Monad combinators that `map`, `iterate`, `fold`, and `unfold` with monadic side effects

For choice and considerations of monads and transformers themselves, refer to the discussion in *Chapter 2, Choose the Correct Data Structures*. Logging with monad-logger and fast-logger is discussed in detail in *Chapter 6, I/O and Streaming*.

Working with monad transformer stacks is most convenient when the actions of used libraries are readily overloaded over a type-class that permits use of an arbitrary monad stack. The `lifted-base` and `stm-lifted` libraries are alternatives to some `base` and `stm` modules. They lift operations from the `IO` and `STM` monad to arbitrary monads overloaded by classes such as `MonadIO`, `MonadBase`, and `MonadBaseControl`.

One monad that hasn't been discussed yet at all is the `Logic` monad and the `LogicT` transformer. This monad has quite specific use cases: in particular, complex backtracking computations can benefit from being written using the `Logic` monad. It has its own overhead, that's more than, for instance, `Maybe` monad's overhead in simple cases.

The `monad-control` package and the `MonadBaseControl` class are especially useful when writing highly stateful applications, where nearly all code has to store and have access to resources. Normally, state control operations such as catch live in `IO`. With `liftBaseWith` from `MonadBaseControl`, it's possible to lift operations that require an `IO` callback to the custom monad, and allow the callback to run in the custom monad as well. Refer to *Chapter 2, Choose the Correct Data Structures* for more information about `monad-control`.

To end our monadic discussion on a lighter note, we note the `monad-loops` package. It's a package which adds lots of general but seldom desired monadic operators, such as `whileM`, `iterateWhile`, and dozens of other variants. They may or may not make your code more expressive.

Monad morphisms – monad-unlift

The `monad-unlift` library exists for two reasons:

- To allow saving the monadic state (monadic side-effects) in case of an exception. Normally, with `liftBaseWith` from `monad-control`, the side-effects are just discarded and there's no way to get them back if an exception is thrown.
- As an alternative to `monad-control`, whose types are extremely general and hard to grasp.

So `monad-unlift` provides much the same functionality as `monad-control`, except for a subset of monads (transformers). In return, monadic effects can be resurrected in case of an exception. This is possible for monads that are isomorphic to `ReaderT`, that is, their effect is not context-sensitive.

In practice, instead of `liftBaseWith` to run a computation with the saved state, we use `askUnliftBase` to get a function that executes actions in the base monad with the same state. The state is shared but must be immutable, in other words, the writer part could be represented by a reference.

Handling exceptions

The libraries in this subsection are as follows:

- `exceptions`: Generalizing extensible extensions to any monad via type-classes (`MonadThrow`, `MonadCatch`, and `MonadMask`)
- `safe-exceptions`: At the time of writing, `safe-exceptions` is a recent attempt at pumping more sense into exception handling in the Haskell ecosystem

When working with custom monads and exceptions, it's advisable to use generalized functions from the exceptions library to conveniently throw, catch, and mask exceptions. The functions work pretty much the same as their originals from `Control.Exception`, unless somehow restricted by the base monad.

There are a few nuisances in the way exceptions are handled in Haskell and GHC. In particular, differentiating between synchronous and asynchronous exceptions is fickle. Plus, with current exception mechanisms in base, it's easy to make unnecessary mistakes, such as throwing asynchronous exceptions unintentionally (with `throw`) or throwing important exceptions away with failing cleanup handlers.

The `safe-exceptions` package tries to encourage better hygiene with exceptions. It's early in development, so radical changes are still possible. However, it seems prominent enough to include it in this list.

Random number generators

The libraries in this subsection are as follows:

- `MonadRandom`: Simple monadic interface for supplying random numbers. Uses `System.Random`. It's rather slow and not very secure.

- `mwc-random`: Very fast pseudo-random number generation. Probably not cryptographically secure.

- `random-fu`: Good support for sampling a wide range of different distributions. Good quality but not terribly slow either.

- `mersenne-random`: Pseudo-random numbers using a **Mersenne Twister**. Probably fastest RNG for Haskell when SIMD is supported.

Random numbers have multiple applications, from simulations to cryptography. Random number generators come with different trade-offs that suit different applications. Others are very fast and not really that random, while others are slower but cryptographically secure.

Haskell doesn't have a shortage of pseudo-random RNG libraries. Cryptographically secure random numbers are hard, however; your best bet is probably in `HsOpenSSL` or `cryptonite`.

For pseudo-random number generation, either `mwc-random` or `mersenne-random` are good choices. If you need a wider range of distributions and don't mind sacrificing speed, use `random-fu`.

Parallel and concurrent programming

The libraries in this subsection are as follows:

- **Control.Concurrent (base)**: The basic concurrency primitives
- **parallel**: Primitive parallel programming and parallel evaluation strategies
- **monad-par**: Provides the `Par` and `ParIO` monads for simple pure and IO parallel programming
- **abstract-par, monad-par-extras**: Add-on libraries to `monad-par`, that add extra combinators and a further abstraction layer over different `Par` implementations
- **repa**: Data-parallel arrays

Parallel programming and the use and features of libraries `parallel` and `monad-par` is considered in *Chapter 5, Parallelize for Performance*. The `RePa` library is also featured in that chapter.

In short, the `parallel` library is used to express parallelism deterministically, and more importantly to separate parallelism from program logic. This enhances modularity and composition. The `monad-par` library, on the other hand, ties computation with its parallel evaluation, in return giving more control over how evaluation happens.

`RePa` focuses on high-performance parallel array programming.

Functional Reactive Programming

The libraries in this subsection are as follows:

- **Elerea**: Discrete-time FRP with a safe monadic interface
- **Yampa**: Hybrid time FRP with first-class signal functions
- **Reactive-banana**: Hybrid time FRP with simple semantics

FRP is handled in depth in *Chapter 13, Functional Reactive Programming*. There are more useful FRP libraries than the three listed here, and the balance between good semantics and performance in FRP is still taking shape.

Mathematics, statistics, and science

The libraries in this subsection are as follows:

- `hmatrix`: Highish-level library for doing linear algebra in Haskell using BLAS and LAPACK under the hood.
- `hmatrix-gsl-stats`: Bindings to GSL, based on `hmatrix`.
- `hstatistics`: Some statistical functions built on top of `hmatrix` and `hmatrix-gsl-stats`.
- `statistics`: Pure Haskell statistics functions. Focuses on high performance and robustness.
- `Frames`: Working with CSV and other tabular data sets so large that they don't always fit in memory.
- `matrix`: A fairly efficient matrix datatype in pure Haskell, with basic matrix operations.

For linear algebra and statistics, there are a few useful packages. The `hmatrix`/`hmatrix-gsl-stats`/`hstatistics` provide pretty good bindings to well-known BLAS, LAPACK, and GSL libraries. The `statistics` package is very different, being a pure-Haskell implementation of a variety of statistics utilities.

Working with large datasets in Haskell is made easy with `Frames`. It provides a type-safe data frame abstraction for streaming data from disk.

Although `hmatrix` is strictly more featureful than the `matrix` library, `hmatrix` has some fairly strict external library dependencies. The `matrix` library has none, which makes it nicer to work with in certain situations. The same applies to the `Statistics` library versus the `hstatistics` library. The latter has extra dependencies and more features, while the former provides basics in Haskell only.

Tools for research and sketching

The libraries in this subsection are as follows:

- **ihaskell**: Haskell backend for the IPython console and notebook platform.
- **HaTeX**: A Haskell EDSL for writing LaTeX documents.
- **H (HaskellR)**: Embedding R computations into Haskell. Passing data between Haskell and R without copying.

The IPython console and notebook software enable wonderful interactive programming, and `ihaskell` brings Haskell to it.

For those who fancy it, writing LaTeX documents is completely possible in Haskell. There is some added syntactic noise from using an EDSL, but the strong guarantees and high-level abstractions made available by Haskell are worth it in bigger documents. As a plus, `HaTeX` makes writing TIKZ images much easier.

The HaskellR project

The HaskellR project enables seamless integration between Haskell and the R language. It makes the big repository of R libraries available to Haskell. In essence, HaskellR provides an interpreter that integrates GHCi with R, called H, and a quasi-quoter that enables writing R code into Haskell code.

The first way to use HaskellR is to install H and run it:

```
$ stack install H
$ stack exec H
>
```

This basically gives a modified GHCi prompt, where we have full access to both Haskell and R:

```
> [1..10]
[1,2,3,4,5,6,7,8,9,10]

> let (x,y) = (5, 10) :: (Double, Double)
> H.p [r| y_hs + x_hs + e |]
```

We access R through the R quasi-quoter. Haskell values simply get a _hs prefix. We can even use Haskell functions from quasi-quoted R expressions, as long as they are lifted to the R monad.

Creating charts and diagrams

The libraries in this subsection are as follows:

- **Chart, Chart-cairo, Chart-diagrams**: Rendering 2D charts in Haskell. Supports multiple backends, including Cairo and diagrams.
- **Diagrams**: Declaratively generating vector graphics. Supports multiple outputs including Cairo, SVG, PS, and more.

There are two excellent libraries for creating 2D graphics in Haskell: `chart` and `diagrams`. The first one is geared towards charting and plotting, whereas the latter is more on EDSL for generative vector graphics.

Both libraries support a wide range of output formats, from vector graphic formats to output directly to GTK windows. Chart even provides some primitive supports for interactivity in charts.

Scripting and CLI applications

The libraries in this subsection are as follows:

- **shelly**: Shell programming in Haskell, similar to Turtle.
- **turtle**: Using Haskell as a shell and scripting language. Very beginner-friendly but perhaps lacking in some ways as a result. Nonetheless portable and exception-safe.
- **cmdargs**: Command-line parsers with a Template Haskell empowered interface. Provides compatibility with **getopt** parsers.
- **haskeline**: Bindings to readline with an easy-to-use interface for use in command-line programs.
- **console-program**: Defining CLI applications with multiple sub-commands, optional and positional arguments. Supports one-off and readline modes.
- **shake**: A build system written in Haskell. A replacement for the make system.
- **propellor**: Puppeting software for servers, using a Haskell EDSL for defining configurations.

Haskell is quite well suited for scripting and shell-programming. Both the Shelly and Turtle libraries define APIs that wrap around shell functions. One of the features of Shelly is "lifting" the Unix pipe operator to the monadic bind (in Shelly.Pipe), which can be convenient in some situations. The Turtle library aims more at user-friendliness.

For writing command-line applications, there are multiple useful libraries. Both cmdargs and console-program provide facilities to define and parse command-line arguments and generate usage info from them. Console-program supports running the same program in interactive mode, taking advantage of readline. The haskeline library provides basic wrapper over readline.

Shake is a build system written in Haskell; it's not really geared towards compiling Haskell programs but rather as a replacement for make and similar ancient build systems.

Propellor is a relatively unknown server configuration system, which features a Haskell EDSl for declaring server configurations.

Testing and benchmarking

The libraries in this subsection are as follows:

- **QuickCheck**: Property-checking with automatic test-case generation
- **doctest**: Writing tests and expected results directly in haddock comments
- **HSpec, HUnit, tasty**: Traditional unit-testing libraries
- **criterion**: Benchmarking time usage
- **weigh**: Benchmark allocation

There are two testing libraries that are rather novel in Haskell: QuickCheck and doctest. QuickCheck lets the programmer just state a property for a function, leaving it to the library to try proving it false.

Doctest builds on the ingenious idea of combining test cases with docstrings. It's especially useful in libraries, because it gives users reading the documentation always up-to-date information about properties and use of functions that have tests annotated in their documentation.

More traditional testing frameworks such as HSpec, HUnit, tasty and time-benchmarking library criterion are discussed in detail in *Chapter 4, The Devil's in the Detail*.

A newcomer library in benchmarking, weigh, measures allocations in Haskell computations. Allocation as such is ignored by criterion, although allocation somewhat correlates with time complexity. Still, allocation benchmarking is a valuable tool in hunting down space leaks.

Summary

In this chapter, we have walked very quickly through a big bunch of libraries in different application areas. New libraries are constantly developed, and current ones are being improved. Lists in this chapter should be taken only as a guideline. It's always a good idea to do a little research before using a new library. The **Haskell-Cafe** mailing list is a good place to be notified about new libraries and major new releases, and is relatively low traffic.

During the course of this book, we have navigated many topics that have hopefully helped you become a better Haskeller.

If you followed closely the first few chapters, you have a good working understanding of lazy evaluation and its traps. You can use seq, bang patterns, and pragmas where necessary. You know many high-performance data structures and are able to use them effectively. In the middle chapters, we learned to test and benchmark, that lazy I/O has drawbacks, to parallelize code, to do concurrency safely and to compile using appropriate flags for GHC and Runtime System. These are the things that form the foundation for productive high-performance Haskell programming.

The last topics in this book were more about specific applications of Haskell: interfacing with foreign code, GPU programming, Cloud Haskell, and functional reactive programming. If you followed through any of these then you have a good overview of that aspect in Haskell programming and are prepared to dive into that subject without friction.

Index

A

abstract data-types
  marshalling 282, 283
abstract loggers 192, 193
abstract-par library 368
Accelerate
  about 285
  matrix multiplication,
    implementing 291, 292
Accelerate, concepts
  backend foreign function interface 300
  conditional execution 293
  elements 288, 289
  flow control 293
  folding 297, 298
  kernels 287
  permutation 299
  reducing 297, 298
  rudimentary array computations 290, 291
  scalars 288, 289
  segmenting 297, 298
  stencils 298, 299
  tuples 297
accelerate-cuda package 294
Accelerate programs
  generated code, inspecting 293
  writing 286, 287
accumulator parameters 12
accumulators 9
acid-state package 350
ad hoc polymorphic 3
aeson library 348
affinity 236
aggressive inlining 17
allocations
  minimizing 15, 16
  profiling 63
anatomy, Haskell project 94-96
array reductions
  via folding 144
arrays
  extending 147-149
  mapping 143
Async API
  examples, timeouts 215, 216
  using 215
asynchronous errors
  handling 105
asynchronous processing
  about 213, 214
  Async API, using 215
  composing, with Concurrently
    type 217, 218
attoparsec
  example 181-183
AWS 357

B

base (module Data.Fixed) library 345
basic-prelude library 361
benchmarking
  about 84
  with criterion 84-88
benchmarks 98
bidirectional channels
  establishing 308
binary and textual data, handling
  about 29
  bit arrays, representing 29, 30
  blobs of bytes, handling 31, 32

builder abstractions, used for iterative construction 34, 35
bytes, handling 31, 32
  characters, working with 33
  strings, working with 33
binary I/O 166, 167
binary library 347
binary serialization, libraries
  binary 347
  cereal 347
  store 347
binary serialization, of Haskell values 347
biographical profiling 83, 84
blaze-html 356
bounded thread 236
boxed types 237
branching 26, 27
buffering modes
  BlockBuffering 166
  LineBuffering 166
  NoBuffering 166
builder abstractions
  using, for iterative construction 34, 35
  using, for strings 35

C

C
  common types 272, 273
cabal file
  about 232
  fields 96, 97
  flags 96, 97
cassava library 348
cereal library 347
C functions
  calling, from Haskell 271, 272
Chan
  used, for broadcasting 206, 207
channels
  using 306, 308
characters
  text library, using 33
charts
  creating 370
charts, libraries
  Chart 370

Chart-cairo 370
Chart-diagrams 370
chunked-data library 364
classy-prelude library 361
closures 304
Cloud Haskell 302
cmdargs library 371
Cmm 248
code optimizations
  common subexpressions, eliminating 229
  float-in 228
  float-out 228
  liberate case duplicates code 230
  state hack 227
Common Subexpression Elimination (CSE) 229
common types, C 272, 273
common types, Haskell 272, 273
compiler code optimizations 17
concurrency primitives 200
conduit library 361
console-program 371
Constant Applicative Form (CAF) 67
containers library 344
control and utility libraries
  basic-prelude 361
  chunked-data 361
  classy-prelude 361
  conduit 361
  convertible 361
  io-streams 361
  lens 361
  pipes 361
Control.Concurrent (base) library 368
control inlining
  about 114, 115
  definitions, specializing 116
  phase control 117
  rewrite rules, using 115, 116
convolution operation
  with stencils 149-151
cost centre-based heap profiling 73-76
cost centres
  about 64
  setting, automatically 68-70
  setting, manually 64-67

C preprocessor (CPP)
  about 232
  use cases 232
criterion benchmark suite 84
cryptography 356
cryptography, libraries
  cryptonite 356
  HsOpenSSL 356
  RSA 356
  SHA 356
  skein 356
cryptonite package 356
CSV input 349
CSV output 349
CUDA backend
  using 294
CUDA platform 285
CUDA programs
  debugging 295
custom Prelude
  using 363, 364

D

data marshal 280
data parallel programming 141, 142
data representation
  libraries 343
datatype fields
  unpacking 23
data-type generic programming
  about 256
  generic sum example 256-258
debugging
  options 241
Decimal (module Data.Decimal) library 345
definitions
  specializing 116
delayed arrays 143
delayed representations 146
diagrams
  creating 370
Diagrams library 370
difference lists
  performance 38
  using 37
  using, with writer monad 38, 39

discrete-time events 327-329
domain specific language (DSL) 264

E

ekg
  used, for monitoring over HTTP 89-91
Elerea
  about 318, 319, 368
  limitations 324
  performance 324
encoding 166, 346
encoding, libraries
  aeson 348
  cassava 348
  json-autotype 348
  xml 348
  yaml 348
ephemeral data structures
  about 49
  mutable arrays, using 50, 51
  mutable references 50
  mutable vectors, using 51, 52
errors
  asynchronous errors, handling 106
  synchronous errors, handling 102, 103
esqueleto DSL 352
esqueleto library 350-352
Eval monad 132
eventlog
  used, for tracing 241
events, and behaviors
  combining 335
  switching 336
examples, from image processing
  about 154
  image, loading from file 155
  letters, identifying with
      convolution 155, 157
  performance, evaluating 159-161
  performance, testing 159-161
  strings, extracting from image 157
exception hierarchy 104, 105
exceptions
  handling 101, 366, 367
exceptions, libraries
  safe-exceptions 366

F

failure, handling
  about 310
  matching on message queue 311, 312
  message-passing performance 312
  monitors, firing up 311
  processes, linking together 312
file handles 165
finger trees 40
FlexibleInstances 121
force
  using 131
foreign function interface (FFI) 271
formats
  encoding from 348
  encoding to 348
FP Complete 99
Frames library 369
functional dependencies 118, 119
Functional Graph Library (fgl) 344
functional graphs 344, 345
Functional Reactive Programming,
    libraries
  Elerea 368
  Reactive-banana 368
  Yampa 368
function pointers 278
fusion 146
futures 138

G

GADTs
  performance 26, 27
garbage collector
  parallel GC 239
  tuning 239
general algebraic datatypes 24
General-Purpose Computing On Graphics
    Processing Units (GPGPU) 285
getopt parsers 371
GHC
  code optimizations, adjusting 227
  code transformations, adjusting 227
  compiling, via LLVM route 230
  Haskell source code, pre-processing 232

  operating 224
  operating, circular dependency
    problem 226
  shared libraries, building 231
  shared libraries, linking 231
  type-safety, enforcing with Safe
    Haskell 233
  using, like pro 224
GHC Core
  considerations 249
GHC extensions
  about 121
  for guards 123
  for patterns 123
GHCi
  Repa, working 142, 143
  tip 15
GHC options
  flags 242
  LLVM backend 242
  optimization, turning off 242
  optimization, turning on 242
  Runtime System (compile-time),
    configuring 242, 243
  Safe Haskell compilation, controlling 243
  summaries 241
GHC PrimOps
  coding in 112
GHC Runtime System
  and threads 211, 212
  asynchronous exceptions, masking 212
GHC's internal representations
  GHC Core, reading 248, 249, 250
  interpreting 248
  Spineless tagless G-machine (STG) 251, 252
GHC-specific features
  about 253
  kinds encode type, representation 254
Glasgow Haskell Compiler. *See* **GHC**
GNU Multiple Precision Arithmetic Library
    (GMP) 28
granularity
  fine-tuning, with buffering 136
  fine-tuning, with chunking 136
Graphics Processing Units (GPUs) 285
green threads 235
guarded recursion 10, 11

H

Hackage 294
Happstack 356
happy library 357
hashtables library 344
Haskell
  about 164
  code lifting to Q, with quotation
      brackets 264
  common types 272, 273
  constN function 263
  data, reifying into template objects 264
  evaluation stack, using 238
  generating 259
  missiles, launching on compilation 264
  names, in templates 261, 262
  quasi-quoting, for DSLs 267, 268
  setters, deriving with Template
      Haskell 265-267
  smart template constructor 262
  splicing, with $(...) 260
  tests, writing for 107
Haskell callbacks, from C 279, 280
Haskell functions
  exporting 275, 276
Haskell programs
  space usage, inspecting 12-15
  time, inspecting 12-15
Haskell project
  anatomy 94-96
HaskellR project 370
HaTeX 369
HDBC 350, 352
HDBC-odbc 350
heap objects, biographical profiling
  state DRAG 83
  state LAG 83
  state USE 83
  state VOID 83
heap profiling
  about 71, 73
  cost centre-based heap profiling 73-76
here library 359

H (HaskellR) 369
hmatrix-gsl-stats library 369
hmatrix library 369
hpc command-line utility 110
HsOpenSSL library 356
Hspec
  about 107, 109
  reference 109
hstatistics library 369
http-client library 353
HTTP clients and servers, libraries
  http-client 353
  http-client-tls 353
  wai 354
  warp 354
  wreq 353
HUnit
  used, for unit testing 108

I

ihaskell 369
indefinite blocking 236
indices 146-149
inlining
  about 17
  considerations 17
International Components for Unicode
    (ICU) 34
Inter-process Communication (IPC) 170
I/O
  about 163
  binary I/O 166, 167
  lazy I/O 164, 165
  lifting, base with exception
      handling 220, 221
  lifting, from base monad 219, 220
  lifting up from 218
  textual I/O 168
  top-level mutable references 218, 219
I/O performance
  with filesystem objects 168
io-streams
  example 181-183

J

json-autotype library 348
JSON-RPC APIs 355

L

lazy evaluation schema
  about 1, 2
  folds 6
  sum, writing correctly 3, 4
  weak head normal form 5
lazy I/O 164, 165
lenses
  using 361, 363
lens library 361
libraries
  installing, with profiling 70
libraries, for data representation
  bytestring 344
  containers 344
  hashtables 344
  mutable-containers 344
  text 344
  unordered-containers 344
  vector 343
libraries, for mathematics
  hmatrix 369
  hmatrix-gsl-stats 369
  matrix 369
libraries, for monads and transformers
  lifted-base 365
  LogicT 365
  monad-control 365
  monad-logger 365
  monad-loops 365
  monad-unlift 365
  stm-lifted 365
libraries, for parallel and concurrent
    programming
  abstract-par 368
  Control.Concurrent (base) 368
  monad-par 368
  monad-par-extras 368
  parallel 368
  repa 368

libraries, for parsing and pretty-printing
  attoparsec 357
  happy / alex 357
  megaparsec 357
  parsec 357
  pcre-heavy 357
libraries, for pretty-printing and text
    formatting
  here 359
  interpolate 359
  text-format 359
  wl-pprint-* packages 359
libraries, for Scripting and CLI applications
  cmdargs 371
  console-program 371
  haskeline 371
  propellor 371
  shake 371
  shelly 371
  turtle 371
libraries, for statistics
  hstatistics 369
  statistics 369
libraries, for testing and benchmarking
  criterion 372
  doctest 372
  HSpec 372
  HUnit 372
  QuickCheck 372
  tasty 372
  weigh 372
libraries, Repa
  repa-algorithms 154
  repa-devil 154
  repa-flow 154
  repa-io 154
  repa-stream 154
lifted-base library 365
logging, in Haskell
  about 191
  with FastLogger 191
LogicT library 365

M

MagicHash language extension 112
manifest representations 145

marshalling
in standard libraries 283
matrix library 369
megaparsec library 357
memoization 7
memory
allocating, outside heap 281
mersenne-random library 367
Mersenne Twister 367
message-passing 302
message type
creating 302, 303
migrator 352
modules
Safe 233
Safe-Inferred 233
Trustworthy 233
UnSafe 233
moments
about 331
observing, on demand 336
monad-control library 365
monadic loggers
customizing 196, 197
monadic logging 195
monad instance 331
monad-logger library 365
monad-loops library 365
monad-par library 368
monad-unlift library 365
monad-par-extras library 368
MonadRandom library 367
monads
catch function, implementing 106, 107
free monads 57-59
list monad 55-57
monad transformers, working with 59
speedup, via continuation-passing
style 59, 60
throw function, implementing 106, 107
transformer 55-57
working with 365
monad stacks
working with 55
monad transformer library (mtl) 59
monad-unlift library
need for 366

monitoring
in realtime 88
monitoring, over HTTP
with ekg 89-91
monomorphism restriction (MR) 122
multi-package projects 101
MultiParamTypeClasses 121
mutable-containers library 344
mutable vectors
bubble sort, using with 53, 54
using 52, 53
mutually recursive signals
about 320
side effects, signalling 321, 322
signal networks, changing
dynamically 322, 323
MVars
about 199, 203
features 204
used, as building blocks 205
mwc-random library 367

N

networking
about 169, 313, 314
above transport layer 173
networking and HTTP, libraries
connection 353
network (module Network) 353
network-uri 353
nodes 313, 314
NoMonomorphismRestriction language
extension 122
non-deterministic parallelism
with ParIO 139, 140
Normal Form Data (NFData) 87
Normal Form (NF) 5, 131
numbers (modules Data.Number.*)
library 346
numerical data
handling 28, 29
numeric data, libraries
base (module Data.Fixed) 345
Decimal (module Data.Decimal) 345
numbers (modules Data.Number.*) 346
numeric types, Haskell 28

O

objects
  outside heap 76-80
  pointing, in heap 281
O(log n) 48
OpenCL 285
Operating System (OS) thread 201

P

parallelism
  diagnosing 140, 141
Parallel library 368
ParIO
  using, for non-deterministic
      parallelism 139, 140
Par monad 136-138
parsec library 357
parsing 357
partial functions 19
partitioned arrays 151
patricia 345
PatternGuards 123
PatternSynonyms 123
pcre-heavy library 357
Perl 5 compatible regular expressions 359
persistent library 350, 351
persistent-odbc 350
phantom types 118
pipes
  benefits 187
  drawbacks 187
pipes library 361
polymorphic 2
polymorphic programs 18
polymorphism performance 18
pretty-printing 359
primitive parallelism 128, 129
primops 247
processes
  about 302
  creating 303
profiler
  unexpected crashes, debugging with 70, 71
profiling
  about 63
  in realtime 88

  libraries, installing with 70
  options 241
promises 138
propellor library 371
property checks 107, 108
pseq 131

Q

QuickCheck 107

R

random-fu library 367
random number generators 367
random number generators, libraries
  mersenne-random 367
  MonadRandom 367
  mwc-random 367
  random-fu 367
raw UDP traffic 172
Reactive-banana
  about 331
  first GUI application 332
  graphical display, with
      wxWidgets 332-334
  input, adding 338
  input, adding dynamically 340
  input, adding via handlers 338, 339
  input, adding via polling 338, 339
  output, adding 338
  output, adding dynamically 340
Reader 55
Reader Writer State (RWS) 59
recursion 9, 337
regular expressions, in Haskell 358
remote process
  calling 309
Repa
  about 141
  working with 142, 143
repa-algorithms library 154
Repa code
  writing 153
repa-devil library 154
repa-flow library 154
repa-io library 154
repa library 368

repa-stream library 154
resources
  handling 164
  managing, with ResourceT 173, 174
  reading 164
  writing 164
ResourceT
  resources, managing with 173, 174
REST API
  programming 355
Rest framework, Silk
  reference 355
retainer profiling 80-83
reverse polish notation (RPN) 10
rewrite rules
  using 115, 116
RSA library 356
RSpec 109
RTS options
  debugging 244
  garbage collection 244
  memory management 243
  profiling 244
  runtime system statistics 244
  scheduler flags 243
  summaries 243
runtime system, GHC
  garbage collector, tuning 238
  green threads 235
  heap management 237, 238
  memory management 237, 238
  profiling options 240, 241
  scheduler threads 235
  stack management 237, 238
  tracing options 240, 241
  tuning 234

S

safecopy package 350
Safe Haskell 223
schedules 136-138
ScopedTypeVariables 124
semantics 337
Seq 40

sequential data, handling
  about 36, 37
  difference lists, using 37
  zippers, using 39
serialization 346
Set Cost Centre (SCC) 65, 71
SHA library 356
shared library
  compiling 276, 277
sharing
  increasing 15, 16
shelly library 371
signal functions
  state, adding to 325, 326
SimpleLocalNet backend
  running with 305, 306
Single Instruction, Multiple Data
    (SIMD) 231, 253
slicing 147
SmallCheck 107
Snap 356
sockets 169
Software Transactional Memory (STM)
  about 199, 208
  alternative transactions 210
  bank account example 208, 210
  exceptions 210
spark pool
  about 235
  dud 130
  fizzled 130
  GC'd 130
  overflowed 130
sparks 130
sparse data, handling
  about 47
  containers package, using 47
  unordered-containers package, using 48
spawn function
  for futures 138, 139
  for promises 138, 139
spawning 304
spec testing 107
Spineless Tagless G-machine (STG) 224
stable pointers 280
stack manual
  reference 100

stack tool
  using 99, 100
state
  adding, to signal functions 325, 326
static addresses
  importing 273-275
static functions
  importing 273-275
statistics library 369
stm-lifted library 365
store library 347
strategies
  about 132
  composing 134, 135
  working 133
stream fusion 33
streaming 175
streaming library
  selecting 175
streaming, with conduits
  about 188, 189
  conduits, resuming 190, 191
  exceptions, handling 189
  resources, handling 189
streaming, with io-streams
  about 176, 177
  combinators, using 179
  exceptions, handling 179-181
  input streams, creating 177-179
  output streams, using 179
  resources, handling 179-181
streaming, with pipes
  about 184
  category theory 186
  exceptions, handling 187
  for-loops 186
  pipes, composing 185
  pipes, executing 185
stream monad 56
StrictData 124
strictness
  annotating 23
strings
  text library, using 33
subtle evaluation
  with pseq 131

sum-type encoding 349
supplementary HTTP libraries
  json-rpc 354
  REST 354
  wai-websockets 354
  websockets 354
switching 327-329
synchronous errors
  handling 102, 103
szipWith 152

T

tabular data, handling
  about 42
  vector package, using 43-46
Tagsoup 359
Tasty
  about 109
  reference 109
TCP/IP client
  acting as 169
TCP server
  acting as 170, 171
Template Haskell
  about 247
  used, for deriving setters 265-267
test frameworks
  about 109, 110
  Hspec 109
  RSpec 109
tests
  writing, for Haskell 107
test suites 98
text-format library 359
text formatting 360
text library 344
textual I/O 168
threads
  about 200
  and mutable references 200
  atomic operations, performing with
      IORefs 202
  thunk accumulation, avoiding 202
ThreadScope 231, 241
Thread State Objects (TSOs) 235

time
  profiling 63
  working with 326
timed log messages 193-195
tools, for research and sketching
  HaTeX 369
  H (HaskellR) 369
  ihaskell 369
tracing
  eventlog, using 241
transformers
  working with 365
Trivia, at term-level
  about 110-112
  coding, in GHC PrimOps 112-114
  control inlining 114, 115
Trivia, at type-level
  about 117
  associated types 120, 121
  functional dependencies 118, 119
  phantom types 118
  type families 120, 121
turtle library 371
type families 121
types
  converting between 363

U

UnboxedTuples extension 112
unboxing
  about 23
  anonymous tuples, using 25
unexpected crashes
  debugging, with profiler 70, 71
Unicode-correct 33
unit testing
  with HUnit 108
unordered-containers library 344
UNPACK
  used, for unboxing 23-25

V

vector library 343
ViewPatterns 123

W

wai library 354
wai-websockets library 354
warp HTTP server 355
warp library 354
Weak Head Normal Form 87
weak references 236
Weak ThreadId 237
Web Application Interface 354
WebSocket applications 355
WebSockets
  using 355
web technologies 356
web technologies, libraries
  amazonka/ AWS 357
  blaze-html 356
  Snap / Happstack 356
  Yesod framework 356
windowing function 44
wl-pprint package 359
worker/wrapper transformation 9
wrappers 278
wreq library 353
Writer 55

X

XML
  parsing 359
xml library 348

Y

yaml library 348
Yampa
  about 324, 368
  events 325
  integrating, to real world 330, 331
  signal functions 324
Yesod framework 356
Yesod web framework 350

Z

zippers
  both ends, accessing with Seq 40-42
  using 39

Made in the USA
Lexington, KY
05 August 2019